REAGAN

Early publicity photo.

REAGAN

THE HOLLYWOOD YEARS

MARC ELIOT

THORNDIKE PRESS

A part of Gale, Cengage Learning

GALE
CENGAGE Learning

Detroit • New York • San Francisco • New Haven, Conn • Waterville, Maine • London

GALE
CENGAGE Learning™

Copyright © 2008 by Rebel Road, Inc.
Thorndike Press, a part of Gale, Cengage Learning.

ALL RIGHTS RESERVED
Thorndike Press® Large Print Biography.
The text of this Large Print edition is unabridged.
Other aspects of the book may vary from the original edition.
Set in 16 pt. Plantin.
Printed on permanent paper.

LIBRARY OF CONGRESS CATALOGING-IN-PUBLICATION DATA

Eliot, Marc.
   Reagan : the Hollywood years / by Marc Eliot.
     p. cm.
   Includes bibliographical references.
   ISBN-13: 978-1-4104-1201-0 (hardcover : alk. paper : lg. print)
   ISBN-10: 1-4104-1201-6 (hardcover : alk. paper : lg. print)
   1. Reagan, Ronald. 2. Actors—United States—Biography. 3.
Large type books. I. Title.
PN2287.R25E45 2008b
791.4302'8092—dc22
  [B]   2008038940

Published in 2009 by arrangement with Harmony Books, a division of the Crown Publishers, Inc.

Printed in the United States of America
1 2 3 4 5 6 7 12 11 10 09 08

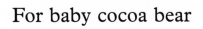

For baby cocoa bear

CONTENTS

Introduction 11
Chapter One: The Next Voice
    You Hear 27
Chapter Two: From Mugs to
    the Movies. 71
Chapter Three: The Irish Mafia . . . 99
Chapter Four: Dutch and
    Button-Nose 139
Chapter Five: The Gamut from
    A to B 179
Chapter Six: Kings Row 215
Chapter Seven: This Is the Army . . 273
Chapter Eight: Mr. Reagan Goes
    to Washington 339
Chapter Nine: Love Is Lovelier . . . 385
Chapter Ten: Falling Upward 427
Chapter Eleven: The Forgetting of
    Things Past 475
Chapter Twelve: Rendezvous
    with Destiny 547
    SOURCES 569
    NOTES 575

FILMOGRAPHY AND TV
APPEARANCES 605
AUTHOR'S NOTE AND
ACKNOWLEDGMENTS 631

Reagan had built up a strong following over the years at Warner Bros. playing mainly the companions of the leading stars, or loyal confidants of the rich and powerful. He hardly ever "got the girl." So when Jack Warner heard that Reagan was running for governor of California, he shook his head dubiously. "Governor, no. Bad casting. The *friend* of the governor."

— JESSE LASKY, JR.

Comedian Bob Hope once asked President Reagan how it felt to actually be the U.S. president — to sit in the very Oval Office where Abraham Lincoln paced during the Civil War. "Well," said Reagan, with his characteristic smile, "it's not a lot different than being an actor, except I get to write the script."

— DOUGLAS BRINKLEY, quoting Ronald Reagan in the published version of *The Reagan Diaries*

INTRODUCTION

Early Warner Bros.–First National publicity photo.

Ronald Reagan holds two unique places in American history, one as a minor cultural figure, the other as a major political one. In that sense, he was a serial populist. In his second incarnation, politics became the driving force of his life, and in 1967 he became the governor of California, an office he used as a springboard to win the presidency thirteen years later. In 1980, he became the nation's oldest elected chief executive and for the next eight years ruled with flash and stature as the most powerful politician in the world and, arguably, the most popular. Future historians will no doubt reevaluate President Reagan's contributions to such remarkable achievements as the fall of the Berlin Wall, the second Russian Revolution of the twentieth century, the arrival of relative peace in his time, and the long-term effects of the policies of "Reaganomics." Yet to understand fully the later political Ronald Reagan, whose personable manner and understated expression of authority allowed him to enjoy the respect of virtually everyone on all sides of the international political spectrum, it is necessary to examine the earlier Ronald Reagan, the Hollywood actor who continually struggled for recognition, success, and, ultimately, relevance. Hollywood helped create the public persona of the man who would eventually lead the free world, and therefore holds the key to understanding Reagan — who he was before who he eventually became. Indeed, if it may be said that as president Ronald Reagan played one character — "President Reagan," the smiling, affable, head-shaking, soft-spoken figure whose frequent utterance of the word "well" became prime turf for comedians the world over — it may also be said that as president the same carefully crafted, head-shaking, soft-spoken character, with all "wells" intact, made him one of the most beloved leaders the nation he led had ever seen.

Any mention of Ronald Reagan the actor usually brings snickers of ridicule, primarily because of the one film everybody remembers more than any of the fifty-three others that he made (only a handful of which are easily seen anymore): Frederick de Cordova's 1951 *Bedtime for Bonzo*. Its comic plot revolves around a man and his relationship to a laboratory chimpanzee. Had Reagan remained in pictures, *Bonzo,* too, would surely have slipped into the obscurity it deserved.

In truth, many of Reagan's films have been largely forgotten, overshadowed by the extensive examination of his accomplishments during his later political era. The reason may be simply one of time pushing his Hollywood years ever deeper into the recesses of the American cultural psyche. Ronald Reagan's career as an actor ended nearly a half a century ago, eons in a culture where lasting relevance is, with rare exception, usually measured in months.

However, Reagan's own reluctance to reflect on this period suggests there may have been some measure of unwillingness on his part to examine too closely just how all the monkey business of his first and mostly unremarkable career could possibly have led to the profoundly successful second one, which saw him heroically guide a nation out of the darkness of its own social, political, cultural, and moral post-Vietnam malaise back into the glorious sunshine of a powerfully chauvinistic national pride.

Like the early studio publicity 8 × 10s of his face, he may have preferred to airbrush the wrinkles of imperfection that marred the myths of his prepresidential Hollywood years. His two official "memoirs," both ghostwritten (the first by Richard Hubler, the second by Robert Lindsey), are, essentially, the same book, save for the expanded time frame of

15

the second, written some twenty-five years after the first, when Reagan's two terms of president had ended. They both share similarly self-aggrandizing distortions and significant lapses of fact — not all that unusual in memoirs when the subject chooses to recollect his own achievements for posterity, something politicians (and actors) often do.

The first, *Where's the Rest of Me?*, originally published in 1965, a year before Reagan made his successful run for governor, takes for its title his character's most famous line from Sam Wood's 1942 *Kings Row*. In it, Reagan, as Drake McHugh, asks the unforgettable question when he realizes his legs have been amputated during emergency surgery following an accident, and that the operation has left him "incomplete" as a man. Unfortunately, the memoir, whose main focus is the political battles Reagan fought before, during, and after his rise to the presidency of the Screen Actors Guild (SAG), a kind of primer for his future political style, is woefully incomplete. Reagan's title references not just his own appointment with destiny in the great American body politic but the political identity that would come with it (he had changed his party affiliation from Democrat to Republican only three years earlier). In the book, he glides through his Hollywood career rather lightly, as if impatient to get to the part of his life's journey that first made him feel truly "whole."

The second, *An American Life,* first published in 1990, runs over 725 pages, of which less than 20 percent, about a fifth, deals with Reagan's Hollywood years, despite the fact that his film and TV career lasted nearly three decades and did not end until 1965, when he was already fifty-four years old — almost thirty years, a full third of his life.[*] Considering Reagan died almost thirty years later — in June 2004, at the age of ninety-three, after several years of suffering from Alzheimer's disease — the span of his active full-time political career (not counting his work as the head of SAG while he was still a working actor), from his election as governor of California in 1966 to his second presidential term ending in 1988, amounts to about twenty-two years, or a little less than a quarter of his life.[†] Granted, serving as the ultimate leading man, the president of the

---

[*] Reagan appeared in fifty-four feature films between 1937 and 1964, and between 1952 and 1965 appeared in dozens of episodics and hosted two series, *G.E. Theater* and *Death Valley Days.* After 1966, he continued to appear on TV variety shows, including *The Tonight Show Starring Johnny Carson,* right up until his presidency.

[†] Reagan's term actually ended with George H. W. Bush's inauguration on January 20, 1989.

United States, was more important to him (and the rest of the world) than playing second fiddle to Warner's extraordinary stable of *über*-leading men (Humphrey Bogart, Dick Powell, Errol Flynn, and Pat O'Brien, among others). There is, nonetheless, in both memoirs, especially the second, a lot "left out," a palpable disconnect, the absence of what actors often refer to as "the motivational through-line," between Reagan's two lives. The biographical, emotional, and psychological connective tissue from one to the other is utterly missing.[*]

Reading Reagan's memoirs, one senses a long-standing dissatisfaction with his on-screen career that falls somewhere between anger and disappointment, with the roles he had (or more accurately, the ones he was denied), his relegation to the B unit for much of his decade-plus exclusive deal with Warner Bros., his inability to make the breakthrough to top-of-the line star. And that once he

***

[*] It was still missing years later, in 1999's *Dutch*, the authorized overstylized and underinformed biography by Edmund Morris. And in Nancy Reagan's 1989 memoir, *My Turn*, Hollywood plays even less of a role. Warner Bros., Reagan's home studio for much of his career, receives two scant mentions. MGM, her home studio, got five, and her entire film career is summed up in a total of twelve pages in her four-hundred-page memoir.

became president of the United States, perhaps the ultimate comeback, his rage and frustration toward Hollywood and the somewhat emasculating effect it had on his self-image — always the loyal pal, rarely the romantic lead — turned softer. If all was not totally forgiven, Reagan often chose to cover his first-career bitterness in a layer of self-deprecating (and self-defensive) humor. Hence, both memoirs, like his performance in *Bedtime for Bonzo,* are too self-consciously stiff and overly literal (but not very literary) to be truly revelatory.

However, away from the strictures of the written word or the movie moment, Reagan's self-deprecating humor always left teeth marks, with its punch lines often telling more about how he saw himself than any of his official chronicles. Rich Little, one of the most dead-on of (President) Reagan impersonators, became friends with his subject during the White House years and often informally chatted with him about the "good old days," something Little quickly discovered was still a sensitive issue for the president. One time, when he asked Reagan if it was true that he had, for a time, been up for the lead in Michael Curtiz's 1942 classic *Casablanca,* Reagan responded with that familiar head shake, automatic smile, quick turn-away of his eyes, and just a hint of a quivering hesitation in his voice: "Well, yes, it's true, but Ingrid Bergman eventually got the part."

During Cabinet meetings or at the many social events and state dinners, which Nancy Reagan produced Hollywood-style, as if they were glittering opening-night premieres of a major motion picture, he liked nothing more than to chuckle and gossip with friends about "the old days," not so much the pictures he made but, and at times quite graphically, the most beautiful women in the world whom he had had the privilege to work with — *Joy, Susan, Ila, Bette, Viveca, Olivia, Ann.* Women, and how he related to them (and them to him), was another complex affair for Reagan largely absent from his memoirs, perhaps another subject too much for him to deal with in autobiographical hindsight.

While his official "best friend" during his presidency was Jimmy Stewart — an actor whom he genuinely admired and knew well from the old days but never acted with, and who, accompanied by his wife and occasionally his children, was among the most frequent guests at the Reagan White House — the actor Reagan talked about the least was one of his closest on-screen "pals," Errol Flynn, with whom he had appeared in two of Reagan's better movies.[*] Flynn, arguably the most notorious ladies' man in the Tinseltown

* Michael Curtiz's 1939 *Santa Fe Trail* and Raoul Walsh's 1942 *Desperate Journey.*

of his time, was the star Reagan had most envied but could not get along with during the Hollywood years. Reagan admired the courtly heroism of Flynn's on-screen persona but strongly disapproved of the brutish way Flynn treated women in real life.

As for Reagan's first wife, the actress Jane Wyman — to whom he was married for eight years (they were married January 26, 1940, and divorced June 28, 1948) and who broke his heart when she had a highly publicized affair with actor Lew Ayres before leaving Reagan for good — in both memoirs he devotes very little space to her, about three paragraphs in his first, and *one sentence* in his second. Only with his second marriage, to Nancy Davis, when he was forty-one years old and she four months shy of thirty-one, does Reagan insist that he finally found emotional closure and completeness.[†] De-

† Reagan was ten or twelve years older than Davis, depending upon which source you consult for the actual year of her birth; it appears she may have shaved two years off in order to extend her youthful appeal to the studio heads of her day. In her unauthorized biography of Nancy Reagan, Kitty Kelley offers convincing evidence that Davis was actually born in 1921. Shaving years for the purposes of extending one's film career was not an uncommon practice in those years. Like today, youth then was everything in Hollywood.

spite their age difference, Davis provided to Reagan what the far more ambitious and calculating Wyman never could: the proper maternal acoustics for the psychologically packed echo left behind by Reagan's cries of longing for his first love, high-school sweetheart Margaret Cleaver. "Mugs," as he called her, had committed the cardinal sin of disloyalty when she left him for another boy, whom she eventually married and stayed with for the rest of her life. This was a deep wound that never completely healed, inflicted by the "gal" who was supposed to be "just like the one who married dear old Dad." From the day he married Nancy Davis until the last days of his life, Ronald Reagan always called his second wife "Mommy."

Politics, Hollywood-style, also played a role in Reagan's conflicted feelings about those years, especially when combined with his complex feelings about women. Reagan originally became involved with the issues of the day at the urging of his first wife, Wyman, who pushed him to secure a position on the board of the Screen Actors Guild, which would eventually lead to his becoming its president (interestingly, it was his second wife, Nancy, who masterminded his elevation in California society that served as entrée for him to national politics). Reagan, while still a Roosevelt liberal, became a strong and outspoken leader of SAG, considered at the time to be one of the most left-leaning unions in forties Hollywood. In that position, he performed the nearly impossible task of keeping the membership working without making them appear to be scabs or strike-breakers during what was perhaps the most volatile strike in Hollywood's history, while at the same time managing to keep the doors of the studios open for business. And he did it with passion, strength, and determination. Even so, despite all that he had done for his studio (one could make a reasonable if not definitive argument that Reagan helped save Warners from going under during these troubling times), once Jack Warner felt he could no longer justify keeping him under his exclusive, high-paying contract, he quickly and coldly cut Reagan loose. Reagan also used his position at SAG to gain advantageous "waivers" for MCA, the talent agency that represented him, owned by the imperious Jules Stein and led by the shadowy Lew Wasserman, and continued to do so even after Wasserman sent him to a humiliating engagement in Las Vegas at the lowest point in Reagan's career.

Upon his arrival in Hollywood as a complete unknown in a crowded field of unknowns, it was his extraordinarily good fortune to land Wasserman as his first agent. Wasserman took an immediate liking to the new young actor and set him on the road to stardom. It was Wasserman, more than any acting teacher ever did or could, who recognized young Reagan's natural talent and then helped to develop it into a commercially viable movie-star persona, the likable fellow, one of the boys, the hero's best friend, the all-around good guy.

It was Wasserman who made him a player in Hollywood; it was Wasserman who stood by him when Reagan fell from cinematic grace; it was Wasserman who orchestrated Reagan's amazing career resurrection, via television, that made possible his remarkable political transformation and eventual leap into history.

And Reagan never forgot it. That was why he could never say no to Wasserman, even when payback came in the form of that humiliating gig in Las Vegas, or the back-door Guild deals SAG president Reagan helped enforce that heavily favored MCA, over not only other talent agencies but also the very performers it and he, Reagan, represented. The last person Reagan had lunch with before heading for Washington, D.C., and the presidency, and the first person he had lunch with after his eight-year two-term tour of duty was over, was Lew Wasserman.

Ronald Reagan managed not merely to survive his Hollywood years, at the end of them he managed to perform an astonishing metamorphosis, from leading man to statesman, from an actor who played minor roles on the soundstages of Hollywood to a man whose greatest role was played out on the center stage of the world. Proving F. Scott Fitzgerald utterly wrong, Ronald Reagan had one of the most spectacular second acts of any American life.

What follows is the story of the first.

■ ■ ■ ■

CHAPTER ONE:
THE NEXT VOICE
YOU HEAR

■ ■ ■ ■

At Eureka, I'd pick up a broomstick, pretend it was a microphone, and do a locker-room interview with some of my fraternity brothers to get some laughs.

— RONALD REAGAN

Ronald Reagan was a lifeguard at Lowell Park Beach in Illinois during the summers he attended high school and college.

It was 1911 and Howard Taft was in the third year of his one-term presidency, a tenure of office so uneventful that on his deathbed he insisted he couldn't remember a single thing about it. In China and Mexico, revolution was in the air. In New York City, a fire in the Triangle shirtwaist factory killed nearly 150 workers and sparked nationwide labor reform. In Los Angeles, the immensely popular novelty of moving pictures was about to be transformed into a full-service industry by the merger of two independent film companies, which became Paramount Pictures, Hollywood's first "major" studio. And on February 6, in Tampico, Illinois, the heart of Chicago farm country, John Edward "Jack" Reagan (pronounced RAY-gun), first-generation Black Irish, and his wife, Nelle, became the proud parents of their second child, a baby boy they named Ronald Wilson.

Like his two-year-old brother, Neil (nicknamed "Moon" for his round face), baby Ronald was born in the cold-water flat the family lived in over a shallow bank on Main Street. There was no doctor available to make house calls for such poor folk as these, but Jack had managed to secure the services of a midwife, who brought the chubby infant into the world with a good old-fashioned smack on the bottom, which set baby Ronnie onto a crying jag that seemed to Jack would never end. Exasperated (and filled with too much booze), Jack declared later that night to the whole world but to no one in particular, "For such a little bit of a fat Dutchman, he makes a hell of a lot of noise!"

The crying eventually stopped, but the nickname stuck. From as early as he could remember, Ronald, whose given name was changed shortly after his birth (no one quite remembers why, but the certificate says Donald) was called Dutch. Jack, like his son, always preferred the nickname because, the father insisted, it made him sound more rugged than did the girlish "Ronnie" that Nelle had chosen.[*]

At the time, the tallest building in Tampico was the grain elevator dominating the single

[*] Accounts vary. According to the official Ronald Reagan website, Reagan's name was changed from *Donald* to *Ronald* while his mother was still pregnant, after her sister had a son and named him Donald, beating her to the punch.

30

commercial main street between the depots of two railroad lines. Jack worked in the general store across from the elevator. His knowledge covered all the departments, not unusual in these Midwest one-outpost towns, but he was especially adept at selling shoes, and his interest in them bordered on the obsessive; he spent his free nights analyzing the bones of feet and filling out forms requesting correspondence courses on how to sell the right shoes to fit them.

Unfortunately, his interest in and devotion to his work not only didn't help him get ahead, but after more than two years it also wasn't enough to keep him from losing his job. The problem wasn't ability; he had a lot of that, along with a good personality, a natural glibness, and an appreciation of when to tell a timely joke to move along a sale. It was, rather, what Ronald Reagan would later describe as the demon in the bottle that brought Jack down. Jack was a fall-down drunk who worshipped at the feet of Irish whiskey.

His wife, Nelle, on the other hand, was a straight-back Protestant, a member in good standing of the Tampico Church of Christ. Born in Illinois from a Scots-English ancestry, she'd met Jack in Fulton and fell fast and hard for the tall Irishman, accepting his proposal of marriage without hesitation despite the fact that he was Catholic. At least, she told herself, he wasn't a "serious" Catholic. He hardly attended Mass and although they were married in the Catholic church in Fulton, she had made it clear to him that their children would be raised Protestant. Jack had no objections.

Now, with two small children to raise — Neil, five years old, and Ronald, three — in the light of his latest firing, Jack, with his family, had to move far enough away to escape the stigma of what Nelle described as their disgraceful circumstances so that Jack could start over again. They moved first, in 1913, to the South Side of Chicago, where Jack worked as a shoe salesman at Marshall Field's department store, then they moved in 1915 to Galesburg, then in 1918 to Monmouth, where he got a job at E. B. Colwell's. They returned briefly in 1919 to Tampico, where Jack managed the H. C. Pitney General Store, a place he'd once sold shoes. Early in 1920, the family moved again, this time to Dixon, a real metropolis ninety-four miles outside of Chicago and situated along the Rock River. Nelle, determined the family would remain in Dixon for the sake of the children's having a stable schooling, insisted Jack lease a three-bedroom house on South Hennepin Avenue. He soon found a job at the Fashion Boot Shop, where for many years he would tell one and all, perhaps even Nelle, that he was a partner, when in truth he was

32

only a manager with a modest override on the percentage of sales he generated.

Although the Reagan family finances remained meager — Jack and Nelle would not own a home until their son became a movie star and bought one for them — the instability of their lifestyle seemed to have had little outward effect on Dutch. Perhaps he was too young to feel the negative social aspects — the lack of friends, the discontinuity of schooling — of constantly being uprooted. In his memoirs, Reagan remembered the family's arrival in Dixon as the first "home to me. All of us have a place we go back to: Dixon is that place for me."

Dutch was nine when the family moved to Dixon. By then he had formulated and developed two essential root characteristics of his personality. From his father he learned the expressive charms of a storyteller, including the value of a smile along with the ingratiating flip of his head, slightly back and to the side; a pat on the back; and a tight and warm shake of a hand. (He'd also witnessed his father's alcoholic stupors, which always left him sprawled out unconscious on the living room floor.) From his mother he learned that a lack of outward expressions of affection did not necessarily mean an absence of love.

And from both of them he learned about tolerance and loyalty. His parents stayed together through poverty, endless and often shiftless moves, and public humiliation due to his father's inability to control his drinking. As young Reagan observed, the bond of love between his parents could not be broken, no matter what. According to his mother, that was the Christian way, and the Christian way always led to Jack's repentance. Even if his promises to give up the bottle never lasted, his well-intentioned attempts made all the difference in the world to Nelle. And it left Dutch with a lifelong aversion to drinking.

One of the first things Dutch did in Dixon was to become active in his mother's newly chosen house of worship, the First Christian Church. Its pastor, Minister Ben Cleaver, quickly became an idealized father figure to him, a simpler and more sober version of the real Jack. For decidedly nonpaternal reasons, Dutch also became interested in the minister's daughter. Margaret "Mugs" Cleaver's face resembled that of her handsome father; she was pretty, with a strong chin and a sharp, slightly upturned nose. Her eyes were set wide apart and, like the minister, she always wore a bright smile on her face. Her brunette hair was cut short in the curl-wave style popular with young girls during the 1920s. If Margaret's physical beauty reminded him of her "perfect" dad, her personality echoed the ship-righting strength and balance of his mother. Like Nelle, Margaret was never at a loss for words — and was very much the aggressor, the organizer, the finger-snapping miniauthoritarian. Her stabilizing if domineering manner appealed to Reagan as much as her good looks and quick wit.

All of these qualities were sharp as an arrow's tip for Reagan, and from the first time he saw her, he fell heart-piercingly, irresistibly in young love. After a few weeks of getting to know each other, they began dating, which allowed Reagan, in an adolescent fashion, to "remake" his father into a better man by casting himself in the role and playing it better than Jack ever could. Margaret was the perfect mother/girlfriend. For Reagan, even at this early age, role-playing was as good as, if not better than, reality.

Dutch and Mugs were soon going steady in that chaste mock-marriage style so in vogue with preteens of the day (hand-holding, movies, popcorn, ice-cream sodas, walks in the moonlight). Before long he was spending more time at the minister's home than he was at his own. Years later, Margaret's sister Helen would recall that "[Reagan] was often in our home and felt the influence of Father's guidance during those formative years." Mrs. Cleaver, a woman wrapped in Christian tradition and a perpetual apron, happily welcomed Dutch's presence in the household. Like her husband, she considered him the right kind of boy for her daughter to be friends with.

The arrival of Mugs into young Ronald's life couldn't have pleased Nelle more, as she, too, had become a familiar figure in the Cleaver home, often consulting with and taking the advice of the minister regarding her lesson books for Sunday-school teachings, her role in the Women's Missionary Society, and her regular dramatic readings in church.

Cleaver, a warm, friendly man with middle-of-the-road politics (that made him something of a liberal in Dixon), was also a strong supporter of the Eighteenth Amendment, the passage of which ushered in the era of Prohibition. Many in the congregation who personally knew the Reagans took Cleaver's incessant support of the passage of the amendment as an indirect but pointed criticism of Jack, who was already distrusted by many of Dixon's prominent Protestants for his insistence on remaining a practicing Catholic.

Rumors of a divorce were whispered like dirty words among Nelle's friends at the church. If she heard them, she didn't care; even if she had to crack the whip occasionally, Jack would always be her man. They were in love and that was the beginning, middle, and end of it. However, the tensions within such a close-knit religious and social community tended to agitate Dutch, who continued to feel embarrassment at his father's inability to control his drinking and who believed the other (Protestant) kids at school poked fun at him because of it. Being the object of their mean-spirited jokes turned him away from after-school activities, Sunday school, and eventually church itself. He much preferred his mother's regular nightly preaching to him and Neil from her *Hostess Reference Book* of enlightened social skills.

But most of all he found comfort in the dark, more secular world of the movies. Every Saturday morning, by himself, Reagan would go to the local Family Theater, where the "kiddie" programs of serials, comedies, cartoons, and Westerns transported him out of his reality and into a world of silver-screen romance and adventure. He especially loved the "cowboys" Tom Mix and William S. Hart, two actors among the biggest movie stars of their day (neither of whom were actual cowboys, a Hollywood tradition that continued with Roy Rogers and Gene Autry, and later on, John Wayne and Ronald Reagan himself). On-screen, Mix and Hart were two-fisted tough, knew right from wrong, always played the heroes, and always defeated the bad guys. They loved the land upon which they rode their white horses, they wore tall if rather impractical hats, and they carried silver six-guns. And with courtly grace and perfect manners they defended the honor of the town's beautiful, helpless, angellike women, more often than not the daughters of one of the fallen sheriffs or marshals, occasionally the "good" daughter of one of the "bad" guys. It was at the movies where Reagan learned all the "enlightened social skills" he would ever need. He would later remember those Saturday mornings as among the happiest days of his youth.

However, Dutch's incessant love for movies sometimes clashed with his duties as a boyfriend (as Margaret put it), especially when it came to church activities. Mugs strongly disapproved of the fact that her boyfriend was spending far more of his weekend at the Family Theater than at church. She also didn't appreciate what she thought of as his clumsy lack of self-control whenever they were alone; his groping at her was something else he must have learned from those movies! Indeed, young Ronald's hormones were raging, and as any boy might want to, he tried to share these new and surging feelings with his girlfriend, who slammed shut these attempts with as much authority as her father did the New Testament at the end of one of his sermons.

Mugs also did not think much of Dutch's new habit of occasionally taking a drink, even though it was never anything stronger than a beer, and would let him know in her typical authoritarian manner that she was not going to tolerate it. This continual criticism of his behavior somehow only made him feel closer to her and reinforced his belief not only that she knew better about these things than he did, but that she was the picture-perfect girlfriend for him. In his first memoir, Reagan wrote that at the time he was "sure" Margaret was one day going to be his wife.

Ronald proved a good student during his years at North Dixon High School, where he tried to keep his grades above average so he could get into college, something he was determined to do. His only apparent shortcomings were, in fact, literal. At the age of thirteen, he was unusually small for his age. He stood all of five foot three, making him ineligible to play on any of the freshman teams, something every Dixon boy dreamed of doing. And his height wasn't his only handicap. After experiencing blurred vision on several occasions, an eye exam revealed what he already feared, that he was severely nearsighted and would have to wear glasses at all times except when reading. His vision and size seemed to rule out any chance he might have had at playing football, the sport he loved most. To him, football was a lot like Westerns: simple scenarios of good guy vs. bad guy, physical strength, and single-minded focus — the ultimate reward for the winners being the respect from the other guys (townspeople) and adoration from the girls (rescued heroines-in-distress). From the sidelines, he watched, through his spectacles, the other boys play, but he imagined that he was the real hero of the game — the great quarterback who threw the winning pass, saved the game, saved the day, saved the season, *saved the world!*

At night in bed he held his breath and literally tried to stretch himself taller.

The one sport where he had any chance at all to compete was swimming, the only one in which his size and slim musculature were an advantage and his eyesight really didn't matter. Just after he turned fifteen, the diminutive Dutch was a good enough swimmer to get a job for the summer that paid $15 a week as a Rock River lifeguard by the beach area at the edge of Lowell Park. It was a job he was to hold for the next seven summers, for all of his remaining high school days and the four years he spent at college. In that time, he put on an astonishing array of heroism by rescuing a total of seventy-eight people from drowning, an average of more than ten every summer, or more than one per week. Even in the roughest of waters, a lifeguard "save" of one or two swimmers a season would be a remarkable achievement for a young man, and impressive for even the most experienced adult lifeguard.

Rather than assuming the role of humble hero, Dutch enthusiastically played up all the attention he received for these "miracles," as the press regularly referred to them. The recognition of his "amazing" feats brought something to his life that he hadn't had before — widespread popularity so intense that it bordered on hero worship. He became Dixon's real-life Tom Mix, or so it felt to him. Because of the stories of his "astounding" feats the *Dixon Telegraph* regularly put on its front page, everyone in town knew about his selfless dives into the cold waters of the Rock. Typical of these is the August 3, 1928, edition that led with this headline reporting Reagan's own, first-person account of his latest "save": PULLED FROM THE JAWS OF DEATH!

After every rescue, Dutch would ceremoniously cut a notch on a nearby piece of heavy driftwood, proof of his accomplishments (after the notches on Tom Mix's six-gun for every bad guy he killed).

The colorful if somewhat fanciful "rescue" stories, which sold a lot of local newspapers, would one day fit neatly into the log-cabin mythos of the future president even if they were about as believable as Washington's confessing to chopping down the cherry tree or Lincoln's walking a mile to return a penny. Nevertheless, throughout Reagan's life, their literal truth remained unchallenged, evidence of his strong virtues and high moral value. (Interestingly, the only actual count of rescues Reagan made was on that piece of driftwood, which did not survive as long as the stories of the rescues it recorded.) It wasn't until after Reagan became president that he even conceded the possibility there might have been some exaggeration involved, but he did it in a way that suggested those whom he pulled to shore didn't know how fortunate they really were to have him watching over them: "People hated to be saved. Almost every one of them later sought me out and angrily denounced me for dragging them to shore. 'I would have been fine if you'd let me alone . . . you made a fool out of me trying to make a hero out of yourself.' "[*]

They didn't know with whom they were dealing. For Reagan, the boy who couldn't make the football team, the need to be seen as a hero was overwhelming. Widespread acknowledgment and praise were not just a social tonic for him but a necessary romantic boost in the eyes of the one person to whom

[*] According to Nancy Reagan, as quoted by James C. Humes in *The Wit and Wisdom of Ronald Reagan,* in Dixon there is a plaque in the park that attests to Reagan's heroic "gallantry." It notes that all the seventy-eight "victims" were women. Years later, even Nancy Reagan was skeptical of the facts of these rescues and suspected they might have been spurred more by hopes of romance than by drowning.

he most wanted to prove his manliness and bravery — his beloved Mugs. If the rest of the world, or at least all of Dixon, loved him for what he did, he was sure Margaret would, too. Hers was the only approval he sought because, in the end, hers was the only approval that mattered.

He didn't get it. If Mugs was impressed with his continual lifesaving, she didn't say so, simply because in her world, heroism was nothing to brag about. It was God-given and therefore expected.

At age sixteen, Dutch experienced a long-awaited and late-in-coming adolescent spurt of growth that by the start of his junior year in high school brought him up to just under six feet. Those few inches made all the difference in the world. This time, despite his eyesight, he easily made the guard and tackle positions on the football team. Even if he still couldn't see all that well, he was now bigger than most of the boys, which made it harder to get around him, and if he had to throw, his teammates would try their best to receive his passes. His biggest advantage was his speed. Although tall, he had yet to fill out, and his well-developed swimmer's body allowed him to fly by most of the others.

Dutch helped his team to a winning 4-3-1

record that year, and that meant a coveted varsity letter. He won another letter playing for North Dixon's "lightweight" basketball team. He was, at the same time, approached by the drama instructor, B. J. Frazer, who had noticed the boy's tall, dark good looks, accentuated by the shock of Irish black/brown hair that hung over the sensitive face. Mr. Frazer persuaded him to join the Dramatic Club, an offer that, in truth, didn't take much persuading. Dutch leapt at the chance to play heroes like his Tom Mix.

Dutch proved so adept that by the end of the year he was elected sergeant-at-arms of the club. His performance in Phillip Barry's *You and I* was praised for its demonstration of emotional sincerity, not hard to understand as it was none other than Mugs who played the female romantic lead opposite him in the play. Now he not only got to kiss his girlfriend — she could not possibly push him away because it was ordained by the higher powers of the invisible but ever-present playwright — but he could do it in front of a packed house and could even take a bow for it while the audience applauded.

In his senior year, he was elected president of the Dramatic Club and was rewarded by being given the best role in that year's annual senior class production, the villainous Ivan Borolsk in George Bernard Shaw's *Captain*

Brassbound's Conversion.[*] Although he performed his part well enough for a high school production, it bothered him to be cast as the villain. When acting opposite Mugs, kissing her was merely an amplification of feelings he already had, but when called upon to play "the bad guy," he just didn't feel right. It was a feeling that was to remain with him for a very long time.[†]

If his appearance in the play left him cold, everything else he did that year caught fire. As the art director of the senior class yearbook, he took it upon himself to design its cover, and wrote two short stories and a poem for the literary section. One of them was called "Meditations of a Lifeguard" and contained this revealing paragraph:

> She's walking toward the dock now. She tips gracefully over to the edge of the crowded pier and settles like a butterfly.

[*] Often referred to incorrectly as *Captain Applejack,* which Shaw did not write; Walter Hackett did. *Captain Applejack* was part of a trilogy Shaw called "three plays for puritans."

[†] Reagan was cast as "the good guy" in all but one, his last, of the fifty-four feature films he made in Hollywood. He often said that Don Siegel's 1964 *The Killers* was his least favorite film (for more on it, see Chapter 12, "Rendezvous with Destiny").

The lifeguard strolls by, turns, and strolls by again. Then he settles in the immediate region of the cause of all this sudden awakening. He assumes a manly worried expression, designed to touch the heart of any blonde, brunette, or unclassified female. He has done all that is necessary. She speaks and the sound of her voice is like balm to a wounded soul. . . .

As he had on stage, Reagan intermingled reality into his world of adolescent imagination and longing, calling upon his private wish and the public's belief that he was a hero by identifying himself as "manly" but in need of caring in the form of a goddesslike woman. It requires little imagination to figure out who the goddess was who supplied the "balm" to this wounded soul. His short story is a love letter in disguise, containing elements of worship and unfulfilled desire for all the world, and Mugs, to read and, hopefully, admire (both story and writer). Things he couldn't say to her in real life he could "think" in the form of his story's character, the lifeguard.

He was also elected president of the Dixon Student Council and president of the boys' Hi Y Club and he participated in several intraclass debates. He also ran track. It seemed everywhere anyone in school looked that year, Ronald Reagan was there. "The fact was," he wrote years later, "I suppose that I just liked to show off."

"Life is just one grand sweet song," according to the assessment of "Donald" Reagan, president of the Class of '28 and president of the Student Council, in the yearbook that featured an unsmiling yet pleasant image of Dutch in a dark suit and striped bow tie. It was, for him, the perfect end to a perfect high school career. He had come from behind, overcoming seemingly insurmountable obstacles, to achieve his class's highest post. He had performed well academically and was a lettered athlete. And the icing on the cake was that he had accompanied Margaret to the Senior Banquet, as sure a sign as any that they were "serious" about each other.

If all of it seemed like those miniatures his mother kept in the showcase cabinet, a smaller-than-life depiction carved in wood of the idyllic Midwestern life, it was also like the set of some simple play he could see in his dreams: He would marry Mugs after they both graduated from college. They would have a family of their own. He would start a business in town and they would live happily ever after.

That September, Dutch enrolled in Eureka College, even as things were beginning to unravel ever so slowly in the fabric of the Reagan household. After having failed to convince the owner of the Fashion Boot Shop to make him a full partner, Jack took a job as a traveling shoe salesman and eventually relocated weekdays to Springfield, Illinois, 141 miles south of Dixon, where he took on a second job managing another retail shoe store when he couldn't make ends meet on his commission-based traveling sales job (a de facto separation Reagan later attributed to the hard realities of the Depression, even though it was still a year away, rather than to marital problems his parents were having or his father's drink-impaired sales abilities). Moon had decided to go his own way as well, rejecting college for practical reasons — the family didn't have the money to send him — and philosophical reasons, believing it was a waste of time anyway. He was eager to get out and make his way in the real world, via Chicago, and a career in advertising.

Dutch, on the other hand, had made up his mind that he was going to be one of the nation's 2 percent who attended college that year. His choice of school was easy because it was preordained, Eureka College, seventy-eight miles south of Dixon, a small school (250 students more or less evenly divided between boys, 130, and girls, 120) run by his mother's favored sect of Protestantism, the Disciples of Christ. And even if other schools had shown some interest in his broad-based academic and physical achievements, he would consider no other place, because Eureka was also the college where Margaret had been accepted, thanks to her father's influence within the Disciples.

He was relatively well prepared financially, having saved enough money from his lifeguard job to be able to make the $180 annual tuition and approximately $400 room and board. A scholarship for half the tuition helped, although it came with a proviso that Reagan perform some work task for the school. During his first two years he was a dishwasher in the girls' dormitory; the latter two he served as a lifeguard at the school's swimming pool and part-time coach for the competitive swimming team he conceived and captained.

Dutch hit the campus running, literally and figuratively. One of Margaret's sister's boyfriends, the school's current football hero, quickly took the freshman under his wing and led him through the easy pledge requirements of Tau Kappa Epsilon, the favored fraternity of the school's athletes. For the next three years, Reagan played football at Eureka. Just as he did in high school, Dutch behaved as if he had something to prove, not just to Margaret but to the world (if indeed there was any difference to him). He took on a heavy load of extracurricular activities. These included reporting for the school paper; cheerleading after he failed to make the basketball team; editing the feature section of *Prism,* the senior school yearbook; and participating in the Student Senate, as president, in his junior year.

All of this extra work eventually caught up with Reagan and took a toll on his grades, but he didn't seem to care. To him, the most important thing was his ongoing courtship with Margaret. He loved doing something called "kegging," the on-campus practice of walking proudly with your girlfriend arm-in-arm.

He also continued to pursue dramatics. He was cast in the lead of most of the plays he tried out for. In his sophomore year he joined Alpha Epsilon Sigma, the college dramatic fraternity, at the same time as Margaret. (So did Neil, who had decided that, with the onset of the Depression and advertising jobs in Chicago nowhere to be found, college didn't sound so bad after all, especially since Eureka was willing to let him work his way through as well.)

Alpha Epsilon Sigma was headed by Ellen Marie Johnson, who took her duties with the Dramatics Society quite seriously. In Reagan's junior year, Miss Johnson put on Edna St. Vincent Millay's fanciful, dreamy antiwar one-act neo–Greek tragedy, *Aria da Capo,* one of the most frequently produced dramas on college campuses. Dutch was cast in the lead role of Shepherd Thyrsis. The production proved good enough to be entered in the annual one-act play competition at Northwestern University's School of Speech, which at the time had one of the most respected dramatic departments in the country, as it does to this day. Entries came from all over the country, and it was considered a high honor to be accepted as one of the dozen productions invited to perform at the university. Traditionally, the prize went to established Ivy League drama clubs such as Princeton's Triangle Club (a student named Jimmy Stewart was a member that year) or the Yale Playhouse.

Eureka's *Aria da Capo* not only made the cut but won third place, and Reagan received a special commendation for his performance, which featured a highly dramatic death scene (his character is strangled by another shepherd). The last night of performances at Northwestern was, according to Reagan years later, more thrilling than "any Oscar show could ever be." At the closing ceremonies he was awarded one of six acting honors. It was a turning point for Reagan, the first time he felt the pull of professional acting.

Dutch then "starred" in a succession of Eureka productions, including *The Art of Being Bored,* playing as usual opposite Mugs. After the final performance of this, the last show of his junior year, he presented her with a long-range plan for their life together and a ring. Five years of engagement, he told her, would be proper and then they could marry. Mugs happily accepted the ring and wore it everywhere she went, off campus and on, and it became common knowledge that the school's best leading man and prettiest leading lady were now officially engaged.

Ronald Reagan graduated from Eureka in June 1932 and chose Chicago as the place to rendezvous with his theatrical destiny. "If I had told anyone I was setting out to be a movie star, they'd have carted me off to an institution," Reagan later said as a way of explaining why he chose Chicago instead of Hollywood or New York. That, indeed, may have been part of the reason for what appeared to have been a choice of compromise, a locale far enough away from home to be considered venturing out but not so far that he couldn't come home when necessary, to visit his family, his friends, and of course Mugs. But there was another reason as well for choosing Chicago. Radio had become show business's newest fad, taking off from the phenomenon of "talking pictures" and bringing into the home the familiar voices that came from Hollywood movies and New York City's Broadway. Although shows like Freeman Gosden and Charles Corell's *Amos 'n' Andy* were legitimate sensations, radio sitcoms and news breaks were not the biggest draw to a public looking for an inexpensive way to be entertained at the height of the Depression; sports were. Games "called" by sportscasters had captured the imagination of home listeners. Everyone — college students, high schoolers, dads coming home after work or relaxing on weekends, even wives and mothers, were entertained by the voice pictures painted by the stentorian voices able to inject drama into college and professional games. For radio stations, sports was a cheap way to deliver drama — no scripts, no royalties, no actors, and no production costs, such as sound effects or props.

Because of its location, Chicago became the first national center of radio. WGN's 50-thousand-watt signal could reach a far greater audience than any live broadcast out of New York City or Los Angeles, as the Midwest flatlands allowed for Chicago's AM stations' broadcasts to be heard without interference as far north as Canada and as far south as Texas. They could be picked up to the east all the way to the Appalachians; and at night, when the sun's gravitational pull could no longer yank the signal away from the earth, as far west as the Rockies.

Chicago sportscasters like Graham Mac-Namee, Ted Husing, and Pat Flanagan became nationwide household names, if not faces, often more familiar than the names of the players whose exploits they so colorfully reported, and far more popular than the entertainers with whom they shared the station's prime time. Reagan chose Chicago because he thought he might be able there to combine his love of athletics with that of theater and become a sports announcer on the radio.

After an unsuccessful job-hunting stint, however, where one sympathetic secretary told the dejected would-be announcer that no one started at the top in this business and that smaller markets were the way to break in, Reagan returned to Dixon to revise his career plan. Jack offered to lend him the family car, a third-hand Oldsmobile, so that he could look for work in the smaller-market tricities of Davenport, Moline, and Rock Island along the Mississippi, about seventy-five miles west of Dixon.

On the way, Dutch looped south and stopped off at Eureka, where Mugs was living. (Moon was, too, staying for the summer before returning to school for his junior year.) If Reagan had hoped, even planned on, Mugs joining him on his job-hunting adventure, that wish evaporated when she told him she had accepted a teaching position at a nearby high school that was to start as soon as she graduated. This time, there was an uncomfortably formal chill to their good-byes. Reagan, standing aside his open car door, his hair blowing slightly in the warm wind, promised he'd come back to visit her again the first chance he got.

It was in Davenport that Reagan would meet the first of what would be a series of mentors who took him under their wing and helped smooth the flight of his life's journey. Things like this had happened to him before, most notably with coaches at school, but they were essentially teachers whose job it was to nurture talent. Peter MacArthur was different. He was a professional in a world of professionals and expected those he dealt with to be talented, knowledgeable, and, most important, experienced. Reagan may have had a certain amount of the first two qualifications, but he had none of the third. Nevertheless, he managed somehow to impress MacArthur enough to talk his way into a job at the Scottish-born chiropractor's radio station.

Peter MacArthur had emigrated to America from Scotland via the show business route, and in doing so became one of the privileged British Isle youths (like Charles Chaplin, Stan Laurel, and Cary Grant, to name a few of the more successful ones) able to use his talents to gain entrée to America. MacArthur did it as a juvenile member of the famed Harry Lauder vaudeville troupe. He remained with Lauder for several years as an acrobat and tumbler, during which time he earned permanent work-status privileges in the States. His career looked unstoppable until he developed a severe case of arthritis in his limbs that forced him from the stage. MacArthur's illness led him to enroll full-time at the Palmer School of Chiropractic as a way to keep his work-status privileges, start a new career, and maybe even contribute to finding a cure for his own illness.

Although his search for a cure remained unfulfilled, he did discover a new field interest at Palmer. Radio. With the money he'd saved from his performing career, MacArthur had purchased a small radio station in Rock Island, Illinois, and moved the antenna to Davenport, where he set it up as WOC (World of Chiropractic, also known as the Wonders of Chiropractic), broadcasting mostly local farm news, weather, medical advice, and stock market information. He did most of the announcing himself, and soon enough the station's strong signal made his signature Scottish burr familiar throughout the Midwest: *"THIS IS WOC, DAVENPORT, WHERE THE WEST BEGINS IN THE STATE WHERE THE TALL CORN GROWS!"*[*]

WOC was Dutch's first planned stop on his

---

[*] MacArthur claimed that his Davenport signal was so perfectly positioned against the flatlands of the Midwest that on a clear day his station could be heard as far away as Stockholm, Paris, Rome,

quest to find work in radio. He tracked down MacArthur, who ran his entire station's administrative operations out of a vacant office he had leased in a Palmer School building located in the modest downtown area of Davenport. MacArthur's office was on the fourth floor, where, from his window, he could enjoy the sight of his giant antenna.

Reagan walked into MacArthur's office precisely on time for his appointment, something MacArthur liked, and when asked why he was there, talked politely about his desire to be in radio. When MacArthur asked him what his other interests were, Dutch mentioned sports and acting. Midway through the interview, MacArthur stood, reached for a fat cigar from the box on his desk, lit it,

---

Manila, even by explorers at the North Pole, although why they would be interested in weather conditions in Davenport remains unclear. Mac-Arthur was part entrepreneur, part hustler, and part P. T. Barnum, according to his son in Stephen Vaughn's *Ronald Reagan in Hollywood* (pages 21–22; see "Sources"). He often referred to himself as "Colonel" MacArthur, a distinction as dubious as the one Tom Parker would give himself a few years later, modeled in part after MacArthur and others like him, cigar-smoking, white-suited, grandiose show-business/carny types, when he managed small-time country acts, including Elvis Presley, who would make "Colonel Parker," world — famous.

blew a plume of dark yellow smoke, stared out at his antenna and excused young Reagan, telling him he'd missed out by only a day; one of the few available announcing jobs had already been filled.

Reagan frowned, shook his head, said goodbye, and turned to leave. It was then that MacArthur shouted for him to "hold on, you big bastard! What was that you said about sports announcing? Do ya know anything about football?"

Reagan stopped frowning. MacArthur asked if he could radio-broadcast a football game and "make me see it"? Dutch assured him he could. MacArthur then took him to an empty studio, told him to start talking when the red light went on, and to re-create a game in his mind's eye that he, MacArthur, would be able to see. Reagan waited, and on cue, proceeded to conjure up a game he'd played in at Eureka. The words came tumbling out of his mouth: "Here we are in the fourth quarter with Western State University leading Eureka College six to nothing . . . long blue shadows are settling over the field and a chill wind is blowing in through the end of the stadium . . ." It sounded like nothing so much as one of his short stories.

MacArthur liked what he heard, especially the dramatic touch Reagan added when he had Eureka win by a last-second drop-kick. He came into the studio, still smoking, and said, "Ya did great, ya big SOB. Be here Saturday, you're broadcasting the Iowa-Minnesota Homecoming game. You'll get five dollars and bus fare."[*]

Reagan couldn't believe it, and at the same time he couldn't *not* believe it. His self-confidence was underscored by MacArthur's instant acceptance of him. His first interview, his first radio job. Even when the football season ended and he was laid off, Reagan left Davenport with a strong and well-deserved sense of accomplishment. He was a radio man now, a sportscaster, a professional.

He returned to Dixon sure he would soon find another job, hopefully in radio, which had become his new field of dreams. He listened to as much of it as he could. He liked nothing better than the live "fireside" chats by the president, Franklin Delano Roosevelt, the first to use mass media as a way to personalize and ingratiate himself to the electorate. Reagan was inspired as much by Roosevelt's use of the medium to com-municate his ideas so effectively as by the

---

[*] Versions of this story vary. Reagan himself pub-lished two differing accounts in his memoirs, and others have published variations with minor changes in details, such as Reagan not being offered one game but the rest of the season on the spot. The es-sential facts are that Reagan made up the game and because of it was able to talk his way into the job.

ideas themselves, if indeed there was any difference.

As fall turned to winter and the gray days grew shorter, the charcoal nights fell fast and heavy like the soot from the many coal stoves that Dixonites used to keep warm eight months out of every year. During this period, Dutch did not pursue any new jobs. He had a feeling, he would later recall, that somehow his next job would come to him, and he was exactly right; it did. Shortly before Christmas, Reagan received a phone call from MacArthur, who offered him a salary of a hundred dollars a week for the position of staff announcer.[†] MacArthur told Reagan that one of the two resident voices of WOC had quit, but in reality he had created a new position to bring the young man he liked so much back to the station.[*]

Reagan left Dixon the next day and re-

[†] Reagan confuses the date in his two memoirs. In *Where's the Rest of Me?,* he says the call came "just before Christmas . . ." while in *An American Life,* he says the call came in February. It remains unclear when the call actually came, but either way, Reagan did return to WOC to do the football games that were broadcast beginning sometime in March.

[*] The other staff announcer, Hugh Hippie, would also go on to have a career in Hollywood films, as Hugh Marlowe.

turned to Davenport.

For the next several weeks, Reagan served as a jack-of-all-trades at the station, sometimes playing records, sometimes making public service announcements, sometimes doing the weather, occasionally reading a commercial. It was during one of these multiple assignment days that he made an error serious enough to get him fired. In a half-hour session of scheduled organ music, Reagan neglected to plug the local mortuary, the program's sponsor. Despite MacArthur's fighting for him, the mortuary insisted Reagan be fired or it would pull all future ads. As much as MacArthur liked Reagan, he liked the money the mortuary paid even more, and so with great reluctance, he had to let Reagan go.

In both his memoirs, Reagan quite candidly calls what took place next nothing less than an act of God: "one of those things happened that makes one wonder about God's having a plan for all of us." Even though he had been fired for his own ineptness, Reagan's final assignment was to teach the new station director the ropes. Along the way they started talking, and when asked why he was leaving, Reagan explained what happened. This made the new fellow go to MacArthur and demand a contract. MacArthur refused, saying no one at his stations ever got contracts. The fellow

61

quit. MacArthur rehired Reagan and decided to personally tutor him in the techniques of announcing (as well as the necessities of paid on-air spots) to ensure he wouldn't have to let him go again. It was one of those instances that would happen throughout his life, with Reagan falling out of an open window in his career and somehow landing on his feet. *On the roof.*

Not long after that, MacArthur got a call from WOC's sister station WHO broadcasting out of Des Moines. They had just contracted to cover the Drake Relays, a major track meet, and needed an announcer to call the event. Did MacArthur have anyone who knew the ins and outs of the sport? MacArthur asked Reagan if he could do it. Dutch, whose track record at Eureka had helped win him one of his letters, said he was sure he could handle the assignment.

Reagan arrived in Des Moines the first week in April and was impressed by the size and décor of WHO, a far cry from the small suite of studios and offices that doubled as MacArthur's base for his many ventures in Davenport. Here Reagan's luck carried him once more. WHO was just in the process of acquiring one of about a dozen newly licensed and extremely powerful 50,000-watt transmitters, along with being named a major new Midwestern affiliate of the New York–based National Broadcasting Company's NBC

Radio Network. By the time his last day rolled around, he was offered the permanent spot as the station's resident sports announcer at a decent salary and the opportunity to make extra money by making guest appearances at sports events, covering them for the local paper, making personal appearances at other events, and doing on-site public-address-system announcements. He became something of a local Midwest celebrity, the sports voice of WHO Des Moines, which meant, in effect, that he was the sports voice of the entire region, a position he held on to for the next four and a half years.

Occasionally Reagan called football games on the air when the University of Iowa played the University of Michigan, despite the fact he was never actually at the games — it was too expensive for the station to send him — but verbalized the play-by-plays via telegraphic reports that came into the station, something he had become quite proficient at doing whenever he "broadcast" Chicago Cubs games over WHO. Baseball, however, was slower than football and he had a bit of difficulty keeping the action going, although he managed to get by.

Calling the games taught Reagan how to tell a story better than anything he had ever written in college. With his voice he acted out, rather than narrated, the games, convincing himself he was there watching it, and in turn convincing the listeners at home they were as well. And when there were lulls, he learned to fill time with folksy stories, down-home anecdotes, whatever he could think of. The confidence with which he learned to communicate gave his broadcasts a heightened sense of believability.

One day in 1934 Reagan received word that his father had suffered a heart attack. After years of minimal employment and long stretches of joblessness, the senior Reagan had managed to get a position with Roosevelt's Works Progress Administration (WPA), created to put able-bodied people like Jack back into respectable jobs while helping to build and rebuild the physical face of America. Unfortunately, Jack did not remain able bodied for long, collapsing one day on the job. Once he was certain his father was going to recover, to make sure he didn't go back to that job, Reagan quietly began sending money home to help his parents make ends meet.

It was also around this time that Reagan discovered what would become a lifelong love affair with horses. One of the other announcers at the studio told Reagan that if he applied for a reserve commission with the Fourteenth Cavalry Regiment based at Fort Des Moines, they would teach him how to ride, something Reagan had never done before. Ever the sportsman (the latent Tom Mix of his cowboy movie fantasies), Reagan tried out for the cavalry reserves, but his poor eyesight prevented him from joining. Having failed his first physical, he waited a few days and went back. This time, while he "covered" one eye to read the chart, he spread his fingers to be able to see it with both and passed.

During all of this, Mugs was never far from his thoughts. As he recalled in both his memoirs, he often thought about her teaching at that school just outside of Eureka, believing she was patiently waiting for him to get that foundation laid for their future.

She wasn't.

One day, early in the winter of 1936, Reagan's fourth year at WHO and second as a cavalry reservist, he received a letter from Mugs. He sat down in the living room of his small apartment and eagerly ripped it open. He loved getting mail from her, but this letter was not like any of the others she regularly sent to him. As he unfolded the single handwritten page, his fraternity pin and the engagement ring he had given her fell into his lap. His heart and head began to pound as he read Margaret's words. She had recently taken a European cruise with one of her sisters, she said, had met a Foreign Service officer there, and fallen in love with him. His name was James Waddell Gordon, Jr., a distinguished member of the U.S. Consular Service. They were going to get married.

Reagan closed his eyes and pressed his fists to his forehead. Gone. Mugs was gone. One of the first things he did, when he could do anything at all, was call his mother. Nelle told him she had been expecting his call. Everyone back home already knew, and she was wondering how long it would be until Margaret broke the news to him. As she listened to the choke in her son's voice, she calmly repeated to him something he had heard her say a million times when he was a child, that he shouldn't despair, that everything always works out for the best. Reagan thanked his mother for her good advice and hung up. A few weeks later Nelle called Reagan to tell him that Margaret had announced the date for her wedding.

That's when it finally became too real and too much for Reagan to bear. Years later he would remember how Margaret's decision had "shattered" him. All the good things that had happened to him in the last four years suddenly meant nothing, because the best thing that had ever happened to him was gone.

Characteristically, he kept much of his sorrow to himself, never letting on to anyone at the station that anything at all was wrong. He came to work smiling every day, did his broadcasts and anything else anyone wanted him to do, then went home at night — the only difference being that now more often than not on his way home he stopped off at the corner tavern for a beer. Or two.

Then, in the midst of all of his private wallowing, another bolt of luck lightning hit him, this one from the side of the angels. The Chicago Cubs, then one of the hottest teams in major league baseball, having won the National League pennant the previous season before losing the World Series in six games to the vaunted American League Detroit Tigers, invited him to cover their spring-training season at Catalina Island, a small tropiclike paradise twenty-six miles off the coast of California. To sweeten the deal, they agreed to let him write exclusive pieces about the team for the *Des Moines Sunday Register* as part of his regular column, "Around the World of Sports with 'Dutch' Reagan."

He couldn't believe his good fortune. In the dead of the Midwest winter he was being offered an all-expenses-paid trip to Los Angeles, land of the fabled Hollywood of his childhood cowboy movie dreams. The first thing he did was pick up a winter vacation catalog from a local department store and buy himself what he thought was a suitable wardrobe — white bucks, linen suit (two pair of pants), white sports coat, two bathing suits, and a straw hat.

And so it was that twenty-five-year-old Ronald Reagan, bags in hand and hat rakishly tilted to one side, caught a train from Des Moines to Chicago, where he boarded the *Los Angeles Limited* (later known as *The Challenger*) that let him out two days later in downtown Los Angeles, at Union Station, the first of February 1936. There he stepped into a gentle Santa Ana breeze that had warmed the temperature to a comfortably dry 81 degrees. Palm trees swayed easily back and forth as he waved down a cab to take him to the Biltmore Hotel, where the team was staying and where a room had been reserved for him.

He was up bright and early the next morning to join the team for breakfast, where he was introduced to everyone by the Cubs' manager, Charlie Grimm, who took an immediate liking to Reagan. After, they all climbed into a bus that took them to the Santa Monica Pier. During the half-hour ride, Reagan eagerly chatted with players he'd only known until then by their pictures and their exploits on the field transmitted to him via Teletype. Here he was, asking last season's National League MVP and All-Star starting catcher Gabby Hartnett about his hitting technique. With his notebook and pencil in hand, he asked Hartnett how he'd gotten the nickname Gabby. The tall, rangy catcher smiled, sat back, put his big foot up against the back of the seat in front of him, and said it was because he never talked to the press. He then spit a chaw into the 'toon, put an arm around Reagan, and smiled, his grin colored by his brown-stained teeth. Reagan grinned back.

Hartnett introduced Reagan to some of the other players, including infielder "Smiling" Stan Hack. Reagan knew all about Hack, who was born in Sacramento, California, but grew up in Dixon. Everyone back home had been thrilled when Hack broke into the majors. There was outfielder and sometime second baseman Augie Galan; regular second baseman and future Hall of Famer Billy Herman, who had also made the All-Star team the year before; first baseman/outfielder Phil "Philliabuck" Cavarretta, in his third of what would be twenty years playing for the Cubs (before switching to the White Sox in 1954 for two seasons); and outfielder and future Hall of Famer Chuck Klein. Reagan was in his own personal baseball nirvana.

At the Santa Monica Pier, a waiting ferry took them for the hour ride over to Catalina. Reagan couldn't take his eyes off the beautiful blue waters of the Pacific. Stepping onto land there, all the players and Reagan went to their assigned lockers and changed. The team donned their summer lights to practice, while Reagan put on a bathing suit. Without saying a word to anyone, he slipped away, went back to the pier, stood with his toes on the edge, put his arms straight up and close to his ears, took a deep breath, and plunged headfirst into the ocean. The water was ice cold, but Reagan didn't mind. He loved it. His years as a lifeguard had made him used to diving into cold waters. Then he effortlessly swam back to the pier, ready for anything.

■ ■ ■ ■

CHAPTER TWO:
FROM MUGS TO THE
MOVIES

■ ■ ■ ■

Although I've managed many illustrious people, the only two letters I have saved, by some quirk of fate, are from Ronald Reagan, both expressing his happiness and gratitude at being signed by Warner Bros. They are signed with the nickname by which I've always known him — Dutch.

— GEORGE WARD

Reagan's first feature film, Love Is on the Air *(1937).*

When the 1936 spring-training encampment came to an end on Catalina, the Cubs left the West Coast via the *Los Angeles Limited* bound for Chicago. Dutch Reagan made the return trip with them and then continued on by himself back to Des Moines. He had had the best time of his life hanging out with these Midwest boys of summer, swimming with them during off days, eating together and hanging out in the hot clubs of Hollywood at night.

They had quickly come to accept him as one of their own, an athlete who announced their games rather than as some microphone nerd who'd never been near a ball field. Over drinks Reagan entertained them with stories of his own playing days, and when women joined the party, he truly became one of the boys. And even though no one recognized the athletes in the days before TV made their faces as familiar as movie stars', this bunch had cavorted as if they *were* movie stars, eating, drinking, dressing in colorful California-style floral short sleeves and short khaki pants, living the boys-night-out fantasy for all it was worth.

Back at the radio station, Reagan discovered he was now considered something of a local hero himself, due to the popularity of many of the newspaper columns he had written and tape-recorded updates he'd filed, which had helped give a "name" to his increasingly familiar voice and the face that ran next to dispatches in the *Des Moines Dispatch*. Not long after he returned, WHO gave him his own early-evening show, live at 5:30, repeated at 10:10, called *The World of Sports with Dutch Reagan*. He had insisted that his name be part of the title. He was no longer an anonymous announcer; he was Dutch Reagan, *the* radio sports voice of the Midwest.

When the 1936 season officially began, he was once again assigned to "call" all the Chicago–St. Louis games, still via Teletype, from the confines of the small Iowa studios with only the telegraph operator beside him. This time, however, he knew all the players personally, and whenever anything went wrong with the telegraph equipment, which was not an uncommon occurrence, he was able to fill the time with anecdotal material, stories he'd heard from the fellows, or his own impressions of them.

One time in the middle of a game, the wire

went dead for a full seven minutes and Reagan simply put the game on hold by having the batter foul off the same pitch dozens of times, filling the long at-bat time with easygoing patter about the game until finally the line was repaired and he was able to get the game back on track: "The Cubs and St. Louis Cardinals were locked in a scoreless ninth-inning tie with Dizzy Dean on the mound and the Cubs' Billy Jurges at bat. I described Dean winding up and releasing his pitch. Then Curly, our telegraph operator, shook his head and passed me a slip of paper and I looked for a description of the pitch. Instead his note read, *The wire's gone dead.'* Well, since I had the ball on the way to the plate I had to get it there. Although I could have told our listeners that the wire had gone dead, it would have sent them rushing toward their dials and a competitor. So I decided to let Jurges foul off the pitch, figuring Western Union would soon fix the problem. To fill in some time, I described a couple of kids in the stands fighting over the foul ball. When Curly gestured that the wire was still dead, I had Jurges foul off another ball; I slowed Dean down, had him pack up the rosin bag and take a sign, shake it off, get another sign, and let him pitch; I said he'd fouled off another one, but this time he'd just missed a home run by only a few inches . . . I described Dean winding up and hurling another pitch;

Jurges hit a foul ball, and then another . . . and another . . . I don't know how many foul balls there were, but I'm told someone reported the foul-slugging spree as a record to *Ripley's Believe It or Not* . . . finally, Curly started typing again and I knew the wire had been restored. Relieved, I grabbed the slip of paper he handed me through the slot and read it: Jurges popped out on the first ball pitched."

It was the stuff Reagan's radio legend would be made of. He liked to refer to the medium as Theatre of the Mind, his own private laboratory of personality where he concocted methods of communication that helped him fine-tune his off-the-cuff, down-home spontaneous familiarity with folksy humor and an uncanny ability to sound sincere even when he was making everything up.

The Cubs came in second that year behind the New York Giants. Although the season was something of a disappointment (they had won the pennant the year before), the team was nonetheless thrown a gala dinner in Chicago that Reagan was invited to. During the party that followed, Hartnett, Hack, Cavarretta, and Klein each individually sought out Reagan to thank him for the way he had called their games, and "Old Man" Grimm assured him he would be invited back again to spring training next year.

■ ■ ■ ■

Reagan lived on that promise throughout the fall, and as February approached he couldn't wait to board a train bound for L.A., where he could escape the icy gloom of the Midwest and indulge in fresh orange juice, the California sun, blondes, and the team of players he now considered his personal friends.

All the big boys were back again — Hartnett, Herman, Hack, Jurges, Galan, Cavarretta — filled with a confidence and swagger from their league victory. They spent as much time together off the field as they did on, and again they always took Dutch along with them to the places usually reserved for players only, like the dimly lit Hollywood clubs filled with flirtatious, beautiful young studio starlets.

Reagan loved it, maybe a little too much; maybe they all did. A few weeks before he was to leave for the Cubs' '37 Catalina spring-training session, an actress named Joy Hodges happened to be passing through town on a publicity tour. As Des Moines was her hometown, she paid a visit to the WHO studios. As she later recalled, "I made only about three pictures in six months [as lead singer for Jimmy Grier's band, which appeared in several musical shorts made at RKO]. One of them was a short in which I had one line — 'Junior forgot to eat his spinach' — and walked in leading a horse. I was the maid. Well, when it played my hometown, Des Moines, you can imagine — I was 'in the movies,' with headlines trumpeting that I was coming home for a personal appearance. So there I was at the WHO mike when in walked this tall, handsome young man with a huge smile and glasses. We were just going on the air, and he ad-libbed, 'Well, Miss Hodges, how does it feel to be a movie star?' I was embarrassed but I flipped back, 'Well, Mr. Reagan, you just may know someday yourself.' "

After the show, Reagan talked for a long time with Hodges, told her about his love of broadcasting and how maybe one day, like her, he could take a shot at the movies. After all, he said, he had had a great deal of success acting in college. She listened politely, wished him luck, and was gone.

When Reagan arrived in California that winter, all of Los Angeles was being socked by one of its worst rainstorms in years. The rain canceled the team's first week of workouts, giving Reagan an extra few days off (the team was already on Catalina, but Reagan couldn't get there because no ferries were running during the storm). Stuck at the Cubs' mainland hotel, the Biltmore, he had dinner by himself and then wandered into the hotel lounge to have a cocktail and maybe check out the evening's entertainment. He slid into a seat at the bar and nearly fell off the stool when he saw a small card on the bar advertising the new lead singer for Jimmy Grier's resident house orchestra — *Joy Hodges.*

To Reagan, this seemed an incredible co-incidence. Here they were, both in Holly-wood, *both in the same room.* He scribbled a note on a napkin and sent it backstage asking if she'd join him for dinner between her two shows. It didn't take long for her answer to come back. She'd love to. Reagan arranged for a table for two, settled in with a drink, watched her first show, after which the pretty, dark-haired young singer came out from behind the small curtain of the tiny band-stand and over to Dutch's table. Before she sat down, she leaned and kissed him on the cheek. He liked that. They exchanged pleas-antries and Reagan signaled the waiter to bring over a round of drinks.

After a drink or two, a loosened Reagan began to openly flirt, telling Joy he was out on the coast not just to cover spring training for the Cubs but also, he added, to maybe try to get himself some movie work. True or not, this story gave him something more to talk about. Joy told him she was shooting a new film during the day.* That's great, Reagan said, smiling and taking another sip of his drink, during which Joy sat back and stared at him. "I don't know whether I wanted him to think I had the pull to get him a screen test or what, but I said, 'Stand up,' " Hodges later recalled. "When he stood, he was so tall and so good-looking, but with those awful horn-rimmed glasses on.

" 'What's the matter?' he said.

" 'Take off your glasses.' "

He reached up with his free hand and slipped them off.

" 'Better,' she said. 'Don't ever put them on again.' "

Reagan wasn't sure if she was talking about him as a potential date or a movie star. Putting a finger to her mouth, she began talking slowly through it, as if analyzing the situation. "I know an agent who will be honest with you. If we're wrong, and you should forget this idea, he'll tell you. Will you see him if I make a date with him?"

"Sure."

"Okay, but for heaven's sake, don't see him with those glasses on!"

Now that he was sure she was talking about his movie ambitions, such as they were, he figured she was just blowing him off. After

---

* Irving Cummings's 1937 *Merry Go Round of 1938,* a Bert Lahr vehicle, in which she had a small part.

dinner Joy politely excused herself to get ready for her second show. "Good luck," Dutch told her, and he smiled as she started across the tiny dance floor and went up onto the bandstand and behind the curtain.

He thought he'd heard the last from her, especially when she hadn't offered to give him her phone number, until, during the second show, for which Reagan had moved to the bar to watch, a waiter came over and handed him a piece of paper with a note on it. It was from Hodges, telling Reagan to call her agent, at ten the next morning, whose number she happily gave him.

Reagan tucked the note into his shirt pocket and ordered another round, stayed until the show was over, then waited to see if Hodges would come out and join him for a nightcap. When she didn't, he quietly slipped out of the club and took the elevator back up to his room.

What he didn't know was that before the start of the second show, Hodges had called her agent about him. "George Ward, who worked for the Bill Meiklejohn Agency, was my agent. I gave George a big, fast sales pitch and he said to have Ronnie call him in the morning." Ward was always looking for new faces.

William Meiklejohn's agency was not the small-time booking joint it has most often been depicted as, nor was he as incidental a player in Reagan's life story as others have made him out to be. In the thirties, dozens of independent agencies had sprung up in and around Hollywood and thrived on the studios' constant need to find fresh faces for its films. With each of the eight major studios producing on average seventy-five features and a hundred shorts each week to supply new product for the movie theaters they owned, the search for talent was constant, and early on the studios figured out it was easier and far more cost-effective to use agents as the discoverers of new talent.[*]

One of the biggest talent agencies at the time was the Music Corporation of America, better known simply by its initials MCA, which had begun in 1924 as the brainchild of Jules Stein, the son of immigrant Lithuanian Jews. At seventeen, Stein had won a musical scholarship to the University of West Virginia, his tuition paid in return for his playing in the school band. To cover his additional living expenses, he played backup fiddle and saxophone for a young night-club performer by the name of Mary Jane West, who would soon become better known to the world as Mae West. He also played for many of the lo-

* The eight major studios at the time were Paramount, MGM, Columbia, Warner Bros, Twentieth Century Fox, RKO (Radio-Keith-Orpheum), United Artists, and Universal.

cal bands being booked by the growing number of speakeasys that had come into existence after the passage in December 1917 of the Eighteenth Amendment.

One night, when he discovered he had accidentally double-booked his band, Stein found a last-minute group to take the second gig. He hired them in return for 10 percent of their fee and realized he could make far more money for far less work by hiring several bands to perform at different gigs the same night. His band-booking business grew so quickly he took on two investor-partners, Fred Hamm and Ernie Young, and the Music Corporation was born. Not long after, Stein recruited his brother, bought out his partners, and renamed his company Music Corporation of America.

By 1936, Stein was the second largest band-booking agency in the country, after the storied William Morris Agency. In 1937, he relocated to Los Angeles, where, increasingly, he had been able to book bands and musicians into the movies. He opened an office in Beverly Hills, bought a home there as well, and set about acquiring other talent agencies for access to their rosters of successful clients. One of those agencies he was interested in was Bill Meiklejohn's.

Meiklejohn represented nearly a hundred clients, mostly journeymen actors and actresses and the occasional writer. While always on the lookout for new talent, once Bill learned of MCA's interest in his agency, he wanted to beef up his clientele list as much and as quickly as possible to increase its market value. That was why, when Ward mentioned Reagan, Meiklejohn agreed to see him, even though the young man had no real credentials, only the suggestion by Joy Hodges, one of his lesser clients, that he just might be the next Robert Taylor.

When Reagan called the next morning, Ward told him to come right over, they were expecting him. He put on his best suit, brushed back his hair, and practiced looking in the mirror without squinting, as he was not going to wear his glasses during the interview. When he arrived at the agency's rather plain Hollywood offices, Ward's pretty young secretary immediately showed him in. Reagan and Ward shook hands, Ward asked the young man to take a seat, and they chatted for a few minutes. It was immediately obvious to Ward that this youngster was no Robert Taylor. He was handsome, to be sure, but he was also a bit . . . soft, Ward thought. He didn't have the granite chin or the sleek, tough but beautiful face that were Taylor's money features. Reagan was more crinkly, with a curiously soft chin that tended to slide to one side whenever this would-be actor let his smile drop. He could play Taylor's good buddy in a pinch but was definitely not the rugged leading man Hodges had made him out to be.

But just maybe, Ward thought, he could be the next Ross Alexander.

Alexander, another Meiklejohn client, had gained a measure of stardom as a juvenile on Broadway, appearing in a number of shows before being spotted by a talent scout for Warner Bros. and signed as their resident sweet-and-innocent kid/young adult, the "male ingénue," a role he played successfully in several Warner films. The studio had big plans for Alexander, seeing him as the eventual replacement for Dick Powell, who was beginning to outgrow those roles, before Alexander, whose mental stability was always tenuous, got caught in a series of increasingly disastrous public scandals overlaid with a relentless homosexual innuendo that caused him to lose his contract at Warner and eventually commit suicide in 1937 at the age of twenty-nine. The studio lost no time looking for someone to replace him, and it occurred to Ward that Reagan just might be the perfect choice.[*]

---

[*] Alexander appeared in several Warner Bros. films, including Frank Borzage's 1934 *Flirtation Walk,* supporting Dick Powell and Ruby Keeler, which was nominated for an Oscar for Best Picture; William Dieterle and Max Reinhardt's 1935 all-star production of *A Midsummer Night's Dream,* which won two

After their brief interview, Ward told Reagan to keep himself available for the next few days in case something came up. As soon as Reagan left the office, Ward got on the phone with Max Arnow, the casting director for Warner Bros., and told him he thought he might have found his new male ingénue. Arnow set up a meeting for the next day.

As Reagan recalled in one of his memoirs, he stood in front of the two men at Arnow's office while they assessed him like a prize side of beef, as if he wasn't even there in the room with them. Arnow was less than impressed, since it was obvious to him that Reagan was

---

Oscars (Editing and Cinematography); Michael Curtiz's 1935 star-making vehicle for Errol Flynn, *Captain Blood,* which was nominated for five Oscars. In 1934, Alexander, who was gay, married starlet Aleta Friele, most likely due to pressure from the studio to deflect rumors of his homosexuality from ruining his career. Friele committed suicide shortly thereafter, in 1935. Alexander then married actress Anne Nagel, again because of studio pressure. Nagel and Alexander had met while filming Ray Enright's 1936 *China Clipper.* They appeared together again in William Clemens's 1936 *Here Comes Carter.* Shortly after the film opened, Alexander was caught in a gay scandal and was abruptly fired by Warner. In January 1937, he committed suicide after completing his final film, Dan Enright's 1937 *Ready, Willing and Able,* playing opposite Ruby Keeler. The film was released posthumously.

nowhere as pretty as Alexander *or* Powell, and was obviously not a singer or a dancer. He, too, noted the imperfect chin, but did like Reagan's resonant voice, which reminded Arnow of Alexander's, who had had a similar early background in radio.†

At the end of the interview, Arnow decided to go ahead and give Reagan a screen test; he handed Dutch a few pages from the original Broadway script of Philip Barry's highly successful comedy *The Philadelphia Story,* which the studio was considering turning into a movie. Study this, Arnow told Reagan, and come back next Monday ready to show us what you can do.

Reagan floated all the way back to Catalina on the buoyant air of his hopes and dreams until he was shot back down to earthly reality when he was greeted on the island by an angry Charlie Grimm, who chewed him out

† In *An American Life* (page 80), Reagan remembered that he was being considered as the next Robert Taylor but doesn't mention Alexander by name, although he does make an oblique reference to him: "For some reason, Arnow said he was impressed by my voice. He said it reminded him of the voice of a young stock player Warners had under contract but, for reasons I can't remember, was giving the studio some kind of difficulty. I guess maybe Arnow thought of me as a kind of replacement for the guy with the voice like mine."

for having missed the first day of practice without permission. Reagan made sure he had Grimm's permission to return to L.A. two days later but didn't tell him what for. He didn't think Grimm would appreciate the notion of a screen test for a young reporter assigned to be covering the Chicago Cubs spring training.

To help him prepare for his audition, Reagan called Hodges. "Ronnie and I rehearsed that Sunday," Hodges later recalled. "Monday he made the test . . . I understand Dutch really 'snowed' Max Arnow with his fantastic gift of gab."

Indeed, the screen test did go well, with Reagan playing opposite one of Warner's starlets and reciting his memorized lines exactly the way Hodges had coached him. From there, however, everything went wrong. Reagan heard nothing from the studio or Ward for several days, and then his tenure with the Cubs was suddenly cut short without explanation. Grimm wouldn't say so to young Reagan's face, but he had no use for anyone who couldn't bother to show up to do his job. Reagan had missed two days his first week due to his auditions and screen test; Grimm, who always had a very short fuse, yanked him as quickly as he would starting pitcher Bill Lee if he got himself into an early jam. Reagan reluctantly packed his bags and bought a return ticket back to Des Moines.

Just before he left town, he decided to call Ward and thank him for all he'd done. Ward thought Reagan was crazy to leave Hollywood now and told him so. Meiklejohn then got on the phone and told him he had heard the screen test went well and insisted that Reagan stay just a few days longer. Dutch apologized, said he couldn't jeopardize his job at the radio station any further. With that he hung up the phone, checked out of the hotel, took a cab to Union Station, and boarded the next *Super Chief* headed east.

On April 20, just two days after he arrived back in Des Moines, he received the following telegram from Bill Meiklejohn:

WARNERS OFFERS CONTRACT SEVEN YEARS STOP ONE YEAR OPTION STOP STARTING $200 A WEEK STOP WHAT SHALL I DO MEIKLEJOHN

While Reagan was chug-chugging it back home, Meiklejohn had met with Jack Warner and personally showed him Reagan's screen-test reel, in which, in truth, Reagan had not come off that well. Under the microscope of the unforgiving camera, his shoulders appeared too wide, giving him an almost sinister, thuggish stance, and his head seemed too small, accentuated by a short neck. However, Jack Warner, who always acted on impulse in matters such as these, liked Reagan's wholesome quality and the sense of honesty he projected — which Garry Wills later described in his study of Reagan as the "heartwarming role of himself" — and decided to sign him, but only for six months. Meiklejohn then agented his client into committing to a long-term contract by telling Warner he had gone back east to accept another offer, without informing him that the "offer" was, in reality, his old newspaper and radio stint. Warner agreed to seven years, with a one-time, end-of-the-first-six-months out clause.

When Reagan got the telegram, he immediately fired one back:

SIGN BEFORE THEY CHANGE THEIR MINDS.

The occasion was noted in a single paragraph in the pages of one of the industry's trade papers, the first time Reagan's name appeared in print in Hollywood:

Ronald Reagan, WHO sports announcer in Des Moines, has been placed under a term contract for pictures by Warner Brothers. The studio tested Reagan while he was here to scout the Chicago Cubs spring training at Catalina. He will report in June. William Meiklejohn Agency handled.

Reagan often recalled with great fondness

the story of his signing with Warner Bros.; it appears in similar versions in both his memoirs, permitting sentiment to mingle with his characteristic self-deprecation that at times served to lessen rather than increase its natural drama. In virtually every retelling of the story, by Reagan and others (for whom Reagan was always the source), there is the suggestion that he left L.A. *on purpose* before being offered the contract, because he believed that unavailability in Hollywood somehow made him more desirable, as if that were part of some clever scheme of his. And he always emphasized the Robert Taylor premise for his audition while leaving out the fact that it was really Alexander he was chosen to replace. It's impossible to know, but not unlikely that Reagan wanted to believe he was more Taylor's type than Alexander's. Nonetheless, the fact that in the space of just seven days, from the first Monday he arrived in L.A. to the following Sunday when he left to return to Des Moines, Reagan had landed a seven-year movie contract at Warner Bros. Studios. And he was determined to make the most of it.

There was little for Reagan to do during his last remaining days in Des Moines except say good-bye to friends, finish up his broadcasting chores, and pack the few belongings he had. There was one extravagance to which he treated himself as a way of celebrating his new deal at Warners. For $600 cash, he bought himself a brand-new Nash convertible that he had been admiring for several months in the company's Des Moines showroom. Reagan chose a beige-colored model because it showed off and matched up well to his thick, dark hair. He also bought a brown tweed suit and a matching brown pipe, very much in the style of the day. He wanted to arrive in Hollywood looking the part of the young actor, or at least what he thought a young actor looked like. He modeled himself after a pictorial in *The Saturday Evening Post* of "The Successful Young American Male." Soon enough, with bags packed tightly into every inch of the car, a loud roar from his engine, and a silent prayer from his soul, he was on his way.

He arrived nearly a week later, on June 1, 1937, the very day his contract officially went into effect. Without a permanent place to stay, he decided to check back into the Biltmore. Reagan always preferred familiar places, and the Biltmore seemed not only that but a talisman as well. He even took the same room he was in the night he'd run into Hodges.

The first thing he did after unpacking was to call Bill Meiklejohn's office. He was put through directly to George Ward, who heard the eagerness in Reagan's voice and told him to relax, that most likely it would be weeks before anything came down that he might be suited for. He suggested Reagan spend some time going out and getting to know the town, and to enjoy himself while doing it.

Three days later he was called in and cast in his first film.

Max Arnow had ordered a script by Warner contract writer Morton Grant, based on a story by Roy Chanslor, that he wanted for one of the studio's new directors, Nick (Nicholas) Grindé. Jack Warner had just signed him away from the Hal Roach Studios, where Grindé had written a couple of highly successful films, including (with Frank Butler) Laurel and Hardy's 1934 version of Victor Herbert and Glen MacDonough's *Babes in Toyland*. It was a huge hit and in years to come would go on to be a TV holiday perennial.

Arnow and Jack Warner knew that Grindé, who had codirected a few early talkies, wanted to get back to full-time directing. Grindé had a reputation as someone who had the patience to work with newly signed Broadway actors, helping them to adjust their talents for the screen by toning down their gestures and their voices and letting the camera do much of the so-called emoting for them. He was also from the Midwest, born and raised in Madison, Wisconsin, and attended university there. For all these reasons, plus the fact that the script was built around the exploits of one Andy McCaine, a crusading crime-busting radio announcer, Arnow thought Reagan would be perfect for the film.

Just after he was assigned to it, the script's original title, *Inside Story,* was changed to *Love Is on the Air.* This had nothing to do with "love" being on the air, whatever that might have meant back then, but served a very practical purpose: The previous month actor Dick Powell had just completed his latest film, William Keighley's *Varsity Show.* Using the movie's popular song, "Love Is on the Air," as the title of his first film was one way Arnow and Warner believed they could plant an association in audiences' minds between Powell and his new heir-apparent at the studio, Ronald Reagan.

The script was actually an adaptation of a Roy Chanslor story the studio had made once before as a vehicle for Paul Muni. In Mervyn LeRoy's 1934 *Hi Nellie!,* Muni plays a newspaper editor stuck writing a column for the lovelorn as punishment for his muckraking anticrime work, which, of course, in the end, allows him to bring down the bad guys and be restored to his former position of journalistic glory.

Warner ordered some changes in the script to showcase its newest player. In the Reagan-tailored version of the story, Andy McCaine is demoted for his anticrime radio broadcasts to the host of a children's show. He replaces Jo Hopkins (June Travis), who becomes his love interest as well as crime-fighting sidekick. When McCaine and Hopkins "trick" the bad guys into confession on the air, they're arrested and McCaine and Hopkins become heroes.

Although it has always been written that the film was meant to be an A picture designed to introduce Warner's newest "star," in fact, from the start it was intended as a B product. The proof of this is that the film was produced by Bryan "Brynie" Foy, known affectionately around the studio as the official "keeper of the B's." Foy, who had his own performing credentials as part of one of vaudeville's most legendary family acts — he was the oldest brother in the father/children act Eddie Foy and The Seven Little Foys — ran a production division at Warner that specialized in original B movies and, wherever possible, remakes of previously owned scripts that could be shot for as little money as possible.

At the studios, the major difference between A pictures and B pictures, besides budgets and placement, was the nature of the scripts and the actors assigned to play them. In Bs, there was little room for performance subtlety, shading, or revelation. Characters were prototypes that reinforce the telling of familiar stories. The stories were simple, straightforward affirmations of legal, moral, and cultural codes — bad guys always got caught, heroes were single-minded lawmen, bad women were sluts, good women were in need of being rescued. They were cinematic comfort food, celluloid popcorn meant to warm up an audience for the main feature (usually a more highly glossed version of the same thing, with bigger names, better sets, and perhaps a little more nuance thrown in for good measure). They also served as curtain-raisers, allowing the audience to drift in after dinner, usually somewhere in the middle of the film. It hardly mattered if they missed the first hour; they had already seen it before in some version or another hundreds of times. Because of the faceless qualities of the actors who played in these films — the less of a noticeable distraction they were, the better the believability of the action — rarely, if ever, did a B movie actor move up to the stature of an A star. (Getting out of Alcatraz was easier, which was one of the reasons that Bogart, who had come from a distinguished career on Broadway, was so angry with Jack Warner for starting him off in B's. Warner did it because he felt Bogart wasn't good-looking or tall enough, had a lisp and was losing his hair. He had all the makings of a villain, Warner insisted, and in Warner Bros. pictures, bad guys were not heroes.)

Love Is on the Air was shot in three weeks for just $119,000 and released as the sixty-one-minute at the bottom end of a double bill.[*] If Jack Warner had any qualms about assigning Reagan to Foy's B unit, he realized ten minutes into the picture that Reagan's potential magnitude as a Hollywood actor was, at best, limited: yes, he was good-looking; yes, he had a nice sound-picture–friendly voice; yes, he moved fairly well, if a little stiffly; and his acting was okay, if a little forced and maybe a touch overly sincere, but he had no comic timing and, even more crucially, *no heat.* He related to comely twenty-year-old costar June Travis, who had originally been signed by Warner's for her pretty face and shapely body, more like a sister than a lover. Arnow liked Travis, who had previously appeared in Howard Hawks's *Ceiling Zero* the year before alongside Pat O'Brien and James Cagney, two A-list stars, and had hoped that she might eventually be moved up to A status.

What may have saved Reagan from being opted out of his contract by Warner were the unexpectedly and exceptionally good reviews the trades gave to both the film and particularly its star. *Variety,* the industry's rag of

[*] The main, or A, feature was Gregory La Cava's *Stage Door,* starring Katharine Hepburn and Ginger Rogers.

record, noted, as Warner had after his screen test, Reagan's "likeability" and "pleasing" quality on screen, while the *Reporter* announced the arrival of "a new leading man, Ronald Reagan, who is a natural, giving one of the best first picture performances Hollywood has offered in many a day."[*]

His growing friendship with George Ward didn't hurt, either. According to Ward, "We became quite close. We were about the same age, only a few months different. He didn't know anyone in Hollywood, so I sort of took him under my wing." Ward assured Reagan he would do everything he could to keep him making movies at Warner.

After all was said and done, Reagan's first feature had landed him higher in the studio rankings than anyone had anticipated, somewhere between the utter darkness of the unknown and the glorious starburst of the limelight.

[*] Arnow had insisted that Reagan drop the *Dutch* and go with *Ronald,* believing that *Dutch* not only did not connote star quality but worked against it on a marquee. Arnow had also objected to *Humphrey* Bogart, but Bogie had absolutely refused to change his first name.

■ ■ ■ ■

CHAPTER THREE:
THE IRISH MAFIA

■ ■ ■ ■

Pat O'Brien would play an important part in
all that has happened to me.
— RONALD REAGAN

Ronald Reagan (in bed) as George Gipp in Knute Rockne All American *(1940).*

Reagan's first film also provided him with his first Hollywood affair. During the making of *Love Is on the Air,* he began an intense and very public romance with his young costar, the dark-haired, green-eyed, round-cheeked June Travis. If they lacked chemistry on the screen, they were highly combustible off it. They quickly became inseparable and spent their three weekends off alone at Reagan's place or shooting clay pigeons at the amusement gallery on the Santa Monica Pier. Jack Warner approved, always believing it was good publicity for a film if the leading lady and the leading man "got together." It helped blur the line of reality and fantasy a little more and made it easier for audiences to suspend their disbelief when they saw a real-life romance happening in tandem with the characters on the big screen.

By the time the film wrapped, however, the affair was over. It's unclear who actually ended it, but likely it was Travis. Reagan's larger agenda included marriage, but Travis was nowhere near ready to make that kind of leap. Later on, Reagan characterized the relationship rather jocularly as symptomatic of a disease young actors were particularly prone to — "Leadingladyitis."*

Indeed, after Travis, he discovered that although his name had yet to appear above the title in any of his credits, just having it anywhere on the silver screen was enough to let him pick and choose from the hundreds of young and pretty starlets always on the studio back lots — either in full costume or in high heels, gray skirts and white shirts, with perfectly coiffed hair. It was part of the Warner tradition and the personal dictum of Jack L. Warner that all the women on the lot and out of costume should be dressed nicely and in full makeup at all times. Reagan loved that tradition.

Harry Warner, the oldest of the twelve children of immigrants Sam and Pearl Eichelbaum, was born in Krasnashiltz, located on the Polish-German border (then in czarist Russia). Jack was born in 1892 in London, Ontario, where the family had settled after fleeing the virulent Polish anti-Semitism of the late 1880s. Sam was born in 1887 in Baltimore. In 1903, their father, Benjamin, a

* Travis soon left Hollywood and movies for good.

struggling cobbler, decided to try to cash in on the new phenomenon of moving pictures. Sam began showing one through a projector he'd purchased (raising the funds for it by pawning his watch) on a sheet in a rented storefront in Niles, Ohio. His sister, Rose, played the piano while Albert and Harry ran the box office and Jack sang illustrated songs. One of the first films they showed was Edwin S. Porter's *The Great Train Robbery,* made that same year, which proved such a success for the Warners that immediately after, Benjamin packed the entire family into a car, took the print, and made a traveling road show out of exhibiting it in storefronts all over the Midwest.

By 1907, the Warner family business owned two hundred films outright — too many to show by themselves, so they started renting their prints to other theaters. They set up their offices in the central location of Pittsburgh, Pennsylvania, where they could do business with other "exchanges," or companies that owned a number of prints, rather than having to deal with individual theater owners. Three years later they were producing their own films rather than buying them from filmmakers or paying expensive licensing fees to Thomas Edison and his restrictive (and to the Warners, anti-Semitic) Trust. The Trust was a notoriously closed organization. Edison's strategy was twofold: to keep the profits from the movie business among himself and a few trusted associates and to keep the Jews, whom he intensely disliked, from diluting the virtues of quality cinema with what he considered their low-grade taste in the performing arts. He blamed them for everything that had gone wrong with his original invention, from the exploitation of sex on the screen to the enormous profits that outside (the trust) distributors, most of them Jews, were making off his invention. Edison's goons regularly went after the independents and eventually drove them out of the East. One of the reasons the Warners and others settled in Hollywood was because it was as far away from New York and New Jersey as they could get, distance being their best protection. In Los Angeles, Carl Laemmle, another independent film producer relocated to Hollywood, formed the Independent Motion Picture Company to distribute the work of non-Trust studios, an organization the Warners quickly joined.

In 1919, the Warners built their first fully functioning film studio, on Sunset Boulevard and Bronson Avenue, to make their own movies without having to rent space from others to do so. By this time, Edison's trust had given in to the reality of the existence of the West Coast studios, and Harry quietly returned to New York City to run the Warner Bros. business affairs, while Jack, Sam, and

Albert remained in Hollywood, to oversee the production side (Albert was the West Coast treasurer and reported directly to Harry).

After a somewhat difficult start, turning out only three pictures in 1921 and four in 1922, not nearly enough to keep the studio running, Warner Bros., desperate for more physical space, bought out Vitagraph and First National Pictures and in 1926 formed an alliance with General Electric to promote its sound-for-movies equipment, patented under the name Vitaphone. Making films with prerecorded sound was a huge risk at the time. It not only entailed making the movies using the new process but equipping theaters all over the country (and eventually the world) to show them. To hedge their bets, they chose the most popular musical talent in America at the time, stage performer Al Jolson, known for his minstrel-style of "black-face," highly popular with white audiences at the time (as opposed to actual black performers who had not yet broken through with the right to play and sing to the mainstream). Already the biggest box-office attraction on Broadway, Jolson was lured to the coast by the most stylishly flamboyant and physically imposing of the brothers, Jack Warner, the one with the pencil mustache and the thousand-dollar suits with silk handkerchiefs, to take his act west and join in the risk and, if successful, the rewards of helping to change the face and the voice of the film industry.

The gamble paid off, and Warner Bros. became the first fully sound studio in Hollywood, the others lagging behind sometimes by years. (MGM, the last to give in — and the most successful among the silent-film studios — didn't convert until late 1929.) Warner quickly became the most profitable studio, partly from its astute choice of sound-friendly scripts and vocally appealing stars and partly from Jack Warner's insistence on low budgets. The need for thrift helped give the largely black-and-white films a gritty quality that perfectly melded with the overwhelming single-minded theme of Warner films — the maintenance of law and order in the service of the American Way of Life (with an occasional musical thrown in to maintain their early dominance of the proven money-making genre they had virtually created with Jolson and continued with Dick Powell).

During the Depression and the years that immediately followed, Jack Warner made his studio the most consistent flag-waver in Hollywood. His films were filled with optimism that affirmed the Roosevelt New Deal era, even when they appeared at times to celebrate the outlaw, the underdog, the downtrodden, and the deprived (the distinctions between these sometimes overly blurred for the sake of a good story). Reaching all the way back to *The Great Train Robbery,* Warner had always been fascinated by the romance and rebellion of outlaws. Perhaps it was a reflection of how the brothers saw themselves, or more precisely how they, as Jews, were seen in the Europe they were forced, like outlaws, to flee. Even while making enormous amounts of money, and turning Democracy into a salable commodity, they did both as if to remind and ensure the audiences as well as the government that they and their product were honest and forthright; the bad guys in their films always "got it" in the end.

Even before the introduction in 1930 of the Motion Picture Production Code and the Hays Office, whose intention it was to enforce the industry to self-regulate its films' content or face government intervention, Warner's was on to its true goal.* The Hays Office may have decried pulchritudinous sex in the cinema but its real concern (like the

---

* "The Production Code (also known as the Hays Code) was the set of industry censorship guidelines governing the production of American motion pictures. The Motion Pictures Producers and Distributors Association (MPPDA), which later became the Motion Picture Association of America (MPAA), adopted the code in 1930, began effectively enforcing it in 1934, and abandoned it in 1967 in favor of the subsequent MPAA film rating system. The Production Code spelled out what was

government's) was political subversion. Both not only wanted films sexually "cleaned up," they wanted them to conform politically (if indeed there was all that much difference between the two), especially during a time when radicalism was rearing its opportunistic serpentine head and reaching into every branch of the mass media at the height of the infamous Depression. Warner Bros. films may have championed the underdog, and glamorized the outlaw sensibility, but more than anything, it reinforced the American way, which had, from the days of the Revolution, made heroes out of rebels and had the "little guy" getting a fair shake by the democratic system.

This is one of the primary reasons for the thematic overview and stylistic rigidity not just of Warner Bros. movies but virtually all Hollywood studio films made in the thirties. Operating in survival mode against a devastated economy and with Washington, D.C., breathing down its neck, the film industry desired to not just give the appearance of conformity but to aggressively promote the status quo, and because of it a very specific vision of the nation's social mores and

---

morally acceptable and morally unacceptable content for motion pictures produced for a public audience in the U.S.A." — *Wikipedia*

patriotic fervor gained physical form in a way it never had before, in literature, journalism, or even on the stage. The mostly Jewish, immigrant moguls who ran the studios knew whom they had to answer to in order to keep their doors open, and made sure they not only played ball, but carefully abided by the rule books of the game. At Warner's and every other one of the majors, all-American white Protestant good looks became a physical correlative to constitutional patriotism. White suits equaled good guys, black suits equaled bad guys. Tall and handsome leading men were heroes. Short, ugly ones were villains. Men with accents were spies. Minorities were relentlessly typecast; Jews were intellectuals, Catholics were priests; blacks were servants or slaves (always either happy with their lot or dim witted and surviving due to the generosity of their owners or caretakers). Virtuous, unglamorous women were heroic. Gorgeous, leggy babes, especially blondes, were "bad." The ultimate leading ladies were really the *mothers,* rather than the *girlfriends,* of the heroes. And, in the end, no matter how flamboyant the lives of the heroes were, once they became involved in "the love story" element, if they got "serious," the romances — if virtuous — always ended happily in marriage or tragically in death (with the survivor left to dutifully mourn, alone, for the rest of his or her life). Conformity, complacency, virtue, belief in a Christian God, and loyalty to the country were the ultimate, if not always obvious, themes of most American movies.

And because of it, Jack L. Warner was constantly on the lookout for a certain image in his players, one that, above all, projected wholesomeness and optimism. He didn't always get it, as the Bogarts of the studio proved. What he got, instead, through the work of actors like Bogart and Cagney and Edward G. Robinson, was the revelation of the charismatic attractiveness of the antihero, and with it came the introduction of irony, or cinematic depth, into the rigid moral characters who peopled their movies. At Warners, these antiheroes only served to highlight the sugary appeal of musical "good guys" like Dick Powell, whom Warner milked until his image was bone dry and then sought to replace with a younger, more attractive model. For every antihero, there had to be a hero to keep the image of the studio in line with the notion of conventional conformity. That was why when Jack Warner discovered Reagan, he believed that, despite his lack of heat — maybe even *because* of it — the natural "all-American good guy" he projected on-screen could very well be worth his weight in box-office gold. Warner stayed with Reagan longer than he would have most actors, convinced the studio would eventually find the right combination to make him a top-ranking star.

For his part, Reagan was happy to go along with the program. Unlike some other Warner stars who periodically grumbled about salaries, scripts, even producers, and very occasionally directors, Reagan never complained about anything. He believed the boss was just that: the boss. Because of that he prided himself on being the ultra–company man. All he wanted to do was get paid, make movies, wave the flag, and chase a few women.

At Warners and every other studio, men (actors) chasing women (actresses) was perfectly okay, as long as it was done within the parameters of the unwritten laws that dictated the lay of this special land. Jack L. Warner was tyrannical about avoiding scandal, as were most of the other studio heads, because of its potentially damaging effect on the box office. Whether his leading men were single or married didn't matter to him; they could carry on all they wanted as long as they did it discreetly, and preferably with the bounty of young starlets corralled within the studio's gates, the best way of keeping tabs on all the boys and girls. Warner had no compunctions about his actors bedding his actresses, especially since he did so himself, as did virtually every employee, from auditioners to casting people to the actual films' directors, giving birth to the term "casting couch."

There were only three off-screen no-nos that could get any actor suspended and ruin a career: sex with children (a starlet over eighteen who got pregnant was no problem; that "situation" could be dealt with by on-site informal abortion clinics, which every studio operated); homosexuality (among men — lesbianism was not only okay but something in which many studio executives shared an intense, if private voyeuristic interest); and anything that smacked of un-Americanism.

In that sense, Reagan fit in perfectly. He was as American as apple pie, a New Deal Democrat, and a "red-blooded" all-American skirt-chasing young man. Jack Warner loved the way Reagan handled the latter off-screen and responded to him with a pride-filled "that's my boy" attitude, meanwhile hoping some of whatever he had that made him so appealing to the starlets on the lot would come across on the big screen. Warner especially liked that when he renewed Reagan's option after the first six months, the young actor sent for his folks back in Dixon instead of buying himself a brand-new convertible. Reagan found them a suitable apartment just around the corner from his own on Sunset Boulevard. Knowing his father's pride would not allow him to accept outright charity, Reagan, at George Ward's suggestion, put him to work answering any fan mail that might come to the studio for him. There was never all that much, but it did give Jack a reason to get up in the morning. If he had any jealousy about his son's success, or if it made him feel even more like a failure, he never said so. The closest he came to expressing any negative feelings about being cared for by his son was his often-repeated dismissal of his new neighborhood, Hollywood, as nothing more than real estate offices and hot-dog stands. Nevertheless, Reagan's generosity and caring deeply impressed Jack Warner.

And if Reagan went through the Warner roster of women, it was with a purpose; he believed he was searching for the girl whose foot could fit the magic slipper left behind by dear departed Margaret. He was prepared to sleep with every pretty, single and available girl in Hollywood, if he had to. He was, after all, on a mission.

Reagan's second movie, Busby Berkeley's *Hollywood Hotel* (1937), appeared at first to be a significant move up. For one thing, it was produced by Hal B. Wallis, who had joined Warner Bros. in 1923 and in eight years had risen from a spot in the publicity department to become the head of one of the studio's elite A production units. He had been given his big break as the producer of Mervyn LeRoy's 1931 *Little Caesar,* the film that made its lead, Edward G. Robinson, a star. When the film proved a smash hit at the box office, Wallis was given his own A production unit.

To direct *Hollywood Hotel,* Wallis chose the highly stylish Busby Berkeley, the so-called king of kaleidoscopic visual cacophony. While working out the choreography for Lloyd Bacon's 1933 nearly all-sung, all-danced *42nd Street,*[*] a remake of Alan Crosland's 1929 *On with the Show,* Berkeley had hit upon the idea of setting the camera on a crane. He began creating precision dance routines for it that made the female dancers' legs resemble the patterns of a kaleidoscope. The movie made a star out of Ruby Keeler and established Berkeley as Hollywood's premier musical chorus-line choreographer. Berkeley went on to do nine more films in the five years between *42nd Street* and *Hollywood Hotel,* many of them vehicles for a resurrected Dick Powell and his leading ladies. (Now in his late twenties, Powell played a character nearly ten years younger than he really was. His growing dissatisfaction with Jack Warner's refusal to let him gracefully mature on-screen eventually led to his successful move to Paramount in 1940, when his contract at Warner's was up. One of the reasons Warner may

---

[*] Aka *Forty-Second Street.*

114

have been reluctant to cut Powell loose before then was that Reagan had not yet proved that he could take over as the studio's resident singing juvenile.)

Hollywood Hotel had a lot of conflict beneath its silvery surface. In addition to the problems the studio was having with Dick Powell, it was also the last musical film a fading Busby Berkeley would be allowed to direct at Warner or anywhere. He would continue on as a choreographer and "special numbers" consultant, *Hollywood Hotel* being one of the last smash-hit musicals from Warner until Michael Curtiz's 1942 blockbuster, *Yankee Doodle Dandy.* Jack Warner's unwillingness (or inability) to compete with MGM's and Paramount's big-budget, Technicolor musical extravaganzas eventually made *Hollywood Hotel* look more like a eulogy for musicals, and because of budget limitations, the movie displayed very few of the trademark Berkeley touches.

Adapted from a popular radio series hosted in the movie by Dick Powell, Reagan's part was so small and incidental — another announcer, but this time without any apparent character or substantial connection to the plot — that he received no billing in the credits. Reagan's second film appearance would have been relegated to the biographical "forget about" file if not for the fact that one of the film's stars was about to have a major effect on his life and career. With *Hollywood Hotel,* Wallis wanted to show the audience what it was really like behind the scenes at an actual radio show. The one he chose to use was a broadcast (starring Dick Powell) that emanated from Hollywood and was heard around the country via syndication; it included regular bits by popular and incredibly influential newspaper gossip columnist Louella O. Parsons, whom he cast in the film to play herself.

Born in Freeport, Illinois, about forty miles to the north/northwest of Dixon, in 1881, Louella Rose Oettinger first became interested in journalism while working for her high school newspaper. After she graduated, she married a young man named John Edwards Parsons and moved to Dixon, where she gave birth to a baby girl, settled down, and didn't see her first movie, Porter's *The Great Train Robbery,* until the age of twenty-five. Fascinated with the new medium of motion pictures, and unhappy in marriage, she decided to change her life. She filed for divorce, moved to Chicago, and got a job writing scripts for Essanay Studios, the former home of Charlie Chaplin, and eventually managed to place her daughter, Harriett, in several movies as "Baby Parsons."

In 1914, Louella Parsons wrote, at the suggestion of the *Chicago Record-Herald,* her first movie-star gossip column, which she kept up for the next four years, until the newspaper was sold to William Randolph Hearst. Then she relocated to New York City and resumed her career in journalism. In 1925, after having married and divorced twice more, Parsons was diagnosed with tuberculosis and told she had six months to live. She quit her job, moved to Arizona to take advantage of the dry climate, and eventually ended up in Los Angeles. When her health improved, she resumed her column for Hearst's *Los Angeles Examiner.* By now her column was being syndicated nationally via all six hundred Hearst newspapers, bringing tremendous readership — at one time it was estimated that Parsons had more than twenty million readers daily — and with it enormous influence. By the late twenties a positive mention in her column could make a star and a bad one could break one. Hearst was always after Parsons to promote the career of his mistress, Marion Davies, which she dutifully did. For her efforts, when Hearst created the radio show for Dick Powell, he insisted that Parsons have a prominent spot on it and in the movie as well.

The long reach of her tentacles into the film industry made her so important, she was able to get a screenwriting deal with Harry Cohn at his fledgling Columbia Studios, for what became George Seitz's 1927 *Isle of Forgotten Women*. But preferring gossip to drama, she turned from writing scripts to hosting her own radio show (all the while keeping her column going full blast).* A grateful Hearst helped her acquire Campbell's Soup as her national sponsor, and the show became so successful that eventually her agent, none other than Jules Stein, convinced Jack Warner to make a movie based on it. That movie became *Hollywood Hotel*.

By now she was a powerful voice in Hollywood as well as one of its strongest moral influences, something the studios, especially Warner Bros., used to their benefit whenever a star stepped out of line or wanted too much money. Jimmy Cagney, constantly at war with Jack Warner, was one of those stars continually hit hard by Parsons, for his pro-union

---

* Accounts differ as to the events surrounding her hiring. Some maintain Parsons's defense of Davies led to her hiring by Hearst instead of resulting from it. According to Davies's memoir, *The Times We Had,* Parsons had encouraged readers to "give this girl a chance" while the majority of critics disparaged Davies; it was on this basis that Hearst added Parsons to his full-time staff. Despite her enormous popularity and influence, Parsons was aware of her own limitations as a hard-news journalist. She called her autobiography *The Gay Illiterate*.

"extra-curricular activities," as she liked to call it. If, on the other hand, the studios wanted to promote someone, he or she was given the white-gloves treatment by Parsons.

Just as it appeared that Reagan's career was about to start its slow fade to black, the final plans were being put into place by Jules Stein to purchase Bill Meiklejohn's agency. Even before the deal became official, Stein, convinced that his new client-to-be Reagan could be a star, quietly went to Parsons and asked her to start talking about Reagan in her column, which, because it was Stein, she happily agreed to do. Parsons was more than happy to help out a fellow Dixonite. With blurb after positive blurb about Reagan, despite his two lackluster performances in films without any discernible luster of their own, he began to get noticed in Hollywood.

Still officially rudderless, with no one able or willing to guide his career at the agency, which itself was in a bit of consolidation turmoil, Reagan worked at the sole discretion of Jack L. Warner, who continued to put him into films that had the potential to be hits but for one reason or another failed to make any dent in the zeitgeist. In 1938, Warner put Reagan into *Swing Your Lady,* an intended A vehicle produced by Ray Enright as a vehicle not for Reagan but for an unhappy Humphrey Bogart, who openly hated Jack Warner,

hated his studio, hated the roles he kept being assigned, hated the whole studio system,
and hated *Swing Your Lady* more than any
other film he had thus far been forced to
make. Years later he would label it the worst
film he had made during his early years at
the studio.

He wasn't wrong. In the film, Bogart rather
unconvincingly plays a small-time wrestling
promoter, and Reagan, a fast-talking sports
reporter with little more to do than make
unwise wisecracks. Five forgettable songs are
improbably sprinkled throughout the plot.
The film opened so poorly, it was pulled in
the middle of its first week and replaced with
another feature, and Jack Warner blamed it
all on Bogart while personally rewarding Reagan's efforts with another feature.

Journeyman house director B. Reeves Eason's *Sergeant Murphy* was another Bryan
Foy B product, a division Jack L. Warner felt
was better suited for Reagan's abilities.[*]
Although Warner did keep him working, it

---

[*] Eason made dozens of silent and sound pictures
in Hollywood. His greatest achievement was as a
second-unit director in charge of filming the
chariot race in Fred Niblo's 1926 silent version (the
second) of Lew Wallace's novel *Ben-Hur*. Later on
he would serve in the same capacity to film the
burning of Atlanta in Victor Fleming's 1939 *Gone
With the Wind*. At Warner, he was strictly B, and oc-

was hard for Reagan not to feel that after the debacle of *Swing Your Lady,* he was being sent back down to the minors, and he wasn't entirely wrong. But he did as he was told, never complained about anything, and continued to vent whatever career frustrations he may have had by bedding as many of his female costars as he could, the latest being Mary Maguire, one of the stars of *Sergeant,* a B actress who had a brief run at Warner before being let go and retiring from films.

Next for Reagan on the cinematic assembly line was William B. Clemens's *Accidents Will Happen,* another Foy B costarring fading A actress Gloria Blondell. Clemens had begun his career as an editor in silent films and was a solid B director who would go on to direct a series of serials, including several of the Nancy Drews and a few years later a couple of the Falcons, neither of which is remembered or seen today (except for occasional matinee plays on Turner Classic Movies). In the film, Reagan plays an investigative insurance adjuster married to the "wrong" girl (Sheila Bromley) in cahoots with an illegal insurance scam operator. As the plot unfolds, Reagan falls in love with a cigar-stand girl

---

casionally was enlisted to direct episodes of the weekly serials the studio made for Saturday-morning screenings across the country.

(Blondell) who somehow helps him bust the gang (and, conveniently, his wife), after which he plans a new life with the "right girl." All of this takes place in sixty-two swiftly paced minutes of all action and no depth. (Reagan reportedly went nuts for Bromley but throughout her life she steadfastly insisted he got nowhere with her.)

The film was successful enough to get Reagan into the cast of Lloyd Bacon's *Cowboy from Brooklyn,* which was a kick back up to the A's and reunited him with Dick Powell, still on the Warner roster. Also in the cast was Pat O'Brien, one of Warner's biggest stars, and Priscilla Lane. *Cowboy from Brooklyn* was a musical satire on the singing-cowboy genre, and Reagan, whose part was not all that big to begin with, was buried on-screen by the scene-stealing veteran O'Brien. It wasn't that O'Brien didn't like Reagan; he did, it was just the nature of the hammy Irishman to try to hog the screen of whatever film he was in.* In fact, O'Brien liked Reagan so

---

* The film was released overseas as *Romance and Rhythm* to enhance its international appeal. Jack Warner felt having *Brooklyn* in the title was too specifically American for foreign audiences. Brooklyn would not become a universal movie symbol of all-American bravado until World War II, when, it seemed, every war picture had a tough, fearless, and ultra-patriotic kid from Brooklyn in it.

much that before the picture ended, Reagan was a junior member of the so-called Irish Mafia (also known as the Emerald Isle Clan), a tight-knit group of Hollywood actors that included O'Brien; Spencer Tracy (his Irish equivalent at MGM — both specialized in playing priests); James Cagney, who fluctuated between tough guys in gangster films and romantic leads in musical comedies; and his pal character actor Frank McHugh.[†]

The only actor in the film who did not

[†] O'Brien (William Joseph O'Brien, Jr.), Warner's "Irishman in Residence," and Spencer Tracy had roomed together as stage actors in New York City. O'Brien's Broadway portrayal of Hildy Johnson in *The Front Page* led to his being cast by producer Howard Hughes for the 1931 screen version of the Ben Hecht and Charles MacArthur play, directed by Lewis Milestone. His performance led to a contract at Warner Bros., where he became one of Warner's biggest stars. Cagney became a star after his appearance in William Wellman's 1931 prototypical sound gangster film *The Public Enemy,* and demonstrated his musical and dancing skills in Lloyd Bacon's 1933 *Footlight Parade.* His best-known "Irish" performance was as George M. Cohan in Michael Curtiz's *Yankee Doodle Dandy.* Frank McHugh, known for his nervous laugh and hangdog look, starred in more than ninety Warner Bros. movies, usually as the sidekick to the leading man, and appeared in several of O'Brien's, Cagney's, and Tracy's films.

especially like Reagan was Powell, who, thanks to Warner's persistence, continued to hear the young actor's footsteps coming up behind him, film after film. Because of that, he made no real effort to help out Reagan when it became clear that the relative newcomer was having trouble handling the film's furiously fast comic pace, set by O'Brien's high-pitched, nasal, hint-of-an-Irish brogue speedball patter. Cast as a small-time show business promoter looking to cash in on Powell's rising-cowboy star, O'Brien plays several scenes opposite Reagan, his "partner," whose real purpose is to allow the audience to hear O'Brien's thoughts as he hatches his plot, a typical foil role. Bacon relegated Reagan to the film's background, where he had little to do other than listen.

Although it broke no box-office records, *Cowboy from Brooklyn* was, nevertheless, Reagan's second straight appearance in a moneymaker, and it helped secure his position at the studio. However, in his second memoir, Reagan hinted that he was more than a little aware that he was not being given a chance to show what he thought he could really do and touched on a very real problem he had faced. Reagan seemed to understand early on that his problem was not so much the films he was being given, but the directors making them: "When I first came to Warner Bros. to the movies, I was certainly a Nobody *[sic]* in,

124

and to, Hollywood . . . The parts they gave me, who cared? But *I* cared. Sure, I was a filler-inner to them. But only to them. To myself, I was a star which had not yet risen . . . I gave [to] them what I would have given [to] them if they'd been starring roles for Capra, Cukor and de Mille, combined . . . no one was going to write a subtitle explaining that Ronald Reagan didn't feel the part was important, therefore he didn't give it very much."

Despite his modest beginnings at Warner, Reagan was a frequent and welcome guest at the best table at the studio's vaunted commissary. That was where the Irish Mafia congregated, as an informal West Coast version of New York's legendary Algonquin Round Table. The commissary was on one side a glorified cafeteria for the off-screen workers and the B players, and on the other a linen café where only the biggest stars ate and hung out. There was also a third, private dining room for the executives.

Most of the bigger-name actors preferred passing the long stretches between takes socializing at the commissary rather than alone in their dressing rooms. Table position, as at any of the show-business restaurants in Hollywood, soon became of paramount importance, and none was more prestigious or difficult to gain entrée to than the one favored by O'Brien and Cagney.

O'Brien was the unofficial place setter, the ordainer of admittance, whose word was final when it came to deciding who could join the party and who couldn't. Along with O'Brien and second-in-command Cagney, the elite roster of those admitted included Errol Flynn, Humphrey Bogart, Dick Powell, Frank McHugh, Allen Jenkins, and . . . Ronald Reagan. Much bigger names who weren't Irish and wanted in were for various reasons kept at arms' distance by O'Brien, actors including Fredric March and Eddie Robinson. March was considered too New York (meaning too much of a stage actor) and Robinson, too Jewish (Warner Jews tended to huddle at their own tables).

O'Brien's allowing Reagan entrée to the inner circle was an anointment of sorts, and he did it for no other reason than he liked him, off-set and on. Reagan was one actor he knew who never chewed scenery; O'Brien never had to worry about "Dutch" trying to steal scenes. And he loved the unapologetic Black Irish in him. For his part, Reagan worshipped O'Brien, another in the growing list of older, father-figure types who welcomed him with open arms and happily took him under his wing. Reagan hung on O'Brien's every word, whether it was acting tips or dirty jokes. Years later Reagan proudly said, "Thanks to Pat O'Brien, I played those B's as if they were

A's. I played every one of them as well as I could, with the idea that it was the most important part in the world."

If his days at the studio were a blitz of acting, hero-worship, and schmoozing, Reagan's nights were reserved for more private affairs. He went out every night with different women, every night, that is, except Sundays. That evening he always reserved for dinner with his parents, always at LaRue's, a local Italian restaurant where the Reagans loved to eat family style, sharing giant portions of spaghetti and meatballs.

Among his most frequent dates on the other nights were Lana Turner, Margaret Lindsay, Mary Jane Crane, Anita Louise, and Joy Hodges, whose own career was going nowhere (many of her film appearances had another voice dubbed over hers — apparently her singing style was better suited to clubs than to the big screen). Turner, considered one of the most beautiful actresses of her day, and one of the hottest, had a hot affair with Reagan that quickly fizzled out. And when Hodges ultimately proved unavailable, Reagan simply turned to the Warner starlet list with all the lust and zeal of a casting director. He preferred brunettes but allowed for the occasional blonde, always with the understanding that their dating was just that, dating, with no long-range expectations on either side.

Reagan also went for the ravenous, rough, and luscious Brooklyn-born Irish beauty Susan Hayward and eagerly posed with her for publicity pictures that showed off both of them in their swimsuit bests, captioned with smirky, double-entendre headlines — RONALD REAGAN SHOWS SUSAN HAYWARD THE PROPER POSITION. Hayward was hot for Reagan as well and was always happy to see him, but their relationship ended rather abruptly when Jack Warner objected to the "cheesecake" the two were generating in the press. Reagan's reputation as a Hollywood love-'em-and-leave-'em type was growing rapidly inside the gates of the studio, and Jack L. Warner was determined to see to it that none of it ever made the gossip columns, at least none he couldn't control. Through Parsons's eyes, Reagan's image was that of the most chaste, well-behaved boy in Hollywood, the boy who'd bought a house for his parents and dined once a week with them, no matter how busy he was.[*]

Next on his list was blond starlet Ila

[*] This consensus was not unanimous. Per Edmund Morris's *Dutch: A Memoir of Ronald Reagan* (see "Sources"), Owen Crump, a writer at Warner Bros. at the time, insisted years later in an interview that "Dutch was regarded as the studio's porch warmer, more gab than grab, and no threat to any virgin," and others, such as his local cavalry commanding

Rhodes, née Ila Rae Corncutt (aka Cornutt), the daughter of a purported (but never proven) part Cherokee Native American, who was, like Reagan, coming up through the Warner Bros. contract player system. Rhodes was a beauty queen who had been spotted by a Warner scout during a Pasadena bathing-suit competition. Her film career was, to this point, less than spectacular, consisting of one bit part, uncredited, in James Flood's *Off the Record,* a 1938 Pat O'Brien vehicle. Reagan began seeing Rhodes during production (he wasn't in the film). For her part, she immediately saw her own starlight reflected in his eyes and took him on a journey of faux-foreign sexual decadence (she claimed to be related to wealthy aristocrats). Reagan liked Rhodes so much that he decided, despite her wild ways, she might be "the one," and went, not to his own parents, but to Jack L. Warner, to make sure it would be all right if he married Rhodes.

Much to Reagan's surprise, the answer was no. Warner's reasons were simple and clear: He didn't like Rhodes or the idea that one of his eligible good-looking young contract players wanted to get married to anyone. It could

---

officer, rather smirkily, with double entendres flying all over the place, said that Lieutenant Reagan was a "greater swordsman than Errol Flynn."

wreck his potential as a leading man. Besides, Warner told Reagan, he was wasting his time with this one. Reagan immediately broke off their engagement.

Rhodes's brief and decidedly unremarkable film career didn't last much longer after that. It came to an end in 1939 after four minor appearances in Warner pictures (because of scheduling, two of them were with Reagan even after their "breakup"). Here is how Rhodes remembered the affair, in which she clearly recalls an official engagement, complete with ring: "I was twenty-one and he was around thirty, tall and cute. Ronnie was very attractive and I didn't want any antidote to ward off this attraction . . . we made B films . . . the short time we filmed together led to lunch-break trysts and weekends out together, snatched from a hectic Hollywood schedule . . . I became engaged to him, with a ring on my finger . . . In all, the engagement lasted eight or nine months, when the studio decided romance between their stars was bad for box-office business."

After she was let go by Warner, Ila Rhodes never made another Hollywood motion picture.[*]

---

[*] Reagan was twenty-nine; Rhodes, twenty-four. It is doubtful the engagement lasted that long, or that she had a "hectic" schedule. The two films Rhodes

■ ■ ■ ■

Early in 1938, thanks to Pat O'Brien's urging, Reagan landed a small role in Hal Wallis's A-unit production of Lloyd Bacon's *Boy Meets Girl,* produced by Broadway veteran George Abbott and intended as a star vehicle for both O'Brien and James Cagney.[†] O'Brien also had a hand in getting Cagney aboard; his box-office power remained high but his battles with Jack L. Warner had caused the head of the studio to punish his star by making him wait until the last minute to be greenlighted for the roles he wanted most.

Loosely based on the private life and creative partnership of Broadway playwrights Charles MacArthur and Ben Hecht, the film was an adaptation of a successful Broadway show Warners had purchased as an intended vehicle for Marion Davies and the comedy team of Olsen and Johnson, the studio's hoped-for answer to MGM's zany and insanely successful Marx Brothers. Neither

---

was making during her affair with Reagan were Noel M. Smith's 1939 *Secret Service of the Air* and Edmund Goulding's 1939 *Dark Victory.*

† Between the productions of *The Cowboy from Brooklyn* and *Boy Meets Girl,* Reagan did the unseen and uncredited voice coming through the radio in Anatole Litvak's *The Amazing Dr. Clitterhouse.*

Davies, who was unsatisfied with the script by Bella and Sam Spewack, or Olsen and Johnson, who had live performance schedule conflicts, appeared in the film. Sweet-faced Marie Wilson replaced Davies in the female lead of Susie. Reagan, meanwhile, was happy to have a chance to work again with O'Brien. And he was also impressed with how O'Brien had handled the Cagney situation in such a smooth, unruffled yet highly persuasive manner, especially with the always-hot Jack Warner. It was something he would not forget.

Cagney had not made a movie for Warner in a while, having run into a political maelstrom for his financial contributions to benefit striking cotton-pickers in the San Joaquin Valley. Jack Warner, whose liberalism extended only as far as the populist stories he put up on the big screen, considered Cagney too much of a leftist as well as a prima donna. The fact that Cagney's check wound up framed and displayed on the wall of the Communist Party office in San Francisco, and a photograph of that wall appeared in dozens of newspapers, didn't help the situation any. Because of it, Cagney's future at the studio was nearly derailed. Ignoring warnings against such actions by Warner, Cagney then contributed money toward the purchase of several ambulances for the Lincoln Brigade fighting on the side of the Loyalists in the

Spanish Civil War. It was that donation that caused him to be called before the Dies Committee investigating communist activities in Hollywood.* It was only after he was cleared and stood up for by O'Brien that Warner okayed Cagney for *Boy Meets Girl,* his first screen appearance in a year.**

*The Dies Committee was the forerunner of HUAC (House Un-American Activities Committee). HUAC was established in 1934 as the "Special Committee on Un-American Activities Authorized to Investigate Nazi Propaganda and Certain Other Propaganda Activities." Congressman Martin Dies, Jr., replaced John W. McCormack as co-chairman in 1938 and initiated the second major phase of HUAC. It had a third major resurgence in 1947, and wasn't officially disbanded until 1975.

** Cagney's previous appearance was in Victor Schertzinger's 1937 *Something to Sing About.* Before that, he had made one film in 1936, seven in 1935, four in 1934, three in 1933, five in 1931, and two in 1930. All but two were made at Warner Bros. Those two, John Blystone's 1937 *Great Guy* and *Something to Sing About,* were made at Grand National, an independent house Cagney had signed a two-picture deal with while on the outs with Jack Warner. It was those five pictures in 1933 that had led Cagney to walk out, and sue Warner Bros., claiming he had only agreed to four a year and was free to sign with Grand National. Many believe the political pressures brought on Cagney during what turned out to

133

Once again, Reagan's role in the film was barely noticeable. He played yet another radio announcer, this time at a Hollywood premiere (the film's plot had shifted the writing locale from Broadway to Hollywood). Despite the film's mixed reviews, it proved a box-office success, due largely to the drawing power of its stars.

However, Reagan felt the film did nothing for him. He had only a tiny part in a big film in which he was completely overshadowed once more by its stars, O'Brien and Cagney. There is not a single mention of the film in either of his two memoirs or in his authorized biography.[†]

Reagan's next film marked a return to Bryan Foy's B unit to star opposite Jane

---

be a year-long stand-off between Warner and Cagney were done in retribution for his contractual dispute and served as a model for what was to come down on Hollywood's liberal contingency a decade later.

† He did make mention of it once, years later, in 1974, when he attended the American Film Institute's Life Achievement Award for Jimmy Cagney. One of the several montages of Cagney's work shown that night included a clip from *Boy Meets Girl*. Afterward, Reagan came to the podium in the ballroom at the Century Plaza Hotel; he joked that he hoped the institute would forget his scene when they got around to preserving the film. He added

Bryan in William McGann's *Girls on Probation*. In this one he plays a young attorney who defends Bryan, a girl falsely accused of stealing a gown. The film's spirited defense of the underdog and the falsely accused, a favorite theme of Jack Warner's, reinforced the studio's paint-by-numbers philosophy of the ultimate fairness of American justice. From the vantage point of the B-movie machine, Reagan was perfectly cast as an idealistic, if a bit naïve, defense lawyer who, in the ritualistic expanse of Hollywood, predictably falls in love with the client whose innocence he truly believes (and believes in).

Next for Reagan was Ray Enright's *Naughty But Nice* (1939). By now, Dick Powell was as eager to part company with Warner as the studio was with him, and this was the movie that was supposed to end it for both. Reagan had a small meaningless "sidekick" part as Professor Hardwick's (Powell's) "honest" music publisher, Ed Clark, who "believes" in him and his music. The professor is an out-of-town hick who comes to the Big City (New York) to publish his symphony and "make it." Sexy Ann Sheridan (Warner's "oomph" girl), as all show-business female cynics do, uses him, while a young female

---

that he not only had known Jimmy for the better part of his life but that "Jimmy Cagney *was* the better part of my life."

lyricist (Gale Page) falls for him and his small-town virtues.

Powell looked at least twenty years too old for his part (which is why he was a professor rather than a helper in his father's small store or a fresh college graduate, which would have made infinitely more sense). The film came and went without much notice, its release delayed several times by Warner before they finally found a slow week in their schedule a year later, in June 1939.

Things finally began to look up for Reagan when Jack L. Warner personally assigned him to his ninth and final picture of 1938, a costarring role in a decidedly A feature, William Keighley's *Brother Rat,* alongside Wayne Morris, Eddie Albert, Jane Bryan (her second feature in a row with Reagan), and a former dancer turned actress by the name of Jane Wyman.

If there had been a preponderance of father figures in Reagan's Hollywood life — George Ward (despite his youth), Pat O'Brien, Bill Meiklejohn, Jack L. Warner — there was a notable lack of eligible, maternal-type women to fill the emotional gap left by Margaret Cleaver. Misadventures such as his affair with Ila Rhodes did not help. Not even the physical presence of his real mother was enough to ease that problem. If anything, her presence made Margaret's absence more poignant.

The more starlets he slept with, the more he was convinced that there simply were no women in Hollywood good enough to marry. Away from the movie screen that beautified them, idealized them, and imbued them with a moral fiber, in real life Reagan found little redeeming about these women. Their idealized, mythic beauty was one thing; their real lives, the side of them the public rarely, if ever, got to see, were too often something that was less than fairy-tale perfect.

Until now.

Jane Wyman took one look at Ronald Reagan and decided he was the man for her. She was out to get him and not just for a one-night quickie. She was determined to marry him. To do so, she would prove to him that she could provide anything and everything he could ever want, that she was trustworthy and faithful and loyal and wholesome and sweet.

Even though she was, at the time, married to another man.

■ ■ ■ ■

CHAPTER FOUR:
DUTCH AND
BUTTON-NOSE

■ ■ ■ ■

I hope my Ronald has made the right choice. I was in hopes he would fall in love with some sweet girl who is not in the movies.

— NELLE REAGAN

Ronald Reagan and Jane Wyman on their wedding day, January 26, 1940.

Sarah Jane Mayfield was born on January 5, 1917, in St. Joseph, Missouri, where she lived until her father, a meal-company laborer, lost his job and moved the family to San Francisco. When her father couldn't find steady work, he arranged for his neighbors, the Fulks (Mr. Fulks was the chief of detectives), to unofficially adopt Sarah Jane, who was still a toddler, as their own. She continued to live with them until 1928, when "Daddy" Fulks died and Mrs. Fulks, a frustrated wannabe actress, took her daughter to Los Angeles.[*]

[*] Wyman's birth date has long been misreported as January 4, 1914. It is likely the mistake was intentional on her part, adding three years to her age so that she could work full-time in Hollywood while still legally a minor. There is also confusion as to her real name. That, too, has been misreported in several places as Sarah Jane Fulks, the last name of the neighbors who "adopted" her after her parents' divorce.

Unable to find any work in film, Mrs. Fulks and Sarah Jane moved back to Missouri, where Sarah Jane shortened her name to "Jane," got a job singing on local radio, and quit high school; then she moved to Los Angeles, changed the last part of her name to "Durrell" and, only sixteen years old, married a traveling salesman by the name of Ernest Wyman.

The marriage lasted less than two years, during which time Jane made her film debut as one of the leggy, scantily clad chorines known as Goldwyn girls, whom Samuel L. Goldwyn used to decorate his independently made features. Her first movie was Leo McCarey's *The Kid from Spain,* a musical produced by the Samuel Goldwyn Company and distributed through United Artists. It was a goofy musical vehicle for Eddie Cantor, a huge musical star at the time cast from the mold of Al Jolson. Five years and seventeen forgettable films later, she finally caught a real break when she was signed by Bill Meiklejohn's agency in anticipation of its takeover by MCA. And, like Reagan, consigned to the B bin.

Wyman was not the tender, tall, blond, blue-eyed WASP type that Hollywood adored. Her face was too leonine and not enough pussycat, but her shoulders were broad enough to carry the enormous if not surprising chip of distrust she harbored toward men.

Hollywood was never a great place for women who believed their fathers didn't love them enough or who sought to find either stable men or stability in men. She didn't particularly like the one she happened to be married to. Her current husband, Myron Futterman, fifteen years her senior and a New Orleans–based dressmaker, was hardly ever around and never missed, at least not by her. He was her security without being a blanket. He gave her respectability at a time in Hollywood when *single* meant "slut" when applied to women (only) over twenty-one and not married. And at the same time he granted her the freedom to sample what was around, which she did quite liberally. There was never a shortage of wannabe Prince Charmings, good-time Charlies eager to slip the glass slipper *off* her pretty feet.

Then she met Ronald Reagan and immediately filed for divorce.

Although Wyman may have had her eye on Reagan for a while as one of the most eligible young working actors in Hollywood, they were first introduced when it was announced they were going to be each other's love interest in the forthcoming *Brother Rat.* Reagan liked what he saw, but when he found out she was married and going through a divorce, he pulled back and focused all his energies on his role in the film, especially since he was, technically at least, still engaged to Ila Rhodes.

William Keighley, the director of *Brother Rat* (1938), had been one of the pioneers of the new talking medium. He had come out of live theater and radio to direct his first motion picture, *The Match King* (1932), which was codirected by Howard Bretherton and was a First National picture (First National was by now a wholly owned subsidiary of Warner Bros., which had gained controlling interest in 1928, mainly for the acquisition of its strong distribution network). Keighley, whose background in radio made him a valuable commodity to the suddenly sound-conscious medium, paid his dues and learned his craft in nine movies over the next three years, sometimes as a dialogue director on more important films and sometimes as a B movie director, until he broke through with *G-Men,* starring James Cagney in one of his signature little tough-guy roles. After the film's critical and box-office success, Jack L. Warner promoted Keighley to a more prominent place on his roster of A directors. He went on to direct, with Marc Connelly, the notable *The Green Pastures* in 1936, and then the Errol Flynn version of *The Prince and the Pauper,* which was a smash, and then a year later *The Adventures of Robin Hood,* the film that struck box-office gold with the reteaming of Flynn with Olivia de Havilland.* Audiences simply couldn't get enough of them.

Brother Rat had begun as a Broadway show directed by George Abbott in 1937 and made its previously unknown lead, a young, likable, and good-looking actor named Eddie Albert, who played one of the three principal "rats," an overnight sensation (in the play military cadets fondly called each other Brother Rat). However, when Warner purchased the rights to the film, they relegated Albert, who was not a big name outside of the New York stage community and proved to be not particularly photogenic in his initial screen test, to a supporting role, and gave the lead instead to Wayne Morris. Reagan was cast as the third member of a trio of young men enrolled at the Virginia Military Institute, the so-called West Point of the South. In the film, Reagan, as cadet Dan Crawford, decides to romance Claire Adams, the commandant's daughter (never a good idea, in Hollywood films

* The two had previously costarred in Michael Curtiz's *Captain Blood,* the film that made Flynn a major star and laid the foundation for his reputation as the successor to Douglas Fairbanks as Hollywood's greatest swashbuckler. Keighley was actually fired from *Robin Hood* during production because he couldn't get along with Errol Flynn, who insisted that Curtiz finish the film. Both Keighley and Curtiz receive directing credit for *Robin Hood.*

anyway), played by Jane Wyman. Sparks immediately flew between the two both off-screen and on, as every chance she got Wyman rubbed up against the flinty Reagan like a giant matchstick looking to be lit. By the time the making of the film was over, they were a real item. Two months after it opened, in October 1938, Wyman's divorce was finalized and Reagan had quickly and quietly ended his engagement to Rhodes.

Soon, every fanzine and column in America was writing about Hollywoods' newest twosome. Here, in a rare interview, Wyman explained the way they began "dating": "Neither Ronnie or I were stars. We were both featured players making $500 a week. I wasn't a glamour queen and he wasn't a matinee idol. We were just two kids trying to break into pictures. . . . When I first met Ronnie I was a night club girl. I just had to go dancing and dining at the Troc [Trocadero] or the [Cocoanut] Grove or some night spot every night to be happy.

"Then Ronnie said to me, 'Don't you ever swim, or play golf?' He was perfectly amazed that I didn't have the slightest conception about either. We were both working on a picture called *Brother Rat.* We'd sit around the set and talk . . . one day the studio took Ann Sheridan, Ronnie and me out to the ice rink to pose for some publicity pictures. I couldn't even stand up on ice skates. Ronnie held me up long enough for pictures. He kidded me so terrifically about it, that Ann and I decided to skate along, too. For two months we'd go out there every morning and we could actually figure skate. That's how Ronnie and I began going together."

Skating on thin ice is a good metaphor for this unlikely duo. According to one of Reagan's biographers, "Small parts. A bad marriage. Janie wore her chips on her shoulder like epaulets. If Ronnie had learned to trust people too easily, Janie's problem was that she did not trust people at all." Wyman told *Movieland* magazine in July 1944, "That was a terrible thing for me, this distrust [of men]. I was so afraid that I should make a wrong move or jeopardize my opportunity in some way! I guarded my budding career so fiercely and with such terrible suspicion of everyone that I made it extremely difficult for anyone to help me. . . . Then of course, Ronnie *really* came into my life. It was *his* easy friendliness which attracted me to him first. Everyone liked him and it seemed to me that he liked nearly everyone."

It had been reported in several newspapers, including the *Daily Variety,* that Jane Wyman had suffered a nervous breakdown of sorts shortly before she'd met Reagan. Emotionally fragile, at best, Wyman was looking for a man to protect her, provide for her, and maybe even help to promote her career. So there they were, the older-than-her-years, hard-as-nails divorcée who trusted no one and the younger-than-his-years bachelor who trusted everyone. In Hollywood, that could only mean they were made for each other.

Although it wasn't a smash, *Brother Rat* did well enough at the box office to keep everybody at the studio happy. Ironically, the only actor to emerge as a legitimate star from it was Eddie Albert, who'd shone in his supporting role. This didn't please Reagan. Although, characteristically, he said nothing at the time. However, in his first memoir, published forty-three years later, he appeared to be slightly bitter if gracious over what happened with Albert. "My part was easily good enough to provide a stepping-stone to stardom. Unhappily I learned another lesson. There is room for only one discovery in a picture. Eddie Albert stole the honors and deservedly so."

The film was promoted by Warners as "just plain fun," involving the antics of the three cadets and their girlfriends. In a time when war was raging in Europe and Asia, and storm clouds were heading for America, popular culture as reflected in the movies (which necessarily lagged at least two years behind the times) was still offering peacetime, frolicky notions of what wartime military service was. Despite Warners' somewhat inflated and oversimplistic reputation as the studio whose feet were firmly set in the social cement of reality (it may be argued, for instance, that Columbia, most notably with Frank Capra, made far more socially relevant movies), military school in *Brother Rat* looks like high school. All the "romances" are so devoid of any sexual heat that it's possible to believe a stork really did bring a baby to the wife of the "shocked" Albert character when he finds out he's about to be a father.

Audiences didn't go completely wild over the film's sunny view of life. After a decade of Depression and the growing threat of war, the American moviegoing audience was not that easily comforted by Hollywood's out-of-date escapism. Bright as the screen and the smiling actors were, darkness rather than prosperity was just around the corner.

In 1939, Ronald Reagan was angry about having to join the Screen Actors Guild. With Jack Warner and Jules Stein looking out for him, he didn't see the need for membership in the Guild, but he soon found out he had no choice in the matter. He was, in reality, entering the theater in the middle of the movie. He had no idea what the Guild was all about, or how hard it had fought for its very existence.

The history of unions in Hollywood is not pretty or simple. The populist films that the studios cranked out during the thirties for the most part did not reflect the views of the rights of the working man. Those films were made for the people buying the tickets, not the actors making the movies. Notions such as equality, justice, and freedom in the dream factories were little more than "product," something sold to audiences shaken by financial ruin, reeling from the unexpected hardships of World War I and preparing to go through it all over again. The factory-run studios cashed in on selling democracy to the public while, in private, they resisted any and all union movements meant to protect their own workers from being exploited.

From the very beginning, Hollywood management, mostly European-born immigrants, were self-starters who built their studios and their fortunes out of nothing more than determination, dreams, and the opportunity to turn what had been an offshoot novelty of the discovery of electricity, moving pictures, into an international industry. All they really knew about management was what they had learned by watching their own parents slave for shop owners, or what they themselves had gone through as children. The fruits of capitalism were, for most of them, a foreign concept, meant for privileged American-born Christians — of which very few of them were — who benefited from the system and looked like the character in Monopoly with the white mustache and tuxedo. Capitalism benefited capitalists. Workers weren't capitalists, and capitalists weren't workers.

By 1929, it was clear film was to become one of the largest and most profitable industries in America (production and exhibition tentacles were already reaching around the globe), with grosses exceeding $1 billion in the Depression era from an annual production rate of more than six hundred feature films. Those who owned the studios wanted their workers, the men and women who acted in, wrote, directed, and built the sets for their salable product, films, to feel as if they were working for one big, happy family — think "Uncle" Walt — rather than in a factory, which is where, in reality, they really were, no matter how glorified that factory was or how glamorous the work appeared. The real family was made up of the banks, who funded the major studios, and those studios — which, despite the fact that there were eight of them, were, in fact, more dictatorial than democratic due to their lockup of distribution and exhibition. They operated as non-union closed shops and wanted to keep it that way.

Although the film industry had been organized into a formal business by the turn of the twentieth century, during the widespread look-the-other-way sweatshop practices of the times, it wasn't until the onset of the Great Depression that the union movement took hold in Hollywood. As early as 1927, studio mogul Louis B. Mayer, sensing the threat of labor unions to the profits of all the film studios — the thought of having to pay decent wages horrified all the moguls — organized what he hoped would be a conciliatory forum among the heads of the major studios to listen to the growing complaints of employees regarding their low rate of pay and generally poor physical working conditions.

Mayer's newly formed Academy of Motion Picture Arts and Sciences, a glorified management coalition meant to unify the competing studios so they could have a united front against labor, put on a sympathetic face but did little to improve the conditions of the workforce. For the first five years, the Academy managed to put off any real progress in union organizing among producers, directors, actors, writers, and technicians. What they had done, and what they felt was just compensation, was to set up an annual prize, a trophy and a dinner to go with it, for all those who had made the most money for the studio. No raises, no unemployment insurance, no paid holidays, no pensions; nothing but a gold-plated statue, an Academy Award, a round of applause, and a couple of trade-paper headlines. In 1931, when box-office revenues took a huge dip, the studios imposed an industry-wide 50 percent pay cut on what it considered the least suffering, most-overpaid group of studio workers, its writers. When their protests failed and their resistance fell, the studios imposed similar reductions on actors, directors, and technicians.

Nonetheless, the heads of the studios couldn't believe it when their employees expressed a united front of dissatisfaction. The Academy saw itself as the watchdog for the workers against management, even if this watchdog was set up and run by management. House unions were fairly common in large organizations in this part of the twentieth century, and the studios felt they were being more than fair with their grievance committees, sympathetic ears, and "investigations." Unfortunately, the workers wanted more, beginning with decent salaries and some form of real job security.

The Writers Guild was the first "talent" union in Hollywood to successfully and independently organize.* It came into exis-

* Two previous attempts at organizing the writers had failed, once in 1914 with the creation of the Photoplay Authors' League, which lasted only two years, and then in 1920 with the Screenwriters Guild in Hollywood, which lasted until 1927, the same year the Academy of Motion Picture Arts and Sciences was formed. Each failed for the same reason: They were unable to win contracts from the studios that recognized the legitimacy of (and therefore legitimized) their unions. For extended

tence in 1933 and once and forever polarized Hollywood's management and workers. Later that same year the Screen Actors Guild (SAG) was formed, with the express intention of limiting or eliminating multiyear exclusive-services contracts, which prevented actors from working freelance if they were signed to a major studio (and no major studio would sign an actor who worked freelance, while they freely loaned out their talent in lucrative deals that in most cases only the studios profited from). SAG also wanted limits put on work hours and taken off benefits, unemployment, and health insurance. Most of all, SAG sought the right to represent its members in collective bargaining, something the studio heads labeled nothing less than Bolshevik-style communism.

Originally formed by six actors, the Screen Actors Guild was kick-started into existence with a publicly touted agreement signed by the studios in which they pledged not to bid against one another for talent.[†] In short

study, the best history of unionism in Hollywood is Larry Ceplair and Steven Englund's *The Inquisition in Hollywood* (see "Sources").

† Berton Churchill, Charles Miller, Grant Mitchell, Ralph Morgan, Alden Gay, and Kenneth Thompson. The Guild was an outgrowth of the Masquers Club, a loose organization of actors trying to unite

order, the Guild attracted first dozens, then hundreds, then virtually every actor in Hollywood to its ranks. Among the more prominent early members of SAG were Edward Arnold, Humphrey Bogart, James Cagney, Dudley Digges, Porter Hall, Paul Harvey, Jean Hersholt, Russell Hicks, Murray Kinnell, Gene Lockhart, Fredric March, Adolphe Menjou, Chester Morris, Jean Muir, George Murphy, Erin O'Brien-Moore, Irving Pichel, Dick Powell, Edward G. Robinson, Edwin Stanley, Gloria Stuart, Franchot Tone, Warren William, and Robert Young. It wasn't until four years later, in 1937, that studios acknowledged the legitimacy of SAG as a union and its right to collective bargaining. It was a major victory, not just for this union but for unionism in America.

All of which makes it that much more startling to know that Reagan, who described himself at the time not just as a Democrat but as a "Roosevelt Democrat," was so opposed to being forced to join SAG whether he wanted to or not. Like a child visiting the

---

against what they felt were the exploitative practices of the studios. It is probably no coincidence that these six actors are largely unknown. The studios avoided using them in important roles and refused to "make stars" out of any of them as retribution for their participation in the formation of SAG.

dentist for the first time, he didn't see the purpose: "When I arrived in Hollywood," Reagan wrote after he had become president of the United States, "actors and actresses had just won a tough five-year battle with studios for the union shop and recognition of the Screen Actors Guild as the exclusive bargaining agent for actors. Like all contract players, I'd had to join the union and wasn't very happy about it. Making me join the union, whether I wanted to or not, I thought, was an infringement on my rights. I guess I also was a little uncertain as to why actors needed to have a union." His largely uninformed attitude, Reagan goes on to explain, gradually changed as he learned more about what some of the older actors had gone through, particularly his new friend Cagney.

Still, what some might describe as his steadfast allegiance to the studios remained. While others in Hollywood prepped for the next round of their increasingly contentious battle against the studios, Reagan was content to play the golden boy, squiring Jane Wyman around Hollywood's most elite social circuit. Rather than attend union meetings, Reagan preferred dining with his newfound socially elite crowd, Mr. and Mrs. Jack L. Warner, and Jules and Doris Stein. Meanwhile, in the press, Louella Parsons, payrolled mouthpiece for Jack Warner and other studio leaders, regularly pumped the careers of Ronald Reagan and his "sweetheart," Jane Wyman, with "breathless" details of their affair. "Two of Hollywood's very nicest young people have fallen in love!" Parsons reported to the world on November 1, 1938, not the first time she would headline their starry-eyed romance with all the excitement, surprise, and wonderment of someone who had just witnessed the arrival of a UFO from outer space.

Reagan's next on-screen appearance was in a film he had actually made before *Naughty But Nice* but that was released after, Ray Enright's 1938 *Going Places,* a chestnut of a script based on William Collier, Sr., and Victor Mapes's play *The Hottentot,* which was regularly trotted out of the vault of well-performing scripts earmarked for profitable remakes. It had first been made into a film in 1922 by James Horne as a vehicle for silent-star Douglas MacLean; it was again in 1929 as an early talkie by Roy Del Ruth as a vehicle for Edward Everett Horton; and was yet again, by Enright, in 1936, as *Polo Joe,* a follow-up to his major 1935 Joe E. Brown comic vehicle, *Alibi Ike.*[*]

Enright, a career journeyman at Warner

---

[*] Brown, an all-but-forgotten film comic of the thirties, is perhaps best known to most filmgoers as the rich pursuer of Jack Lemmon (in drag) in Billy Wilder's 1959 comedy classic *Some Like It Hot.*

Bros. who made his bones directing Rin Tin Tin (*Tracked by the Police,* 1927), was the logical pick to direct, having already done well with Powell (and costar Olivia de Havilland) earlier that same year with the romantic comedy *Hard to Get,* as well as with Reagan a year earlier in *Swing Your Lady;* he was now called upon to helm *Going Places.* Produced by Hal B. Wallis, *Going Places* was an A project, and Reagan was thrilled to be a part of it, even if his part, as usual, was smaller than the lead, played by the slow-fading Powell.

The film was a romantic comedy with songs by Johnny Mercer and Harry Warren; their best for it, "Jeepers Creepers," became a popular hit with audiences, most unaware it was actually about a horse, as a flirty love song — "Jeepers Creepers, where'd you get those peepers . . . where'd you get those eyes . . ." The plot of the film is from the fake-identity rack; Peter Mason (Powell) poses as a famous gentleman jockey to get inside the gates of wealthy Maryland horseman Colonel Withering (Thurston Hall) to woo the colonel's niece, Ellen (Anita Louise), where he befriends Jack, the colonel's happy-idiot son (Reagan).

Reagan especially enjoyed working on this film because a lot of it was shot at Will Rogers State Park, a favorite spot for Hollywood's polo set, including Walt Disney, and where

Reagan loved to go riding on weekends. Otherwise, his performance was quick paced but heavy-handed, overheated but never steamy, labored, full of manneristic overreactions, including, worst of all, a slightly feminine fret-frown combined with the raising of one eyebrow and a slight shake of his head. He used the same reaction in the film whenever he was supposed to be upset, annoyed, puzzled, angry, or reconciling. It wrinkled one side of his chin and made him seem more hapless than heroic. Not Academy Award material. Except for an appearance by the always great Louis Armstrong, and the then awkward fact that the hit song was not sung by Powell (happily, Armstrong did it), the film was utterly forgettable and did nothing to advance the careers of anyone, including the horse who played Creepers.

The career yo-yo continued for Reagan when he was once more demoted to Bryan Foy's B unit for his next assignment, Noel Smith's 1939 *Secret Service of the Air*. The studio had decided to make a series of inexpensive black-and-white (in character complexities as well as film stock), never-skip-a-beat adventure films, of which the sixty-one-minute *Secret Service of the Air* was to be the first (Warner hoped audiences would note the similarity between the titles of Reagan's *Love Is on the Air* and *Secret Service of the Air*).

Reagan tried to make the best of a role that had all the weighted reality of a Flash Gordon Saturday-morning serial, somehow believing that he was being groomed to become the Errol Flynn of the B's. "I was as brave as Errol, but in low-budget fashion," he told one friend years later.

Well, not exactly. He didn't have Flynn's swashbuckling athleticism (Reagan was athletic, but not nearly as graceful as Flynn) or his beautiful facial features that made him as pretty as he was handsome. Flynn was a bad drinker; a reformed thief (according to his memoirs); a relentless womanizer (a reputation that gained him the moniker "In like Flynn!" after being tried and acquitted in 1943 by an all-female jury of the charge of statutory rape of two sixteen-year-old girls); a tough guy and a night-side brawler. But he was something else as well — one of the biggest stars in Warners' stable, the reason they kept him under contract through scandal after scandal. Everyone wanted to see Flynn on the screen, especially women, who were more often than not responsible for choosing the weekly movies for their dates or their husbands, while, apparently, nobody wanted to see Ronald Reagan. The films that he was in to this point that had made money were vehicles for other stars, or low-budget bottom-of-the-bill features that profited from their cofeatures. And nobody knew it more than Reagan.

Wyman's career wasn't doing much better. Her next film was Roy Del Ruth's *Tailspin,* a forgettable (and forgotten) Alice Faye vehicle costarring Charlie Farrell, a fading silent-film sensation.

During their off-hours, Wyman and Reagan comforted each other on the mud-stuck status of their careers, although at the time Wyman was more content than Reagan. She had another goal besides becoming a star. Even if she didn't particularly like or trust men; even if she hated the annoying little things Reagan did, like his annoying Midwest habit of imposing a nickname on her — "Button-Nose" — that sounded to her condescending and demeaning, as if she were his rag doll rather than his girlfriend. Nonetheless, she felt that, like no other man who had passed through her life, she could trust Ronald Reagan. "I went around all the time with a mild form of hate eating into me," Wyman told her biographer, Anne Edwards. "I was constantly on the alert . . . for signs that someone was trying to spoil my job for me. I suspected the hairdresser for trying to ruin my looks . . . a press agent for trying to make me look silly in print . . . [but] I trusted Ronnie. For the first time in my life I truly trusted someone." Trust, to Wyman, translated into love, and love in the parlance of the day meant marriage. For her, that was the only starring role that really mattered.

When Bryan Foy was first given the material to make *Secret Service of the Air,* even he was disappointed with how little there was to work with. To make it, Jack Warner had acquired the rights to the memoirs of William H. Moran, a former head of the Secret Service, and since Moran's agreement with the agency precluded him from revealing very much about what had gone on in his life, there was virtually nothing left on which to base a meaningful movie. Despite the studio's publicity campaign that had declared the film was actually a thinly disguised version of Moran's private files, Foy had to tailor a story out of whole cloth into the adventures of a former army air corps lieutenant making a living as a commercial pilot before deciding one day, with no apparent reason (none is given in the film) to join the Secret Service.[*] Just like that, he is assigned to bust a ring of opium smugglers bringing illegal aliens into the United States (the original script had him busting up a conventional drug ring, but those in charge of the government censorship of Hollywood films disapproved. Joseph

---

[*] Moran's deal included a consultancy position on the film for $250 a week. He was used mostly in the film's publicity campaign.

Breen, the tough new head of the reinvigorated Hollywood Production Code Administration, designated to crack down on the studios for their lax enforcement of the Hays Office's rules of ethics, apparently didn't think the American drug dealer was a sufficient enemy to show off Bancroft's inherent patriotism, something foreign smugglers would). To accomplish this, he decides to go undercover to infiltrate the gang (a little more difficult when they're all Asians), posing, of all things, as a counterfeiter.[†]

Despite a script totally lacking in reality, the studio okayed a higher-than-usual budget to film the aerial shots, rather than relying on its vault of stock footage. Unfortunately, this left no money for a stunt double for Reagan, who wound up with two black eyes filming his own action sequences (no actual flying, lots of fistfighting), something he was not at all pleased with. He was also left with permanent hearing damage after someone fired a

† Joseph Breen was appointed in 1934 to crack down on those studios continuing to ignore the rules of ethics and morality created by the Hays Office. Interestingly, in *Secret Service of the Air,* several of the villains were Asians. American neutrality policies prevented specifically identifying villains as Nazis, which the original script called for, but there was no problem in suggesting that Asians (Japanese) were the bad guys.

163

blank .38 too close to his head.

Nor did he appreciate the fact that Ila Rhodes was still in the film. In the Rolodex raffle that was the casting system of the B's, it was only a matter of time before the two would wind up working together. Now that he was dating Wyman, Reagan was a bit uncomfortable working with the woman to whom he had so recently been engaged.

Foy cast his brother, Eddie Foy, Jr., to play Reagan's sidekick, "Gabby" — sidekicks were often the equivalent of girlfriends in action films, meant to broaden their appeal to young male audiences that didn't go for all the "mushy stuff." The "kid" audience was so desired that on Saturday afternoons the film was actually the A movie on the bill, with the intent of attracting the young boys who went to the movies on those weekend mornings to see the serial adventures of Flash Gordon and dozens of other wishful warriors of American adolescence.

The film took all of twelve days to shoot and was pretty much a stinker, but due to its clever marketing campaign, it made enough money for the studio to green-light a sequel. Reagan was ambivalent about that; he was grateful for the work, but hated the assignment.

Before he got to make it, though, he was unexpectedly (to him) pitched back up for a small role in a Bette Davis vehicle, Edmund

Goulding's *Dark Victory,* produced by Wallis's A unit. Despite decent-to-terrific supporting performances by George Brent, Humphrey Bogart (in a role almost no one remembers him in), and Geraldine Fitzgerald, the film is all Davis, in a role that was originally played on Broadway by one of her arch screen rivals, Tallulah Bankhead.

It didn't help matters any that Goulding didn't particularly like Reagan, and that Reagan didn't like him either, most likely because Goulding was bisexual and never tried to hide it.[*] Reagan had no use for homosexuals, didn't like being around them, and certainly did not enjoy taking directions from them (Goulding had a notorious reputation in Hollywood for throwing unbounded sex orgies, something that personally repulsed Reagan).[†]

[*] Neither the film, Bette Davis, nor Goulding are given a single mention in either of Reagan's two memoirs, and Davis is given only two scant mentions — the film none — in Reagan's authorized Morris biography.

[†] A 2004 biography of Goulding, *Edmund Goulding's Dark Victory* by Matthew Kennedy, claims that it was widely known in Hollywood that Goulding was bisexual, and hosted wild parties for all persuasions. (See "Sources" for more information on this book.)

Goulding's films tended to lean toward the soap-operatic — 1932's *Grand Hotel* — but he could also direct high-style black-tie comedy cut with low-style slapstick, such as his 1935 Marx Brothers vehicle *A Night at the Opera* (Goulding was uncredited; the director was officially listed as Sam Wood). *Dark Victory,* with a then-colossal and much ballyhooed budget of just under a million dollars, is a black-and-white brain-tumor tragedy, generally credited with being the first of a series of Hollywood films with unhappy endings, and one of the very few of its time to deal overtly with the subject of death, in which the audience is treated to the dread creep of advancing mortality, step by star-killing step (weakness, blindness, deathbed). The film's then-controversial and for the most part taboo subject matter — death being considered by the government an inappropriate storyline for American audiences — created a frenzy in the Breen Office, which insisted on dozens of changes made to the script before the film could receive an approval code. Apparently Breen had no problem with Davis's costumes, however, many of which revealed a great deal of skin, something the actress pushed for as a way to deepen the film's drama by showing how alive her character was. She referred to one outfit her character wore throughout the film, designed by Orry-Kelly, as "my naked dress."

In *Dark Victory,* Reagan plays an inebriated suitor of Davis who is barely noticed by her. Adding insult to injury, Goulding pared down Reagan's already small part because he found his acting unacceptable. Later on, Reagan had this to say about their clash: "We came to our moment of truth near the end of the picture. In the scene George Brent comes to my apartment, desperate because of his failure to convince Bette that he loves her (in one of the film's better touches, during her treatment she falls in love with her doctor, the vivid personification of life's ongoing battle over death). She, in turn, thinks his love is pity because when she finds out he knows she is dying. My part in the scene is to tell George she is on her way to the apartment and before I disappear I ask him to be kind to her because I love her too. It was a well-written scene, and a nice moment in the picture. I still insist there is only one way to play a scene and that is simply and with great sincerity. [Goulding] hit the ceiling. He demanded, 'Do you think you are playing the leading man? George [Brent] has that part, you know.' In the matter of studio standing, I was outweighed. He was a top director, doing only top pictures. I was up in that class on a raincheck. He didn't get what he wanted, whatever the hell that was, and I ended up not delivering the line the way my instinct told me it should be delivered. It was bad."

Years later, the director Irving Rapper, who would direct Reagan in 1942's *The Voice of the Turtle,* told one interviewer that Bette Davis didn't even remember Reagan was in the film: "I was in London one time and went over to Bette Davis's house for a drink. We were reminiscing about the old days, and she had done a beautiful picture called *Dark Victory.* Bogart played a horse trainer in it and Reagan was in it, too. And I said to Bette, 'Do you remember that Ronald Reagan had two or three scenes with you in that picture?' And she said with a furious puff of smoke, 'Was he in it?' "

Despite Reagan's frustration with Goulding and the entire production, *Dark Victory* went on to become one of the major Hollywood success stories of 1939, a year already crowded with extraordinary cinematic achievement, including William Wellman's *Beau Geste,* George Marshall's *Destry Rides Again,* John Ford's *Drums Along the Mohawk,* his *Stagecoach* and also his *Young Mr. Lincoln,* Victor Fleming's *Gone With the Wind* and *The Wizard of Oz,* Sam Wood's *Goodbye Mr. Chips,* George Stevens's *Gunga Din,* Frank Capra's *Mr. Smith Goes to Washington,* Ernst Lubitsch's *Ninotchka,* Howard Hawks's *Only Angels Have Wings,* Raoul Walsh's *The Roaring Twenties,* George Cukor's *The Women,* and William Wyler's *Wuthering Heights,* all of which were milestones in the careers of their directors and, respectively, among the best screen work of Tyrone Power, Jimmy Stewart, Marlene Dietrich, Henry Fonda, Claudette Colbert, Clark Gable, Vivien Leigh, Olivia de Havilland, Hattie McDaniel, Leslie Howard, Robert Donat, Claude Rains, Jean Arthur, Greta Garbo, Rita Hayworth, James Cagney, John Wayne, Judy Garland, Joan Crawford, Laurence Olivier, Merle Oberon, and Henry Fonda. In this prestigious company, *Dark Victory* was nominated for three Academy Awards, including one for Bette Davis, but did nothing for the careers of George Brent, Humphrey Bogart, or Reagan, all of whom went unnoticed by Oscar.[*]

Indeed, Reagan finished up 1939 making three more fast, frenzied, and completely forgettable movies. The first was Lewis Seiler and E. A. Dupont's *Hell's Kitchen,* another Bryan Foy B production (coproduced by Mark Hellinger). It was the next of what was to become an endless and endlessly cheesier

[*] The film was nominated for three Academy Awards, including Best Actress (Davis), Best Picture, and Best Music (Max Steiner). Vivien Leigh won Best Actress for her performance as Scarlett O'Hara in *Gone With the Wind,* which also won Best Picture. Herbert Stothart won for Best Music (original score) for *The Wizard of Oz.*

series of films starring the so-called Dead End Kids (aka East Side Kids, Bowery Boys, etc.), a group of actors headed by Leo Gorcey. A short, fat, twenty-year-old mustachioed, cigar-chomping lout, Gorcey had originally appeared in Sidney Kingsley's original Broadway Depression-era sociopolitical drama *Dead End,* made into a movie in 1937 by William Wyler as a vehicle for Humphrey Bogart. Eventually, the "kids" became favorites of the kids who went to the Saturday-matinee marathons. They made a total of eighty-nine "gang" movies and three serials, the best film of which, by far, was the sequel of sorts to *Dead End,* Michael Curtiz's *Angels with Dirty Faces,* starring Jimmy Cagney as a gangster who allows his own state execution to save the "bad" kids of the neighborhood (the Dead End Kids) who idolize him by demonstrating in a highly graphic death scene that crime doesn't pay.

In *Hell's Kitchen* the boys have been let out of the reform school they've been sent to and relocated to a city shelter. Reagan and Margaret Lindsay play their social workers who just happen to fall in love while they're trying to help the boys reform.

Lewis Seiler had difficulty handling the "gang," who were on a major star trip by this time, and a second-unit director had to be brought in just to direct their scenes. Reagan, too, had trouble with them. He resented their attitude and their cockiness and what he perceived as their lack of respect for authority, that they had somehow confused their roles with their own identies. He wasn't entirely wrong. According to Huntz Hall, one of the "kids," "We used to give [Reagan] 'hot hats.' We got a piece of paper, rolled it into a cone, put it on him and lit it." Reagan was not amused. At one point during the filming, on the back lot he ran into Cagney, who had starred with the boys a year earlier in *Angels with Dirty Faces.* Reagan asked Cagney how he could stand to work with the boys, especially Gorcey. Cagney laughed and told Reagan to say to them that he "looked forward to working with them but you'll slap hell out of them if they do one thing out of line." Apparently, on his next run-in with Gorcey, Reagan did just that (threatened, not slapped) and for him at least, the rest of the movie went smoothly.

Next for Reagan was Ray Enright's *Angels Wash Their Faces,* yet another sequel to Wyler's original 1937 filmed version of Sidney Kingsley's *Dead End,* this one with Ann Sheridan and Reagan and those increasingly lovable (to moviegoers) Dead End Kids. In this one Reagan plays the son of the district attorney who falls in love with one of the kids' sisters (the kid, Gabe, played by Frankie Thomas; the sister, Joy, by Ann

Sheridan). Gabe is framed for arson. The D.A.'s son, Pat (Reagan), helps the boy because he loves his sister. The boy is eventually exonerated and Pat and Joy get married. It was the last time Reagan had to work with "The Kids," which was fine with him and fine with them.

Reagan went right back to work in another quickie Foy B project, the second in the projected series of Secret Service movies, which had been delayed because of his assignment in *Dark Victory.*

In Noel Smith's *Code of the Secret Service,* Reagan, as "Brass" Bancroft, this time chases Mexican counterfeiters. The finished film ran only fifty-eight minutes. Even the starring Reagan could no longer pretend that these films had anything at all going for them. All he wanted to know was when the fights came and who they were with. The film was so awful that Reagan made an unusually strong appeal to Jack L. Warner to tank it before it was released. Warner compromised and did not release it theatrically in Hollywood, to spare Reagan the embarrassment of having to live it down among his peers (to this day, the film has never had a commercial theater release in L.A.).

Reagan's film year ended with his role in Terry Morse's *Smashing the Money Ring,* produced by Bryan Foy, the third in the "Brass" Bancroft Secret Service series. Fifty-seven more minutes of counterfeiting, on every level. Much of the script was made up along the way. It is artificial, thin, forced, unrealistic, predictable, boring, and hackneyed. In a word, dreadful.

So instead of preparing to go to the 1940 Academy Awards ceremonies, Reagan decided to get married. Just after the film was completed, Reagan popped the question to Wyman, complete with a fifty-two-carat amethyst ring — Wyman's birthstone. Wyman said yes, although the exact circumstances of the proposal remain cloudy.

Her divorce had become final that December, and barely a month later, on January 26, 1940, she and Ronald Reagan tied the knot at the Hollywood-Beverly Christian Church, in Glendale, California, in a ceremony performed by the Rev. Cleveland Kleihaur; the reception was at the lavish Beverly Hills home of Louella Parsons. It was Parsons who first alerted the world in her Hearst-syndicated column, reporting that "two of Hollywood's very nicest young people" had fallen in love and that "Ronnie and Janey" were to "be married as soon as they return from a personal appearance tour with me later this month." Unreported in her gushing column was the Hollywood rumor that just before Reagan's proposal Wyman had attempted suicide, officially reported as a "stomach disorder," in order to get Reagan to agree to make her his bride. Several Hollywood friends, including Eddie Albert and Owen Crump, later hinted to several reporters as to the veracity of the story (reportedly, Reagan popped the question to Wyman before she was checked out, although one of Wyman's friends, Ruth Waterbury, remembered the whole occasion differently: "The next thing Ronnie and Jane knew, they were one night at the Trop in the middle of a proposal . . .").

And at the end of Parsons's piece came this curious observation: "It being Jane's third marriage and Ronald's first, they recognize that they have certain snares to guard against. We even pointed out that his ceasing to be one of the few bachelors of the screen might affect Ronnie's popularity. 'You see what I'm giving up?' he said, turning sternly on Janie. 'But look what you're getting,' Jane said."

In the endless mill that turned out the studio's publicity fodder, here was a reminder to the audience that Reagan had never been married before, giving him a slightly heroic stance in the mores of the day. He was rescuing the lonely divorcée from a life of bitterness and solitude. He was not only welcoming her to his side, but back into the mainstream of society. There is also an amusing attempt to suggest that Reagan is somehow a matinee idol, the adored male figure of single women all over the country — *the world*

— who will be losing out on their chances to snag him, as well as his chance to snag them! And finally, in keeping with the studio's so-far-failed attempt to turn Wyman into a major star (they'd removed her glasses after *Brother Rat* and were about to dye her hair vavoom blond), they gave her the titillation of a closing line to remind him that he was getting much more than he was about to give up (if he was, indeed, giving up anything, as his career wasn't exactly on fire). The Hollywood industrial substrata of misinformation, promotion, and publicity had kicked in big-time for Reagan and Wyman, with the strings being pulled by Jack Warner in the hopes it would increase their popularity.

With a salary now at $1,650 a week, a wife (who was making about $75 a week), his parents and brother nearby, and surrogate parents Jack Warner and Louella Parsons firmly in place, for Reagan, everything felt almost completely right in his world.

After returning from a brief Palm Springs honeymoon capped by a night of festivities at Hollywood's celebrated Cocoanut Grove nightclub, Reagan, amid much press coverage, showed up smoking a pipe, looking quite husbandly for the lens. Wyman, ever ready to please, publicly promised Reagan he could have a special place in the den of their new home to keep his growing collection of pipes.

It was as if they were dressing a set of a movie of the perfect marriage.

Reagan, all too happy to accommodate Louella Parsons for all she had done for him and Jane, agreed to join her latest studio-sponsored caravan tour of movie theaters that had begun in November 1939 and continued on through the winter of 1940, with the biggest actors and actresses appearing as needed for opening nights while the lesser ones went along for the whole thing at the directive of the studio and for the extra cash it provided.[*] In the days before television talk shows, this was the best method of promoting a film. Radio helped, but no one could see the faces of the stars on it.

Known since childhood for his thriftiness, Reagan was determined that he would provide for Jane Wyman the way his father, Jack, had never quite been able to for Nelle (the only one). When Reagan discovered early on that Wyman was flat broke, he gallantly promised to get her back on her own two feet.[†]

---

[*] Newlywed Reagan joined the second, winter leg of the tour along with Wyman, Joy Hodges, and Susan Hayward.

[†] "I don't know how I ever did it," Wyman recalled in an interview with Virginia Wood for the November 1941 issue of *Screenland.* "I was up to my neck in

Reagan had joined the tour after Parsons gave him a good buttering up, telling him how much she needed his and (later) Jane's presence on it, and how good it would be for both their images and careers. Not that there was anything wrong with his image, she emphasized, but women might appreciate both of them even more if they could see them live, and their careers might likewise benefit. Traveling around the country for free, plus expenses, was, in Reagan's eyes, a sort of second, extended honeymoon. Wyman didn't agree. She felt put upon by the whole thing but went along only because Reagan was so insistent and enthusiastic.

Married and with eighteen films under his belt, Reagan still dreamed of landing that one, so-far-elusive great role in a big film that would turn him into a top-of-the-line star.

As it happened, he wouldn't have to wait

---

debt [when we got married] and knowing the way Ronnie [felt] about debts, I decided the best thing to do was to pay every last living bill before the big event. After it was all over, I had exactly $500 to my name.

"Our system was so simple, it doesn't sound like anything. It's just that we save half of everything we make . . . Ronnie has a phobia about bills. If a bill is ten days old, he starts having a fit. As a result, every bill is paid and out of the way by the 10th of the month."

very long, for that and a whole lot more he never dreamed of.

■ ■ ■ ■

CHAPTER FIVE:
THE GAMUT FROM
A TO B

■ ■ ■ ■

Until I got the part of George Gipp in *Knute Rockne All American,* I was the Errol Flynn of the B pictures. I usually played a jet-propelled newspaperman who solved more crimes than a polygraph machine.
— RONALD REAGAN

Lobby card for International Squadron *(1941).*

One night in Philadelphia while on the Parsons holiday promotional tour, Reagan left his hotel room to take a walk and found himself "mobbed" by women, at least according to Jon Landon, who wrote about it in *Motion Picture* magazine: "It took the police about fifteen minutes to get him out of his hotel. When the women did get near him, they'd practically disrobe him. Several times he heard them ask, 'Please, may I just touch you?' And they'd touch him whether he liked it or not and then breathe deeply and exhale an impassioned 'Oh!' Even his hotel door became the knocking board of every woman in town who could get past the clerk.

"Ronnie didn't honestly enjoy this display . . . It was the first time in his life that a public demonstration like that had happened to him. It did have one effect on Warners, though. It showed the producers (who used to say 'Reagan for a real love scene? Impossible!') that he did have something that women admired. And it helped to bring about the current build-up of the new and romantic Ronald Reagan."

Was the whole thing staged for the sake of publicity, the way it sounds? Likely. It was just the kind of thing that the studios were so adept at. The question is, Who was behind this incident? Who arranged it and made sure there was a Hollywood reporter there to see it? Certainly not Reagan; he didn't have the clout or the inclination, especially with Wyman along. Evidence points instead to Reagan's new agent, Lew Wasserman.

Early in 1940, Jules Stein's acquisition of the Meiklejohn Agency was finally completed and all of Bill Meiklejohn's clients were absorbed into the larger and ever more powerful MCA. Meiklejohn's deal included a position for him in MCA's studio talent department, meaning he would still handle much of his original roster of clients, but now he would have to answer to Lew Wasserman, who was a genius at promoting his clients as far as they could go.

Lew Wasserman was the third son of Isaac and Minnie Weiserman, Russian Orthodox Jews who had fled Odessa for the New World during the last days of the czar's brutally anti-Semitic purges. The Weisermans American-ized their name to Wasserman (water carrier, a sign of the zodiac), and Isaac took on a partner and began what became a struggling restaurant business in Cleveland, Ohio. When he was old enough, Lew took a part-time job at one of the city's many burlesque houses and spent whatever extra money he had on his first love, the movies. He managed to shed burlesque completely when one of his father's friends and frequent diners, who happened to own a movie theater, agreed to let the boy become an usher.

Young Lew quickly became the theater's chief usher, then quit the job to work for a movie advertising company that created lobby cards and billboards. That led to a stint as a publicity runner, someone who helped place people's names in the right newspaper columns.

It was during this period of his life, when he was still in his early twenties, that he came under the close guidance of Harry Propper, who had made his fortune running speakeasies during the height of the Depression. Eventually Propper became the front man for the Mayfair Casino, an extremely popular Cleveland gambling emporium that was secretly owned by four local Jewish mobsters — Moe B. Dalitz, Lou Rothkopf, Morris Kleinman, and Sam Tucker — all veterans of the local and notorious Road Gang, a small-time syndicate made up of immigrant Italian and Russian Jews that controlled all gambling, prostitution, bootlegging, and loan-sharking in the lawless stretch of eastern Cleveland. Propper had taken a liking to the young and eager Wasserman and took him under his wing to teach him the trade of entertaining people in exchange for a very hefty paycheck. The beauty, Propper liked to say, was when they didn't even know they were paying.

Most of the talent that passed through the Mayfair Casino was represented by Jules Stein's MCA talent agency. Word got back to Stein that the young Wasserman was particularly adept at handling musicians, making sure that performers and bandleaders like Tommy Dorsey showed up on time even if they were stone drunk an hour before they were scheduled to go on.

It was true. Wasserman had an interesting combination of hard and soft persuasiveness, a good mix of muscle and charm, that allowed him to float easily between undisciplined talent and unwieldy management. Stein, who wanted to expand his reach into film, had spent several years acquiring smaller talent agencies like Meiklejohn's and needed someone to handle that side of MCA. He chose Wasserman after a single meeting, in which he was impressed by his low-key manner and assured modesty. Stein loved low-profile representation, agents who knew how to shift the spotlight off the agency and onto the talent.

Stein arranged for Wasserman and his new wife to move to Hollywood and put him to work immediately maximizing the ready roster of film talent that awaited him, with certain names earmarked for special attention. Among those were Jane Wyman and Ronald Reagan.

Wasserman, whose antennae were as sensitive as those of a giant insect, immediately realized two things: that Reagan was growing increasingly dismayed at his inability to land an "important" role and that the studio had one such important-and-as-yet-uncast role that was just perfect for him. Ten actors had already tested and been passed on for the small but key role of George Gipp in Lloyd Bacon's upcoming biopic and star vehicle for Pat O'Brien, *Knute Rockne All American.* Out of that group, which included William Holden, John Wayne, Robert Young, and Robert Cummings, only two relatively minor stars, Dennis Morgan and Donald Woods, were still left in the running. Wasserman began to lobby Jack Warner to add a third name to that list — his new client, Ronald Reagan.

To overcome Warner's objections that, despite his personal fondness for Reagan, he believed the actor had no on-screen romantic appeal, Wasserman countered with the fact that this part was not essentially a romantic lead, and reminded Warner that Reagan's tour with Parsons had produced hordes of screaming women. Warner told Wasserman he'd think it over, but the final decision would have to be the producer's, in this case Hal B. Wallis, who had already worked with Reagan on several occasions without noticing any cinematic sparks. Warner, knowing Wallis was going to be a much harder sell, decided to let him be the bad guy.

Meanwhile, there was more pressing business for Reagan. Next up was a sequel to the hugely popular *Brother Rat.* The studio concocted a quickie, *Brother Rat and a Baby,* which Ray Enright was to direct (William Keighley, who'd helmed the original, and whose career at Warners never fully recovered from his *Adventures of Robin Hood* debacle, had by now left the studio and film business in favor of directing episodic radio). In this version, the focus of the story was away from the saga of Bing Edwards (Eddie Albert) and Billy Randolph (Wayne Morris) and put squarely on the shoulders of Reagan and Wyman, and Dan Crawford's continuing attempt to romance and marry Claire, the commandant's daughter.

While no great shakes as an original drama, the first film, with the Reagan-Wyman subplot used as a light diversion rather than as a prime story–developing element, had a surprising, rhythmically pleasing feel. This time, Reagan felt Midwest-uncomfortable kissing his wife in public (as it were), was awkward about shoving Albert, who had become a good friend, out of the starlight (at least for this film), and gave a disappointing performance in a film where, about to turn thirty in real life, he was still playing a cadet trying to woo someone's daughter.

For the film, Wyman's hair was bleached a much deeper blond in an attempt by the studio to make more of a sex goddess out of the sultry but subtle actress, who moved on-screen like the dancer that she was but came off more librarian than hottie. The glasses she'd worn in *Brother Rat* didn't help. For the sequel, they were removed, on-screen and ritualistically, a symbolic deflowering during this heavily censored period.

As for the film itself, besides the fact that everyone looked too old for their parts in a script that took place a year after the boys had graduated from VMI, it had pretensions to screwball comedy at a time when that genre was being dominated by Cary Grant in Leo McCarey's *The Awful Truth* (1937), Howard Hawks's *Bringing Up Baby* (1938), and *His Girl Friday* (1940). Ronald Reagan was no Cary Grant, and the film disappeared quickly.

On its heels came another Reagan-Wyman

quickie, as the studio still hoped to make some kind of successful movie mirror-image couple out of the two. Once again Ray Enright was assigned to direct. *An Angel from Texas* was taken from a George F. Kaufman play, *The Butter and Egg Man,* and again included Wayne Morris and Eddie Albert, this time in supporting roles, in the hopes that the audiences that "missed" *Brother Rat and a Baby* would discover this time around all that cinematic chemistry up there on the silver screen.

While the studio trumpeted the use of such elite talent as Kaufman as a way to express how important they thought this film was (and how successful they believed it would be), in truth this was serious hedge betting. For one thing, the Kaufman play was something of a chestnut, having first been made into a silent movie by Richard Wallace, with William Demarest, for First National in 1928. After the acquisition, Warner remade it in 1932 as a vehicle for comic Joe E. Brown (opposite Ginger Rogers), directed by none other than Ray Enright. *The Tenderfoot* kept the heart of the story, an innocent young man looking to invest in a Broadway play about to be swindled by a smarmy producer until his secretary steps in, saves the day, and winds up starring in the hit show.[*]

The *Angel* of the title refers to the innocent but wealthy young investor, this time played by Eddie Albert, who wants to produce a Broadway play for his girlfriend (Rosemary Lane) to star in. Albert was the undisputed star of this film and, not surprisingly, totally eclipsed Reagan, who had little to do in it but work on his hem-and-haw frown, complete with the familiar one upraised eyebrow, his short-cut way of expressing doubt, suspicion, anger, and moral outrage. The film was yet another flop.

That left only one more "Brass" Bancroft film Reagan was committed to make before *Knute Rockne* went into production. The role of George Gipp was still not cast, and Reagan still badly wanted it, even though he knew his two previous bombs did not help his chances. Lewis Seiler's *Murder in the Air,* the fourth and last Brass Bancroft movie, was

* Three years later, Warner assigned its British division to make a version that featured the West End rather than Broadway. The script was then remade again in 1937 as *Dance, Charlie, Dance,* directed by Frank McDonald and starring Stu Erwin, and was revived once more after *An Angel from Texas,* in 1953 as *Three Sailors and a Girl,* directed by Roy Del Ruth, with Jane Powell and Gordon MacRae in the starring roles. None of the film versions of the play, including Reagan's, was a box-office success.

put into production within days after *An Angel from Texas* finished shooting its last scene. Bryan Foy was in charge of the production. While Harry Warner prided himself on the fact that this film, like so many of Warner Bros.' prewar products, served to educate the public about the high-minded, morally unambiguous ways of maintaining peace and freedom, Jack L. was skeptical of not just this film but the whole notion of flag-waving as the best way for the studio to make money. The problem wasn't that his Warner films were too political, but that they weren't political *enough,* neither sufficiently sophisticated nor artistically provocative in the manner of, say, Frank Capra's 1939 smash hit for his main competitor (as Warner saw it), Columbia Pictures, *Mr. Smith Goes to Washington.* As far as Jack Warner was concerned, Bryan Foy's main talent was his ability to "stretch a four-line [newspaper] clipping into five or six reels." He didn't mean that as a compliment.

The film itself (originally titled *The Enemy* and then *Uncle Sam Awakens* before the studio settled on the less political, more action-oriented *Murder in the Air,* again echoing Reagan's first and to date most successful action flick, *Love Is on the Air)* offers what one might expect from a fourth-go-around sequel: Flash Gordon–level action without any discernible drama, heroes who never sweat, might equaling right, stolen blueprints, a brief (but ominous) appearance by a heroic group of men calling themselves the House Un-American Activities Committee, and innumerable threats to the isolationist-favoring hero, the financially utilitarian-named Bancroft (Reagan).[*]

There is a story, almost certainly apocryphal, told by Reagan himself in nearly identical versions in both of his memoirs and in numerous other places, that when he heard the part of the Gipper was still available, he "ran" all the way to Hal Wallis's office and asked for "a shot" at the role (although, according to all accounts, he had already been rejected by Wallis, via Wasserman, at least twice). Reagan continues the story this way: "I got in my car and drove home as fast as I could and dug into the trunk I had brought from Dixon. I found a yearbook photo of myself in my college football uniform, raced

---

[*] In the hopes of building a following for the film among the Saturday-morning set, Warner Bros.' marketing division issued "Junior Secret Service Club" memberships, for a nominal fee of course, in the lobbies of the theaters where this Saturday-morning special played. "Original" autographed 8 × 10s of Bancroft, presigned as "Ronald Reagan, Chief," were also available for purchase. While the campaign went nowhere, today these are rare, expensive, and highly coveted items on the collectibles circuit.

back to the studio and put it on the producer's desk. He studied the picture, looked up at me, and said, 'Can I keep this for a while?' I hadn't been home more than an hour when the phone rang. It was a call telling me to be at the studio at eight in the morning to test for the role of George Gipp."*

Lou Cannon, one of Reagan's more thorough biographers, correctly describes Reagan's quest for the role of "The Gipper" as being a little more complicated and a little less direct. According to Cannon, it was not Wallis whom Reagan approached, but Bryan Foy. By now, he and Reagan had become good friends — Foy called Reagan "Ronnie," and Reagan, employing his incessant Midwest habit of nicknaming, always referred to Foy as "Brynnie." Reagan believed that if Brynnie put in a good word for him, it would signifi-

---

* According to Reagan in his *An American Life,* he had actually started writing his own screenplay of the life of Rockne, one of his personal heroes, and that it was possibly "stolen" from him because he talked about it during lunch at the Warner commissary. Even more astonishingly, he claimed to have first heard about Warners' planned film from reading a blurb in the *Daily Variety.* There is no evidence to be found of any such screenplay, in whole or in part. In *Where's the Rest of Me?* Reagan says he "broke a few speed laws" rushing back to his house to get those photos of himself.

cantly increase his chances. Foy laughed out loud at Reagan's lingering inability to understand the politics of the studio system. Patiently, he explained to Reagan, as he had many times before, that as head of a B unit, he, Foy, had less-than-no influence on the head of an A unit. The implication was that Reagan's chances of landing such a key role were not good. Reagan then went to the head of the studio's Irish Mafia, Pat O'Brien, who had already been cast as the legendary football coach, to plead his case, and that's where things became a bit more complicated.

O'Brien had, indeed, been selected to play Rockne, although he, too, had not been the first choice of either Foy or the screenwriter, Robert Buckner, who, because of his close ties with the Rockne family, held an unusual amount of power and influence on the production that gave him nearly as much say as Wallis and even Jack L. Warner. It was Buckner, a journeyman screenwriter at the studio, who was able to enlist the services of Rockne's widow and immediate family and get them to agree to allow Warner to make the movie, while every other studio had been pushing each other out of the way to make an offer for the rights to the story. As part of the deal, Buckner was entrusted by the family (and several Notre Dame officials) to tell it in a way that avoided some of the more complex situations in which the real-life

Rockne had been involved. While Wallis was not all that pleased to have a medium-to-low–level screenwriter so intimately involved with the production, he nevertheless understood the film's potential and allowed Buckner as much leeway as possible. One of the first decisions Buckner made, that normally would have been decided either by Wallis or Warner, was the casting of the lead. The writer insisted that only James Cagney could do justice to the role of Knute Rockne.

Wallis and Warner agreed. At the time, Cagney was a much stronger draw at the box office than O'Brien was, and had a rougher, more combative movie persona, having played "tough guys" for the better part of a decade. However, it was precisely that image that hurt Cagney's chances with yet another unofficial partner on the film — the Catholic Church. Already displeased with the fact that the young New York–bred actor had made his career playing gangsters, what finally eliminated him from contention was the Church's outrage at Cagney's open support of the leftist (and anti-Catholic) volunteer "Lincoln Brigade" during the Spanish Civil War.[*]

* Cagney's gangster image is most memorably on display in William Wellman's 1931 *Public Enemy,* William Keighley's 1935 *G-Men,* Michael Curtiz's 1938 *Angels with Dirty Faces,* Keighley's 1939 *Each Dawn I Die,* Raoul Walsh's 1939 *The Roaring Twen-*

194

Although there is no mention of it in Cagney's woefully incomplete 1983 memoir by Doug Warren, the actor had been at the forefront of Hollywood's liberal support of the so-called Lincoln Brigade, actually called the Abraham Lincoln Battalion, a group of volunteers from the United States who served in the international brigades fighting Generalissimo Franco in Spain. At the same time, a coalition of Roman Catholics, industrialists, and landowners had backed Franco's attempted overthrow of the Madrid-based government. Because of it, Notre Dame, perhaps the biggest and most powerful Catholic institution in America (outside of the Church itself), and the professional home of Knute Rockne, vehemently opposed Buckner's choice of Cagney for the role. Wallis, who had never gotten along well with Cagney, made no move to lobby to have him in the film, nor did Warner. With no studio support, Cagney was dead in the film's waters.

---

ties, and Walsh's 1949 *White Heat.* His musical and comic films during this period include Lloyd Bacon's 1933 *Footlight Parade* and William Dieterle and Max Reinhardt's 1935 *A Midsummer Night's Dream.* One further note: Gipp was Protestant, and his real-life deathbed conversion to Catholicism was a sensitive issue to both the Protestant and the Catholic churches. They clashed over what religion the priest should be who would give Gipp his last rites.

Notre Dame's first choice to play Rockne was Spencer Tracy, who, like O'Brien, played priests more often than any other type of role, and was the number one box-office attraction in the country at the time, coming off two consecutive Best Actor Oscars (Victor Fleming's 1937 *Captains Courageous* and Norman Taurog's 1938 *Boys Town,* in which he played the celebrated true-life hero Father Flanagan). It was, in fact, Tracy's portrayal of Father Flanagan that had made Notre Dame want him so much (the "family," ever-savvy of things like marketing and box office, also knew that Tracy could deliver a huge audience). Tracy was actually offered the role but MGM, the studio he was signed to, would not lend him out, and he had to be eliminated. Warners' next choice for the role was Pat O'Brien. Buckner liked him as well, but Wallis said no. He didn't think the actor could handle the part. Jack Warner then demanded Wallis cast O'Brien, but Wallis hesitated until the Legion of Decency, a Catholic Church–dominated organization that issued regular bulletins of approval and rejections that often made the difference as to whether a film became a hit at the box office, threw its support behind O'Brien.

Once he got the part, O'Brien immediately began a campaign to get Reagan the role of the Gipper, again over the objections of Buckner, who wanted Donald Woods for the part. Woods, a genial character actor who stood well over six feet four, had already appeared in more than thirty Warner features, mostly B's, had the right physique, and was not above turning down a relatively small role.* Buckner also liked the fact that Woods wasn't particularly good-looking, in the conventional Hollywood "pretty-boy" style, which he felt would add more authenticity to the film.

At a casting meeting, O'Brien ramped up the pressure: "There weren't many contract players at Warners who were athletically inclined. [I told Jack Warner] a lot of the people you have under contract don't know a football from a cantaloupe. This guy [Reagan] does." O'Brien volunteered to do a screen test with Reagan (the scene in which Gipp is ordered to carry the football by Rockne and replies, "How far?"), something stars rarely did. O'Brien's presence at the test sent a message to Wallis that he meant business. The next day Wallis called Reagan and told him he was going to play the Gipper.

* Although Reagan liked to call himself "The King of the B's," it was actually Woods who coined the term in describing his own career at Warner Bros. Woods eventually went into TV and had a second career in Palm Springs real estate after his acting days were over.

Knute Rockne All American proved a career milestone film for Wallis, O'Brien, Warner, and Ronald Reagan. It cemented Wallis's hold on the A division of the studio's films. His post-*Rockne* career at Warner would include dozens of major movies, including 1940's *The Letter* (directed by William Wyler), *Santa Fe Trail* (directed by Michael Curtiz), 1941's *High Sierra* (directed by Raoul Walsh), *The Maltese Falcon* (directed by John Huston), 1942's *Kings Row* (directed by Sam Wood), and *Casablanca* (directed by Curtiz), several of which would use Reagan in important roles.

Rockne made O'Brien an even bigger star than he already was, although he rarely played another screen figure with such dynamic personality and physical strength. Instead, O'Brien, who was already forty-one years old when the film was produced, became increasingly docile on-screen, most often playing the wise Irish priest with a high sweet voice and a twinkle in his eye.

As for Jack Warner, the film confirmed his studio's unspoken political commitment to the growing movement for America to enter World War II on the side of the Allies. *Rockne* was different from the other socially conscious movies the studio had turned out in the thirties. Most of those had sought to affirm the audience's belief in a political and social system that seemed to be failing them.

Law and order proved its own point, and poverty symbolized youth, freedom, and, most crucially, love.

In *Rockne,* football served as an obvious and powerful metaphor for war. Played with a one-note ferocity unlike anything O'Brien had done before (and mercifully never did again), the story is less factual than symbolic, a mostly mythic tale of immigration, assimilation, and success, all-American style. The love of football comes to Rockne while he is still a young boy, small and unprotected on the fierce streets of Chicago. As an adult, he looks for a job and eventually lands at Notre Dame, where he begins as a postal clerk — starting at the bottom, working up the ladder, step by step. Even as his heavily accented parents react with amusement, horror, a total lack of understanding, and even less compassion for their son's chosen sport, their love of family, religion, and the American way — an unbeatable cinematic combination — holds them all together.

The film preaches involvement, assimilation, and spiritual and moral values of victory. With the Depression subsiding and America's entry into the world war all but inevitable, the film uses football as a strategizing weapon, suggesting that an army of properly trained men will be unbeatable no matter who the enemy is or where the battlefield. The sense of God-on-Our Side is all encompassing, with Donald Crisp as Notre Dame's Father Callahan, a man so righteous he comes off less representational of the faith in God than God himself. Whenever Rockne expresses anything like self-doubt, or uncertainty about his team, or anything, really, it is Father Callahan who provides the soothing reassurance that with God on his (America's) side, no battle is too great, no victory out of reach, no setback a permanent defeat. This was the ultimate Christian-ethic film, one that all but declared war on Hitler, Mussolini, Hirohito, and anyone else who thought they could tackle America. Rockne's death in a plane crash all but elevates him to the level of a saint (in real life as well as the movie), in a church funeral even more spectacularly visual than any of the football sequences that precede it.

Today, *Knute Rockne All American* looks flat and moves with a jerky awkwardness that suggests the physicality of silent movies. The football players and their game come off to modern viewers as too pristine. The film's blunt edge was not helped by Lloyd Bacon's direction, his slavish adherence to the paint-by-numbers story that makes its visual narrative seem as elementary as a Dick and Jane reader. It is only within its zeitgeist that the film roars to life, the Four Horsemen taking on biblical proportion as the embodiment of an isolationist-ending generation eager to run headstrong onto the world's arena and reestablish America as a world power. As drama, it bordered on the hokey; as political dogma, its level of inspiration was staggering.

For all of that, without question, it was Ronald Reagan who made the greatest impact on audiences with his performance in *Rockne* (and, conceivably upon whom the film had its greatest impact). George Gipp was a personal childhood hero to Reagan (as was Rockne). He had often talked about the heroics of the Gipper on his radio sports shows back in Iowa. After hearing about the movie being made at his studio, he was convinced that if he could only play him, he would finally get the chance to let Hollywood and the rest of the country see what he could do.

He wasn't wrong.

Although the part is small, about ten minutes' worth of screen time (for which he was paid a total of $2,667 for one week's worth of shooting), it fit Reagan perfectly.* As the young, eager halfback who dies prematurely, his final words are those of utterly selfless inspiration; Gipper whispers to Rockne,

---

* O'Brien received $30,000 to play the role of Knute Rockne, the same amount the studio paid Mrs. Rockne for the rights to the production. The budget for the film was $543,000. Very few films were allowed to exceed a half-million-dollar budget in those days — this was one of them.

who is at his bedside, "Some day when things are tough, maybe you can ask the boys to go in there and win just one for the Gipper." Thus was created one of the most unforgettable utterances in the annals of film history, up there with *Citizen Kane*'s "Rosebud" and *Casablanca*'s "Play it again, Sam" (even if the latter was never actually said in the film). At that point the Gipp is transformed from an athlete dying young to the personification of every American boy soon to die in battle trying to "win one for America." Culturally, he became the poster boy for self-sacrifice, teamwork, humility, and ultimately, the American Way.

Unsuspecting 1940 audiences were stunned by Reagan's surprising athleticism that made his character's death even more shocking. Because of it, few supporting-role performances of the day matched Reagan's for its emotional impact. It was a career-altering turn that was to move Reagan's name above the title (and years later provided the unforgettable campaign slogan — "Win one for the Gipper!" — he used during his successful runs for governor of California and president of the United States).

Critics raved about the picture and Reagan's brief but electrifying performance. *Variety* said "it carried both inspirational and dramatic appeal on a wide scale," the *Holly-*

wood Reporter called it "a beautifully done picture," and *Film Daily* noted Reagan's "finely shaded" performance. The *New York Post* said the film was filled with "soaring ideals" that "can't be improved upon." And the *New York Times* gave it the official imprimatur of greatness when it declared that the film was Pat O'Brien's finest hour, so much so that Rockne's widow had "almost expected him to make love to me!" It cheered Reagan for having given a performance that was "superbly enacted." Interestingly, both (and only) O'Brien and Reagan were invited by what was then the official almanac of Americana, the Bible of the Bible Belt, the *Saturday Evening Post,* to describe why their respective roles in the film were their favorites to date. O'Brien called his performance a tribute to Rockne, while Reagan took a more jocular view of the film and his own career: "I [had] always played a jet-propelled newspaperman who solved more crimes than a lie detector. My one unvarying line which I always snapped into a phone was 'Give me the city desk; I've got a story that will crack this town wide open!' . . . I welcomed the chance to get away from this pattern, especially as it was to play the part of a man I had always admired."

Knute Rockne All American was given a special World Premiere in October at Notre Dame's vaunted South Bend, Indiana, campus, the highlight of "National Knute Rockne Week," a public relations gimmick concocted by Warner that won the approval of eighteen state senates. Everyone in the cast attended the opening, including Reagan, who took along his bride, Jane, and his father, Jack, who treated the journey as nothing less than a pilgrimage to heaven on Earth.

Privately, Reagan was worried about Jack. His old drinking habits had returned, and he had developed another serious heart condition. It didn't help matters any that O'Brien had befriended Jack and that both of them got plastered on the *Super Chief* in one of the special cars designated for the film's stars on the way back from the promotional star-studded opening in South Bend, Indiana.

The event itself was nothing less than spectacular. More than a quarter of a million people poured into the streets to meet the train's arrival. The president of the United States sent his son, FDR Jr., as his personal emissary. Kate Smith broadcast live the opening speeches of Reagan, O'Brien, and FDR Jr. on her then top-rated national Mutual radio network program.

The film barely opened before Reagan, now hotter than a freshly fired pistol, was thrust into the long-planned A production of Michael Curtiz's *Santa Fe Trail.* For this depiction of abolitionist John Brown, Hal B. Wallis wanted an all-star cast behind Errol Flynn, set to play Jeb Stuart. The cast included Raymond Massey as John Brown, in one of the most frighteningly demented performances of the decade (which vaguely echoed the horror of Hitler's evil, murderous charisma; Jack L. Warner personally supervised the makeup for Massey, to make sure it was horrible enough in a Nazi kind of way); Olivia de Havilland, Flynn's costar of choice as Kit Carson Holliday; and Ronald Reagan, as the infamously doomed George Armstrong Custer.

Both Wallis and Warner had wanted John Wayne to play Custer. Wayne had knocked around for years before being cast as the Ringo Kid in John Ford's *Stagecoach* in 1939, the film and role that had turned him into a star. Despite being offered as much money as Flynn, Wayne turned down the role of Custer because he didn't want to play a supporting role to Errol Flynn (or to compete on-screen with Flynn's extraordinary charisma), with whom he did not get along. Warner then turned to Reagan, a decision that surprised everyone, including Wallis. But Warner knew what he was doing. With the war coming, Warner understood there was going to be a shortage of male leading men and knew that Reagan's poor eyesight might keep him out of the draft altogether. Red-hot Reagan represented the studio's future, and

Warner wanted to keep him happy. So, with great fanfare, he and Wasserman got together and jointly announced that Ronald Reagan would play the much-coveted part of George Custer.

Ronald Reagan was in heaven, or as close as America had to one: in Hollywood of the 1940s, young, successful good-looking men had it made. Their cars were big, their taxes low, their smokes unfiltered, their drinks undiluted. Their beautiful women had hair piled high, legs sheathed in perfumed nylon, and a desire to please that seemed a natural extension of what celebrity was all about. For male stars, preening, indulging, basking, and sunbathing were as important, if not more so, than the drudgery of actually having to make movies. They were treated like spoiled children by the studios, even if they were the ones who had done the spoiling. They wanted to keep their moneymakers happy. And now, post-*Rockne,* Reagan was considered one of the happiest and least spoiled. And because of his new popularity, Jack Warner wanted to accommodate him any way he could. That was one of the reasons that even before production began on *Santa Fe Trail* Warner wanted to flood the market with as much unseen Reagan product as he had. His method, however, proved problematic. He threw into release a few B films that Reagan

206

had stockpiled before *Knute Rockne* that might otherwise have seen limited bottom-bill release, if they were released at all.

Tugboat Annie Sails Again was one of the standbys the studio had put Reagan into before *Knute Rockne,* a fast seventy-seven minutes of filler. A product of the Foy machine, it was directed by Lewis Seiler and continued a series that had long since grown stale with the public and represented the losing end of a speculation bid on Jack Warner's part. The original *Tugboat Annie* had been made at MGM, which had used part of its endless roster of big names to be in it, including Wallace Beery, coming off his Oscar-winning performance in King Vidor's *The Champ* (1932); Maureen O'Sullivan, fresh from the smash, and smashing, *Tarzan, The Ape Man* (1932, W. S. Van Dyke); audience favorite Robert Young; and, most of all, Marie Dressler, who'd won a Best Actress Oscar in 1931 for George W. Hill's *Min and Bill.* Based on a series of short stories by Norman Reilly Raine, today the film resembles nothing so much as one of those rural half-hour sitcoms that ruled American television in the sixties and seventies. It had scored big with audiences, and a sequel was in place when Dressler died. Unable to find a suitable replacement, MGM eventually let the rights to the character drop; Jack L. Warner snapped them up for Marjorie Rambeau, betting she would find the same box-office magic in *Tugboat Annie Sails Again.* She didn't. With Reagan in the role of Annie's protégé, Alan Hale in the comic role of Annie's competitor (a loose echo of Beery, whose character had been written out), and Jane Wyman as the wealthy young socialite who falls in love with Reagan's poor but ambitious commercial sailor, Warner rushed the film into release as an A feature, but it failed to catch on. Most critics felt that Rambeau had done a poor imitation of Marie Dressler rather than trying to create her own version of Annie. Few noticed the lack of on-screen chemistry between the two romantic leads. Despite Warner's good intentions, Reagan was not pleased with the film's appearance post-*Rockne,* but said nothing about it.

(Reagan made one other appearance on-screen before *Santa Fe Trail,* a cameo for a Warner Bros. short, *Alice in Movieland,* directed by Jean Negulesco and written by Owen Crump from a story idea by Ed Sullivan, then a young newspaper and radio reporter. This was an "every girl's dream" bit of black-and-white fluff the studio could use if a double feature ran a little short after coming attractions, the newsreel, and the cartoon, filled with as many famous faces as the director could squeeze in. This one, like so many other films Hollywood made about itself, deals with the fantasyland myth of how local beauty contest winners gravitate to Tinseltown to see their movie-star dreams come true. In this case the local beauty is Joan Leslie, playing Alice Purdee, with Hollywood a kind of Wonderland, with stars like Reagan, Wyman, Hale, Frank Faylen, Alexis Smith, and Craig Stevens.)

The anticipation for *Santa Fe Trail* was enormous. It came from the typewriter of Robert Buckner, who had also done the screenplay for the military-schooler *Brother Rat.* And, as with *Rockne,* the message here was more than what appeared on the surface. Now, with America's entrance into the world war all but inevitable (production started in late November 1940), Warner felt it could throw caution to the wind and push even harder on the side of blood-and-guts glory, even if this time the film was set safely in the receded history of the Civil War.

Although the film was originally conceived as a broad-stroked tribute to the expansion of the Santa Fe Railroad, the secondary storyline, at Jack Warner's insistence, became the main one: the pursuit, capture, and hanging of abolitionist leader John Brown. Even if the film made no historical sense, it made for rousing saddle drama and remains one of the most exciting "cavalry charge" films ever made. The reason for that, quite simply, is because it was directed by the great and vastly underrated Michael Curtiz.

Hungarian-born Curtiz was a veteran of silent films with sixty-two European films already under his belt when he arrived in Hollywood in 1926, at the relatively late movie-making age of forty, dressed in high boots and chaps with a riding crop tucked under one arm (à la Erich Von Stroheim) and quickly found a home at Warner Bros., where throughout the thirties and forties he turned out some of Hollywood's greatest movies, including before *Santa Fe Trail, Mammy* (1930), *Dr. X* (1932), *20,000 Years in Sing Sing* (1932), *Female* (1932), *Jimmy the Gent* (1933), *Go Into Your Dance* (1935), *Anthony Adverse* (1936, uncredited, signed by Mervyn LeRoy), *The Charge of the Light Brigade* (1936), *Marked Woman* (1937), *Kid Galahad* (1937), *Angels with Dirty Faces* (1938), *Blackwell's Island* (1939), *Dodge City* (1939), *The Private Lives of Elizabeth and Essex* (1939), *Four Wives* (1939), *The Sea Wolf* (1941), *Yankee Doodle Dandy* (1942), *Casablanca* (1942), *Mission to Moscow* (1943), *This Is the Army* (1943), *Mildred Pierce* (1945), and another thirty-one films into the sixties, when he made his last film, *The Comancheros,* in 1961, a year before he died. Dismissed by most film critics as nothing more than a journeyman, he was, in fact, anything *but.*

It didn't help his reputation in Hollywood

at the time that nobody on-set particularly liked him — Errol Flynn and Jimmy Cagney especially detested the director. And he felt the same way about them and all actors, but he managed to get great performances in great movies and, in the case of *Santa Fe Trail,* he could depict Americana the way only a foreign-born director could, with an awe enhanced by a style of exotica that was the equivalent of an immigrant family room — burnished furniture with a glint of greatness and a visible flag everywhere possible. Especially in his films that dealt with the coming war, *Santa Fe Trail* indirectly and, after Pearl Harbor, *Casablanca* directly, Curtiz provided the perfect *been there* for Jack Warner, who believed Curtiz was one of the greatest film directors to ever grace Warners' lot, and to hell with factual accuracy. As Curtiz often said to his studio boss, "Vell, Jock, the scenario isn't the exact truth but ve haff the facts to prove it."

The film proved a smash hit when it debuted on December 28, less than three months after *Knute Rockne,* giving Warner another big moneymaker to close out the year. Much of the accolades went to the action sequences, with a general attitude of, It isn't history, it's a movie, by the critics, allowing for its many lapses in accuracy. Flynn was a sensation and his presence on-screen was enough to enchant critics and audiences alike. Every other male performance in the film except Massey's seemed to fade into the background, including Reagan's, disappearing into the mist of Flynn's spectacular effervescence.

Santa Fe Trail would gross more than a million and a half dollars in its initial theatrical release, an enormous amount in the days before television and video (reportedly nearly a third more than *Knute Rockne,* one of the few films of the era to break the "magic million mark"). And critics loved it as much as audiences. *Variety* began its review by noting that "Once in a great while there goes forth from Hollywood a celluloid epic built on story material that so firmly grips the imagination with entertainment, production and histrionic values in such full measure and with dramatic action, comedy and romance so deftly woven that customer eyes never waver from the screen. *Santa Fe Trail* is that kind of a picture and more — it is a picture that leaves spectators regretful that the final fade has come even after the clock has ticked off its 112 minutes of running time."

Even Bosley Crowther, the *New York Times*'s resident curmudgeon, after a little bit of carping about the film's geographical and historical inconsistencies, went on to say that the film had "everything that a high-priced horse-opera should have — hard riding, hard shooting, hard fighting, a bit of hard drinking and Errol Flynn." *The Hollywood Reporter* joined the cheering bandwagon and called the film "impressive" and "thrilling."

As for Reagan, he was more of an afterthought in most reviews rather than a revelation. Having raved on about Flynn, *Variety* added that "Ronald Reagan, too, scores." Crowther singled out Flynn, Massey, and Van Heflin for praise and lumped the performances of the rest of the cast, Reagan included, as "routine."

Nonetheless, as 1940 ended, twenty-nine-year-old Ronald Reagan was at the top of his game. After less than three years in Hollywood, he had a lucrative contract at a major film studio and appeared in twenty-five feature films; he had made a name for himself by playing his own real-life hero; he had reunited the family by bringing his parents to Hollywood; and he had married a beautiful actress. From here on out, he believed, nothing could possibly go wrong.

Until the morning of May 18, 1941, when Reagan received a phone call informing him his father Jack Reagan had just died.

■ ■ ■ ■

CHAPTER SIX:
KINGS ROW

■ ■ ■ ■

The first thing you must realize about him is that he is all at once living in another world, totally different from the one he has already known and inhabited. A different world, but he has only the old equipment that he had and used.

> — From a letter written by Parris (Robert Cummings), referring to Drake (Reagan), in the film *Kings Row*

Lobby card for Kings Row *(1942).*

He and Jane were in Atlantic City on an MGM promotional tour for *The Bad Man* when he got the call from Nelle that Jack had collapsed the night before and died. Reagan was at once furious, crushed, frightened, and confused.

The emergency services ambulance had been late to arrive because of something that seemed unbelievably trivial to him, a jurisdictional dispute between Beverly Hills and the adjoining West Hollywood. A Beverly Hills ambulance could have arrived within three minutes, but because his parents' house was out of its designated zone, it would not respond to the call and it took twenty minutes for a West Hollywood unit to do so. By then Jack, fifty-seven years old and suffering through a hangover from his latest drinking binge with his newest best pal, Pat O'Brien, was stone-cold dead.

After getting his mother to agree to delay the funeral until his arrival, Reagan caught the next train back to Los Angeles. He had wanted to make the trip by air, via Jack L. Warner's personal plane, a TWA DC-2, part of the corporate fleet that the head of the studio had graciously offered to him, but Nelle pleaded with him not to fly. Jack was dead, she reasoned; he could wait the extra three days. Her fear was that if the plane crashed, she would have to bury her son and her husband on the same day. As much as he wanted to avoid having to spend all that time cramped on a train, including a Chicago layover for a connection to the *Super Chief,* he agreed.

The services were held at St. Victor's Catholic Church in West Hollywood, walking distance from the house Reagan had bought his parents after moving them from their first apartment. His recollections of the funeral were vivid and revealing, showing how crushed he was by his father's sudden death and the particular mechanism of denial he used to deal with it: "My soul was just desolate, that's the only word I can use. Desolate. And empty. And then, all of a sudden I heard somebody talking to me, and I knew that it was Jack, and he was saying, 'I'm OK, and where I am it's very nice. Please don't be unhappy.' And I turned to my mother, who was sitting with me, and I said, 'Jack is OK, and where he is he's very happy' . . . the desolation wasn't there anymore, the emptiness was all gone."

The man he both dearly loved and was severely disappointed in was gone, having lived long enough to see his son become more popular and financially secure than either of them could ever have imagined. There was something essentially Freudian in Reagan's having moved his parents into what was, in reality, his turf (Hollywood); it was a primal father/son role reversal from his childhood when he had lived in his parents' home and was the one being taken care of. Moreover, Jane had given birth just four months earlier to their first child, a cute, smiling towhead named Maureen. Now he was the real as well as symbolic father.

After the burial, Reagan wasted no time in returning to work, resuming his place on the publicity tour he had been on for Richard Thorpe's *The Bad Man,* which he had filmed in February. Jack L. Warner had arranged a "loan-out" for Reagan to make the film for MGM. It was a star vehicle for Wallace Beery and Lionel Barrymore, with important second leads for Reagan and MGM leading lady Laraine Day. What was good about this for Reagan was also what was bad about it; the policy of loan-outs had become a gold mine for the studios. They sold the services of their players to other studios for hefty prices, sometimes as high as six figures, with the actors and actresses receiving nothing more than their regular salaries. It was a way for the studios to "borrow" talent without having to engage in complicated and expensive bidding wars, and all bonuses and buyouts went to the studios.

Reagan was happy to move to MGM, even if only for this one picture. It was like he had been living in a nice house and now had a chance to stay in a mansion for a few months. There was no question in anyone's mind among those who worked in Hollywood that MGM, with the biggest stars ("more stars than there are in Heaven!"), the best producers, and the grandest and most popular movies, was the most sparkling jewel among the majors. To be working with the likes of Academy Award winners Wallace Beery and Lionel Barrymore (of the famed Barrymore "dynasty" of actors, writers, and directors) was undoubtedly a thrill, though not to be paid anything extra for it was less so.* That this could happen to actors bothered Reagan. Something ought to be done about it, he told himself.

Reagan liked doing anything that gave him a

---

* Barrymore had won the Oscar for Best Actor in 1931 for Clarence Brown's *A Free Soul,* and had been nominated for an Oscar as Best Director in 1930 for *Madame X.*

sense of purpose. It was a feeling that reached all the way to the deepest core of what he defined as success. He got it from making movies, from personal appearances to promote them where he could see the audiences live, and he got it from, of all places, civic responsibility. Or at least what passed for it in Hollywood. Reagan regularly attended meetings of the Screen Actors Guild, the very organization he had so resented being forced to join upon his arrival at Warner two short years before but whose burgeoning popularity he now believed could serve as an influence, if not a force, on the side of the workers of his industry. Nothing like resentment or rebellion was brewing inside of him, just a vague, still-undefined sense that there was something out of balance with the current system. In some ways he was starting to feel a little like the ballplayers he had gotten so friendly with during his spring-training sessions with the Chicago Cubs. They could only be traded by the owners, for the owners' profits. The players had no say and made nothing from it. The reserve clause gave all the power (and the money) to the owners and none to the players.

In his first memoir, Reagan reflects on his early interest in and gradually increasing involvement with the Screen Actors Guild. It began around the time he was loaned out to MGM, not long after his marriage to Wyman:

"I suddenly found myself on the board of SAG. The reason for it was not my fame nor fortune nor talents — but simply that the board had created a policy of a broad representation of all segments of the actors' world . . . one of the vacancies happened to fit my classification: new, young contract player. I accepted with awe and pleasure." In truth, he didn't "suddenly find himself" on the board of SAG at all, but was urged to run for it — by Jane Wyman.

Having gotten himself more involved in the union, Reagan became fascinated with everything about SAG, how it was formed, its daily operations, its place in the life of its dues-paying membership. He toyed with the idea of possibly organizing the membership into a stronger, more effective lobby, aware that he would have to walk a fine line so as not to anger Jack L. Warner, not one of the union's stronger supporters. Unfortunately, being a contract player at Warner at the time did not allow much time for Reagan to immerse himself too deeply in union politics or anything else — part of the reason there was a need for a union. He was still quite taken with his new real-life role as father and with the business of fulfilling his obligation to MGM, and therefore to Jack Warner.

MGM had owned the story for *The Bad Man* since 1922, having purchased the rights to

Porter Emerson Browne's play, which had been a vehicle for Holbrook Blinn, a well-known Broadway actor who starred in the original 1923 silent version, directed by Edwin Carewe, which had enjoyed enormous success at the box office. The studio had remade the film in 1930, this time as a vehicle for a young Walter Huston, and scored yet another winner with it. Now it had wanted a newer version, this time as a vehicle for Wallace Beery. Beery had won his only Oscar nearly a decade earlier, and his luminosity had begun to fade among MGM's celestial roster of superbright megastars. To try to extend his viability, the studio searched for an inexpensive project that could turn a profit without a big investment. Hence, the next resurrection of *The Bad Man.*

And because Reagan was hot, MGM hoped he might generate additional box office behind the film's two older stars, without having to put up any of their own leading men, such as Clark Gable or Spencer Tracy, in a relatively low-budget film (and if the film bombed and stalled Reagan's momentum, it wouldn't be any skin off the snout of Leo the Lion).

While Reagan would never publicly criticize either actor, he found both Barrymore and Beery difficult to work with. Lionel Barrymore had become a temperamental nightmare on any set in which he acted, often in a drunken state of prolonged anger and frustration, while Beery embarrassingly overacted, as he tended to do when *he* was drunk, which in this case, with Barrymore beside him, was during the entire shoot. In the end, the film did well for MGM, not a blockbuster but not a bust, though it did nothing for Reagan, who, not surprisingly, got lost among the fuss and bluster of his two hammy costars and a less-than-alluring Laraine Day, who looked more than a little uncomfortable playing opposite her overly earnest and uncomfortable leading man.

When the promotional tour for it ended, Hal Wallis wasted no time in bringing Reagan back to Warners for the A list *Million Dollar Baby,* directed by Curtis Bernhardt, a German-Jewish refugee recently arrived in Hollywood after miraculously escaping the grip of the Gestapo. He had been offered a contract by MGM but turned it down in favor of what he felt were the grittier, more socially aware movies being made at Warners. He quickly gained a reputation as being good with difficult leading ladies, having successfully navigated through the rough waters of Olivia de Havilland's *My Love Came Back* during a troubled time in her life. Wallis, the executive producer on the film (which also starred Jane Wyman, Eddie Albert, and Jeffrey Lynn), slotted Bernhardt to direct Casey Robinson's highly regarded screenplay of *Mil-*

lion Dollar Baby, which Wallis envisioned as a lush musical love story with Reagan and Priscilla Lane in the romantic leads.

Reagan was eager to return to his home studio and start work on the new film. Before production actually started, Jack Warner put him into one more quickie B in which he felt Reagan would do well. The film was A. Edward Sutherland's *Nine Lives Are Not Enough* (1941), a sixty-three-minute murder mystery set in a boarding house that put Reagan in the lead opposite Faye Emerson and Joan Perry. Sutherland, who had directed Laurel and Hardy's *The Flying Deuces* (1939) and W. C. Fields in *Tillie's Punctured Romance* (1928), was a B movie stalwart: dependable, fast, and forgettable. Reagan gives one of his more relaxed performances in the film, even if the pace reflects the kind of super-speed world of all movement and no depth that was the very definition of the bottom of the bill.

Wyman, meanwhile, continued to work as well, although none of her films was nearly as notable at the time as her husband's, nor was she being handled with the kind of kid gloves that Ronald was, by Lew Wasserman. Shortly after taking over as president of MCA, Wasserman had brought Herb Rosenthal to Los Angeles from the agency's New York office precisely because he was an outsider and Wasserman wanted to prevent the outbreak of power plays among the ever-growing stable of former agency heads who were now accountable to him and Jules Stein. Wasserman also had to necessarily pare down his hands-on guidance of clients. He kept Reagan for himself but delegated Wyman to Rosenthal, with the directive to make sure she was kept busy. Wasserman promised he would keep a close watch over her assignments, but in truth he had little time for the B actress who, unlike Reagan, had shown little evidence of ever being able to break onto the A list.

As a result, her films continued to be nondescript B filler, like Lewis Seiler's *Flight Angels* ("These women are tough angels — they can handle anything but a pilot!"), George Amy's *Gambling on the High Seas,* Curtis Bernhardt's *My Love Came Back,* his *Tugboat Annie Sails Again* (with Reagan), and his short *Alice in Movieland* (in which she cameo'd alongside Reagan), Lloyd Bacon's *Honeymoon for Three,* Ray Enright's *Bad Men of Missouri,* Lewis Seiler's *You're in the Army Now,* and D. Ross Lederman's *The Body Disappears:* all of them stockpiled in 1940 while she was in the early stages of her pregnancy, with their releases stretched out through 1941 to cover the time she was away to care for her and Reagan's new baby girl.

Wyman was continually cast as the beautiful and tough single woman, more often than not against such weak or borderline leading men as the aging former silent-film star Gilbert Roland *(Gambling on the High Seas)*, Dennis Morgan *(Bad Men of Missouri)*, Phil Silvers *(You're in the Army Now)*, and Jeffrey Lynn (both dead *and* invisible in the Edward Everett Horton so-called comedy vehicle *The Body Disappears*). In this rash of B movies (the lone exception being *You're in the Army Now)*, Wyman found herself with little to do but act tough and sexy in front of the camera. (The lobby card for *The Body Disappears* featured an unattached stockinged leg coming out of a casket.) By 1941, she was more than happy to take a break from it all and stay home to care for her new baby. Reagan insisted that they hire a live-in Scottish nanny to help.

The nurse turned out to be an unexpected blessing for Wyman, as the euphoria of giving birth quickly cross-faded into the hard reality of day-to-day motherhood. Domestic life had never held any real charm for Wyman, neither as a child nor as a newlywed (both times) or as a new mother. She quickly grew weary of diapers, and, this being the early forties, had no real outlet for her homebound frustrations. But the last thing she wanted to do was complain to her husband about anything. He was the main breadwinner of their household; his star, unlike hers, was decidedly on the rise. Still, things she had once found so comforting, such as Reagan's ever-present pipe, now bothered the hell out of her. The smell of burnt ashes, the sticky residue left in the ashtrays by those hideous pipe cleaners, the clear bags of tobacco all over the place, and most of all the sickly sweet bluish haze of smoke that permeated every inch of their house made her want to throw up as much as her postpartum morning sickness.

And if that wasn't enough, her husband's habit of pontificating about the headlines of the day was starting to drive her crazy. He had opinions on *everything,* and often made what amounted to speeches, right there in the living room even when she was putting the baby down for a nap or changing its diaper. Puffing away, he'd book-end and break up his pontifications with a few "Button-noses" that made her roll her eyes and shake her head. She *hated* that nickname. One time she thought of calling him "Barrel-nose" but thought better of it. What's more, he had taken to calling the baby "Button nose number two."

Months of having to listen to Reagan's living-room speeches day after day and night after night had driven her to the brink. Although throughout her marriage she was carefully guarded about giving anything away to the press about their home life, probably because she feared too much information might lead to some unwanted investigations into her less-than-perfect past (that the studio had carefully glossed over in their biographical PR releases), there were occasional glimpses of their married life that slipped through to the public. While talking to Earl Wilson, a midcentury gossip columnist who covered Hollywood and Broadway for both newspapers and radio, she let drop this commentary of Reagan's habit of homeland speechmaking: "You ask what time it is and he'll tell you how the watch was made!" It was supposed to be a joke, but Reagan didn't laugh when he read it in Wilson's column.

Part of being in the studio system meant that their home life was not entirely their own; nor entirely real. The studio PR machine's job used the Reagan name and image of his family life as another means of extending the public's fantasy about their lives. This made life even more difficult for Wyman, especially when, two months after Maureen was born, the studio sent cameramen to their home to take stills and movies of her, Reagan, and their new baby. The scene was as well scripted as any feature, with Reagan and Jane doting over their newborn, a cutesy moment Wyman knew was pure fiction and would never have happened if the lensmen weren't there to chronicle it.

On the rare occasions that she complained to her husband about any of it, Reagan would put his hands up to stop it. He didn't want to hear anything but good things from her. He had a suggestion for Wyman after she had fallen into one of her sullen funks: "We'll lead an ideal life if you'll just avoid doing one thing: *Don't think.*"

When the studio released its midyear report, the latest Gallup survey ranked Ronald Reagan number eighty-two among Hollywood's top Hollywood stars. Wyman was unranked. Number one at the box office was Clark Gable, based largely on his curiously unrewarded role as Rhett Butler in Victor Fleming's 1939 *Gone With the Wind,* which had stayed in theaters for most of 1940 and was still going strong around the world.[*]

A more relevant gap than the distance between Reagan's and Gable's popularity rankings was the disparity in their earning powers. Under his contract at MGM, Gable was pulling down $210,000 per picture and

[*] The Best Actor Oscar for 1939 went to Robert Donat, for his performance in Sam Wood's *Goodbye, Mr. Chips,* over Gable, who had been the odds-on favorite. Also nominated that year were Laurence Olivier for William Wyler's *Wuthering Heights,* Mickey Rooney for Busby Berkeley's *Babes in Arms,* and James Stewart for Frank Capra's *Mr. Smith Goes to Washington.* Many felt that if Gable somehow didn't get it, Stewart would.

230

averaging four films a year. At Warner, Errol Flynn, who was ranked number two, was earning $157,000 per picture, and was slated to make three features that year. Reagan's salary paled by comparison, averaging out to about $50,000 per film in a schedule that had leveled out at four films per year, which amounted to less than half of Flynn's annual take and about a quarter of Gable's.

However, to Reagan, his numbers actually sounded pretty good for someone only four years removed from the relative obscurity of the Midwest. Warners thought so, too, and used those statistics and a few more of their own to determine the direction and staying power of Reagan's future at the studio. The upside of Warner's tracking and research showed that he was extremely popular with boys eighteen years old and under, something they attributed to the continual re-releases of what had become a Saturday-morning staple, Reagan's "Brass" Bancroft series. The downside was his startling lack of appeal to female audiences. He was no Errol Flynn, Warner knew. But as Flynn's nonthreatening pal, he was perfect.

Late that summer, with Reagan riding relatively high in the polls, Louella Parsons, who was being feted by her hometown of Dixon with a "Louella Parsons Day," invited fellow Dixonite Reagan to share in the honors. He was delighted to do so. Warner gave him his official okay as long as the visit — which would interrupt production on Reagan's new film, Sam Wood's *Kings Row* — could be tied in to a promotion for *International Squadron,* a film directed by Lothar Mendes that he had completed earlier that summer. Parsons had no problem with that, and the studio hastily put together a "world premiere" event for it to be held in Dixon on Labor Day.

A crowd estimated at just over fifty thousand showed up at Rock River Valley to cheer them. The festivities began with a ten-block parade complete with five bands and fifteen floats, atop which some of the biggest stars in Hollywood rode, hats and hands waving at the enthusiastic cheers. Bob Hope, Joe E. Brown, Ann Rutherford, George Montgomery, Bebe Daniels, and others all showed up, some to honor Reagan, most to genuflect in public before the all-powerful Parsons.

A rubber-chicken lunch (catered by Warner Bros.) for two hundred "special" guests was served on the riverfront lawn, during which time the Louella Parsons Wing of the local hospital was officially dedicated. So prestigious was the occasion that old-man Hearst himself, the head of the newspaper empire that Parsons had helped gain such an influential foothold in Hollywood, called in to express his congratulations. The day was capped off with a dinner banquet at the

Masonic temple and a screening of *International Squadron* at the old Dixon Theater, where Reagan had passed Saturday mornings watching Westerns.

Just before the lights went down, Parsons and Reagan were brought to the front of the theater and given special awards. The Queen of Rock River, a seventeen-year-old local beauty, beautifully blushing in her bathing suit, handed Reagan a bouquet of roses, an extra surprise for him arranged by Parsons.

The film was an update of Howard Hawks's 1935 *Ceiling Zero,* a Jimmy Cagney vehicle in which he plays a test pilot whose recklessness causes the death of a fellow flyer. He then dedicates his life to testing dangerous new equipment for the betterment of the entire world. In Reagan's version, he's a test pilot who delivers a bomber to England, witnesses the death of a child during an air raid, and devotes himself to winning the war for the betterment of the entire free world.[*] Reagan received a standing ovation when the film ended.

After, he called Wyman, who had chosen to

[*] The plot is remarkably similar to Twentieth Century Fox's *A Yank in the RAF,* directed by Henry King with Tyrone Powers in the Reagan/Cagney role, released two months earlier, as the studios scrambled to prepare audiences and themselves for America's expected entrance into the war.

stay home and take care of the baby, to tell her all about it.

Back in Hollywood, Reagan immediately resumed filming *Kings Row*. Based on the highly popular if a bit overrated 1940 Henry Bellamann novel that was the *Peyton Place* of its day (and may indeed have served as the inspiration for Grace Metalious's scandalous 1956 book); *Kings Row* is the story of a seemingly all-American town whose outwardly upright citizens are in fact busily engaged in incest, unmarried sex, unfaithful sex, sex of every type imaginable except satisfying. In its rogues' gallery cast of characters, Reagan had been cast as Drake McHugh, a good-looking young trust-funded philanderer. It was a role no one at first thought he could play.

In truth, it was a role almost nobody got a chance to play, because the entire production was nearly shut down before it ever began when highly respected screenwriter Casey Robinson could not find a way to translate the plot of the story to the screen. During an extended vacation to Asia with his wife, a slow boat to China as it were, Robinson had taken a galley of the book with him prior to its publication. The story he read was a real page-turner, set in a typical small town in the American Midwest at the turn of the twentieth century dealing primarily with the relationship between two boyhood friends, Parris Mitchell and Drake McHugh, the women they love, and the fate that awaits them all.

Robinson's initial reaction to the novel was one of outrage and revulsion, yet he couldn't put it down. When he finished it, he interpreted the story as an attack on the moral foundation of the country, that saw beneath its civilized veneer a jungle of repressed sexuality, incest, and evil; he tossed the book into the Sulu Sea somewhere near Bali. Even if he'd wanted to make a movie of it, given the ever stricter parameters of the Production Code, he believed it simply could not be done.

It wasn't until Robinson, still on vacation, discussed the book's plot out loud with his wife that he came up with a brainstorm to change the primary subject matter and theme from incest, which was, at best, of peripheral interest to the general public (or so it was generally believed at the time), to insanity, making it a much easier sell for the studio. Lunatics and the bins that held them had become a popular genre for Hollywood ever since the silent German expressionist *Cabinet of Dr. Caligari* (directed by Robert Weine, 1921) had caused a sensation in America. Robinson wired Wallis his story-change suggestions, and Warner immediately purchased the rights to the novel for the then-hefty price tag of $35,000.*

It took several months for a workable script to be written that would satisfy the preliminary demands of the Breen office. The primary shifts in plot were crucial and changed the entire nature of the story into one of non-explicit sexual sadism, unmotivated suicide, and requited love. All suggestions of incest were removed. Dr. Tower became a more humane character who fears his daughter, a neurotic social misfit who cannot survive in a normal social atmosphere, and makes her a shut-in for her own good. Parris Mitchell became an all-around good guy, with any suggestion of the latent homosexuality between him and Drake that the novel had hinted at obliterated. The revised Parris is devoted to medicine and general goodness and eventually sacrifices his own career opportunities to help save Drake's life. Cast in the crucial role of Parris was the two-dimensional actor Robert Cummings, a genial comic actor who had made a breakthrough in Henry Koster's 1939 comedy, *Three Smart Girls Grow Up,* and become a star with his turn in Sam Wood's 1941 *The Devil and Miss Jones,* a prewar isolationist comedy set in a department store, a favorite setting for thirties and forties films — the world is a

* The film cost $76,000 to make and took seven weeks to shoot.

store, the store is the world. (Cummings would not have been cast if Wood's first choice, Tyrone Power, had been available. Power wanted to make the movie but was under contract to Twentieth Century Fox and the studio couldn't come to an agreement with Warner.) The role of Drake went to Reagan.

In the movie version, like the novel, Parris is by far the more sensitive and intelligent of the two leading male characters, having been raised from infancy in modest circumstances by his adoring grandmother after the early death of his mother and father. His grandmother's death leads Parris to devote himself to a life of healing. Eventually he goes to Vienna to study medicine, where he becomes interested in psychiatry. Drake, who also lost his parents while still a little boy, assuages his pain by using his inheritance to live the life of a playboy, until his bank is caught in an embezzlement scam and he loses all his money and is thrown into a life of poverty and hard work. The nature of their individual characters is further reflected by their relationship to the town's local doctor, Alexander Tower. Although bitter and private (and in the novel sexually twisted — he is having an incestuous affair with his daughter, Cassandra), Dr. Tower takes a liking to the young Parris and tutors him in preparation of a career in medicine.

At the same time, Parris has a childhood crush on Cassandra (Betty Field), Dr. Tower's sheltered daughter. When Dr. Tower (beautifully underplayed by the always superb Claude Rains) realizes that Drake likes Cassandra, he takes her out of school and forces her to become a virtual recluse (in the film the incestuous theme was replaced with that of insanity, the reason the doctor gives for removing his daughter from school and shutting her up in her room). As soon as she is old enough, Cassandra rebels against her father's short leash and begins to see Parris. Not long after, in a move that shocked the residents of Kings Row (and theater-going audiences then and today whenever the film is revived or seen on TV), Dr. Tower kills both his daughter and himself. As if that were not enough, later on it is revealed that Cassandra was pregnant when she was killed. The identity of the baby's father is purposely left vague as directed by the censorship board, allowing for a perhaps unintended twist, with both the doctor and Parris as possible impregnators.*

Young Drake, meanwhile, prior to his

---

* The film was fraught with controversy. The American Medical Association tried to prevent *Kings Row* from being shown because it believed it portrayed doctors in a bad light. Nothing came of the AMA's campaign.

disastrous financial losses, takes up with two other girls, Randy Monaghan (Ann Sheridan), a working-class tomboy who has blossomed into a beautiful young lady, and the attractive but haughty Louise, who happens to be the daughter of another Kings Row physician, Dr. Henry Gordon (Charles Coburn). After the death of Cassandra and Parris's departure for Vienna, when Drake loses his money, he also takes up with Randy, whom he had dismissed while romancing Louise.

When Drake can't find work, he is forced to go down to the (other side of the) railroad tracks, where he begs the foreman, who happens to also be Randy's father (Pat Moriarty), for a job. Despite his dislike for Drake and the disrespectful way he has treated his daughter, Mr. Monaghan hires him. Drake slowly integrates himself into the Monaghan household until he is seriously injured in an accident. It falls to Dr. Gordon to care for him; in yet another incredulous and appalling turn of events, the doctor, in a fit of vengeance, decides to punish Drake for being attracted to his daughter by amputating both of his legs, another horrifying twist to this tale and a viciously symbolic castration that permanently cripples and all but kills Drake.

It falls to Randy to nurse him back to health; when Parris hears of the accident, he immediately returns from Vienna to try to help his friend. In the film (unlike the novel, in which Drake develops cancer and dies), Parris and Randy help Drake rediscover the will to live despite being filled with despair and feeling his life is over.

With a film certain to be as controversial as *Kings Row,* even considered socially subversive by some, Wallis wanted a director at the helm who was absolutely above reproach, and Wood (riding high at Warner because of his success with the 1940 tearjerker *Kitty Foyle,* which had won a Best Actress Oscar for Ginger Rogers and a Best Director nomination for Wood, and with *The Devil and Miss Jones* the following year) was that man.[*] He had been in Hollywood from the beginning of feature films, knocking around as a silent-movie bit player until he came under the wing of Cecil B. DeMille. After serving as his A.D. (assistant director) for several years, he was

---

[*] *Kitty Foyle* was Wood's second nomination. His first came in 1939 for *Goodbye, Mr. Chips,* which he lost to Victor Fleming for *Gone With the Wind* (interestingly, Wood directed, without credit, several scenes for *Gone With the Wind*). He lost Best Director in 1940 to John Ford, who won for *The Grapes of Wrath.* Wood also directed the 1940 film version of Thornton Wilder's *Our Town,* which was also nominated for Best Picture, but it lost to Alfred Hitchcock's *Rebecca* (the award went to David O. Selznick, the film's producer).

given the chance by DeMille himself to direct for Paramount. He moved to MGM in the late twenties and worked with some of the studio's biggest stars before signing on with Warners on a nonexclusive basis. Wood was a talented director, personally trained in film and tutored in the ways of the industry by DeMille, and had a reputation for being one of the most conservative, promanagement, antiunion men in the business. Besides liking the way his movies looked, Wallis cannily figured Wood was the smart choice to direct a movie that intended to lift the crinolines of so-called proper American small-town society.

In turn, Wood wanted an actor for Parris who projected a sense of infallible wholesomeness, which Cummings did. Playing opposite Reagan, Cummings also projected something between callow and shallow. It was a choice that would ultimately flatten the moral dimension of the characters of Parris (intellectual, sexually repressed) and Drake (nonintellectual, sexually free) and lessen the implications of the film's stylistic technique of "doubling" its major characters to help define their inner characters through contrasting behavior: Parris and Drake, Louise and Randy, Dr. Gordon and Dr. Tower.

If Reagan fared better than Cummings in the film, it was because his lack of acting depth was more appropriate to his character's

corresponding shallowness. Parris has to pull
Drake through, something audiences ultimately found hard to believe. Cummings
simply didn't have that kind of strength or
conviction on-screen, which is why he fared
better in light comedies than intense dramas.
Wood, of course, loved the film's upbeat ending because, unlike the novel, in which
Drake's death might suggest the death of
individualism in a repressive and restrictive
society, he believed that Drake's ability to
overcome his tragic setback suggested the
indomitable strength and endurance of the
individual as well as of the American system.
And, lastly, the script's simplistic final "conversion" scene simply did not play as a
convincing resolution to the complexities of
the film's plot. It may have been uplifting,
but ultimately it did not fly.

To play the crucial, and difficult, role of
Cassie, Wallis's first choice was Ida Lupino,
who read the script, hated it, and bowed out
"because of prior commitments." Wallis then
turned to Bette Davis, who said no because
despite the fact that Cassie dominates the
first hour of the film, Davis felt that the
female lead really was Randy, whom Ann
Sheridan had already been cast to play
(necessarily "de-oomphed" for this film, according to Reagan biographer Lou Cannon).
The part of Cassie eventually went to the
relatively unknown Betty Field, Wood's first

choice all along after seeing her play Mae in Lewis Milestone's 1939 film adaptation of John Steinbeck's *Of Mice and Men.*

A number of actors were considered for the key role of Drake McHugh, but Reagan got the part because of Wasserman's relentless pressure on Wallis, over several other studio contract players, including Dennis Morgan, Jack Carson, Jeffrey Lynn, and Eddie Albert. It was Reagan's surprising success in his relatively small role as the Gipper in *Knute Rockne* that helped Wasserman convince Wallis that Reagan could play Drake. What had given that performance its poignancy was how Reagan, as the Gipper, had delivered his and the film's single most memorable line from bed. In *Kings Row,* Reagan's character was also bedridden, and Reagan had demonstrated he was a pretty good actor lying flat on his back. When Drake awakens from his surgery and utters his first words, they, too, would become a national catchphrase (and eventually, the title of Reagan's first memoir), the equally unforgettable "Where's the rest of me?" Wasserman insisted that Drake was a kind of natural extension of George Gipp in *Knute Rockne,* and convinced Wallis of it, who in turn convinced Wood to cast Reagan.

Lew Wasserman, meanwhile, had been pushing Jack L. Warner to renegotiate Reagan's contract before the original ran out (its seven years ended in 1944), at which time, he warned, there would be no renegotiation, and he would take Reagan, who had come to Warner an unknown but would go out a star, the freelance route. The other possibility, Wasserman knew, was that the coming war meant Reagan might be drafted into military service. In wartime, Reagan's poor eyesight might not be enough to keep him from being chosen for duty. If that happened, Wasserman wanted Reagan's new contract in place prior to his service.

Unexpectedly, at least to Wasserman, Warner jumped at the opportunity to renew Reagan, but not solely because of Wasserman's clever agenting. During their negotiations, Warner had secretly arranged to see a rough cut of *Kings Row,* and realized that once again, as he had in *Knute Rockne,* Reagan was going to steal the film, and this time likely emerge as one of the biggest stars in Hollywood. He wanted to be sure he had Reagan signed to a long-term deal before the film was released.

Reagan, however, was far less confident of the outcome of the film. Going into rehearsals, he was worried about playing his crucial scene, how he could play waking up and realizing he had no legs with just five words of dialogue. As an actor with little technical training besides the mandatory daily lessons at the studio (and disregarding the amateur-time plays he did in college), Reagan felt he was at a loss. As Reagan later recalled, "I rehearsed the scene before mirrors, in corners of the studio, while driving home, in the men's room of restaurants, before selected friends. At night I would wake up staring at the ceiling and automatically mutter the line before I went back to sleep. I consulted physicians and psychologists; I even talked to people who were so disabled, trying to brew in myself the cauldron of emotions a man must feel who wakes up one sunny morning to find half of himself gone.

"The night before [filming the scene] I could not sleep. I appeared wan and worn on the sound stage, still not knowing how to read the line. Without hope, with make-up pasted on and in my nightshirt, I wandered over to the set to see what it looked like. I found the prop men had arranged a neat deception. Under the gay patchwork quilt, they had cut a hole in the mattress and put a supporting box beneath. I stared at it for a minute. Then, obeying an overpowering impulse, I climbed into the rig. I spent almost that whole hour in stiff confinement, contemplating my torso and the smooth undisturbed flat of the covers where my legs should have been."

Lost in concentration, Reagan didn't notice how the crew had lit the scene and that Sam Wood, now standing beside him, wanted to know if Reagan was ready to shoot the scene. "Without rehearsal?" Reagan asked, breaking into a cold sweat. Wood nodded. The cameras were cued, and the scene began. To his credit (and his own astonishment) Reagan managed to get it in a single take. Wood shouted "Cut it and print it" and it was over. Reagan had risen to the occasion, as it were, and everyone on set knew it.

It would be the finest moment of a sustained performance that would serve as the hallmark of Reagan's entire acting career. He had reached deep into himself to connect to a feeling that he would later describe in his memoirs as a metaphor for his ultimate sense of limitation and his inability as an actor (an "incompleteness" that would serve as the springboard for his eventual rejection of acting as a career, in favor of the world arena of politics). It was, in truth, a perfect moment of Method acting, what students of Stanislavski (and later a host of American derivative teachers) were taught — to connect their real emotions to those of their characters and to let that bridge take them to a deeper level of truth in their performance. This one time, Reagan had managed to touch both ends of his "self," the external, expressive performance side and the internal, emotional engine that fueled it.

According to Robert Cummings, "He was a hell of a good actor — a far better actor than most people give him credit for. In *Kings Row* he had the sympathetic role of having his legs cut off, and he was just great. The producers asked both myself and Ronnie and all the cast not to read the book because, they said, 'We're not making the book — we're doing a screenplay adaptation by Casey Robinson.' The doctor cut his legs off, and I believe the implication was that he also cut his genitals off. We were not allowed to say that in the movie because it was deeply censored.

"But I believe in the book it said he got his genitals cut off, too. So in the movie, when Ronnie sat up in bed and said, 'Where's the rest of me?' you knew that since this doctor was a sadistic character, you got the feeling that he probably took everything off."

Reagan's performance would serve as a model for dozens of future movies built around physical and metaphorical "incompleteness." There would be distinct echoes of it in the young Marlon Brando's screen interpretation of the wounded war veteran who loses the use of his legs in Fred Zinnemann's 1950 *The Men,* in Jimmy Stewart's psychological broken-leg neurotic voyeur in Alfred Hitchcock's 1954 *Rear Window,* and in Gary Sinise's legless Vietnam War veteran Lt. Dan Taylor in Robert Zemeckis's 1994 *Forrest Gump.* In *Kings Row,* Drake's panicky cry of recognition that his legs have been amputated is a frightened scream of the theft of manhood, of becoming socially inept and sexually deprived (in a character that has until now been taken on a lifelong joy ride run on his sexual energy). And it was precisely Drake's (and Reagan's) lack of understanding for the deeper consequences of this tragedy that allowed him to journey into the darkest side of his own moral imperfection, until, at the film's climax, his open arms more than compensate for his missing legs. It was, finally, a performance by Reagan of grandeur and mystery that towers above all his others.

For the rest of his life, Reagan gave all the credit for it to Sam Wood. Not surprisingly, by the time the film was finished, Wood had taken his place among the pantheon of Reagan father-figures alongside Lew Wasserman and Jack Warner (and in death, the idealized ghost of the mortally and morally imperfect Jack Reagan himself), men of authority who held influence and emotional powers of persuasion over him.

As they grew closer, among the many things Wood and Reagan often talked about during the making of *Kings Row* was politics. As Cummings recalled, "Ronnie did expound on the set a lot . . . he was a passionate Democrat then and our director, Sam Wood, and I were Republicans. There was always a lot of good-natured political banter going on between Sam and Ronnie."

Another time, Cummings said, "All the cast used to sit around waiting for the cameraman to light the scene — sometimes it was long, tedious hours, because almost all of the entire outdoor scenes were shot indoors. So we'd listen to Ronnie talk about foreign affairs and the economy and things like that. He was so articulate on the subjects — he understood what the government was all about. I didn't. He was always interested in world affairs, and always well-imbued with the spirit of trying to make America better. Whether he knew what he was doing at the time or not, I don't know . . . it wasn't a lecture — but he took the center of the stage."

Wood and Reagan also frequently discussed an ongoing and increasingly ugly strike taking place at the Disney Studios that had lasted much of the late winter and spring of 1941 and showed no signs of being settled anytime soon. Wood, a hard-edged conservative, was completely opposed to it, and especially to its leader, Herb Sorrell, the head of the painters' union, a new name to Reagan. A SAG board member, Reagan remained sympathetic to those manning the picket lines. He listened and occasionally, politely, questioned Wood's points. They never openly disagreed, but somewhere within he connected to Wood's strongly conservative position about the striker, and his strong support of management, in this case Walt Disney. He would not forget these discussions.

When Jack Warner and Lew Wasserman sat

down to hammer out the details of Reagan's new deal, Warner offered to roughly triple his star's salary, to a total of $758,000 over seven years, for forty weeks' worth of movie work a year. Wasserman immediately agreed, but, nobody's fool, he left a tiny window open to allow for a renegotiating fine-tune after *Kings Row*'s release. If the film was extremely successful, as Wasserman believed it would be, he wanted the right to bump the deal up. If Reagan was drafted — to adjust his suspension clause, which, as it stood now, would have put all lost studio time on the back end, meaning that Reagan would not be paid while serving his country — his salary (and time lost) would resume upon his release from the military.

The issue of military service was a real one. The summer of 1941, just prior to the start of the making of *Kings Row,* Reagan's cavalry reserve status had been revoked and he had been called to immediate active duty. Reagan did not want to go. He was newly married with a baby and after years of toiling in the cinematic dream factories, he believed he was finally in reach of major stardom after a long and slow buildup of career steam that might be released by the military's long and mandatory reach.

Reagan certainly wasn't alone in this respect. Despite the Hollywood newsreels that continually showed its stars happily slipping into uniform and going off to service in the months immediately preceding and following the country's formal entrance into World War II, in truth, with a few notable exceptions (Jimmy Stewart was one, although he, too, was drafted rather than volunteered), there weren't many actors who appreciated their careers being interrupted by having to fall into lockstep for their Uncle Sam, even if almost none of the big names of Hollywood were ever in danger of actually being put into combat situations. Their higher value, the government knew, would be service on the propaganda front.*

Wasserman wrote a letter he wanted Jack Warner to send on behalf of the studio to the assistant secretary of war in Washington, D.C., requesting a deferment for Reagan on the grounds that his being drafted would create a serious financial loss to the studio and

---

* This didn't become official policy until 1942, when Col. Lewis B. Hershey, the director of the Selective Service, the draft, declared that the film industry was "essential to the national health, safety and interest, and in other instances to war productions" and granted regular deferments to "actors, directors, writers, producers, cameramen, sound engineers and other technicians" whose induction "would cause a serious loss of effectiveness." (Details of Colonel Hershey's directive are from the February 9, 1942, *New York Times*.)

to him. Wasserman understood the government's intended use of the studios as perhaps the most effective propaganda tool available and wanted Reagan to take advantage of it. In an industry where an actor's wardrobe in a scene could immediately change the stylistic trends of the times, as when the sales of T-shirts plummeted after Clark Gable revealed he didn't wear one in Frank Capra's 1934 *It Happened One Night,* the effect of seeing an actor in uniform, the government knew, was invaluable. Wasserman had already seen to it that Reagan's upcoming schedule of films included at least one military war picture, still to be chosen, that would go a long way in justifying his deferment. "Therefore," Wasserman's letter concluded, "in view of these facts we respectfully request that said Ronald Reagan be placed in the War Department reserve pool. In the event that this cannot be done, we also request that he be placed in a deferred class for so long a reasonable period of time as will be necessary to adjust our production schedules and rearrange our plans."

Warner copied the letter word for word in his own handwriting on studio stationery, signed his name to it, and sent it off. Less than a week later, Reagan was assigned the rank of second lieutenant and given a provisional, or temporary, deferment. As a favor, Wasserman also got Warner to raise Wyman's salary from the $150 a week she was still earning to $750 a week, no small potatoes for someone stuck in the B boat making instantly forgettable (if modestly profitable) films.

To celebrate the new deals he had negotiated for the both of them, Warner messengered a bonus-on-singing check for $600 and a bottle of champagne to the Reagans' new home, a comfortable $15,000 seven-room two-bedroom/two-bathroom shingled ranch high in the Hollywood Hills they had bought with an FHA twenty-year, $125-a-month mortgage. They had applied for it the day after they'd gotten married, but it had taken nearly two years to get approved.

The studio, fearful that Reagan might be drafted at any time, wanted to stockpile as many films with him in them as they could. After *Kings Row,* they applied for an extension of Reagan's deferment, got it, and immediately re-paired him with Ann Sheridan, the actress with whom he'd always had the most on-screen chemistry. The somewhat misleadingly titled *Juke Girl,* directed by *Million Dollar Baby*'s Curtis Bernhardt, an A production from Hal Wallis, was not at all a musical as the title might suggest but a socially aware melodrama dealing with the rights, or lack thereof, of itinerant crop workers in Florida. In the film, Steve Talbot (Reagan) and his pal, Danny Frazier (Richard

Whorf), are a pair of drifters who have headed south for the winter to pick tomatoes. Inseparable when they arrive, they soon find themselves on opposite sides of a labor dispute. Steve opportunistically sides with Henry Madden (Gene Lockhart), the owner of a fruit farm and packing plant, while Danny is righteously sympathetic to the workers, led by Nick Garcos (George Tobias). Everything comes to a head at the local juke joint (the forties equivalent of a modern nightclub, with recorded music instead of a live band), where a girl hired to "entertain" the fieldworkers touches off a brawl between workers and management over low wages.[*]

All of this serves as a very elaborate "meet not-so-cute" for Reagan and Sheridan who, in short order, become involved in a plot to break the monopolistic practices that have all but enslaved the migrant workers. They eventually endure (as all struggling heroes and heroines did, their success mandated as

[*] The film was based on an original story by Theodore Pratt, "Jook Girl," a fictionalized version of a story he also wrote for the *Saturday Evening Post,* called "Land of the Jook." *Jook* was a variation on a slang term, *Juke,* for jukeboxes (the latter spelling the one used for the film version), "Jook girls" were described in the articles as young women employed by local taverns "to dance and make love with the patrons."

much by the Production Code as the nuances of storytelling), but only after a series of violent clashes, corporate betrayals, mob thuggery, and wholesale destruction of acres of farmland.

The film was all Wallis (and very little Bernhardt), a Hollywood liberal who saw in the story an opportunity to cash in on the then-current, quite successful trend in the studios to take a harder look at the Depression years.[†] Far from being a cultural trendsetter, studios always feared being on the wrong side of an issue. Films made during the early years of the Depression were really last-gasp celebrations of the Roaring Twenties, even if they suggested the end came with a crash (Fred Astaire dancing penniless in a tuxedo). Movies that dealt with the harsh realities of those years — the economic, social, and political ramifications — came only as those years (but not those issues) were fading with America's inevitable entry into World War II. Forties "noir" is, in reality,

---

[†] Bernhardt had very little use for this film and another he directed with Reagan. According to Charles Higham and Joel Greenberg's *The Celluloid Muse,* Bernhardt said, "I [didn't] like these films, despite [the fact] that they starred Mr. Reagan, a sort of an unimportant, pleasant, typical, healthy American boy. One was *Juke Girl.* Another was *Million Dollar Baby.*"

Hollywood's decade-late stylistic depiction of the country's mood during the Depression.

Wallis had noted with special interest the financial success of two recent "socially aware" films: John Ford's award-winning adaptation of John Steinbeck's novel *The Grapes of Wrath* that Twentieth Century Fox had released, examining the plight of migrant workers in a realistic, decidedly nonglamorous way that nevertheless caught the attention and ignited the passion of audiences the world over, and Raoul Walsh's *They Drive by Night,* dealing with the plight of Depression-era wildcat truck drivers, made at Warners.[*] Both Ford's and Walsh's movies were only tangentially political (Steinbeck's novel, in particularly, had been severely watered down for the screen version, transformed into a family melodrama all but devoid of a larger

---

* Both films were huge financial successes. *The Grapes of Wrath* won Oscars for Best Director (Ford) and Best Supporting Actress (Jane Darwell), and was nominated for Best Picture, Best Actor (Henry Fonda), Best Editing (Robert Simpson), Best Sound Recording (Edmund H. Hansen), and Best Screenplay (Nunnally Johnson). *They Drive by Night* starred George Raft, Humphrey Bogart, Ann Sheridan, Ida Lupino, and Roscoe Karns. It was not nominated for any Oscars but did even better at the box office than *Wrath* and helped push Bogart to the top of the list of Hollywood's most popular actors.

political overview, rendering Tom Joad's [Henry Fonda's] final monologue without a sense of specific social outrage, only a vaguely moral one, that took much of the time and place as well as the soul out of the movie).

Juke Girl was something else again. Wallis had been able to make it only because he was Warners' biggest and most successful producer, and Warner, not nearly as liberal, did not want to do anything to upset him. Jack Warner did not at all like the film's blatant observation about the proliferation of hookers meant to appease workers like a drug in a dress (or out of one), which in and of itself was a pretty good reflection of the way women, especially starlets, were treated at Warner and every other major in town, gorgeous playthings without power. However, as Jack L. Warner knew as well as anyone in Hollywood, sex sold tickets, even when, *especially* when, it had a whiff of the lurid about it. MGM hadn't done so badly with Jean Harlow, and even if Ann Sheridan was no Harlow, she came off more sexual than usual opposite the upright (and uptight) Reagan.

Even as *Juke Girl* was in production, the seeds were being planted for what would be the biggest strike in Hollywood's history, even bigger than the one that Disney had endured; it would have far-reaching effects on virtually everyone working at the time in film, both on camera and off, and would be the first major step in the permanent altering of the structure of the business as well as of the art of Hollywood.

Those seeds were sown in the fall of 1940, when Disney's full-length feature *Fantasia* had opened, although not in the way Disney had wanted. For the film, Disney's creative in-house technical wizard, Ubbe Iwerks, had devised a unique widescreen format and a ninety-six-speaker stereophonic sound system that needed special installations in every theater the film was to be shown in. When Disney insisted the film could only be exhibited in that format, a conflict over the rights to handle the special installations broke out between opposing factions of IATSE (the International Alliance of Theatrical Stage Employees) and IBEW (the International Brotherhood of Electrical Workers). The battle was supercharged because IBEW openly supported the Disney cartoonists' move to join the independent Cartoonists Guild, which "Uncle" Walt had vehemently opposed. He believed that he treated his workers better than any union ever could, like "family," and reacted to their attempt to unionize not only as a personal rejection but also as a warning that communism had managed to infiltrate not just his studio but the studio system itself. Disney was further infuriated when the government indirectly settled the dispute by refusing to allow the manufacture of "Fantasound" because of the need to conserve raw materials for the coming war. To Disney, that was a sign that the whole country was in on the plot, and that the problem was now not only Hollywood's but all of America's.*

After the animators went on strike against Disney in the summer of 1941, the question of how to handle the industry's growing labor problems became unavoidable. At this point, the struggle had been, for the most part, an internal one, kept behind the walls of the studios, even as they turned out countless movies glorifying and idealizing the working man. It was the studio heads' belief that the public didn't know and didn't care about anything that happened in the industry, as long as the movies kept on coming; that nobody in the world was watching what happened behind the scenes, unless it involved the love lives of the stars.

Meanwhile, the level of union discontent in Hollywood intensified as the moguls insisted

* The film opened without its special processing or the need for any augmented theaters. It was, in its initial release, a commercial flop, which Disney attributed to a conspiracy against him that he believed had been originated by the unions and supported by Washington. For more information and details about Disney and *Fantasia* see the author's *Walt Disney: Hollywood's Dark Prince.*

the hired help (what they considered talent and technicians alike) should be grateful they had jobs at all in an industry that provided a better quality of life for them than any other in the country.

To the outside observer (then and now) it is tempting to believe the image of Hollywood that the studios project, a culture of privilege, which was written, produced, and directed by those who reflected their own lives. The moviegoing public of the thirties and forties, according to critic and cultural historian Wilfrid Sheed, "did not expect [writers] to write about the very top people, the Cabots and the Biddles, but only about imitation top people like Fred and Ginger and occasionally Bing Crosby, two hoofers and a groaner dressed up in evening clothes to constitute a kind of take-out aristocracy of *make-believe.*"

It was a take-out aristocracy that was selling a way of life that most who were helping to sell it were not, with a few notable exceptions, privy to. The great majority of actors and off-screen talent barely made enough money to live on. Almost none thought what they were doing was art and were more concerned with making their rent than any lasting, let alone meaningful, statements. They had fought bitterly for the right to organize, only to find their unions, such as they were, corrupt practically from the moment of inception by so-called leaders who made themselves susceptible to the favors of management in return for keeping their membership working, and, in some cases, outside goon-squads (funded by the studios) that operated with ease beyond the law. The only immediate relief from the foul odor of corruption came in the form of communism, the then socially fashionable, idealistic alternative to a system that appeared to have fallen off the high wall and, like old Humpty Dumpty, was having difficulty putting its own pieces back together. The workers believed the whole world was watching.

That unions existed at all was the result of years of struggle against the studio heads just for the right to organize, and the situation had become infinitely more complicated when, along with the unions, organized crime followed in its footsteps with the arrival of Willie Bioff and George Browne, two roughnecks who were part of Frank Nitti's gang of enforcers sent to Hollywood at the behest of the studios to keep the members of IATSE in line. When, during the filming of *Kings Row,* IATSE challenged the picketers outside the Disney studios, and the NLRB (National Labor Relations Board) sided with strikers, Disney remained adamantly opposed to union representation at his studio and threatened to fire any employee who joined it. The strike, led by Herb Sorrell, lasted for months and further divided those in Hollywood demanding uncorrupt union representation from those in management who were against it and supported importing organized crime thugs like Bioff and Browne to fight it.

The Disney strike was finally settled late in the summer of 1941, but the wound it had opened had only just begun to bleed.

Because of the upheaval it caused in the way business was done in Hollywood, Wallis's blatantly prounion *Juke Girl* resonated throughout the industry in a way it no longer does among contemporary viewers, who see it today as nothing more than a simple adventure movie. Despite the fact that it was, at least on the surface, following in the tradition of proworker Warner Bros. films, Jack L. Warner, who had been a supporter of Walt Disney through all his union troubles, intensely disliked it, and when it was released, did nothing to help promote it, even if its failure affected his own studio's bottom-line. *Juke Girl*'s treatment by Jack Warner would be so internally contentious, it signaled the beginning of the end of the Wallis era at the studio.* And if Reagan was not completely aware of all the film's political implications, he couldn't find any answers from Bernhardt, the film's director, but did from his newest

---

* Wallis would leave Warner two years later, after producing his final picture at the studio, 1942's *Casablanca*.

mentor, Sam Wood, who, like Jack Warner, did not like the film's political message and was more than happy to point out its flaws to his newest pupil.

Meanwhile, every night during the filming of *Juke Girl,* Reagan and Wyman could be seen around town having dinner at their familiar haunts: Chasen's, the Brown Derby, or Ciro's, usually with either the Steins, the Wassermans, less often with the Warners, and lately and with increasingly regularity, with Mr. and Mrs. Sam Wood. While the others liked to schmooze with Reagan about films, deals, and food, Wood was strictly about politics. Wood, like Disney (and Charles Lindbergh and many others prior to Pearl Harbor), was decidedly against America entering the war, believing a second front would strengthen the Soviets' postwar position. What was happening in Hollywood, and the rest of the country, Wood maintained, was nothing less than a power grab by the communists, who needed America to help them defeat the fascists. As far as Wood was concerned, it was more important to stay out of the war and let the chips fall where they may, than to get suckered into being an ally of the Soviet Union and fight their battles for them.

Reagan didn't agree with Wood's extreme opinions, about either the war or the so-called communist infiltration of the Hollywood unions, nor did he endorse them as policy as a board member of SAG, but some of it did make more than a little sense to him, particularly the part about the communists. As a member of the board of the Screen Actors Guild, he had witnessed for himself the growing and, to him, completely justifiable dissatisfaction the membership had over issues such as wages and working conditions, but he had never heard it expressed from Wood's political perspective.

Still, at this time in Reagan's career, no matter how spirited Wood's arguments were, to Reagan it was all and only after-dinner conversation. Personally, Reagan liked Wood a great deal, and frequently invited him and his wife over for dinner, after which the conversation would inevitably turn to the business and politics of Hollywood.

Wyman, on the other hand, couldn't stand Wood. She found him to be nothing more than a right-wing extremist, and one with a surly manner. She couldn't stand to be in his presence and soon enough began to find excuses not to join the party whenever the Woods were going to be present.

Recalled Cummings: "I did another film right after *Kings Row* called *Princess O'Rourke* [made in 1942, directed and written by Norman Krasna, released in 1943] with Janey Wyman, who was still married to Ronnie at that time. I liked Janey very much, she was a hell of an actress, with that little turned-up button nose of hers. I'll never forget one night I was talking to her about Ronnie and I said, 'You know, he amazes me — his grasp of politics.' And she said, 'Ooh, politics. He gives me a pain in the ass. That's all he talks about! If you had to sit at home and listen to him like I do — that's all he talks about, how he's going to save the world.' "

Reagan never pressed Wyman to come along or questioned how she spent those evenings without him, even when the occasional item appeared in the gossips that Wyman, on those very nights she was supposed to be home with the baby, was seen having dinner in some dim-lit café, most often with MGM rising star Van Johnson (one of Hollywood's "eligible bachelors" prior to his marriage in 1947 to Eve Lynn Abbott). Reagan preferred not to acknowledge the items, or their implications. As far as he was concerned, gossip was all part of the Hollywood game, the price one paid to be a player.

As always, he let it go and continued to do his job, finishing *Juke Girl* and, despite a notable fatigue he admitted to feeling from the nonstop treadmill of work — nine movies in the year and a half since he'd finished *Knute Rockne* — going directly into Raoul Walsh's *Desperate Journey,* another Hal Wallis production that was put on the fast track by Jack Warner after having successfully obtained yet another deferment for Reagan.

Desperate Journey, whose main lead was Errol Flynn, was an early version of the type of war picture that would dominate the first half of the forties, a flat-out propaganda movie where the enemy, the German fascist army, were depicted as imbeciles ("nincompoops" was the way Tony Thomas described them in his *Films of Ronald Reagan* compilation), while the heroic, internationally flavored "good guys" were all impossibly good-looking or ridiculously amiable — Flynn an Australian pilot, Arthur Kennedy a Canadian navigator, Alan Hale a Scottish veteran of World War I, and Reagan as a Yankee in the RAF. They're all shot down while flying a mission over Germany and encounter a series of side missions while working their way back to the free world.[*]

While the film's intentions were nobly heroic, even if it was out-and-out propaganda, it had about as much depth and sophistica-

[*] Another, perhaps more insidious, tradition is continued in this film. Warner Bros., like every major studio, seemed reluctant to depict the Nazis as the evil mass murderers they were; issues like the Jewish mass exterminations, the prison camps, and the murder of Catholics and Gypsies were, for the most part, glossed over, while the Japanese were relentlessly shown to be bloodthirsty subhuman torturers capable of the most inhuman acts imaginable.

tion as Reagan's old "Brass" Bancroft series. Despite uniting much of the male cast of *Santa Fe Trail,* an equally preposterous and inaccurate view of history, the feeling among them, including Reagan, was that they had a real bomb on their hands that would do more damage to the box-office receipts of Warner Bros. than all the German bombs being dropped on England during the life of the film.

The making of it also reignited Reagan's curious jealousy of Errol Flynn. According to costar Kennedy, "Flynn and Ronnie didn't get along very well. Ronnie had wanted to play General Custer in *They Died with Their Boots On* because he felt he was entitled to the part. In a bit part, when he was just getting started, he had played Custer as a young cadet at West Point [in *Santa Fe Trail*] and he just couldn't get it through his head why Flynn played Custer in *They Died with Their Boots On.* When we did *Desperate Journey,* all the actors, not just Ronnie, were unhappy with the fact that they were required to work on Saturdays, and this particular Saturday Flynn arrived on the lot with a case of bourbon. As it happened, there were quite a few heavy drinkers on this set, including Alan Hale, Raoul Walsh, the director, and Flynn, of course. And Ronnie, of course. But he would surreptitiously, he thought, dump his drinks in a spittoon.

"Anyway, I was playing Flynn's number one gun boy, and I was wandering around with all this equipment on. I didn't know where I was or anything, and Flynn was standing in the middle of the set in one of his usual heroic postures, with a gun in his hand, a .45, and Ronnie gave the first line. Flynn looked at him and responded, 'Why don't you go fuck yourself?' and Walsh said, 'Print it; it's fine for me.'

"The next shooting day, Monday, Ronnie came to the set and said he'd see a great picture last night and I said, 'I know what it was — *Knute Rockne* — and he really got mad. He had quite a temper, but then, as always, it blew over. In those days there was something terribly ingenuous about Ronnie that left him open to all kinds of kidding."

On February 7, 1942, two months after Pearl Harbor had put an end to all further talk of isolationism and "America First," *Kings Row* opened to mostly rave reviews, with Reagan getting his fair share. *The New Yorker*'s Russell Maloney called his performance more than capable, *Life* magazine heaped heavy praise on it, and even the *New York Times*'s Bosley Crowther gave a begrudging nod to the film he described as "gloomy and ponderous" with "moments of pathos," and while he let Reagan and Sheridan off with light smacks, he blasted Robert Cummings, describing his performance as "a musical comedy juvenile trying to find his bearings in a heavy Ibsenesque part."

Audiences, however, were unequivocal in their enthusiasm, and the film went on to become one of the year's highest grossing, an out-and-out smash.

With the government having set an April 19 deadline for Reagan to report for active duty, Wasserman wasted no time in returning to the bargaining table. Wasserman insisted that Reagan's new contract be torn up for an even newer one. This time the deal was to be for $3,500 a week, matching the highest salary Warner Bros. paid anyone, including Flynn, and his with forty-*three* weeks of movie-making a year. Warner agreed to it all. When Wasserman called in Reagan to sign the papers, it was the first time he had actually heard about the details of the deal and wondered why Wasserman had added three weeks to his already overloaded workweek. "Because," Wasserman explained, "I knew [Warner] wouldn't go higher than $3,500 a week and I've never written a $1 million deal before — so those three extra weeks for seven years makes this my first $1 million sale."

Ronald Reagan made history putting his signature on that contract, becoming the first actor in Hollywood to sign a contract worth a million dollars. For his part, Jack Warner wanted his money's worth, and quickly put together the next intended project for his newly high-priced star, one he hoped would cash in on the Reagan tsunami that was washing across America. So sure was Warner that he could get Reagan another deferment, that even before *Kings Row* opened, he had leaked the new project to the *Hollywood Reporter,* which announced the planned third re-pairing of the film's two costars on the front page of its January 5 edition:

> Ann Sheridan and Ronald Reagan will co-star for the third time in Warners' *Casablanca* with Dennis Morgan also coming in for top billing. Yarn of war refugees in French Morocco is based on an unproduced play by Murray Burnett and Joan Alison.

Despite pulling every string he could think of, Warner was unable to get Reagan another deferment and, even as talk began to build for an Academy Award nomination for his performance in *Kings Row,* Reagan was preparing to report to Fort Mason, in San Francisco, the traditional point of departure for soldiers assigned to overseas duty. He was convinced that by the time next year's Oscars were handed out, he would be overseas fighting in the trenches.

April 18, 1942, the night before he was

scheduled to leave, Wyman threw a surprise going-away party for him that seemed more a celebration than a tearful farewell. There to share in the champagne were Reagan's closest Hollywood friends and co-workers — Pat O'Brien, Ann Sheridan, Jack and Mary Benny, Barbara Stanwyck, and Robert Taylor.

The next morning, at the crack of dawn, uniformed and polished, with a smile and a final wave of his hand to his wife standing in a robe in the doorway, Reagan got into a waiting car supplied by the studio to take him to the airport. And just like that he was gone.

■ ■ ■ ■

CHAPTER SEVEN:
THIS IS THE ARMY

■ ■ ■ ■

Ronnie Reagan is ready and standing by. Just when his career and his personal life are rich with fulfillment, comes every indication that his services may be needed as a reserve member of the United States Cavalry. If he is called, the one hindrance may be the deficiency in his eyesight. Without his glasses, like Joan Bennett, Martha Scott and many others, Ronnie can't see clearly over five feet from him. Ronnie's adoring wife, Janey Wyman, isn't saying a word. But there's a hurt something in her face, as she goes gaily around Hollywood these days. Little Maureen Elizabeth, the baby Reagan, is too young and healthy to realize the drama that's going on around her.

— "Hot from Hollywood,"
Screenland magazine, January 1942

Lobby card for This Is the Army *(1943).*

Despite the massive troop buildup taking place, Ronald Reagan barely had time to unpack his duffel when a requisite wartime physical determined that his eyesight was so poor he could be assigned only to limited duties in noncombat situations. After just five weeks of boarding others onto transports headed off to battle in the Pacific, Reagan found himself back in Hollywood, assigned to the Army Air Corps' newly created First Motion Picture Unit (FMPU). The officer in charge and the one responsible for deciding who qualified for duty in it was none other than Lt. Col. Jack L. Warner.*

None of the major studios, and few of the independent ones, had escaped the government's virtual taking over of their operations

* It is widely believed that Lew Wasserman also played some part in getting Reagan transferred to the FMPU, although the author was not able to fully substantiate this.

to make propaganda and training films for the duration of the war. Therefore, commercial production schedules were, by necessity, either severely cut back or in some cases completely wiped out. Warners was hit particularly hard. In 1942, the studio produced just forty commercial feature films, down from its average of one hundred during the late thirties. Along with the drop in production came a drop in profits.

Jack Warner had worked during peacetime with Gen. Henry "Hap" Arnold, chief of staff of the Army Air Corps; whenever any studio needed the cooperation of the military in making a movie, it fell to Arnold to supply personnel and equipment, once he approved the scripts. When, shortly after Pearl Harbor, Arnold went to Warner about the possibility of acquiring the studio's help in making army training films, Jack Warner went him one better and floated the idea of the First Motion Picture Unit.

Because Warner didn't have enough physical space to devote to it and continue making commercial movies, the FMPU acquired space at the independent Vitagraph, which had plenty of unused acreage and the Hal Roach Studios in Culver City near MGM's headquarters, which was, because of the war, sitting vacant. Fort Roach (Fort Wacky to the self-titled "Culver City Commandos" who worked there) became the center of production of propaganda films for the FMPU, and at the same time something of a playground for its thirteen hundred actors, producers, and directors. Many of them were draftees like Reagan, who now found themselves drafted a second time, with a deferment that put them back in Hollywood to make movies for the government. If they had a little fun along the way, well, this was still Tinseltown, and as long as it got what it wanted, the army was more than willing to look the other way.

Unlike the private studios, which watched every cent and pushed productions deep into the night, before union regulations eventually put an end to that practice, Stateside military operated under a chaotic anarchy. Although Jack Warner and General Arnold were the titular heads, nobody was really in charge of anything and as long as movies were turned out — at its peak, Fort Roach made nearly ninety movies per year — because the government was paying, nobody really cared how much they cost or who made them. Reagan was thus able to spend most nights at home, doing pretty much what he had done before active duty, making military movies during the day and sleeping in his own bed at night.

That was not, however, the impression of the FMPU that the studio wanted to project to the public, and with Reagan especially, Jack Warner wanted to protect and preserve his actor's familiar and popular image for when the war ended. He insisted that Reagan only play enlisted or "everyman" roles, rather than officers and heroes. He saw to it that Reagan was on the front cover of every magazine, always in full uniform, smiling, and with a flag waving behind him, an image that became ubiquitous across America during the first years of the war. The FMPU also promoted Jane Wyman to the public as the dutiful war wife, sitting at home, alone, taking care of the children and worrying about the safety of her heroic husband with a patriotic smile on her face.

In truth, Wyman never came close to being anything like a housewife. Despite the onset of the war, she continued to work; she was in the middle of making a film when Reagan had first left for San Francisco. The movie was Gregory Ratoff's escapist Broadway-set comedy, *Footlight Serenade,* in which she played the sexy chorine opposite John Payne, with Phil Silvers thrown in for laughs. In July, two months after Reagan had quietly returned to Hollywood, the press was still running stories about the Reagans that had little to do with reality. The July 1942 edition of *Modern Screen* magazine reported "Jane breezed into [the Brown Derby] wearing a tailored suit and sun glasses and clutching a handful of business letters. She'll personally handle the Reagans' finances while Ronnie's gone. She showed us a letter she had received from Ronnie only this morning. It was full of the old Reagan pep and enthusiasm. There were long passages about Dr. Margaret Chung, the famous American-born woman surgeon he met in San Francisco. Dr. Chung, who is known as 'mother' to 475 leading American flyers, has 'sons' winging over Germany, Australia, China and every far corner of the world. Ronnie can't be a 'son,' but he hopes she'll accept him into a separate unit for friends of flyers."*

Jack Warner had good reason to want Reagan seen by the public as a war hero. Even the slightest hint that his man was getting an easy ride while others were going off to war could be disastrous for his career. The slightest whiff of any type of avoidance of duties could be catastrophic. Lew Ayres, who had become a star in Lewis Milestone's 1930 *All*

---

* The interview was done by Sylvia Kahn, who noted she'd met with Wyman on May 15, which, technically, was only four days before Reagan's actual return to Hollywood. The piece, however, ran in July, two full months after he was transferred to the FMPU. In September, the PR spin continued when *Photoplay* magazine, a competitor of *Modern Screen,* broke the "inside news" that "Jane Wyman and wee daughter are probably the happiest people in town since husband and daddy Ronald Reagan has been temporarily sent back to Burbank to make Government shorts."

Quiet on the Western Front, a film based on the antiwar novel by Erich Maria Remarque, became a conscientious objector and refused to be inducted into active military duty when World War II broke out. His career suffered irreparable damage because of it.

Frank Sinatra avoided the draft and never served in the military. A controversial recording he made in the forties later nearly got him blacklisted, and his career took a nearly ten-year hiatus from the top spot he had occupied in music during the midforties.*

And John Wayne, the celluloid hero of a thousand battles, whose movies came to neighborhood theaters complete with recruiting desks in the lobby to snag young boys who wanted to be just like "the Duke," managed to avoid conscription, even though he was still in his early thirties. His evasive ac-

* The song was "The House I Live In (That's America to Me)," written by Earl Robinson and Lewis Allen. It appeared in a ten-minute short of the same name written by Albert Maltz, who would later be blacklisted and jailed as one of the notorious "Hollywood Ten," and produced by Frank Ross and Mervyn LeRoy. Its intent was to oppose anti-Semitism and racial prejudice. It received an Honorary Academy Award, but several years later the message was reinterpreted as a call to a communist way of life, an especially sensitive topic as Sinatra, in the film, is singing to children.

tions were said to have caused a lifelong rift between him and his good friend and mentor, John Ford. It is also believed by many that Wayne's subsequent loyalism and his desire to portray military heroes on-screen was a form of personal atonement, and one of the reasons that (except for one nomination in 1949 in Allan Dwan's *Sands of Iwo Jima*) he didn't receive any nominations from the Academy for such landmark roles in films including Ford's 1952 *The Quiet Man;* his 1956 western classic, *The Searchers;* and his 1962 *The Man Who Shot Liberty Valance;* Howard Hawks's 1948 *Red River;* and dozens more outstanding performances from the more than two hundred films he made. It wasn't until Henry Hathaway's 1969 *True Grit,* a minor film in the Wayne canon, released at the height of the Vietnam War and Wayne's resurrection as uberpatriot, that he finally received his Oscar, as much a statement of older Hollywood's rejection of the new crop of antiwar and foreign-born filmmakers as it was an acknowledgment of Wayne's cartoonish performance.[†]

Errol Flynn, Warners' single biggest mon-

† Wayne won out over Dustin Hoffman and Jon Voight in John Schlesinger's *Midnight Cowboy,* Richard Burton in Charles Jarrott's *Anne of the Thousand Days,* and Peter O'Toole in Herb Ross's *Goodbye Mr. Chips.*

eymaking machine prior to the war, also avoided conscription; in 1942, he was brought up on rape charges that resulted in a trial before his acquittal. Flynn always maintained in private that those who opposed his reluctance to serve in the American armed forces set him up. Flynn still made movies but his career never fully recovered.

Laurence Olivier, part of the expatriate group of British actors who lived in Malibu as part of what was known as the Brit Pack, was slow to return to England in the late thirties when his country was already at war and only did so when the British government threatened to charge him with treason. His American film career never fully recovered. Cary Grant managed to avoid service by claiming an informal dual citizenship until he was officially too old to be drafted; once he acquired official U.S. citizenship, he made a few commercial films in which he played a submarine hero or a spy for the good guys. Others who served honorably included Jimmy Stewart, Robert Montgomery, Tyrone Power, David Niven, and Robert Taylor. Clark Gable enlisted and saw action after the death of his wife, Carole Lombard, in a plane crash in Nevada during a War Bonds drive. Although virtually all of them had trouble reestablishing their careers after the war, their war service made it more difficult for the studios not to make it seem as if they were at least trying to use them in movies.

Even those who didn't serve because of health, age, or other reasons not having to do with war resistance sought (or were ordered to by their studios) to find ways to contribute, for example, by volunteering in the Hollywood Canteen. Begun by John Garfield and Bette Davis, with the help of Jules Stein, it was a local stop for soldiers that offered them the chance to mingle with celebrities for a night. Some actors entertained troops domestically and overseas. This regular group included, most famously, Bob Hope, Bing Crosby, and Al Jolson. All in all, over a thousand Hollywood stars did one form or another of public service and played a crucial role in unifying America's civilian population against the Axis powers. That unification would never again be felt as strongly as it was during World War II, nor would entertainers ever again seem so unified behind the American armed forces.

If Reagan served in the FMPU with relative ease, he also had great enthusiasm for it, believing he was doing important work. He heeded Jack Warner's warning to never be seen around town at night looking as if he was having any civilian fun, and to make sure he always wore his uniform if he had to go out.

His most notable on-screen appearance during this period was in the short film *Rear*

Gunner (1943), made by the FMPU and directed by Ray Enright, which also starred Burgess Meredith, Tom Neal, and Dane Clark. Filmed outside of Las Vegas and Tucson, Arizona, the film tells the story of an innocent, shy farm boy (Meredith) who is drafted, trained as a gunnery, and comes under the influence of a friendly lieutenant (Reagan). The boy goes on to become a war hero and wins the Distinguished Service Cross, all in twenty-six action-packed minutes. The film caused thousands of young boys to enlist.

It struck a chord with American audiences, and its success resulted in dozens more like it with Reagan playing either himself on-screen or using his radio voice to serve as narrator. These short films include *Jap Zero** and Lewis Seiler's *Beyond the Line of Duty,* both made in 1942 (the latter most memorable for having the live voices of both future president Ronald Reagan and then president Franklin Delano Roosevelt in the same film), *For God and Country* (uncredited, 1943; Reagan plays a Catholic chaplain whose best friends, a Protestant and a Jew, both die in battle trying to save an Indian!), *Target Tokyo* (no directorial credit; 1945), *The Fight for the Sky* (no directorial credit; 1945), *Land and Live in the*

---

* Aka *Recognition of the Japanese Zero Fighter.*

Desert (uncredited; 1945), and *Fighter Bomber Against Mechanized Targets* (an uncredited and undated training-manual film).

Because of these movies, which were always shown in theaters in place of the first film or between it and the main feature, bagloads of fan mail for Reagan began arriving at Warner Bros. He became the second-most-written-to actor on the lot, surpassed only by Errol Flynn (whose mail, despite his legal troubles, usually contained dozens of proposals of marriage). To handle the load, this time Reagan arranged for Warner Bros. to pay his mother an additional $75 a week to answer them, the money to be deducted from his contract.

The studio's PR machine, at Jack L. Warner's personal directive, kept Reagan's name in all the popular movie magazines, such as *Modern Screen.* Here is an excerpt from one such piece that appeared in January, 1943: "It's nine months now since Ronald Reagan said, 'So long, Button-nose' to his wife and baby and went off to join his regiment! Poor Lieutenant Reagan ordered an expensive gift for Jane, only to be told by the shopkeeper that his charge account has been closed when he entered the service. His pockets revealed a mere $2.24. 'Charge it to my wife,' said he. 'She's still in pictures!' "

As usual, accuracy had little in common

with publicity. Nothing was true in the *Modern Screen* piece. Reagan was home and if "Button-nose" was "still in pictures," the word "barely" would have made that a more accurate depiction. The severe cutback in commercial film production meant that fringe actresses like Wyman were even less likely to find much new work. Because Reagan's million-dollar contract didn't kick in until he was discharged, she, Nelle, and the baby were barely able to get by.

In late 1942, Jack L. Warner resigned his commission to be able to return to making commercial movies. His studio, like every other one of the majors, was feeling the pinch and he successfully pled his case to the military. If he didn't start turning out films for profit, he warned, Warner Bros. would have to go out of business. The military agreed to a compromise; he could return to commercial films as long as he kept making ones for the government as well.

Once back at the studio, one of the first commercial features he made was Michael Curtiz's *Casablanca,* starring Humphrey Bogart. A World War I veteran too old to serve in World War II, Bogart was cast in the role Warner had originally designated for Reagan, whom the government insisted could not make for-profit movies while in the military.[*] Besides, he had no operating contract with the studio until he returned to civilian status. Jack Warner insisted to Reagan that he had tried to get him a special waiver for *Casablanca* but had been turned down (no evidence to support this has been found). More likely, by this time Warner felt Bogart was better suited to play Rick, which meant that Reagan was out and Bogart was in.

It was the first time Reagan felt the business fangs of Hollywood take a bite out of his own hide. Until now, he had believed, and with good reason, that as a favorite son of Jack Warner, he would always be cared for and protected by him. Now, here was Bogart playing a role that he, Reagan, had dearly wanted as his follow-up to *Kings Row.* And Reagan feared Bogart's costar would be Ann Sheridan, his own best, most compatible on-screen leading lady. However, with Reagan out, so was she; the part of Ilsa eventually went to Ingrid Bergman.

Casablanca would go on to win the Oscar

---

[*] According to most (but not all) sources, Bogart was not the first choice after Reagan. George Raft had turned down the part, and, reportedly, so did John Garfield. Bogart's age made it necessary to create the Paris back-story that justified his character's being an older man, for a film that was literally written as it was being filmed.

for Best Picture in 1943 over an unusually crowded wartime field of ten nominees. It permanently reignited Bogart's career, turning him into one of the hottest actors in Hollywood. Reagan was further disappointed because after all the anticipatory buzz, he wasn't even nominated the previous year for a Best Actor Academy Award for *Kings Row*. He attributed at least part of the reason to the lack of campaign support from Warner Bros., which had instead thrown its weight behind James Cagney for his performance in *Yankee Doodle Dandy,* a political self-purge and highly fictionalized biopic of Broadway legend George M. Cohan. It was well known in the industry that Cagney had made the film to prove to Jack Warner and Washington that despite his liberal-leftist views he was still a true red-white-and-blue American. Cagney conceived *Yankee Doodle Dandy* (with Michael Curtiz directing), as a way once and for all to put an end to the rumors that he was a communist. The public, eager for revenge after the bombing of Pearl Harbor, went wild over the film's relentless flag-waving. *Yankee Doodle Dandy* was an overwhelming success, restored Cagney's reputation as both a patriot and an actor with star power, and returned him to the front ranks of Hollywood movie stars.

As Reagan put it years later, "*Kings Row* was the only picture I was in for which there was ever any talk of getting an Academy Award. But that year, Warner Bros. also made *Yankee Doodle Dandy,* and in those days the studios usually got behind only one picture in the Oscar race, and it picked *Yankee Doodle Dandy.*" It was the closest Reagan, now a captain, had and ever would come to publicly expressing anything like disappointment toward Jack L. Warner.[*]

Wyman, meanwhile, was becoming more and more antsy, lonely, and worried about money as she anxiously awaited her next film assignment.[†] With her initial seven-year contract nearing its end, she wondered if she

---

[*] Cagney won the Oscar over Ronald Colman in Mervyn LeRoy's *Random Harvest,* Gary Cooper in Sam Wood's *Pride of the Yankees,* Walter Pidgeon in William Wyler's *Mrs. Miniver,* and Monty Woolley in Irving Pichel's *The Pied Piper.* Often forgotten is that Reagan was in a film nominated for Best Documentary that year, a short he had starred in, *Mr. Gardenia Jones,* directed by George Seitz, made at MGM for the War Activities Committee of the Motion Picture Industry.

[†] A little-known fact is that in August 1942, Wyman was commissioned in the army air corps as a second lieutenant. This was a highly promoted public-relations assignment that allowed cutesy comments like the one that appeared in *Screen Guide*'s August 1942 edition under the heading of "We're in the Army Now," which noted the contributions of the

might never work again, not only at Warner but anywhere, a concern shared by all the actresses in Hollywood whose career arcs continue to be always shorter and sharper than their male counterparts. They were and are like bubble gum to those who called the shots — easily unwrapped, immensely tasty for however so briefly a chew, and, with rare exception, spit out as soon as all the sugar was gone. She was, therefore, pleasantly surprised and greatly relieved when, most likely to take the pressure off Reagan, Jack Warner cast her in Peter Godfrey's 1944 *Make Your Own Bed,* a comedy about servants and Nazis; followed quickly by James Kern's 1944 *The Doughgirls,* another war-related sex comedy; and William Clemens's noirish 1944 *Crime by Night* (all of which were made in 1943). None of these films was memorable, but Wyman didn't care as long as the studio kept her on salary.

That same year, at the height of the war, Jack Warner settled on another film designed to at once wave the flag as high as *Yankee Doodle Dandy* had the year before and generate a lot of income (to quash any hint of war profiteering, a portion was donated to the

---

wives of stars who had been drafted. In reality, there was virtually no commitment required of Wyman, and she was not paid for her commission.

war effort). The vehicle was an adaptation of Irving Berlin's *This Is the Army,* which had just completed a successful run on Broadway. Berlin's show, for which he wrote the book, music, and lyrics (and produced, although he gave that credit in the program to "Uncle Sam"), was a collection of old or unused songs he had pulled out of the trunk, some of which had originally appeared in his 1917 Broadway musical *Yip, Yip, Yaphank,* updated to capture the fervor of patriotism sweeping the country; he even appeared in the show himself to sing what he considered his personal anthem, "Oh How I Hate to Get Up in the Morning." For the film's rousing finale, "This Is the Last Time," Warner sought a chorus of 350 real soldiers dressed in battle gear to do the job.

To convince the army to let him make the musical and lend him all the soldiers he requested, Warner, together with Berlin (who wanted the movie made as much for the continuation of his own, somewhat stagnated Hollywood career as any patriotic concerns), promised the film's first million dollars would go to the army's relief fund to help needy soldiers and their families. The army was so delighted they even okayed Jack Warner's personal request to let Reagan be the non-singing star of the decidedly commercial movie, which Warner hoped would put to rest any lingering ill will over *Casablanca* and

Yankee Doodle Dandy that Reagan might still be feeling.

Reagan was thrilled to be back on a soundstage in a first-class, big-budget Hal Wallis production with a top-drawer screenplay adaptation by *Kings Row*'s Casey Robinson. Despite the fact that his nonsinging performance all but disappears behind Berlin's grand score, as far as Reagan was concerned, Warner had done him right by getting him into this movie of a play-within-a-play and giving him a real character, the son of a Broadway producer (played by George Murphy), who is drafted and put in charge of producing an army show with real soldiers. At its completion, the cast marches off the stage and goes directly to war.

Warner musicals were particularly good at blurring the realities of the stage and screen. In *This Is the Army,* just as in *Yankee Doodle Dandy,* both directed by the versatile Michael Curtiz, the stage numbers would be impossible to do on any stage. In both, during big production numbers, the scenery falls away and somehow becomes the place that the songs are singing about; in other words, they changed from filmed theater into *movies* (in *Yankee Doodle Dandy* this worked especially well in numbers like "Grand Old Flag" and the final scene in the picture, when Cohan [Cagney] joins a parade in Washington in which the soldiers are singing "Over There," a scene that looks less real than it is). In the finale of *This Is the Army,* it feels as if the entire armed forces are onstage, about to march off it into war.

If there was any downside for Reagan during all of this, it was in the Ides of March comment made to him during production by none other than the legend of lyrics and melody himself, Irving Berlin. Having been introduced to the aging and increasingly aloof legendary composer, Reagan was unexpectedly pulled aside one day by Berlin, who wanted to give him a compliment. Having confused him with all the real soldiers on the set (and Reagan, of course, *was* a real soldier), he told the young actor, "You really should give this business some consideration when the war is over. It's very possible you could have a career in show business."

Reagan thanked Berlin and walked away, stunned. What was Berlin saying? That he had never heard of him? Or that he had simply forgotten who Reagan was? It was at this moment that Reagan began to wonder if he would ever get back to the prewar level of popularity he had attained with *Kings Row,* if his audience would still be waiting for him when the war finally ended, if it ever did.

He had good cause to be concerned. Four more years were to pass before Reagan would appear in another commercial feature.

■ ■ ■ ■

By the end of 1943, however, because of *This Is the Army,* Reagan found himself for the moment still riding high, wide, and handsome atop Hollywood's wartime-thin list of most-popular actors. On the strength of *Kings Row,* which grossed about $3 million in its initial domestic release, and *This Is the Army,* which quadrupled that, taking in a fantastic $12 million, Reagan moved slightly ahead of Cagney, Flynn, and Bogart to the top of one of the most important industry popularity polls.*

Reagan was thrilled but wary; he had been in the business long enough to know what these numbers really meant. They were reflections of the past, interest paid on the pictures he had already banked for Warner Bros. With 1943 coming to an end and nothing for him to do but appear in more propaganda films, he found himself with plenty of downtime, which he hoped to spend with his wife. Unfortunately for him, she had other plans.

* According to *Box Office Records,* for the movie season 1942–1943, Reagan scored 195 percent, a relative score that placed him at the top of a list whose top five included Jimmy Cagney (186), Bing Crosby (176), Clark Gable (171), and Cary Grant (169).

Wyman was now spending every minute of her day at the studio, making movies.

For a number of reasons, this made Reagan increasingly uneasy. His vision of a wife had always been that of the little woman at home wearing an apron with the broom in one hand and a baby's bottom cradled in the other. The fact that his wife was working was bad enough; the fact that he wasn't made it all that much worse. He had been brought up that the man of the house was the one who was supposed to bring home the bacon, not the other way around. With nothing but time on his hands, he searched for something worthwhile to do. (Reagan considered his military service patriotic duty rather than a job.)

If his wife was no longer available to sit and listen to his political speeches, there were plenty of organizations in Hollywood that were. Like all the other members who had suspended their memberships during military service, he still had access to the headquarters bulletin boards, where new and ad hoc groups posted daily invitations to meetings. These organizations were either left over from the thirties, when it seemed that everyone was the member of something, or new ones that had formed around the increasing polarization of the growing union discontent in Hollywood, a situation the war and its unifying sentiments had somewhat muted but by no means eliminated.

While trying to decide which ones he might want to look into, he happened to run into Sam Wood and, after meeting a few times, was personally invited by him to join the Motion Picture Alliance for the Preservation of American Ideals (MPA), made up of some of Hollywood's most important and talented citizenry. The group had secretly formed in late 1943 and had not officially introduced itself to the rest of the industry until February 1944, when its members held a news conference in a suite at the Beverly Wilshire Hotel to announce their organization's existence.

Although many of its founders were good friends of Reagan's, people he had worked with ever since he'd arrived in Hollywood, he turned down Wood's offer. It was the secrecy aspect that had bothered him. He didn't understand why an organization that was trying to have its voice heard had originally chosen to operate covertly, unless they had something to hide.

It was a tactic that had been used before by the MPA's founding members, Wood, Wayne, Disney, art director Cedric Gibbons, director/writer Norman Taurog, director Clarence Brown, screenwriter Casey Robinson, and columnist Hedda Hopper. Other early supports of the MPA included actors Adolphe Menjou, Ward Bond, Clark Gable, Ginger

Rogers, and Robert Taylor; and labor mediator Roy Brewer (who replaced Bioff and Browne as IATSE's official representative in Hollywood after both were convicted of extorting $550,000 from five major studios to prevent union disruptions; in 1955, Bioff was killed by a bomb rigged to the starter of his car). Brewer eventually became the official government enforcer of the notorious industry-wide blacklist of the late forties and early fifties.[*]

[*] The secrecy was part of the legacy of something called the Committee of 21, an anonymous strike-breaking organization that had formed during the Disney strike that accused the strikers, led by Herb Sorrell, of being communists. Several ads appeared in the trades during the strike that were paid for "anonymously," signed only by "The Committee of 21." It has long been believed but never definitively proven that Disney and Sam Wood were the only members of the committee. One such ad that ran in several local newspapers on May 21, 1941, stated the following: "We are continuing our investigations of your [strikers'] leaders and of some of you. We are not yet ready to disclose our identity or to turn over our findings to the proper authorities. We are not yet willing to report on what you have been doing and saying until you yourself answer the question of your own conscience: 'AM I A LOYAL AMERICAN OR A LOYAL DUPE.' The COMMITTEE OF 21 holds this conviction that anyone

When the MPA finally did go public, it announced its existence with the following statement (which strongly resembled those first issued by the "Committee of 21"): "In our special field of motion pictures, we resent the growing impression that this industry is made up of, and dominated by, Communists, radicals, and crack-pots . . . we pledge to fight, with every means at our organized command, any effort of any group or individual, to divert the loyalty of the screen from the free America that gave it birth."

Despite Wood's attempt to recruit him, Reagan, who considered himself a mainstream Roosevelt liberal, politely declined the offer. Instead, he sampled one group after another, attending meetings of those he thought might interest him, two, three, sometimes four times a week. Eventually, one of them did catch his eye: the more correct-sounding (to him) Hollywood Democratic Committee (HDC).[*]

He discovered the HDC through Bernard

---

who knows the facts and fails to speak out in this hour of our national emergency must be judged as equally guilty with those who are seeking the destruction of DEMOCRACY."

[*] The Hollywood Democratic Committee, one of the older organizations in Hollywood, originally formed in the thirties, alongside the American Com-

Vorhaus, an older writer-director veteran who had worked in film alongside Cecil B. DeMille since the industry's inception. Vorhaus's commercial career, like Reagan's, had been suspended when his services were acquired by the FMPU. Vorhaus was a New York–born, Harvard-educated filmmaker who had made a breakthrough with *The Last Journey* in 1936, followed by a number of undistinguished films until he was enlisted by the government to make propaganda movies. Like Reagan, he was ambitious and uneasy with the amount of free time he had on his hands. And, like Reagan, he was liberal leaning, only much more to the left. (Vorhaus had joined the anti-Nazi league in 1938, one of several organizations later named by the MPA as a communist front. It was a move that eventually earned him a place alongside many others on the notorious blacklist. This

---

munist Party, as the Motion Picture Democratic Committee. After the country entered World War II, to separate itself from the growing problems of the prewar American Communist Party, many of whose members had also been members of the MPDC, the group, which was considered one of the three most important left-wing organizations (along with the Hollywood Anti-Nazi League and the Motion Picture Artists' Committee) changed its name to the Hollywood Democratic Committee.

would cut short and permanently end his American filmmaking career and set him among Hollywood's most gifted but "forgotten" talent. After the war and the HUAC investigations, Vorhaus lived the rest of his days in England, traveling to Italy to work on films and TV shows produced there, and apprenticing a young David Lean, who would go on to direct such Hollywood blockbusters as 1962's *Lawrence of Arabia.*)

However, in 1943, Vorhaus was still a Hollywood mainstream player and an active recruiter for the HDC, as persistent and persuasive as Wood was for the MPA. Reagan liked the more liberal message, joined the HDC, and became the newest of HDC's thousand-plus members, whose board of directors consisted of a number of known Hollywood liberal/left including Gene Kelly, Olivia de Havilland, lyricist Ira Gershwin, screenwriter Howard Lawson, and union leader Herb Sorrell, who had successfully led the animators' strike against Disney that had made him one of Sam Wood's most avowed enemies.*

* Reagan makes no specific reference in either of his memoirs to his 1943 membership in the HDC. Lou Cannon confuses Reagan's membership in HDC with his later membership in the postwar Hollywood Independent Citizens Committee of the Arts, Sciences, and Professions (HICCASP), which

Reagan stayed mostly in the background of HDC, because he had lately been assigned to work on a secret military mission to make training and survival films specifically for those pilots who would be assigned the dangerous task of bombing the Japanese all the way back to Tokyo. That assignment took most of 1944 to complete. The only time during this period he did take any active part in HDC activities was on the eve of the 1944 presidential election, when Roosevelt was perceived to be the most vulnerable he had been at any time in his three-term presidency for having dumped his popular vice president, Henry Wallace, for the far less liberal Harry Truman. The night before the polls opened, the HDC ably assisted the Democratic National Committee by urging its members to participate in a pro-Roosevelt radio broadcast that ran live on all four radio networks. Those members who did included Humphrey Bogart, who served as the narrator, Judy Gar-

---

was formed out of what remained of HDC. In his memoirs *(AAL)*, Reagan identifies his "brief" membership in HICCASP as beginning after the end of the war, and alludes to HDC only indirectly, by including it, unnamed, as among "other organizations" he had previously joined. Upon his discharge from the military, Reagan joined only one other political organization, the American Veterans Committee.

land, Groucho Marx, lyricist "Yip" Harburg, Tallulah Bankhead, Joan Bennett, Irving Berlin, Claudette Colbert, Joseph Cotten, John Garfield, Rita Hayworth, George Jessel, Danny Kaye, Gene Kelly, George Raft, Edward G. Robinson, Lana Turner, and . . . Jane Wyman. At her urging, Reagan gave $100 to the Roosevelt reelection campaign committee shortly before the broadcast took place.

Whenever he did have any free time, he preferred the always lively political discussions held at either Jack Benny's or George Burns's homes in Beverly Hills, where the drinks flowed and the rhetoric overflowed. Most often, it was Reagan, occasionally joined by his brother Neil, who would commandeer the floor at one end of the pool and lecture about political issues of the day until the crowd slowly dispersed.

In 1945, the war finally ended and on September 12, after nearly four years of active service, Capt. Ronald Reagan was officially discharged. As per the terms of their contract, Jack Warner immediately reinstated him at full salary and also promised to put him in a new movie as soon as a suitable script came along. Reagan was relieved to finally be earning more than military pay and was more than eager to resume the commercial film career he had been forced to leave at the peak of his popularity.

He waited, patiently at first, for that suitable script, and while doing so hosted, along with Wayne Morris and Bette Davis, a huge "Welcome Home" ceremony thrown by Warner Bros. on its Hollywood back lot for all employees who had been in the armed forces or done voluntary service during the war. Unfortunately, for Reagan, there was relatively little attention paid that night by the press to the returning, veteran actors. Instead, they were all focused on the new and upcoming kids in town — Van Johnson, Peter Lawford, Robert Walker, Tom Drake, Cornel Wilde, Gregory Peck, and dozens of others in attendance who had come into their own while their older and more established counterparts had been taken out of cinematic action by the military.[*]

This and other welcome-home parties

---

[*] Van Johnson had been in a serious car accident in 1942 that left him with a metal plate in his head, exempting him from military duty. Peter Lawford went through a plate-glass window as a child that severely limited the use of one of his arms, making him ineligible for military duty. Robert Walker did not serve in the military for reasons that are not clear but may have had to do with his lifelong bouts with mental instability. Tom Drake was exempted from duty in the military because of a chronic heart condition. Cornel Wilde's parents were European-

ended soon enough, as the euphoria of victory that had swept across America, from Times Square to Hollywood and Vine, quickly morphed into the paranoia that would fuel the coming Cold War, with an American government led, after Roosevelt's death, by the far more conservative Harry Truman. As early as Potsdam, the postwar Soviet threat had been widely perceived by the West as one that would have to be dealt with, sooner rather than later. Within a year of the bombings of Hiroshima and Nagasaki, the threat of Stalin's Soviet Union and its intention to spread communism throughout the world would light the fuse that reinvigorated Washington investigations into internal subversive activities. The stage was set for the return of a more powerful HUAC to Hollywood, and in its wake the infamous industry-wide blacklist. The new fear of being tainted for past actions was pervasive among Hollywood's liberal faction. Organizations like the HDC changed their names, in this instance to the Hollywood Independent Citizens Committee of the Arts, Sciences, and Professions (HICCASP), and tried to move their political foundation away from the fringe left

---

born and he spent much of World War II overseas with them. Gregory Peck received a deferment because he was a medical student in college.

and closer to the mainstream center. Slowly but surely, they continued to try to purge any remaining communists from their midst before the government did it for them.

While Reagan sorted out his political affiliations, and continued to wait for a phone call from the studio that would put him back to work, he tried to pay more attention to family life and fatherhood. Wyman wanted to have another child, but with a schedule that kept her busier than ever as the studios cranked themselves back to full operating levels, she did not want to become pregnant again and halt the momentum of her invigorated career. Instead, she tried to convince Reagan that they should adopt a baby. He finally agreed, and on March 21, three days after he was born and several months before Reagan was actually discharged, newborn Michael was welcomed into the family.

The studio PR machine, always looking for a way to get the names of the studios into the papers with "good news," immediately ratcheted up, running numerous "cute" stories about the happy addition to the perfect Reagan household. One of them headlined the news that four-year-old Maureen had wanted to buy a baby brother on a shopping spree the previous Christmas in Beverly Hills and wondered why it had taken so long to be delivered.

However, it was well known by this time throughout Hollywood that the Reagan marriage was anything but perfect. Reagan's military service had put a far heavier financial burden than either of them had anticipated on Wyman's shoulders. She didn't tolerate it well. She believed she had married one of Hollywood's most popular up-and-coming stars and felt secure that he would be the breadwinner of the family. Considering Wyman had always relied on older, father-figure men who appeared well to do but in fact were deadbeats, her fear that Reagan had turned out to be a better-dressed, better-looking, better-meaning version of all the others led to some dicey domestic times. As early as 1944, the following excerpt ran as part of a story that appeared in *Modern Screen:* "It's Ronnie who's Irish, but Jane who's moody. Up in the clouds or down in the depths of gloom — never a happy medium, no matter how she tries, and she tries hard — 'My husband and I,' says Jane, 'are like Scotch and Soda (their dogs).' . . . If things at the studio upset her, she gripes about them at home. She flies off the handle. She knows she shouldn't, but she does. When Ronnie's around, he tries to calm her down. But she doesn't want to be calm, she wants to storm — 'You don't know what things are like. You've been away too long' [even though Reagan lived at home for almost the entire duration of the war] . . . Time passes and she cools off — realizing that Ronnie has his own problems, that it can't be fun to come home on a week-end pass and listen to her beef. Her conscience smites her."

In January 1946, amid growing talk in Hollywood that, despite the arrival of little Michael, there was still trouble between the Reagans, *Modern Screen* revisited the marriage. This time the reporting was more blunt: "When rumors started that all was not well with the Reagans, Ronnie got to the base of it, found the culprit and warned him that, uniform or not, he'd throttle him if he didn't retract statements." *Modern Screen* was being kind, probably at the behest of the studio, downplaying the impossible-to-ignore rumors and declining to name Wyman's "secret" lover (believed by most to be Van Johnson) in favor of a sympathetic description of an increasingly frustrated but resolutely two-fisted Reagan looking to defend his marriage the good, old-fashioned American way.

Despite all their denials, the problems between the Reagans were deeper and more difficult even than third-party affairs. Work, or the lack of it, was driving Reagan crazy; as his star continued its rapid fall from its dizzying heights of 1943, even as Wyman's continued its amazing ascension into the Hollywood stratosphere. By 1945, the distance between them stretched beyond the professional; they were barely speaking to each other and technically no longer living under the same roof.

Wyman had taken the two children and relocated for the summer to Lake Arrowhead in the San Bernardino Mountains, where she was shooting Clarence Brown's *The Yearling,* based on the Marjorie Kinnan Rawlings novel about a young girl who falls in love with a deer that she eventually adopts. The book and the film owed a great deal to the international popularity of Disney's *Bambi.*

The Yearling was a top-of-the-line MGM production, the second film of a two-picture loan-out for Wyman that Jack L. Warner had arranged for her in 1944. Needing to raise cash, Warner lent out as many of his stars as possible. The first picture sent her to Paramount and Billy Wilder for *The Lost Weekend,* his film based on Charles R. Jackson's powerful story that dealt with the ravages of alcoholism. Made in 1944 and released in '45, it proved a tremendous hit with audiences and had — quite unexpectedly to everyone in Hollywood, but no one more than to Jack L. Warner — made a major star out of Wyman, who played the long-suffering fiancée opposite the brilliant Ray Milland, in one of the best performances of his long and distinguished career. The film struck an emotional nerve with audiences as it looked under the covers of a seemingly successful, stable, handsome young man whose life was ruined by his addiction. They sensed, on some metaphorical level, a correlation between the alcoholic, Austrian/Hungarian-born, German-raised Jewish refugee, and the surface euphoria in America that had prevailed for most of the war years and the cracks in it that the Cold War was about to split wide open.

In truth, *The Lost Weekend* was, like all film, less emotionally prescient than intellectually reflective. Wilder rightly described the inner conflicts of his symbolic "hero" as the way most Americans felt during the long years of the war. After the early chauvinistic fervor that followed the bombing of Pearl Harbor, disappointment in the war's length and its devastating numbers of casualties as well as doubt about the eventual outcome caused many to question the leadership of Roosevelt. (This contributed to the Republican strength in the 1942 midterm elections and the ongoing influence of the American Communist Party, the two politically opposed extremes of the public's discontent that both benefited from.) The uncomplicated screen heroes depicted during the war years, including *Casablanca*'s seemingly rebellious Rick (who was, in reality, just one more heartbroken patriot carrying a dimmed but still glowing torch), were being replaced by younger actors who played even more neurotic, conflicted, well-meaning but hopelessly damaged good bad guys, manifestations of the war's real American rebels. Wilder's real message in *The Lost Weekend* (the title itself suggestive of the years spent at war) was not that the country's soldier-boy heroes had changed, but that Hollywood's ability to portray them in a more dramatically realistic, adult fashion had.

Although Wyman wasn't nominated for her role (the film would win four Oscars), after a decade and a half of struggling for recognition, her on-screen suffering, which perfectly reflected the feelings of the women left behind by the soldiers of World War II — a helplessness cut with rage — resonated so deeply with female audiences that it thrust her into the front ranks of Hollywood's leading ladies.*

Wyman's decision to relocate to Lake Arrowhead for the duration of the filming of *The Yearling* wasn't just for convenience. By the time shooting began, her hard-won success brought with it a marked reduction in her need for father figures to care for her. Fame became her only and best parent and husband, the adulation of millions of men of all ages far more meaningful to her than the

---

* *The Lost Weekend* won Best Picture, Best Director (Wilder), Best Actor (Milland), and Best Screenplay (Wilder and Charles Brackett).

love of one. Playing perfect women on-screen more than made up for her own self-perceived imperfections of real life.

In *The Yearling,* Wyman played the role of Ma Baxter, opposite Gregory Peck as her husband, Ezra "Penny" Baxter; they are the parents of the story's central character, Jody Baxter, played by Claude Jarman, Jr. The film was an MGM deluxe vehicle, a first postwar extravaganza, the studio's biggest and most expensive production since 1939's *Gone With the Wind.* Every leading lady in Hollywood wanted the part of Ma Baxter but Wyman, on the strength of her performance in *The Lost Weekend,* got it. Even before it was finished, there was Oscar buzz for both the film and Wyman.

Meanwhile, Reagan couldn't get a job. No matter how hard he tried to press Lew Wasserman (which was not very hard; nobody ever successfully "pressed" Wasserman), who in turn tried to get Warner to find that perfect script for Reagan, nothing came his way. And when he visited the set of *The Yearling,* he purposely stayed as far away as he could from Wyman while she filmed her scenes, allowing himself to get pushed into the background of the shoot's enormous on-site location camp. When he decided to stay on location for the duration, he was quickly relegated by Wyman to the role of glorified babysitter while she sizzled on-screen opposite one of the post-war's newest and brightest leading men, the dark-haired, youthful, and manly Peck (whose good looks made Reagan feel even older, his face having aged into full adulthood during his years in the army). Peck had been pulled up to prominence in 1944, when the war had created a vacuum of leading men in Hollywood, after he starred in John Stahl's neoreligious *The Keys of the Kingdom,* for which Peck, still a relative unknown, was nominated for a Best Actor Academy Award.

"All I wanted to do," Reagan later wrote of his time at Lake Arrowhead, "was to rest up awhile, make love to my wife, and come up refreshed to a better job in an ideal world. As it came out, I was disappointed in all these postwar ambitions." Indeed, the more his star fell, the more Wyman's rose. After he was reportedly addressed as "Mr. Wyman" by a crew member on the set of *The Yearling,* he simply couldn't take any more and returned to Los Angeles by himself, to the site of a new ranch he and Wyman had purchased but not as yet moved into, an eight-acre spread in Northbridge, in the San Fernando Valley. He hoped to pass the time putting up rail posts for enclosures to hold what would one day be a stable of breeding horses.

Reagan named the new ranch "Yearling Row," a combination of his wife's present film project and his most successful past one.

The only other thing that kept him busy was politics. Upon his discharge he had reactivated his membership in SAG and reclaimed his seat on the board, this time as an alternate, first for Rex Ingram and then Boris Karloff, both of whom had taken his place on it while he'd been away.* After putting up railings all day, he would drive into Hollywood to attend meetings for SAG, the American Veterans Committee (AVC), and HICCASP. Unlike the latter, which, to Reagan's way of thinking, was becoming increasingly polluted with unrepentant leftists, he considered the AVC untainted and untaintable because it was made up of veterans. Among its many notable and politically unimpeachable members were such war heroes as General Eisenhower and Audie Murphy, Franklin D. Roosevelt, Jr., the celebrated cartoonist and actor Bill Mauldin, and the theologian Reinhold Niebuhr.

In March of that same year, 1945, just as the studios were planning to ramp up their production schedules to recover from the stagnation the war had imposed on their

---

* He did not regain his full board position until September 1946, when he was elected vice president of the Guild.

industry, a massive stagehand strike hit the industry, one of the reasons, upon his discharge, Reagan believed Jack Warner had been unable to prioritize his obligations and find a film for an actor he was paying $3,500 a week to stay home and put up fences. The strike was led by none other than Herb Sorrell, the big, burly rough-and-tough stage worker who had successfully united the opposition against Disney during the animators' 1940 strike. Flush with that victory, the pugnacious Sorrell had continued to challenge IATSE's (International Alliance of Theatrical Stage Employees) dominance and unified several other industry unions into a consortium he called the Conference of Studio Unions (CSU). Sorrell's goal was to eventually replace IATSE, which he and others considered hopelessly corrupt and infiltrated with members of organized crime, with his upstart CSU. The March strike against the studios that remained aligned with IATSE, which was all of them, was how he intended to do it.

This time Sorrell's strikers immediately came up against IATSE's new, post-Bioff-and-Brown mob leader, Roy Brewer, who refused to acknowledge the legitimacy of the CSU while at the same time pledging to clean up any remaining bad elements in IATSE, to rid it of the last vestiges of mob affiliations and corruption as a way to maintain his union's position with the studios and keep any of its members from defecting to the CSU. Trying to get rid of the striking CSU picketers, he wound up employing many of the same thug tactics as his predecessors — scabs, tear gas, fire hoses, private studio police forces, fire department–supplied hoses, and local precinct police forces.

Brewer's methods only made Sorrell's picketers dig in that much deeper. The strike, in its various stages, would last for the better part of two years and polarize Hollywood as it had never been before. In September, the seventh month of the increasingly bitter and hostile strike, Brewer, sensing he was losing momentum to Sorrell, resorted to the lowest kind of retreat, the usual last resort in Hollywood in those days. He declared that not only any members who left IATSE for CSU but *anyone* in Hollywood who supported Sorrell were revealing themselves to be communists because the CSU was nothing more than a communist front and its leader a hard-core Communist Party recruiter.

In a letter sent to all Hollywood union members (which was virtually everybody in Hollywood), Brewer officially threw down the political gauntlet when he wrote, "Do you, as an individual, support the campaign of slander, vilification, lies and scurrility now being carried on against our officers and

315

those loyal American workers who believe in and support the IATSE, and who, by doing so, have incurred the enmity and hatred of the entire communist *'apparat'*?" The letter set off a blistering round of accusations and cross-accusations and had the opposite effect of what Brewer had intended by further dividing, rather than uniting, Hollywood's unions.

It was into this maelstrom of alphabet-soup warfare that Reagan had blithely stepped, having been out of the loop since his years in the military, during which time he had remained largely unaware of the growing intensity of the situation. After attending a meeting in January 1946 of HICCASP, he was surprised to learn that despite Brewer's letter, there was still a great deal of support among its membership for the CSU. While Reagan had always been sympathetic to Sorrell and his cause, he had nonetheless been disturbed by the charges hurled against the CSU by Brewer (as a member of SAG, Reagan had received a copy of the Brewer letter, which he considered at the time nothing less than Red-baiting) and wanted HICCASP to announce its support for Sorrell, or at least his right to strike without being branded a communist for doing so.

To make that happen, he invited de Havilland, James Roosevelt, and a few other of HICCASP's more influential members up to the still-unfinished ranch house for a strategy meeting. Working through the night they came up with an idea to formulate a compromise statement of sorts that declared HICCASP's support for CSU's right to strike, and at the same time denounced communism. At the end of its Statement of Ideals, HICCASP declared, "We reaffirm our belief in free enterprise and the democratic system and repudiate communism as desirable for the United States." To Reagan's surprise, it would take several more months for HICCASP's membership to decide whether or not it could support that statement because of the inclusion of the communist repudiation.

While members of HICCASP debated which side they were on, Reagan finally returned to his paying job, that of being an actor for Warner Bros., when Jack L. Warner personally called him to come in from the cold and start work on a new film. As reluctant as he was to cross the CSU's picket lines, which had gone up around every major studio including Warner's, he did so at the urging of Lew Wasserman.

At first, Reagan had been thrilled with his assignment, a film called *Stallion Road*, directed by James V. Kern and produced by Warners' new A unit, following Wallis's departure to form his own independent production company, after the runaway success of *Casablanca.*[*] Kern, a onetime singer and screenwriter, was strictly a B director, a *metteur en scène* type who simply allowed the shots of his shooting script to tell the story by describing the plot, with no stylistic overlays (like writing in block letters rather than cursive).[**] The film was to star the ultrahot Hollywood couple, Humphrey Bogart

[*] *Casablanca* won three Oscars: Best Picture, Best Director (Michael Curtiz), and Best Screenplay (Julius Epstein, Philip Epstein, Howard Koch). Although Wallis had made his decision to leave after *Casablanca*'s Oscar success in 1943, he stayed on at Warner Bros. long enough to complete the several projects to which he was already committed, including *This Is the Army* and a sequel of sorts to *Casablanca,* Curtiz's 1944 *Passage to Marseilles,* which reunited Wallis, Curtiz, Bogart, and Claude Rains. Wallis's first independently produced film was William Seiter's *The Affairs of Susan,* a comic vehicle designed to show off the talents of Joan Fontaine. It was distributed by Paramount.

[**] To understand the difference between an *auteur* and a *metteur en scène,* think of the original document of the Declaration of Independence and the difference between the same words written in plain block letters and the flowing, beautiful script of Thomas Jefferson. The content is the same, but the style of the presentation makes all the difference in the world (as the signers of the Declaration understood).

and Lauren Bacall. Media darlings, their story was made all the more fascinating by the wide gap in their ages; they'd first met during the filming of Howard Hawks's 1944 adaptation of Hemingway's *To Have and Have Not* when he was forty-four and she was nineteen. He had been married and divorced three times by then; she had never been married.

Then, suddenly and without any explanation, other than saying *Stallion Road* was not the kind of picture they wanted to make, Bogart and Bacall withdrew from it. Although no real explanation has ever been given (years later Bogart unconvincingly claimed he had a natural aversion to Westerns), it was hard to avoid the fact that Reagan and Bogart had serious differences over HICCASP's position regarding its Statement of Principles. Bogart and Bacall had not wanted communism to be repudiated as the price paid for supporting the CSU strike. Moreover, Bogart, who did not think much of the script, the director, or the producer, was not eager to work with an actor like Reagan, whose reputation was increasingly that of a Hollywood has-been.

With Bogart and Bacall literally out of the picture, it quickly fell from its perch of importance. Warner demoted it from an A to a B, Zachary Scott and Alexis Smith replaced Bogie and Bacall, and the budget was cut so deeply that the film, originally scheduled to be shot in Technicolor, was made in black and white.

Stallion Road is about the life of a horse breeder (Reagan) who is also a veterinarian involved in a triangular love affair (Scott and Smith) while battling an outbreak of anthrax. He then comes down with it himself, only to be miraculously saved by Smith and an experimental serum.

The script was a troubled one from the start, and after the departure of Bogart and Bacall, one of the writers Jack Warner hired to try to fix it was William Faulkner. He had been lured to Hollywood for the money he always seemed to need, but hated the film. When first informed that he was being assigned to a Western, a modern-dress one of all things, he asked original scriptwriter Stephen Longstreet who was in it. "A horse," Longstreet said, wryly. "I mean the human," Faulkner replied. "Who's the lead?" "Ronald Reagan." Later on, when the film opened, Faulkner sent Longstreet a note that read, "If you're a horse, you'll like the picture."

The film went nowhere and Reagan found himself back on the Warner fringe, with all the heat and momentum he had built up from *Knute Rockne* and *Kings Row* gone with the wind.

During the making of *Stallion Road,* Reagan

tried as best he could to keep abreast of what was happening with the strike. At a HICCASP meeting that July, the first Reagan attended after the filming of *Stallion Road,* screenwriter John Howard Lawson (who would later be blacklisted), Bogart, and several others opposed the part of the statement that denounced communism and demanded it be put to a vote by the entire board. To Reagan's surprise and dismay, his Statement of Ideals was resoundingly defeated (de Havilland was the only board member of HICCASP who voted for it). As a result Reagan, de Havilland, and Roosevelt all resigned their membership in HICCASP. Years later, in his memoir, Reagan would imply that his resignation was immediate, from an organization that was hopelessly infiltrated by communists at the time of his withdrawal and about to "give its last groan and expire."*

* In fact, HICCASP did not expire. It continued to centralize within the mainstream and merged again, this time with the National Citizens Political Action Committee (NCPAC), which in turn became the Progressive Citizens of America (PCA), an extremely liberal/left organization that nevertheless supported Henry Wallace's 1948 unsuccessful Progressive Party campaign for president. The exact date of Reagan's resignation is not clear. No official date is recorded and reports vary, although Rea-

While a defeat for Reagan's more moderate faction of the organization, it was a resounding victory for the communist faction that managed to retain a strong postwar union presence, not only in HICCASP but throughout Hollywood, despite the disastrous wartime German-Russian nonaggression pact and the growing chill between the Soviet Union and the United States. After Reagan left, HICCASP replaced the departed moderate Roosevelt with the more liberal producer Dore Schary, and (then) liberal/leftist Frank Sinatra took over moderate de Havilland's place as vice chairman.

At the same time HICCASP was undergoing its shift to the left, the Society for Motion Picture Interior Decorators (SMPID), a small contingency of studio laborers, switched its allegiance from IATSE to the CSU, a move that rippled through the entire industry. Despite SMPID's relatively small membership, this was considered a major victory for the feisty, barrel-chested Herb Sorrell, who was becoming as well known for his colorful

---

gan's account in his memoir *(AAL)* indicates that it may have happened that July, immediately after the controversial Statement of Ideals had been rejected by HICCASP. The organization's records indicate he did not officially resign until late August, suggesting that Reagan gave his resignation more thought than the instantaneous decision he recalled.

rhetoric and fist-waving brand of leadership as many of the actors sympathetic to his cause.

Energized by SMPID's move, Sorrell called for an intensification of the ongoing strike, this time pushing for SAG's support, even as the studios continued to support IATSE and wanted SAG to side with them. SAG was by far the largest and most influential union, and its support was crucial for either side. If SAG went with CSU and honored its picket lines, it almost certainly meant an industry-wide shutdown; Hollywood could not make movies without movie stars.

Reagan, meanwhile, was being pressured by SAG's president, Robert Montgomery, to join him and George Murphy, the Guild's second in command, in a statement that declared SAG's position as neutral because the strike was essentially a jurisdictional battle between IATSE and the CSU as to which organization had the right to represent Hollywood's workers, and not a general workers' action against the studios themselves. Therefore, under the orders of the American Federation of Labor (AFL), SAG members should continue to cross the picket lines and report for work. Reagan now found himself facing the same type of polarizing dilemma he had at HICCASP, forced to take a stand in an increasingly divisive and hostile union environment.

Sorrell, meanwhile, called for a national boycott of the studios by the moviegoing public audiences — a blacklisting, as it were — of any picture that featured a star who was, in Sorrell's words, a strikebreaker. Despite his threats, very few actors honored the picket lines and even the most liberal, including Bogart, Judy Garland, and Lucille Ball, kept making movies.

SAG now wanted to make it clear that its neutrality wasn't a disguised endorsement of the extreme left and drafted a statement of principles that condemned both communism and fascism, but couldn't get a majority of the membership to approve it. The internal debates over the statement continued through the next round of SAG elections, during which Reagan, a strong supporter of the statement, was elected the third vice president of the Guild.*

In his new position of increased authority, Reagan met with Roy Brewer to see if he could not get him to back off from a direct confrontation with Sorrell, at least until the AFL's national convention that October, when the issues of the CSU's legitimacy and domination could be dealt with once more. At the same time, Reagan also secretly met

* This was September 1946, and the first SAG office to which Reagan was actually elected, rather than appointed.

with Sorrell and asked him not to continue to pressure SAG into striking, and to stop raising the bar throughout the industry until the AFL could decide the issue.

When both sides refused to back down, Reagan, Montgomery, and Murphy intensified SAG's position of neutrality.

In early October, Reagan and William Holden, a good friend from the FMPU days when they had worked together making propaganda films, attended a meeting of a group of SAG members who wanted to support the CSU despite SAG's official position of neutrality and strike. The meeting was held at actress Ida Lupino's house, and although neither Reagan nor Holden had been invited, they went anyway.

Actor Sterling Hayden, a staunch left-winger and on-the-record Communist Party member, led the meeting. Hayden denounced IATSE as being as corrupt as it ever was and urged these members to openly support the CSU. Reagan then stood up and started speaking in defense of neutrality; he was met with a chorus of jeers and boos, led by actor John Garfield and actor Howard Da Silva, both of whom tried to shout Reagan down (and both of whom would later be blacklisted).

The next day, Reagan attended an open SAG meeting of all its membership and demanded the Guild take immediate disciplinary action against Lupino, Garfield, Da Silva, and Hayden. That night, home alone, Reagan received an anonymous midnight phone call warning him that he was going to be "taken care of," that the next time he spoke out against the CSU, he would receive a face full of acid. When Reagan got the acid threat, according to Brewer, he eventually turned to him for protection and support, and Brewer made the most of it, later claiming credit for Reagan's beginning to move to the right, declaring, "I was the man who persuaded Reagan he was on the wrong side."

According to Reagan, however, it wasn't Brewer but the studio he turned to, first thing the next morning. Although he was supposed to be neutral, he went directly to Warners' security department and convinced them to issue him a .32 Smith & Wesson pistol. "Thereafter, I mounted the holstered gun religiously every morning and took it off the last thing at night. I learned how much a person gets to lean on hardware like that. After months of wearing, it took a real effort of will to discard it. I kept thinking, the very night you take it off may be the night when you need it most."

There is no record to be found of Warners ever having issued a real gun to any actor, including Reagan, to protect themselves. The story is likely apocryphal, something Reagan probably made up to cover where he really got the gun. The weapon, however, was real. As Jimmy Stewart later recalled, "I remember Ron at that time was very active in the Guild and they were having trouble with the mafia — the Chicago gangsters. This was a very difficult time for everybody out here, though I really never got to know what it was about other than that the mafia evidently was trying to take over the picture business or something. At least that's the way I remember it. The big studios were really together on getting this thing out of town, and Ron was one of the big driving forces in helping to achieve this . . . Anyway, I was just leaving his home one night, he had just been at a meeting with the board members of SAG, and I remember he was carrying a gun — he showed it to me."

By now, Reagan and other union leaders were being closely watched by J. Edgar Hoover's Red-baiting FBI, which was keeping extensive files on all their activities. As Reagan's influence in SAG grew, Hoover marked him as a potential domestic spy for the Bureau. At Hoover's request, Reagan, code name T-10, secretly met with the FBI before and after his resignation from HIC-CASP and handed over not only the names of members he suspected were subversive but also information as to how they had voted in favor or against the communists. As he would admit several years later, proudly claiming he was doing his patriotic duty, and confirmed by his FBI file, on at least those two occasions (most likely the meeting at his house prior to the HICCASP vote and the one at Lupino's house by the SAG left) and probably several more, he acted as a secret informant for the Bureau, although what he specifically did and whom he named has all been redacted from his file. When he became concerned about the threats to his personal safety, if he did request a weapon, it certainly wouldn't have been from the studio, but the FBI, although no such request, if it exists, remains unredacted in his FBI file.[*]

* Reagan's FBI file #100-382196 shows that the FBI considered HICCASP nothing more than a communist front. Neil Reagan, Ronald's brother, who was an advertising executive, had joined HICCASP and been recruited by the Bureau as a spy. Before the FBI recruited Ronald Reagan, Neil warned him to resign from the organization. It was at that point, according to the file, that Reagan decided, instead, to join his brother in the FBI's espionage program. According to the file, Reagan used to call his brother from a pay phone on Sunset Boulevard to pass along information that he, Ronald, felt needed to get to the FBI. Later on he held nighttime meetings in his house to report on members of communist cliques he felt had infiltrated the Screen Actors Guild.

■ ■ ■ ■

A few weeks earlier, on September 12, 1,200 carpenters and painters aligned with the CSU were summarily fired by the studios for refusing to report to work. Sorrell then called for an immediate, industry-wide general strike intended to shut down all fifty films in production at the majors. On September 26, violence between those who wanted to cross the picket line and those who wanted to keep them out erupted outside the gates of several studio lots. The police were called in with riot gear and shots were fired both into the strikers' crowds and back at the police. More then two dozen injuries were reported, although there were no fatalities. The next day, the AVC came out in support of the strikers, a move that shocked Reagan, who was convinced it meant the communists had managed to gain a foothold in that great, patriot-filled organization. If they could do that, he feared, they were in reach of a complete takeover of Hollywood.

After his election, he was asked by the board of SAG to speak to a general meeting of the entire membership, to encourage them to cross the CSU picket lines and report for work. Three thousand SAG members showed up at the Hollywood Legion Stadium to hear what Reagan had to say. In order to get in, they had to cross an angry picket line of CSU workers. Reagan was convinced that this was the night he was most likely to be hit and made sure he passed through the crowd surrounded on all sides by bodyguards, as he remembered it in his second memoir, with one hand under his suit jacket firmly gripping the .32.

That night, Reagan stood in the center of the arena's boxing ring and gave an impassioned speech that implored the membership to do the right thing and continue to show up for work. Reagan was superb as he commanded the stage. He was articulate, emotional, powerful, and, most of all, persuasive. He was like the character of Lt. "Brass" Bancroft, only this was a far better scenario than that character had ever been given. It was in fact, by far, the best performance Reagan had ever delivered, infinitely more nuanced than anything he had ever done on screen.

While he was speaking to the crowd, someone slashed the tires of his car.

When it came time to vote, the membership voted 2,748 to 509 to cross the CSU picket lines and report for work the next day.

It had been an emotional night, but nothing had really changed because of it. Not long after, the union members of Technicolor voted to leave IATSE for the CSU, a clear victory for Herb Sorrell, and the seesaw continued. Then, in late October, Reagan was again asked to speak at a SAG event, this time held at Hollywood's Knickerbocker Hotel. To everyone's surprise, Sorrell himself showed up.

After Reagan spoke, offstage, Sorrell and Gene Kelly, whom Sorrell towered over, got into a shouting and shoving match. A furious Reagan separated the two and then confronted Sorrell, just like he would have if this was a movie, dressing him down as a self-serving troublemaker more interested in his own glory than the welfare of his followers.

Despite Sorrell's ability to keep the strike going, without SAG's support, which it was not going to get, the CSU could not survive. In 1946, Sorrell had been named the defendant in a series of court cases stemming from the September 26 confrontations that resulted in his being convicted on charges of contempt of court and failure to disperse his men from their illegal gathering. Although he was eventually acquitted of any felony charges, his spirit had been broken by the trials; the final nail in his coffin came when he was named on the record by Walt Disney as a communist during his 1947 testimony before HUAC. Not long after that, the CSU was dissolved and Sorrell disappeared from the mind-set of Hollywood. By then, IATSE, with Brewer still serving as its leader, had become the largest and most powerful labor union in Hollywood.* Sorrell, who was either in his late thirties or early forties, died shortly after from a heart attack.†

The first to acknowledge the importance of Reagan's role in helping to break Sorrell's union was Jack L. Warner. In a statement he released to the press shortly after SAG members had made it clear they were not going to back Sorrell, Warner declared that "Ronnie Reagan has turned out to be a tower of strength, not only for the actors but for the whole industry, and he is to be highly complimented for his efforts on behalf of everyone working in our business." Warner had a good reason to publicly commend Reagan; in his opinion, in those troubled economic times for Hollywood, he had done nothing less than keep his and every other studio in business.

However, not everyone thought Reagan had done such a great job or shared Warner's lofty

---

* In May 1984, seventy-four-year-old Roy Brewer was appointed by president Ronald Reagan as chairman of the Federal Service Impasse Panel, whose purpose was to arbitrate disputes between federal agencies and the unions representing federal workers.

† Sorrell's exact age at the time of his death is not known.

and exaggerated opinion of Reagan's efforts, a role that Reagan himself inflated and distorted quite a bit in his two memoirs. According to film historian and director/ producer William Gazecki, "His first significant entrée onto the scene was at that meeting in '46, where he spoke at length against the CSU. Prior to that he was not recognized as a leader in the SAG/CSU situation. George Murphy was far more active earlier on. Reagan was not that involved in the strike in '45. While he was indeed developing into the anticommunist crusader he became later, he was still steeped in the liberalism that characterizes his early years. In congressional hearings after the strike was over, the Kearns Committee did find that SAG had collaborated with IATSE and the studios to lock out the CSU. However, Reagan's role in this was likely minimal."

George Dunne, a liberal Jesuit priest who reported on the strike for *Commonweal,* had this to say about Reagan's actions during the strike: "I never had much use for him ever since my dealings with him in the Hollywood strike. Because he played a key role in cooperation with what, in my judgment, were the thoroughly immoral Chicago gangster Outfit . . . at least. The union had been controlled by those gangsters and, in my judgment it was still. And it was operating in conspiratorial cooperation with the Hollywood producers to destroy what was the only honest and democratic trade union movement to Hollywood. Reagan played a key role in that destruction. It's been difficult for me to believe that he wasn't aware of what he was doing and with whom he was cooperating. And I also have been convinced that he was rewarded for it. I don't pretend to charge that he had a prior arrangement with the producers, that the producers agreed, 'We will do this for you if you do this for us.' No, I don't charge that, but he was at the end or near the end of his acting career, such as it was, and it's from this period on, after having done this very effective job in the interest of the producers, that his whole success stems . . . the producers don't forget their friends any more than the crime syndicate people forget their enemies. They didn't forget Willie Bioff and the producers didn't forget Ronald Reagan."

Despite Dunne's feelings, a great majority of SAG actors appreciated how Reagan's sense of practicality and fairness had made it possible for them to keep working without appearing to be scabs or strike-breakers. Robert Montgomery resigned the presidency and withdrew from SAG in March 1947 to avoid any potential conflict-of-interest scenarios when he, like many others were doing, formed his own, independent production company. Gene Kelly, grateful for Reagan's having defended him that night against the much bigger and stronger Sorrell, nominated Reagan to replace Montgomery as interim president until the next election.

A week after that, Ronald Reagan, the man who ten years earlier had, with anger and reluctance, joined the Screen Actors Guild, was elected its president.*

* With the government's antitrust lawsuit against the "monopolistic" studios, independent production companies that previously could not get widespread distribution became the industry's wave of the future. According to the SAG board minutes of March 10, 1947, all the letters of resignation, including Montgomery's, stated the same reason: Each of the actors now had a financial interest in the production of the pictures in which they were scheduled to appear. Other SAG board members, including several of its founders (of which Montgomery was one) quickly followed him out the door, all with similar plans to produce movies. They included Franchot Tone, the first vice president; Dick Powell, the second vice president; and James Cagney (who formed a company with his brother, who had produced the phenomenally successful *Yankee Doodle Dandy*). Nonoffice-holders also resigned, including John Garfield, Harpo Marx, and Dennis O'Keefe. Gene Kelly nominated Reagan even though he, Kelly, had also been nominated, along with George Murphy.

■ ■ ■ ■

A few days later, on March 13, 1947, Reagan attended the Academy Award ceremonies with Wyman and Mary Benny, Jack Benny's wife. The Bennys, Beverly Hills neighbors of the Reagans before they'd moved to their ranch, had invited the Reagans to sit at their table at the Shrine Auditorium, just outside the campus of the University of Southern California (USC). Benny was the master of ceremonies that night.

Despite all the attention he had received for his union activities, Reagan didn't want to take anything away from the big story of the awards, Wyman's nomination for Best Actress for her performance in *The Yearling.* Everyone in Hollywood figured she had a lock on the Oscar, despite some very strong competition, as payback for her not even being nominated the prior year for her superb work in *The Lost Weekend.* Also nominated were Olivia de Havilland for her role in Mitchell Leisen's World War I melodrama *To Each His Own,* Celia Johnson for David Lean's wonderful *Brief Encounter,* Jennifer Jones for King Vidor's neo-Western *Duel in the Sun,* and Rosalind Russell for Dudley Nichols's nun drama *Sister Kenny.* The smart money was on either Wyman or, riding a strong place position, Johnson.

Reagan had been asked to introduce and narrate the evening's filmed Parade of Stars and reluctantly did so, again not wanting to take anything away from his wife's spotlight. Dressed in black tie and tails, Reagan stepped to the stage to thunderous applause — the audience treated him like a hero, which to many in attendance he was — and began his narration without realizing that a mishap in the projection booth had caused the film to be shown upside down and backward. As a low laughter rolled through the audience, an increasingly nervous Reagan ignored it while continuing to read from his notes: "This picture embodies the glories of our past, the memories of our present, and the inspiration of our future." It wasn't until after he was through that he realized what had taken place. Humiliated and angry, he nevertheless smiled, waved, shook his head, made his way back to the table, and ordered a double bourbon. By the time the Best Actress was about to be announced, he was comfortably numb.

Onstage, Ray Milland, the winner the previous year for his performance in *The Lost Weekend,* opened the envelope and called out the name of . . . *Olivia de Havilland.* The crowd roared its approval.

Although losing was a personal disappointment, it did not hurt the upward momentum of Wyman's career. She had already completed two more important films (Raoul Walsh's *Cheyenne* and William Wellman's *Magic Town*), and was about to begin work on Jean Negulesco's *Johnny Belinda,* in which she was to play a deaf-mute, with Lew Ayres as the heroic doctor who tries to teach her how to communicate with the rest of the world. It would be Wyman's role in *Johnny Belinda* that would change everything for the Reagans again, this time in ways that neither of them could have anticipated.

Ronald Reagan, second from left, at approximately four years of age, with his father, Jack Reagan, his brother, Neil, and his mother, Nelle, 1915.

Joy Hodges, who helped Reagan break into movies by introducing him to her agent, in a still from Merry-Go-Round of 1938.

An early Warner Bros./First National Studios publicity photo of Ronald Reagan, emphasizing his physical prowess.

Another Warner Bros./First National Studios publicity shot, 1937.

Sergeant Murphy *(1938) was Reagan's fourth movie.*

Lobby card for Brother Rat *(1938), with Wayne Morris and Priscilla Lane. The film also featured Reagan's future wife, Jane Wyman, whom he met on the set.*

In Secret Service of the Air *(1939), Reagan was cast as "Brass" Bancroft, in the first of what would be a series of B movie adventures loosely based on the memoirs of William H. Moran, former Chief of the U.S. Secret Service.*

With Bette Davis in Dark Victory *(1939). The film, a star vehicle for Davis, featured Reagan and Humphrey Bogart in minor supporting roles. Reagan played Alec Hamm, a rich, spoiled, alcoholic playboy, anticipating his appearance three years later in what many consider his best film,* Kings Row.

Smashing the Money Ring *(1939) and*
Murder in the Air *(1940; next page), two*
more films in the "Brass" Bancroft series.

Reagan as George Gipp in the film that made him a star,
Knute Rockne All American *(1940). With him is Pat O'Brien*
(in the title role), a member of the so-called Irish Mafia that
ruled the Warner Bros. commissary.

In a scene from Santa Fe Trail *(1940), literally standing in the shadow of Errol Flynn (with Olivia de Havilland). The film established Reagan as best suited to play the "pal" of the romantic leads at Warner Bros. Despite their onscreen camaraderie, Reagan and Flynn did not get along in real life.*

COURTESY OF THE ACADEMY OF MOTION PICTURE ARTS AND SCIENCES

Ronald Reagan in Tugboat Annie Sails Again *(1940), the disastrous sequel to the hit film* Tugboat Annie. *Released immediately after* Knute Rockne All American, *it helped stall the forward momentum of his career.*

On his wedding day, January 26, 1940, with Jane Wyman and his parents, Nelle and Jack.

Ronald Reagan and Jane Wyman (also next two pages) in staged publicity photos taken by Warner Bros. to show how happy the couple was in real life.

COURTESY OF THE ACADEMY OF MOTION PICTURE ARTS AND SCIENCES

Ronald Reagan in his Cavalry reserve uniform, Los Angeles, 1942. That April he would be called to active duty in the U.S. Army.

A staged publicity photo of Reagan leaving for Fort Dixon.

Capt. Ronald Reagan and, from left, Lt. Col. Johnny Meyers, number one American Ace; Lt. Col. Jack L. Warner; and American war hero Col. James Stewart, during a broadcast over the Mutual Radio Network for Air Force Day.

Juke Girl (1942) was one of Reagan's better efforts. It costarred his favorite leading lady, Ann Sheridan, as a "Juke Girl," a Hollywood euphemism for "prostitute."

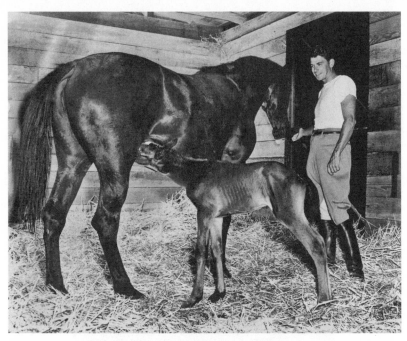

Reagan with the horses on his farm, c. 1944.

Reagan and daughter Maureen enjoy the family swimming pool while Jane Wyman looks on, c. 1944.

REBEL ROAD ARCHIVES

Out on the town, c. 1945. Jane Wyman was on the verge of major stardom while Reagan's career was on the descent.

At the 1946 Academy Awards table for The Lost Weekend *with Ray Milland, a tense Ronald Reagan looks on as his wife flirts with Lew Ayres, soon to become her lover.*

With his career in decline, Reagan was forced to appear in That Hagen Girl *(1947) as the romantic lead opposite Shirley Temple. The film was a disaster at the box office.*

In The Girl from Jones Beach *(1949), featuring Virginia Mayo, Eddie Bracken, and Dona Drake, Reagan played a glamorous photographer/playboy. The film was made during his divorce from Jane Wyman.*

Ronald Reagan on a date with Nancy Davis. The occasion was a movie premiere, necessitating the eyeglasses that Reagan almost never wore in public.

COURTESY OF THE ACADEMY OF MOTION PICTURE ARTS AND SCIENCES

Mr. and Mrs. Ronald Reagan relaxing at home.

COURTESY OF THE ACADEMY OF MOTION PICTURE ARTS AND SCIENCES

Publicity still and lobby card for Bedtime for Bonzo *(1951), the film that made Reagan a running joke on Johnny Carson's* Tonight Show. *Other stars had made movies costarring animals, but Reagan's was usually cited as the worst of the bunch.*

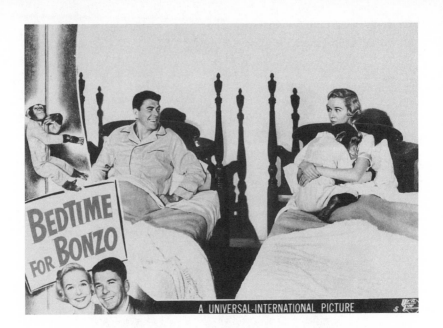

Following the unfortunate Bedtime for Bonzo, *Reagan broke another show-business taboo by playing opposite a child.* Hong Kong *(1952) went nowhere.*

By 1953, Reagan was out of Warner Bros. and freelancing. *Tropic Zone* *was his third film for Paramount.*

A lobby card and publicity still (next page) for Law and Order *(1953). Westerns were Reagan's favorite genre.*

The low point in Reagan's Hollywood career came in February 1954 when he played an engagement at the Last Frontier Hotel in Las Vegas, at the behest of Lew Wasserman.

The Reagans celebrating Christmas, c. 1955.

Mr. and Mrs. Reagan at a black-tie event in mid-1950s Hollywood. Under Nancy Reagan's guidance, the couple rose to prominence on the California social scene.

A publicity still from Tennessee's Partner *(1955).*

Ronald Reagan with Frank Sinatra and Cyd Charisse. Despite the smiles, Reagan and Sinatra had a very tense relationship, exacerbated in later years by their political differences, The Godfather *movie, and rumors of an affair between Sinatra and Nancy Reagan.*

Nancy, Ronnie Jr., Patti, and Ronald Reagan in the late 1950s.

A copy of a cover of a rare album Reagan recorded in 1960 to fight against what he believed was John F. Kennedy's platform for broadening medical coverage.

The Killers *(1964; also next page)*, Reagan's *last film and the only one in which he played a villain. He hated having to "slap" co-star Angie Dickinson.*

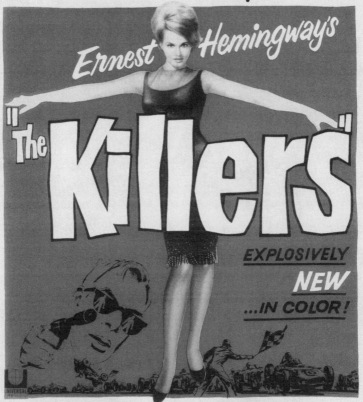

Reagan in the 1960s paying tribute to Jack Warner.

With Barry Goldwater during the 1964 presidential campaign.

■ ■ ■ ■

CHAPTER EIGHT:
MR. REAGAN GOES
TO WASHINGTON

■ ■ ■ ■

The night before, Jane had told a friend, "We're finished, and it's all my fault." Three times before, Jane had said good-bye to her marriage, then reconciled. Is this the last round in the marriage ring that has encircled the fighting Reagans for ten sometimes stormy but all the time, we believe, in-love years? That Ronnie is still deeply in love with Jane is very evident . . . "It's a strange character I'm married to. But I love her."

— GLADYS HALL

*Ronald Reagan testifying in Washington, D.C., before the
House Un-American Activities Committee, October 1947.*

The real action for Ronald Reagan now, and what saved him from the giant shadow of Wyman's huge career, was his rise to the presidency of the Screen Actors Guild. It wasn't, as has always been thought, the communist fringe itself, but their methods of infiltration and the boorish, bullying ways of Herb Sorrell that had pushed Reagan to take action. Even when he chose to become a domestic spy, he saw it as something heroic, even patriotic, like the hero "Brass" Bancroft he had played so often in the movies. The best explanation as to why he did it is also the simplest: He thought it was the right thing to do. If it was sometimes difficult to tell the difference between Ronald Reagan the man and Ronald Reagan the actor, or the characters that he played, this blurring of the line between real and role-play, or what he did and how he did it, was an essential part of the action for Reagan. He had discovered the best venue for his dramatic talents — the reality of the drama happening outside of the soundstages — and it was an arena that would remain his favorite venue of performance the rest of his life.

Perhaps more than any other faction in Hollywood, the Screen Actors Guild knew that despite Sorrell's fall and the collapse of the CSU, the economic struggles that had become hopelessly intertwined with ideological battles had not been resolved at all. For the moment, everyone was working, but that wasn't going to be enough. The word was that HUAC was coming back, sometime that summer or fall, this time with both barrels loaded, hunting for commie bear, and this time they meant business.

As Hollywood braced for the political storm it knew was coming, Ronald Reagan waited for his chance to make another charge onto the battlefield. While doing so, the day after Wyman had lost her bid for the Oscar, he went back to work.

This time, he had no illusions about the script, the cast, the budget, or the quality of the picture to which he was assigned. He hated *That Hagen Girl* from the moment he first read the script, a mindless soap opera starring the thirty-six-year-old Ronald Reagan opposite Hollywood's former child sweetheart, none other than Shirley Temple, all grown up (or at least filled out) at nineteen, and on loan from independent producer David O. Selznick, who had no idea what to do with her anymore. The plot of the movie, based on the novel by Edith K. Roberts, concerns the trials and tribulations of an adopted, illegitimate girl and the small town where she lives that ostracizes her to the point of suicide. Just before her darkest hour she is rescued by a man (Reagan) who has long been suspected of being her father, but isn't, and winds up marrying her.

Reagan believed that because of the difference in their ages — seventeen years — and the unforgettable child-star image Temple had, it was a bad idea for him to play a romantic lead opposite her (interestingly, Cary Grant, seven years older than Reagan, had done the same thing earlier that same year at RKO, in Irving Reis's *The Bachelor and the Bobby Soxer,* where the teaming of Grant and a loaned-out Temple proved extremely popular with audiences). While Temple had been thrilled to play opposite Grant (as the daughter of Myrna Loy, Grant's real love interest in the film), she was anything but with Reagan. "If only he looked younger, or I older," she thought to herself when they met the first day of rehearsals, knowing he was going to have to play a father figure and a lover and that, according to the script, she was supposed to choose Reagan over the young, hunky Rory Calhoun.

343

Despite his unease with the role, he was friendly and charming to Temple on-set. The first day they met, Reagan cheerfully reminded her that she had once been called to testify by HUAC, back in 1938, when she was all of ten years old, and suspected of being a communist dupe. They both had a good laugh over that one. Temple's mother and manager, however, found nothing funny about her daughter, who had been the number one box-office draw as a child, cast in a movie with Reagan, someone she considered "long on quips, short on talent, and mired permanently in the never-never land between anonymity and success." She took it as a sure sign her daughter's film career was nearing its end.[*]

During the shooting of the film, directed by Peter Godfrey, a British-born mannered B actor without any noticeable flair for comedy, Reagan tried in vain to get the Charles Hoffman script altered to make the casting a little more believable. He implored Jack Warner to at least make the screenwriter remove the "I

[*] Temple's mother was right. This was Temple's fifty-second feature-length movie (eighteen of which were shorts). She would make only six more features, none memorable, before her film career ended two years later, in 1949. There is no mention of *That Hagen Girl* in Reagan's second memoir and only a few sentences about it in his first.

love you" line he was supposed to say to Temple. Warner eventually did, but only after one audience greeted the moment with a collective cry of "Oh no." Hoffman then wrote a new and ambiguous ending to the film — Temple leaves town carrying a bouquet of flowers — which nobody understood. Godfrey, in particular, had no idea what all the fuss was about; he himself was married to a girl young enough to be his daughter, one of the reasons, presumably, that Warner had assigned him the film in the first place. No amount of fixing could save it and *That Hagen Girl* proved an enormous dud at the box office.

During production, Reagan had had to jump into a lake to save Temple when she tried to commit suicide, a familiar film scenario in those days (think Frank Capra's *It's a Wonderful Life,* then remove the magic). Numerous takes were required to get the shot just the way Godfrey wanted it, and by the time he did, an exhausted, frozen Reagan retreated to his bed, with stabbing pains in his chest. He was admitted to the hospital and diagnosed with viral pneumonia. For several days, Reagan actually hovered near death. Wyman, who was at the time preparing for *Johnny Belinda* by studying sign language and lip-reading with a deaf Mexican girl the studio had hired to live with her for a few weeks, rushed to his bedside.

Reagan's fever reached 104 degrees before it broke after six touch-and-go days. Just as he was preparing for his release, Wyman's water burst, and she was admitted to Queen of Angels Hospital. Her pregnancy was something both she and Reagan had kept secret, at her insistence, so she could continue to work. The next day, June 26, Wyman gave premature birth to a baby girl they named Christine.

Christine died nine hours later.

On July 2 the baby's body was cremated, and an exhausted Reagan returned to making his film. He looked as if he had aged five years during his week-long stay in the hospital.

Labor Day weekend, the couple entertained friends; Reagan spent much of Monday night pontificating on politics and also screened *Kings Row,* something that caused Wyman to turn in early, claiming she had an early pickup in the morning. In truth, Wyman couldn't stand to watch that movie one more time. Reagan showed it almost every time they had guests.

The next day, a studio limousine took Wyman to Mendocino, north of San Francisco, where *Johnny Belinda* was to be filmed.

Reagan didn't see her off, having left before she did, since he was already on to his next film, *Night Unto Night,* directed by a young, still unknown Don Siegel. Reagan's costar this time was the exotic Viveca Lindfors, the future Mrs. Siegel. In the film, Reagan plays an epileptic biochemist who falls in love with a young widow (Lindfors) but is afraid to commit to her because of his disease. The film might have caught on as a metaphor for the psychological baggage and physical war wounds returning veterans of the day could identify with, but it was deemed unreleasable by Warner and held back for three years, finally dumped into theaters in 1949 in an attempt to earn back production costs. Lindfors was no longer with the studio by the time *Night Unto Night* saw the light of day.

Wyman, meanwhile, was on location, living in an abandoned lumber camp the studio had rented for the duration, Wyman and her costar, Lew Ayres, huddling every evening in front of a campfire, began a passionate love affair and made no attempt to hide it from the others. Wyman was taken by Ayres's manner, his intelligence, his good looks, and his ability to shut up once in a while and actually listen to whatever it was she had to say. He was in every way the opposite of Reagan, an aesthete who, unlike her flag-waving husband, had been a conscientious objector for the duration of the war.

While Wyman was on location, Reagan finished *Night Unto Night* and knocked off two more hastily made movies. The first was Irving Rapper's *The Voice of the Turtle,* based on the 1943 wartime play that was still on Broadway when the film opened. Reagan didn't particularly want to do a sophisticated comedy, and he'd never felt particularly good or comfortable having to make those kinds of movies. At the same time, John Huston had offered him the small but effective role of Cody in *The Treasure of the Sierra Madre,* a film Reagan really wanted to do. Jack Warner rejected it, he said, because he had purchased *The Voice of the Turtle* with Reagan in mind to play the lead, a role he thought was perfect for Reagan. The role in the Huston film went instead to Bruce Bennett.

The Voice of the Turtle is a slight story about a soldier on leave in New York City who becomes involved with a Broadway actress — another in a seemingly endless flow of postwar comedies in which soldiers wore suits as tailored as tuxedoes, their hair was longer than the military would have ever allowed, and they were never seen in anything resembling army barracks, military training, or actual combat, just in women's wildly extravagant, impossibly large New York City apartments, which no one ever explained how they could afford. The film did okay at the box office and nothing for Reagan's career, while *Treasure of the Sierra Madre* won three Oscars (John Huston for Best Director and

Screenplay and his father, Walter Huston, for Best Supporting Actor).

Although he never liked to criticize any authority figure, in his second memoir, Reagan recalls this period of his Hollywood career as being far more successful than it really was and comes unusually close to blaming Jack Warner for keeping him from the type of film he really wanted to make: "I'm especially proud of several of the postwar pictures, particularly *The Voice of the Turtle,*" Reagan wrote in 1990. But in an unidentified, typewritten interview that may never have been published, circa 1962, Reagan sang quite a different tune about that film and others of the late forties, with his frustration aimed directly at Jack Warner, for not letting him make *The Treasure of the Sierra Madre:* "My only beef [with Jack Warner] was I thought I had done too many comedies. There was *The Voice of the Turtle* [and others]. It was the start of mammoth Westerns — the start of the John Wayne push — and I wanted action stuff."

It wasn't that Jack Warner tried to keep Reagan from making Westerns. Ironically, Warner believed that Reagan was better than that and he continued to look for projects he thought the actor might use to regain his star status. Clearly, the triangular chasm between who Reagan thought he was, who Warner thought Reagan was, and who Reagan really was had become deep and wide.

Reagan continued to make movies during the day and spent most evenings alone (during the weekdays, the kids were cared for by live-in nannies; on weekends, by his mother, Nelle) while his wife remained upstate. To occupy his time, as much out of loneliness and boredom as anything else, he once more turned his attention and energies back to the Guild.

In light of HUAC's anticipated arrival, Reagan sought to remind everyone of the role he had played during the 1945 strike, a role that he greatly exaggerated as he would in both his memoirs, and the one he anticipated possibly playing in defense of Hollywood the industry in the coming months. He set up a preemptive defense of his membership in HICCASP, which could have been seen as a defense of its communist faction, something he felt he needed, especially since, at the time, he wanted to keep his involvement with the FBI secret.

To do so, he enlisted the help of Hedda Hopper, who, that May, had published a new profile on Reagan in which she quoted him, in defense of his actions during the strike, this way: "Right now the liberal movement in this country is taking the brunt of the Communist attack. The Reds know that if we can make America a decent living place for all of

350

our people their cause is lost here. So they seek to infiltrate liberal organizations just to smear and discredit them. I've already pulled out of one organization [HICCASP] that I joined in completely good faith. One day I woke up, looked about and found it was Commie-dominated. You can't blame a man for aligning himself with an institution but you can blame him if he deliberately remains with it after he knows it's fallen into the hands of the Reds. I can name you one organization that is so obviously controlled by the Communists that all members must be aware of it. So I must believe that any who choose to support it must be aware of it. So they must be at least Communist sympathizers. Otherwise, knowing what they must know, why don't they get out?"

This was extraordinarily revisionist history and marked a significant turn in Reagan's philosophical stance. The enemy was now the communists, not the CSU or Herb Sorrell (who had never been proven to have ever been a communist). More than anything else, it painted Reagan as the one thing he hadn't been before — a "commie-hunter." His entire stance prior to this statement was that the democracy worked *because it could withstand the presence of communists.* Now Reagan's idealistic pragmatism had taken over, a method as much as a belief that would serve him well in the coming months and far into the future.

In August of that year, 1947, amid the growing rumors of trouble in their marriage, Wyman published an "open letter" to Reagan that appeared in a popular movie magazine, a public reiteration of her love for him and a belief in the lasting value of their marriage, tinged with a bit of sadness and finality, as if she were thanking him and saying good-bye at the same time. It said, in part, "You and I have been married for seven years, Mr. Reagan. During this period, at least once a week you've reminded me (kiddingly) how lucky I am to have you, for a husband. I think I *am* lucky . . . all kidding aside, there isn't a single thing about you I'd want to change. You've been wonderful for me in many ways."

That fall, only weeks before HUAC was to begin its new round of hearings in Washington, D.C., word began leaking from the set of *Johnny Belinda* about the affair going on between Wyman and Ayres. Just as he was packing for Washington to testify under subpoena before the Committee, Reagan received a phone call from Wyman; she informed him that while the production was coming to an end, she wasn't coming home, that she needed some time by herself to think things over. When he asked her what things, she said their marriage.

Reagan arrived in Washington October 17,

1947, two days before the hearings were to begin. They were generally divided into two sections: friendly and unfriendly witnesses. As president of the Screen Actors Guild, Reagan was considered a friendly witness and scheduled to testify in the first headline-grabbing wave of star-studded, filmed, and recorded cross-examinations.

The first session was held on October 20 in the Caucus Room of the Old Office Building, the largest space on Capitol Hill outside the Senate and the House. It was chosen because of the huge amount of media that had requested access. HUAC was more than happy to accommodate the press, believing that any publicity only made the hearings, and their chairman, the pompous J. Parnell Thomas, even more important.

The first to testify on the friendly side was Jack L. Warner. Yes, he admitted under oath, he had made all those working-class-hero films that glorified criminal elements by shining a social spotlight on their motivations, and, yes, two of his biggest stars, Bogart and Cagney, were under the investigative microscope. But Warner managed to fully acquit himself when he declared that he believed subversive elements had, indeed, infiltrated the film industry and he was more than happy to help dig them out and get rid of them. After he left the stand, he declared to the waiting and eager press that his studio would never again make the kind of socially aware movies it had in the past.

Louis B. Mayer was the next to take the stand; he went even further than Warner among Hollywood's power elite in what was rapidly turning into a cavalcade of flag-waving and righteous outrage cut right through the middle with fear. It was no accident that the first two "witnesses" were studio heads, the very men who had had the most to lose by the strikes Brewer and others had insisted were led by organizations such as the CSU that been rotted from within by communism. Mayer used the opportunity to call for new laws that would allow for the prosecution of anyone associated with the Communist Party: "Legislation establishing a national policy regulating employment of Communists in private industry! It is my belief they should be denied the sanctuary of the freedom they seek to destroy." It was an interesting theory — destroy freedom so that those seeking to destroy freedom wouldn't be able to. That pretty much set the tone and the tenor of the hearings.

Next to come were several founders of the Motion Picture Alliance. Sam Wood took the opportunity to rail against his "enemies, insisting that if you pulled the pants down of a communist you would find a hammer and sickle tattooed on their rear ends." Walt Disney went so far as to name four "communists" that had infiltrated his studio during the animation strike. One of them, David Hilberman, an animator who had gone out on the picket line during the strike, had no connection to the Communist Party, but had studied at the Leningrad Art Institute for six months in 1922. That was enough to mark him as a subversive, and because of it, Hilberman never again worked in Hollywood. Disney had also named Herb Sorrell as a communist without a shred of evidence.*

Reagan, who had had no love for Sorrell, nevertheless was not thrilled with what he was hearing and seeing. The hearings seemed, to him, less interested in justice than in vigilantism. The night before he was to appear, he was summoned to a secret meeting by Robert Stripling, the Committee's chief investigator, who, at the outset of the hearings, had publicly declared his intention to expose to the nation and the world the enemy's plan to "communize" the nation.

During the meeting Stripling implied that if Reagan fully cooperated, meaning naming names, he would also get an opportunity to make an uninterrupted defense of the film industry. That would make him look like a real hero, Stripling said. Reagan liked him

* Disney also named William Pomerance and Maurice Howard, both former business agents for the cartoonists' union.

even less after the meeting.

The next day, the fourth of the hearings, Reagan showed up amid the popping light-bulbs and general crush of media. The tone was set even before he took the stand, during Robert Montgomery's testimony; Montgomery was another designated "friendly witness." He was questioned by Thomas. Montgomery did not feel that the communist minority in Hollywood was anything more than minuscule, with no chance of "taking over." "They appear at public meetings tremendously well organized and with a complete program for the evening," he said, with a slight smile on his face. That was wiped off when Thomas added, "Mr. Montgomery, they even appear at congressional hearings."

It was Reagan's turn next. He was to be questioned by Stripling. He wore a white gabardine suit (the obligatory uniform of the good guys), complete with thick glasses, something he rarely wore in public. They were less an aid than a prop to make him look even more sincere to the public as well as the committee.

After being sworn in, Reagan was asked a series of opening questions by Stripling, one of which, rarely reported, offers a sharply more personal insight to Reagan's strong dislike of communists. Stripling asked Reagan if he could provide any instances of communist tactics that he was aware of, and Reagan related the story of a phone call he received one afternoon by a woman who announced a Paul Robeson concert recital. The money for the tickets, she said, would all go to a charity hospital. Would Reagan lend his name to the cause? Reagan paused to let the suspense build, as if he were waiting to find out if the runner was out or safe at home. "I felt a little bit as if I had been stuffy for a minute and I said, 'Certainly, you can use my name.' I left town for a couple of weeks and, when I returned, I was handed a newspaper story that said that this recital that was held . . . under the auspices of the Joint Anti-Fascist Refugee Committee . . . I did not . . . see one word about the hospital."

He was also asked if, as SAG's president, he had been aware of the presence of subversives within the organization:

MR. STRIPLING: You have no knowledge yourself as to whether or not any of them are members of the Communist Party?

REAGAN: No, sir, I have no investigative force or anything and I do not know.

MR. STRIPLING: Mr. Reagan, what is your feeling about what steps should be taken to rid the motion picture industry of any Communist influence?

This was the money question, one that

Stripling felt confident Reagan would answer with at least as much fire and brimstone as Mayer and Disney. To get the head of a major union to concur with their testimony, Stripling knew, would be a major victory for HUAC.

Reagan, however, had other ideas. The room fell into a hushed silence as Reagan, looking up frequently from his prepared words, to give the impression to the cameras that he was looking Stripling right in the eye, began to speak into the microphone.

Well, sir, ninety-nine percent of us are pretty well aware of what is going on, and I think, within the bounds of our democratic rights and never once stepping over the rights given us by democracy, we have done a pretty good job in our business of keeping those people's activities curtailed. After all, we must recognize them at present as a political party. On that basis we have exposed their lies when we came across them, we have opposed their propaganda, and I can certainly testify that in the case of the Screen Actors Guild we have been eminently successful in preventing them from, with their usual tactics, trying to run a majority of an organization with a well-organized minority. In opposing those people, the best thing to do is make democracy work. In the Screen

Actors Guild we make it work by insuring everyone a vote and by keeping everyone informed. I believe that, as Thomas Jefferson put it, if all the American people know all of the facts they will never make a mistake. Whether or not the Party should be outlawed, that is a matter for the government to decide. As a citizen, I would hesitate to see any political party outlawed on the basis of its political ideology. We have spent a hundred and seventy years in this country on the basis that democracy is strong enough to stand up and fight against the inroads of any ideology. However, if it is proven that an organization is an agent of a foreign power, or in any way not a legitimate political party — and I think the government is capable of proving that — then that is another matter. I happen to be very proud of the industry in which I work. I happen to be very proud of the way in which we conducted the fight. I do not believe the Communists have ever at any time been able to use the motion picture screen as a sounding board for their philosophy or ideology.

It was an altogether stunning performance, as powerful and effective as anything he had delivered during the strike, only this time the whole world was watching. The silence lingered for several seconds as the message sunk in. Reagan had once again, daringly, evoked the right of the communists to exist, and said that that was the truly democratic way. His reference to Thomas Jefferson sent a clear message to those looking to slam shut the doors of democracy for their own political gain.

Reagan hurriedly left Washington the next day amid a flurry of congratulations, eager to get back to Hollywood to try to save his marriage. When he did see Wyman, she remained distant, agitated, and decidedly nontalkative but agreed to remain in the house for the sake of the children while she tried to figure out what to do next. For his part, Reagan believed being seen in public together was good for both their careers and might somehow work in his favor.

The detente didn't last very long. One night the Reagans attended a dinner at the Beverly Club, where, according to Hedda Hopper, "Jane blew a fuse. As Ronnie helped her into the car, she was talking loudly and angrily. 'I've got along without you before,' she cried, 'and I certainly can get along without you now!'" The "spat," as Hopper later described it, was overheard by everybody within earshot.

Not long after, Wyman asked for a legal separation. It happened following another explosion, this one taking place in their living room while Reagan was reenacting the testimony he had given before HUAC. "YOU BORE ME," she screamed at him in the middle of it. An argument developed and before it was over, she demanded a formal separation. To hasten the process, she told reporters, she was establishing residency in Las Vegas.

Until the end, Reagan had hoped for reconciliation. In what read more like a eulogy than a report of a split-up, Louella Parsons took the opportunity to take credit for the couple having met on one of her promotional tours, and to explain to her readers what had broken up the two: "The trouble started when Ronny [sic] accepted the presidency of the Screen Actors Guild and devoted much of his time to the issues that are now troubling Hollywood and the world. Jane said no one could do the job as well as Ronny and she understood his interest. But, although she said that, she told other people that politics had broken up their home. I've never known any divorce to come as such a surprise. Jane and Ronny have always stood for so much that is right in Hollywood." Nowhere in the article was the name Lew Ayres mentioned.

When Hedda Hopper heard about it, she went directly to Reagan to find out what was really going on between him and Wyman. "Well," Reagan told her somewhat disarmingly, "if this comes to a divorce, I think I'll name *Johnny Belinda* co-respondent."

This next rather startling statement, also reported by Hopper, is the closest Reagan ever came to publicly admitting that his wife had had an affair with Lew Ayres. Even more startling, he implied that he understood why and that it was okay with him. "[Jane] is very intense, but she's been a wonderful wife and unsure because of that very thing. The trouble is she hasn't learned to separate her work from her personal life. Right now, Jane needs very much to have a fling and I intend to let her have it."

Dick Powell summed up the Reagans' real-life *A Star Is Born* scenario quite succinctly: "They would not have gotten a divorce had their careers not been going in opposite directions — hers up, his down."

Jack Warner may have thought he was doing Reagan a favor when he announced that Wyman had been taken off *John Loves Mary,* a movie the two were scheduled to appear in together (something that would have helped Reagan more than Wyman). She was replaced with up-and-coming twenty-three-year-old Broadway stage ingenue Patricia Neal (who that year would also make a strong impression opposite Gary Cooper in King Vidor's adaptation of Ayn Rand's controversial and epic novel *The Fountainhead*). It is difficult to understand any logical reason for Warner's taking his hottest actress off his coldest actor's next film if it wasn't done for purely humanitarian purposes, especially in the case of Jack Warner, who was not known for his individual grace and generosity. A much more likely scenario is that Wyman took herself off the film and, not wanting to confront one of his biggest stars, Warner had no choice but to replace her. To save Reagan from further embarrassment, he let it seem as if it was his decision, not hers. Figuring to save a little money, Warner gave her role to the low-salaried Neal.

Neal remembers that one night, after shooting, Reagan "wept and wept . . . He didn't want a divorce. He was heartbroken. He really was."

John Loves Mary, directed by David Butler, best known for his 1942 comedy vehicle *Road to Morocco*, a Hope/Crosby/Dorothy Lamour vehicle, the third in the lucrative Paramount "road movie" franchise, was assigned to Jerry Wald's A unit because of the anticipated box-office bonanza the pairing of the Reagans would create. However, with Wyman out of the picture and it being too late to reconfigure the production, Warner was faced with either canceling it or continuing with it as an A feature; he chose the latter. A hit when it was first produced on Broadway in 1945 (and still running when the film version opened),

John Loves Mary resembles nothing so much as a downgraded redo of *The Voice of the Turtle,* with postwar Reagan again in uniform playing a returning vet. It was already an outdated genre, and a film that Reagan didn't want to do without Wyman.

With no promotion budget to speak of, the movie slipped in and out of theaters with very little fanfare.

With Wyman continuing her affair with Ayres and production finished on *John Loves Mary,* Reagan packed his bags and checked into the Garden of Allah, a show-business home and hideaway better known for its bevy of starlets dressed as genies and a favorite hangout for, among others, Errol Flynn. Then, as if to twist the knife into him a little deeper, on February 6, 1948, as a birthday present, Wyman gave Reagan a brand-new turquoise Cadillac she had ordered for him before their split. She put the kids' name on the card, to make it seem it had come from them. It was an ambivalent message, a push-pull and slightly sadistic act that had the presumably desired effect. Reagan nearly had a nervous breakdown over it.

A week later Wyman filed for divorce.

Reagan didn't attend the court hearing. His friends claimed he simply couldn't bear it. Wyman wanted and got full-time custody of the children, Reagan got weekend visitation rights — for the children to come to his house (Maureen was now seven, Michael three). It didn't seem as if Reagan was all that upset about this part of the arrangement. Being a father did not mean all that much to Reagan, who wasn't around the children that often and didn't show much in the way of paternalistic skills. He was only really interested in the private, just-the-two-of-them intimacies offered by Wyman. He used to write her little notes when they were still together hoping that no one and nothing could interfere with their nights alone in front of a fire, sipping wine. Wyman asked for $500 a month child support and "horseback-riding privileges" at the "Yearling Row" ranch, which Reagan could otherwise keep. Their primary house was to be sold and the proceeds evenly split. Reagan agreed to everything.

In the April 1948 issue of *Photoplay,* Louella Parsons wrote what was, for all intents and purposes, an obituary column for marriage: "It is unfortunate but true that Hollywood can shrug off most marriage crack-ups. But when they are Jane Wyman and Ronald Reagan — well — we just can't take that . . . for eight years they have shared a beautiful life that has earned them the respect and admiration even of people who did not know them personally. To those of us who are close friends, they were an ideal Mr. and Mrs. That's why this hurts so much!"

Wyman refused to make any comments, other than the few she made privately to friends, about Reagan, some of them more hateful than others. Among them reportedly were some jokes she made about Reagan's not living up to her sexual standards. She also told a friend, Father Robert Perrella, something that was eventually reproduced in a book published when Reagan was running for governor a generation later and picked up again by Lou Cannon in one of his biographies of Reagan: "[Wyman] admits it was exasperating to awake in the middle of the night, prepare for work, and have someone at the breakfast table, newspaper in hand, expounding on the far right, far left, the conservative right, the conservative left, the middle of the roader."

Reagan, meanwhile, couldn't bear to go back to the house, even to prepare it for sale. Instead, he moved out of the Garden of Allah and took a bachelor pad at the Londonderry Apartments, the complex he'd lived in when he first moved to Hollywood. Having settled in, he sent for his desk, some books, a few other necessities, and little else, except, in an interesting quirk (especially since his father was a shoe salesman), dozens of pairs of brand-new shoes. Reagan, since his first job in radio, changed his shoes at least two and often three times a day. He believed that the source of one's energy came from the feet and that new, clean, and neat shoes invigorated them, and him. And he retreated emotionally, not unlike the way he did when Margaret Cleaver had left him. He sulked and stayed to himself, dated little, and kept his social card empty — except for an occasional get-together with Bill Holden, whom Reagan liked to drink with at Ciro's until closing time.

The studio had only one film for him, another light comedy he had no interest in but consented to make. He just wasn't up to a fight, with Warner or anybody else. *The Girl from Jones Beach,* directed by Peter Godfrey, who had directed *That Hagen Girl,* with a script by I.A.L. Diamond, was an intensely unfunny comedy about a commercial artist (a woefully miscast Reagan in a part Cary Grant could have phoned in, and which Robert Cummings played to perfection a few years later in a TV series, *Love That Bob,* more or less based on this film) in search of the perfect beauty — "The Randolph Girl" — whom he discovers at Jones Beach wearing a bathing suit that could effortlessly raise the dead (played by Virginia Mayo, one of the late-forties variations on the Betty Grable platinum blonde before Marilyn Monroe took over the franchise).* Reagan, posing as an intellectual to win the cooperation of the gorgeous but chaste schoolteacher, falls in love with her along the way. She falls in love with him and they live happily ever after.

It was a thoroughly dopey movie, redeemed only by the suggestive near-nakedness of Mayo, who showed enough thigh to push the pulse rate of male America into a near frenzy and the box office into the black. Although it did nothing for Reagan's career, *The Girl from Jones Beach* was one of the few films he made in this era that turned a healthy profit. However, his patience with Jack Warner was

---

* "The public," Mayo said during the making of the film, "seems to believe that an actress is a girl entirely without humility or self-doubt . . . the idea of having to spend much time before the camera in a bathing suit bothered me. It's true that I have worn dozens of abbreviated costumes of various types, but a bathing suit is the most unfriendly of outfits. It can't keep a secret. One day I walked out of my dressing room wearing one of the daring white swim suits required for the part and a wonderful thing happened. Ronnie Reagan, who has the manners of a grand duke under ordinary circumstances, WHISTLES at me. That wolf call did more for my ego and self-assurance than a hundred words could have done!" — From "Men Have Given Me Confidence," an article signed by Virginia Mayo that appeared in the April 1950 issue of *Movieland.*

by now wearing extremely thin.

Reagan spent the summer doing SAG work and riding his horse up at the ranch. Then, that October, he received a call from Wyman, who wanted to know if he would accompany her to the gala opening of *Johnny Belinda.* He was as thrilled as he was surprised, and immediately believed it was a first step toward reconciliation.

He showed up in his best tuxedo for the occasion.

The film opened to rave reviews and Wyman was the toast of the town. There was no further contact between her and Reagan other than the obligatory ones for the kids. Apparently, she had used Reagan as a beard to deflect the rumors of her romance with Ayres. But the next month she attended a dinner party with Lew Ayres during which she publicly declared him the love of her life. Reagan's heart broke all over again when he heard about it, and then again when the gossips started speculating on when Wyman and Ayres would get married.

It looked to be a gloomy, lonely holiday season for Reagan, whose only distraction now were his duties at SAG and an upcoming industry-wide meeting chaired by the Motion Picture Association of America at the Waldorf-Astoria in New York City, to discuss the question of what to do about the investigations into communism that were tearing

Hollywood apart. While he had every reason to be at the meeting — called to decide whether or not the film industry was going to tolerate the politics of not only anyone who was a confessed communist but also anyone even suspected of being or having ever been a communist — he had another and, to him, equally important reason for being in New York: Wyman was going to be there, with Ayres and the children. She had scheduled the trip to celebrate the Christmas holidays and had had to get his permission to travel out of state with the kids.

The agreed-upon declaration that came out of the meeting, the Waldorf Statement, which had been issued the year before, officially began one of Hollywood's darkest eras. It is generally acknowledged as a frightened and intimidated Hollywood's official endorsement of what would be a decade-long and illegal guilty-until-proven-innocent era of blacklisting anyone the industry deemed politically unfit to participate at any level in the business of making motion pictures.

No one who "made it" could consult any actual list, other than opportunistic power-hungry rags like *Counterattack* and *Red Channels,* run by a couple of grocery-store owners who were the sole deciders of whose name was listed in their publications, an event that meant immediate industry-wide blacklisting (with considerable backdoor influence-peddling going on, to be sure, along with the assumption of power that *Counterattack* and *Red Channels* enjoyed because they were, supposedly, supported by the general public, the people who shopped at grocery stores and therefore the target audience for advertisers).

The lockouts were all done by word of mouth, with the victims — some communists and some not — sometimes not knowing or realizing or willing to believe for months that the reason they weren't getting work was because they were blacklisted. Some went to jail. Others committed suicide. Still others went broke in the wake of their shattered careers. Some who were listed had committed no crime whatsoever. Others were barred from earning a living simply because their last name happened to be the same as someone else's who was blacklisted.

Ironically, Reagan supported the enforcement of the blacklist by seeming to deny its power. In a speech he made at a meeting of SAG, he explained why: "They agreed none of them would knowingly employ communists or those who refused to answer questions about their affiliations" even though that was a fundamental, constitutionally guaranteed right of American individuals. "The communists were among those who reacted in Hollywood by distorting facts they got, claiming they were victims of a 'blacklist' — when they were actually working members of a conspiracy directed by Soviet Russia against the United States. In war, that is treason and the name for such is a traitor; in peace, it is apparently martyr. It is easy to call oneself a 'political party' and hide other motives behind it: the Mafia can do it, so can a Chicago mob of gangsters. My own test for the time when the communists may call themselves a legitimate political party is that time when, in the USSR, an effective anti-communist political party wins an election. At that time, I shall withdraw my objections to labeling communists 'political.' "

This was an altogether astonishing speech, one that would be inconceivable (and undeliverable) any other time in America's history, filled with inaccuracies, false associations, assumptions, and self-congratulatory rhetoric. It clearly shows the breadth of Reagan's ideological shift, from a tolerance of communism to an intolerance of it, in a time when tolerance toward communism could warehouse an actor's career faster than anything. In the speech, his denunciation of the Soviet system's intolerance of anyone who was not communist was a mirror-image of what the Waldorf Statement endorsed as a way of doing political as well as economic business. And it ignored the real thugs of the industry, the corrupt union thugs who still operated in the wake of Bioff and Browne.

Playing the popular rather than the populist

card brought Reagan even more glory and respect from the industry than ever before as a major Hollywood player in 1948, even though he had no movie in production and the ones in theaters were only those he would like to forget. His movie career had stalled for a more fundamental reason than his political persuasion — he just wasn't that castable as a middle-aged, former action star whose always tenuous romantic onscreen curve had dipped dramatically as he approached his forties.

After the first of the year, Reagan was back in Hollywood, where he passed the time keeping a close watch on SAG's roster of who could work and who couldn't because of the blacklist, and presiding over ceremonial affairs, such as representing the Screen Actors Guild at the opening of the Motion Picture County Hospital at Calabasas, California, alongside such notables as Dinah Shore, Robert Young, and the mayor of Los Angeles, Fletcher Bowron. Reagan was proud of the hospital, which had been built entirely by voluntary contribution.

From Sidney Skolsky's February 2, 1949, column in which he "tyntyped" Ronald Reagan: "His favorite food is steak. His favorite color green. On his cooking abilities, he comments, 'I can fry an egg and boil some tea. Just give me an egg and a tea bag and I'll be busy in the kitchen for hours.' He sleeps in a big bed, wearing both the jacket and trousers of his pajamas. He is not a fresh-air fiend in bend. He is awakened by an alarm clock. He frankly admits that he finds the big bed lonesome."

As expected by virtually everyone in Hollywood, Wyman was once again nominated for Best Actress by the Academy, this time for her performance in *Johnny Belinda*. The twenty-first year of the presentation of Academy Awards was held on March 24, 1949, in the AMPAS Theater of the Academy of Motion Picture Arts and Sciences, a reflection of the hard times that had befallen Hollywood. No longer able to afford the cavernous Shrine Auditorium, which easily held nearly seven thousand Academy members, the AMPAS auditorium could barely accommodate nine hundred. The reasons for the downturn were many — the political acrimony that continued to split Hollywood into factions, the new union problems over the right to residuals by actors, writers, and directors whenever their films were shown on television. The issue wasn't how much they should get, but, according to the studios, whether they should receive anything at all. The unions looked to their leaders for guidance and support, and Reagan promised the membership of SAG that after the Academy Awards, he would seriously look into the matter.

Johnny Belinda had been nominated in all four of the major categories — Best Picture, Best Actor, Best Actress, and Best Director. Presiding over the awards that night was former SAG president Robert Montgomery, who had, since leaving the board of the Guild, become a successful independent film and television producer.

The ceremony progressed at its usually crawling pace, until it was time for Best Actress. The crowd hushed as it did before every announcement and the names of the nominees were read: Ingrid Bergman for her performance in Victor Fleming's *Joan of Arc;* Olivia de Havilland, in Anatole Litvak's *The Snake Pit;* Irene Dunne, in George Stevens's *I Remember Mama;* Barbara Stanwyck, in Litvak's *Sorry, Wrong Number;* and Jane Wyman for *Johnny Belinda.*

The envelope was opened. *Jane Wyman!* She leapt out of her seat and leaned over to kiss and hug Lew Ayres for all the world to see.[*]

---

[*] Wyman was the only winner that night for *Johnny Belinda.* The director, Jean Negulesco, lost to John Huston, who won for *The Treasure of the Sierra Madre.* Best Actor went to Laurence Oliver for his self-directed performance in *Hamlet.* Best Picture also went to *Hamlet.*

■ ■ ■ ■

Dana Andrews, a popular actor and friend of both Wyman and Reagan, remembered one last attempt to get the two back into each other's arms: "After he and Jane split up, a group of their friends got together and tried to patch things up. One group of friends, including SAG board member Dick Carlson and his wife, held a gathering, and both Jane and Ronnie were invited. Well, Ronnie started talking and talking and talking, and there wasn't any dialogue going on — he was just talking and holding forth. Finally Jane turned to Ronnie and said, 'I came here hoping that you had changed, but you haven't changed a bit. You're still the same loudmouth. Talking, talking, talking. I might as well go home.' And with that, she got up, walked out, and as far as I know that's the last time they were ever together."

On July 18, 1949, the Reagan-Wyman divorce was finalized. Reagan received the news in the hospital. He had broken his right thigh in five places sliding into first base during a charity softball game. Five days later, he was supposed to start work on a film Wasserman had managed to get for Reagan, a one-off at Universal that Jack Warner had okayed, Michael Gordon's *Woman in Hiding,* costarring Ida Lupino. Because of his injury, the role went instead to Howard Duff.

The next day Wyman left for England to prepare for her role in Alfred Hitchcock's *Stage Fright.*

Reagan returned to Warner Bros. in 1949 for two pictures. The first, David Butler's *It's a Great Feeling,* paired him with Doris Day, in a film about Hollywood that costarred the always reliable Jack Carson, who could flip back and forth with ease from good-guy comic and song-and-dance man to villainous lout. Carson played an egotistical actor having difficulty finding a director who would put up with him. Despite being light, funny, and breezy with several one-day cameo appearances by Reagan and several other Warner stars of the day, including Gary Cooper, Joan Crawford, Sydney Greenstreet, Danny Kaye, Eleanor Parker, Edward G. Robinson, Errol Flynn, and . . . *Jane Wyman,* it's an enjoyable, instantly forgettable film that did nothing to advance Reagan's career. When it was over, Reagan implored Lew Wasserman to find him a Western.

Warner put him right back to work in Vincent Sherman's *The Hasty Heart,* in which he had a real part, opposite Patricia Neal again. On the plus side, it was a serious postwar drama rather than another ditzy star-parade comedy. *The Hasty Heart* was adapted by Ranald MacDougall from the highly regarded John Patrick play that had been a hit on Broadway and the West End. Set in Burma (but filmed in England), the story concerns a bitter Scottish soldier named Cpl. "Lachie" MacLachlan (Richard Todd) and an American soldier, "Yank" (Reagan), who tries to reach out to Lachie while he is recovering from malaria. The nurse in charge of the hospital unit is Sister Parker (Neal), who knows what the others and MacLachlan don't: Lachie is dying. Yank and the others succeed in bringing him around until he discovers that he is indeed dying, and he relapses into the cold, detached fellow he was at the beginning of the film. Yank makes one last attempt to pull Lachie back into society, if only in the limited realm of the hospital . . . and succeeds.

Reagan had a good relationship with the film's director, whom he'd known from his earliest days at Warner. Being put through his paces by the American Sherman made it easier for Reagan to work abroad and have a shoulder to cry on. As Sherman later recalled, "We were in London for almost six months during the coldest and most bitter winters ever in England — *and our story was set in a hot Burmese jungle!* A chauffeur would pick Reagan up at the Savoy Hotel, along with Patricia Neal, then pick Todd and myself for an hour's journey to the studio at Elstree. [When we weren't shooting] I didn't see too much of him but I think he used to attend the soccer matches and visit various points of interest. When we first arrived in London we spent an evening or two together and he told me about his recent divorce from Jane Wyman, and from what I could gather, it hurt him considerably."

Reagan won good reviews for the film. Bosley Crowther gave it a positive nod in the *New York Times,* singling out Reagan for being "amusingly impatient and blunt." However, his character suffered from a lack of a female interest, which limited the film's appeal (Neal is a nun in the film), and the majority of the plaudits went to Todd's flashier performance (Crowther called his performance "eloquent and irresistible"), and he went on to win a nomination that year for a Best Actor Oscar (he lost to the blistering performance given by Broderick Crawford in Robert Rossen's sociopolitical drama *All the King's Men*).

Being overlooked for his performance bothered Reagan less than the actual making of the film, which had been shot in England for purely financial reasons. After the war, the British government retained all foreign monies in an attempt to rebuild its shattered economy, which meant that any studio that had significant money banked in England, which was all the majors, including Warner Bros., could only get their hands on it if they spent it in England. Hence, a slew of British-

American dramas, including Cary Grant's *I Was a Male War Bride* (Howard Hawks), shot in Germany and England, were concocted to justify the use of that money.

At first, Reagan had been eager to go to England in hopes that there might still be a chance to reconcile with Wyman, on the Hitchcock set (where Richard Todd was now costarring with Wyman). However, once there, he found he had no time at all to visit and wound up fairly miserable, alone in the cold, damp, black-and-white atmosphere of burned-out postwar Britain.

While he was away, Jack L. Warner made another one of his "special purchases" for Reagan (who personally contributed part of the money), a film called *Ghost Mountain.* Reagan was energized about it, because the film was a Western. But when he returned to America, he was informed by the studio that he had been taken off *Ghost Mountain,* replaced by Errol Flynn. Reagan was enraged and went directly to Wasserman demanding to know why. Wasserman explained that the poor box office of *The Hasty Heart* was the reason. Jack Warner didn't want to risk A money on a Ronald Reagan picture.

Reagan demanded that he either be allowed to make his own decisions about which movies he appeared in or be let out of his new contract. Surprisingly (to Reagan), Wasserman was all for the latter. He went to Warner and got him to quickly agree to a one-picture-a-year nonexclusive contract, at half Reagan's former rate (down from a million to a half-million annually.)*

Less than a week later, Wasserman personally delivered to Reagan a nonexclusive five-year, five-film deal with Universal. Although it appeared that Wasserman was a magician, able to perform miracles for his client, he was really thinking five moves ahead with the Universal deal. He had big plans for the studio, for himself, for Jules Stein, and for Reagan. For now, though, Reagan was thrilled with the new deal.

That November, he was reelected to a full term as SAG president on the platform of change that he had campaigned on, that the "problem" of the blacklist could be remedied if all SAG officers were made to sign loyalty oaths and that SAG should continue to support the "Waldorf Statement" doctrine of blacklisting anyone deemed politically "unworthy" of working in Hollywood. Reagan also promised to grant permission to work to any applicant, blacklist notwithstanding, who could somehow "prove" their loyalty to

---

* Reagan had made eight movies for Warner in the four years since his discharge from the army. Cutting him down from two a year to one at half the salary translated into major savings for Warner.

America.[†]

Nonetheless, despite all his political activity, nothing much was really going on in his life. His deal at Universal had not yet produced any scripts, and there was even less happening socially. It wasn't that he didn't go out, but because most of his friends were by now married, rather than being the odd man out, he chose to spend most evenings with young, willing, and always beautiful studio starlets. His phone rang regularly. If it wasn't some young thing calling him back to say she could get away that night to meet him, it was an actor's agent looking for an official okay so his client could go to work. Reagan never knew which starlet he was going to be with on any given night and didn't much care. They were all the same to him.

One morning he picked up the receiver

[†] Although the "Waldorf Statement" had been made by the Motion Picture Association of America (MPAA), all the guilds quickly fell into lock-step behind it. They formalized their allegiance by creating an organization called the Motion Picture Industry Council (MPIC), a so-called public relations committee set up by Louis B. Mayer, to help determine who could work and who couldn't. Reagan was its co-chairman, one of the key "go-to" guys with sufficient power to grant permission for questionable applicants to gain the right to be hired by a studio.

expecting it to be from his date for the evening and was surprised to hear the voice of his friend director Mervyn LeRoy, who said he had a favor to ask. There was a young woman on the set of his newest movie, *East Side, West Side,* whose name kept showing up on communist mailing lists and lists of "left-wing actors" that were being published regularly in *Counterattack* and *Red Channels.* LeRoy said he was sure it was a mistake and wondered if Reagan could check her out and give her a clearance if she proved okay.

Reagan said he would, and after making a few phone calls — including one to Louella Parsons, who kept her own charts of acceptability and published weekly "nays" or "yays" in her column, with inclusion on the wrong side of her personal approval rating enough to kill a career — discovered the actress had the same name as someone else who was on all the blacklists. He called back LeRoy and told him it was all right to use this one in his picture.

LeRoy thanked him profusely and then added that he knew the young actress would be so grateful, she'd probably want to thank him in person. Reagan liked the sound of that. He told LeRoy to have the actress give him a call.

Her name was Nancy Davis.

■ ■ ■ ■

CHAPTER NINE:
LOVE IS LOVELIER

■ ■ ■ ■

When I opened that door for our first date, I
knew he was the man I wanted to marry.
— NANCY REAGAN

Ronald and Nancy Reagan at home.

Davis didn't want to call Reagan directly, believing it was not the proper thing for a single woman in Hollywood to do, even if the circumstances were completely upstanding and all business. Instead, she asked Dore Schary, the vice president in charge of production at MGM, where she was signed as a contract player, to arrange a meeting for her with the president of the Screen Actors Guild. She said she wanted to thank Ronald Reagan in person for all that he had done in helping to clear her name. Schary was all too happy to do it.

Nancy Davis had come to know Schary quite well, an unusual circumstance for an entry-level contract player. She had come to Hollywood with great credentials and unbeatable connections for an actress with ordinary (at best) looks and not a great deal of acting ability. Hollywood, like every other industry in America only more so, was all about whom you knew, and that was Davis's great advantage.

She was the daughter of the lovely and attractive Edith Prescott Luckett, born Anne Frances Robbins in Washington, D.C., into a family of what at best may be called modest means. Edith managed to find work in a local theater and have enough talent and tenacity to eventually make it all the way to Broadway, or close enough, when, with the help of one of her brother's well-connected friends in Boston, she appeared in the road production of what was to be George M. Cohan's farewell to the Great White Way, *Broadway Jones.* Touring the United States with the show, Edith gained a reputation among the large cast as a raucous hot-to-trot "Broadway broad." She loved every minute of it.

While passing through Pittsburgh, she met and fell in love with Kenneth Seymour Robbins, a wealthy scion of a New England manufacturer, who was even crazier about her. So much so that against his parents' wishes, the handsome young Robbins married Edith Luckett on June 27, 1916, the only condition being that she give up her theatrical ambitions.

She did and they lived happily and properly, if uneventfully, on a gentleman's farm in the Berkshires, and without benefit of any of his family's money. When America entered World War I, Robbins eagerly enlisted, was sent overseas, and was one of the lucky ones who returned unharmed after the war ended, only to find that in his absence Edith had grown lonely and bored with life down on the farm. Robbins suggested it was time they started a family. Edith became pregnant but she knew motherhood simply wasn't going to be enough for her.

By (or around) 1923, although the divorce wouldn't become final until five years later, the marriage was over and the Robbinses separated. Kenneth returned home to his father and the family business, his tail hanging ruefully between his legs, while Edith went to New York City to give birth to her baby. When Nancy was two years old, fast city life and single motherhood had proved too much for Edith and she asked her sister, Virginia, married and living in Bethesda, Maryland, if she would take the child for a while.

A while turned into six years. Nancy lived with her aunt and uncle until she was eight years old, when they moved to Atlanta; apparently having had enough of babysitting, they shipped the young, by now slightly overweight and extremely lonely child to Chicago, where her mother had recently moved.

In Chicago, Edith had met and was now about to marry Loyal Davis, an up-and-coming doctor and wannabe actor eight years

389

her junior. He was charming, he was skilled, and he was broke. Edith knew he was going to need some direction, a good coat of social polish, a sharpened focus, and someone to give all of that to him while taking him to greatness. They were married in 1929, and she worked tirelessly to bring him with her love, guidance, and nurturing to exactly where she wanted him to be.

By the early thirties, they were living a privileged life on Chicago's fabled East Lake Shore Drive, socializing with the cream of Chicago's high society. Nancy, a teenager now, adored Dr. Davis, despite some of his quirkier and more distasteful habits, like his outspoken hatred for blacks, Jews, and Catholics. Nor was he overly affectionate toward Nancy; affection was just not his game. As soon as she was of age, Dr. Davis arranged for his stepdaughter to attend Smith College in Massachusetts.

Nancy had wanted to follow in her mother's footsteps and pursue a career in theater, but Dr. Davis would have none of it. He chose Smith for two reasons: It was far enough away that he could have Edith all to himself, and it lacked a theater department. Nancy dutifully packed her bags and, in the fall of 1939, left Chicago for her first year at Smith College.

Nancy shared all the familiar debutante rituals with the other wealthy society girl students in the class of '43, including "coming out." Her parents regularly sent her money and clothes to make her feel at home among her privileged classmates. Even the war, which took away most of the eligible Princetonians and made life at Smith a bit more inconvenient (the girls had to peel their own potatoes!), did not interfere all that much with the pampering that came with being a Smith Girl.

Toward the end of her senior year, Nancy's theatrical ambitions reawakened and, upon graduation, she returned to Chicago with a degree and a renewed determination to have a career in show business. Her parents, however, had enrolled her in the Junior League of Chicago, one of the society prerequisites to finding the right man to marry. Soon enough, she was engaged to James Platt White, Jr., Amherst, class of '42. All went according to plan, until, without warning, Nancy broke off the engagement, returned the ring, and announced to one and all that she was going into the theater.

Despite her stepfather's continuing disapproval, Nancy was able to get Edith to pull some strings from her earlier other life to help her daughter land a role in *Ramshackle Inn,* a Zasu Pitts comic vehicle bound for Broadway. After a brief run in Chicago, the play came to Broadway, opened with much advance fanfare, and closed in a week. Rather than returning home, Nancy chose to stay in New York City; she quickly landed a nonspeaking role in *Lute Song*, starring Yul Brynner and Mary Martin. Martin, another old friend of Edith, had used her star power to get Nancy into the show.

By the end of its five-month run, considered long and successful in 1946, Nancy was comfortably set in a luxury apartment on Manhattan's tony Beekman Place. After a short tour with Pitts on a show that took her around the Northeast, Nancy returned to New York City and began a brief but heated affair with Broadway star Alfred Drake, then the king of the American musical with his triumphant runs in *Oklahoma!, Kismet,* and *Kiss Me, Kate.* After Drake, she moved on to Max Allentuck, an older, well-connected theatrical figure who was, at the time, the general manager to Kermit Bloomgarden, the most successful Broadway producer of his time.

She also had a fling with Clark Gable during one of his publicity passes through the city. When he was finished with her (which didn't take long for the sexually insatiable star), he passed her on to Benjamin Thau, vice president of Loew's and head of casting for MGM.

On one of their dates Thau took Nancy to see Spencer Tracy, who was appearing on Broadway in a play called *The Ragged Truth.*

After, they went back to meet Tracy, and the next day Thau informed Nancy that Tracy had urged him to set up a screen test for her. This came as no surprise to her. The night before she had called her mother to tell her that she was meeting Tracy, who happened to be yet another "old friend of the family." Tracy's son had suffered from nerve deafness, and Dr. Davis had not only treated him but helped Tracy's wife set up a foundation to help treat other, less fortunate children with a similar affliction. When he discovered that Nancy was Dr. Davis's daughter, Tracy, who was one of MGM's biggest stars and money-makers, used his influence to arrange a screen test for her at MGM and made sure that no matter what the result she would be offered a contract. "With that kind of power behind her, the fix was in," according to former MGM producer Gottfried Reinhardt.

As if to ensure the studio understood that he meant business, Tracy asked director George Cukor to handle the screen test, something that directors of his caliber simply did not do. But Cukor, who had just directed *Adam's Rib* with the celebrated Tracy-Hepburn duo (and who had directed several other Hepburn movies, and lent the couple his estate whenever they needed to be alone) was more than happy to accommodate Tracy.

Despite all the advantages going in, Nancy's screen test was only marginally passable and if Tracy hadn't insisted, MGM would never have offered her a contract. She didn't have the sophistication of Hepburn, the heat of Ava Gardner or Lauren Bacall, or their youthful appeal. She didn't pump sex like Dietrich, her body wasn't pin-up material like Betty Grable's, she couldn't sing like Doris Day, and she couldn't dance like Ginger Rogers. She was too polished to be raw, too thin to swivel, too demure for come-hither, and too Smith to get down and dirty.

On March 7, 1949, Nancy Davis began work on her first movie, Pat Jackson's *Shadow on the Wall.* British-born Jackson, who'd worked himself up from the MGM writing department to a position as a second-unit director before he moved on to television episodics, was put in charge of this pseudopsychiatric mystery about a child who witnesses the murder of her mother. Ann Sothern played the romantic lead; Nancy Davis, the psychiatrist. The film was instantly forgettable (it does not receive a single mention in Nancy Reagan's memoirs) and did nothing to propel her career. Her next film, Curtis Bernhardt's *The Doctor and the Girl,* an only slightly better film starring Glenn Ford and a young Janet Leigh, was still bottom-of-the-bill fodder.

All the while she continued to see Thau, who tried to get her into as many films as he could. Dore Schary helped, too, and cast her in one of his productions, Mervyn LeRoy's *East Side, West Side,* an upscale, well-budgeted right-side/wrong-side-of-the-tracks murder mystery in which Barbara Stanwyck and Ava Gardner go at each other's catty throats over the sexual favors of the always dashing James Mason. Against that kind of heat and talent, Nancy was completely over-shadowed.

When the movie was finished, so was Benny Thau, at least as far as Nancy was concerned. Whether it was because his usefulness to her had come to an end is an open question, but soon enough Nancy was dating Robert Walker, the handsome, charismatic, but disturbed young leading man who had ap-peared the year before in William Seiter's romantic fantasy *One Touch of Venus* op-posite Ava Gardner, who had introduced the two.

Walker was considered part of the new youth movement in Hollywood, with the same qualities and good looks as Mont-gomery Clift. Nancy began dating Walker just before one of his numerous losing bouts with drinking forced Dore Schary to send him to the Menninger Clinic, which dried him out but couldn't clean him up. Despite his wounded-bird frailties (perhaps because of them), Nancy was attracted to Walker and undeterred by a past that included two failed marriages, one to Barbara Ford, John Ford's daughter, that lasted only a few weeks, and one to Jennifer Jones. Jones had left him to be David O. Selznick's mistress and eventual wife, a rejection that led Walker to have a nervous breakdown for which he was committed for nearly two years before making what amounted to his comeback in *East Side, West Side*. But Walker's illness ultimately proved unconquerable. After achieving enormous popular success in Alfred Hitchcock's 1951 *Strangers on a Train*, during the filming of Leo McCarey's *My Son John*, he died at the age of thirty-three of an "accidental sedative overdose," the official explanation that many believe was a cover-up for his suicide.

It was during the making of *East Side, West Side* that Nancy ran into trouble when she was identified as one of 208 who'd signed an amicus brief in support of reversing the contempt convictions of writers John Howard Lawson and Dalton Trumbo, two of the celebrated Hollywood Ten who were not only blacklisted but had actually spent time in jail. Thus Schary's rescue phone call to Reagan, the quick "resolution" to her "problem," and the subsequent dinner invitation. Nancy was thrilled by the prospect of meeting such a powerful man who also happened to be one of the most handsome and eligible bachelors in Hollywood.

■ ■ ■ ■

Schary's staff, closely supervised by his wife, prepared a beautiful dinner for the occasion. After everyone had eaten, they all moved to the parlor, where, standing in front of the fire, holding a glass of sherry, Reagan gave an impromptu lecture about the current state of the Guild's affairs, about which Schary was more than a little interested. It was common knowledge throughout Hollywood that Louis B. Mayer was on the way out as head of the studio, and when that finally happened, his successor was most likely going to be Schary. Throughout Reagan's discourse, Davis watched his every move with her eyes wide open and a neat smile that flashed at him like a lit-up billboard.

A couple of days later, Reagan called and asked Davis out for a date. She immediately accepted, believing she was well on her way to developing a meaningful relationship with Reagan. What she didn't know was that he was still burning over Wyman and venting his rage by dating everything that moved, sleeping with and then discarding them. To him, she was just another possible conquest in a long list of recent conquests.

There was Adele Jergens, a tall Brooklyn-born blonde with a tough but pretty face who, before heading for Hollywood, had been a Rockette at New York's famed Radio City Musical Hall, during which time she was named the number one show girl in the city. In the late thirties, she was signed by Columbia and dubbed "The Eyeful" by the publicity department. Her greatest cinematic moment and the one that caught Reagan's eye was playing starlet Marilyn Monroe's mother in Phil Karlson's 1948 *Ladies of the Chorus,* the best of the nearly forty films she made before moving into television. She and Reagan had a short but passionate affair and after, neither pined for the other.

There was Kay Stewart, a beauty who'd played small parts in big films, including Ernst Lubitsch's 1939 *Ninotchka,* and several of Preston Sturges's classic Paramount Pictures comedies. Blond and leggy, she had the looks to qualify her for Reagan's list.

There was Ruth Roman, a more serious, dark-haired contract player with star potential who projected cool if detached sophistication.

There was Monica Lewis, fourteen years Reagan's junior, who would go on to become a regular on several TV shows, including one of the first appearances on *Ed Sullivan,* in his original chorus line of women who promoted his auto sponsor's product every Sunday night. She had been married to agent Jennings Lang, who had been unfortunately incapacitated when producer Walter Wanger suspected Lang of having an affair with his wife, Joan Bennett, and shot his testicles off.

There was Penny Edwards, blond haired and blue eyed, with a smile that defined the word *vivacious,* whom Reagan had first met on the set of *That Hagen Girl* and whose company he much preferred to that of Shirley Temple. Edwards, seventeen years Reagan's junior, was originally a Ziegfeld girl signed to Warner as a second lead and appeared in a number of minor musicals before signing with Republic, where she temporarily replaced Dale Evans as Roy Rogers's (sometimes) lover and (always) sidekick. Edwards was, reportedly, enamored of Reagan, but her mother, who was a Christian zealot, did not approve of the relationship. No matter. Reagan loved the fact that she was gorgeous, young, and believed in God. It didn't have to last forever.

There was Ann Sothern, a tart redhead turned blonde who played in the Maisie series in the forties before making her real name in television. She was two years older than Reagan, slightly overweight, and short, but her snappy personality appealed to him. For a month or so.

There was Evelyn Knight, a popular singer of the time known as "the lass with the delicate hair." She was blond, five years younger than Reagan, and had several hit songs during the forties, including two that went to number one ("A Little Bird Told Me" and "Powder Your Face with Sunshine").

There was Betty Underwood, a blond starlet he'd met on the set of *The Girl from Jones Beach,* who had Reagan's flavor of choice for nightclubbing, something he especially enjoyed when he had a drink in his hand and a bombshell on his arm. "I had just arrived in Hollywood from New York in 1948," recalled Underwood. "I started dating Ronnie after starting the movie. I had been a Powers model. Ronnie was surrounded by girls like Virginia May and Joy Lansing and Lola Albright, and the gossip columnists had fun with that. Not too long after *Jones Beach* I went back to New York to do television, and Ronnie would come to New York to do public appearances and we dated until I started dating my future husband. He was always a gentleman, very charming, and we had a lot of fun together. . . . He was very romantic and he wrote me a lot of letters. I threw them all away, but I do remember him writing about how he missed me. I still have a French bird in a golden cage that he gave me as a gift when we were dating. . . . He seemed to be serious about me, but in all frankness, I was never really pushy about that. Security was very important to me and Ronnie was an actor, but we did date for a couple of years. He got married in '52, I got married in '53 . . . let's just let it go at that."

There was Dorothy Shay, ten years Reagan's junior, who was a popular singer with the Spike Jones band before going into television, where she had a solid if unexciting career. Her southern accent and manner charmed Reagan.

There was Peggy Stewart, twelve years younger than Reagan, who acted mostly in television but was often used as a double in films because of her ability to ride a horse. Reagan liked that. He met her through her brother-in-law, actor Wayne Morris.

There was Piper Laurie, twenty-one years younger than Reagan, whom he had met at Universal. Laurie was more mature looking than her age, and although she played his daughter on-screen, away from the camera she was one of his favorite flings.

Reagan also dated actresses of greater stature, including his costars Patricia Neal, Rhonda Fleming, and Doris Day.[*] It didn't matter to Reagan what their status was, as long as they were players.

Reagan's love life, or more accurately, sex life, was no secret. It was, in fact, the talk of the town, a place where who dated whom

[*] "There was a little place on La Cienega that had a mall band and a small dance floor where [Reagan] always took me." — Doris Day, from her autobiography, *Doris Day: Her Own Story.*

was at least as important a topic at breakfast as the impending threat of nuclear war with the Soviets, if not more so. Actors were like perennial teens, lauded for their physical beauty and treated more or less like children. They threw tantrums and slept with each other like life was one long summer camp. And once Reagan had been burned by Wyman, his method of vengeance was as juvenile as anyone else's in town; he just wanted to screw his way through it and didn't seem to care who knew or who got hurt.

While Louella Parsons and Hedda Hopper purposely steered clear of Reagan's love life, Sidney Skolsky, among other columnists, regularly updated his profile on Reagan with enough "juicy" tidbits to satisfy his Sunday breakfast audience:

HE WAS A FORMER SPORTSCASTER WHO BEGAN HIS CAREER IN PICTURES BY PLAYING THE ROLE OF A SPORTS ANNOUNCER . . . HE COMES ON THE SET AND ALWAYS WALKS AROUND WITH A PORTABLE RADIO . . . HE IS KNOWN AS RONNIE TO HIS FRIENDS, BUT HIS "INTIMATES" CALL HIM DUTCH. . . . HE SAYS HIS TEMPER IS MILD BECAUSE HE'S TOO LAZY TO WORK HIMSELF UP TO A PITCH OF ANGER . . . HE WAS RECENTLY

DIVORCED FROM JANE WYMAN AND IN TRUE HOLLYWOOD FASHION, THEY REMAIN FRIENDS . . . HE HAS BEEN GOING WITH NANCY DAVIS, A PRETTY MODEL . . . HE HAS ALSO BEEN LINKED WITH MONICA LEWIS, ADELE JERGENS AND PATRICIA NEAL . . . THEY ARE ALL JUST DATES . . . HE RESIDES IN A RANCH STYLE HOUSE IN THE HOLLYWOOD HILLS.

Nancy could not have been pleased with being listed among her competition (some of them, anyway) or that she was a model rather than an actress. It was going to take all the skills of an expert to get Reagan, who, while emotionally wounded, in her eyes stood on the brink of greatness. To her he was a healthier version of Robert Walker, only with far more potential.

Reagan was not oblivious to Davis's strong attraction to him, though he may have gotten his signals somewhat crossed. He took her "Come hither" to mean "Let's get it on." Nancy knew the difference; if Reagan did, he didn't think about it all that much. In her memoirs, she tacitly acknowledged the truth of the existence of other women in Reagan's life while she was dating him: "I wish I could report that we saw each other exclusively, and that we couldn't wait to get married. But

403

Ronnie was in no hurry to make a commitment. He had been burned in his first marriage and the pain went deep. Although we saw each other regularly, he also dated other women . . . my mother reminded me that Loyal Davis had been badly burned in his first marriage. He had been terrified of making another mistake, and she had had to wait until he was ready."

In that remarkably frank paragraph is both the recognition that she had competition and, at the very heart of her devotion, her desire not only to rescue Reagan but, like her mother had with Dr. Davis, to redeem him. And she wasn't about to let a few "dalliances" stand in the way of what she had in store for him, meaning of course for them.

Greatness.

Reagan's first film under his new contract at Universal, Alexander Hall's 1950 *Louisa,* didn't thrill him. Having left his exclusive deal at Warner Bros. because of the seemingly endless flow of light comedies they continued to put him in, he now found himself in a goofily limp "romp" about the pursuit of a grandmother (Spring Byington) by an aging local grocer, a geriatric romance that becomes a nuisance to married architect Hal Norton (Reagan), his cute daughter (Piper Laurie, whom Reagan dated during the making of the film), and his wonderful wife (Ruth Hussey). Problems arise when Norton's boss also inexplicably goes into heat over the elderly Byington. The film is essentially a role-reversal comedy, with the parents acting like the kids and the kids acting like parents, with all the humor that implies, which, in this case, was none. While the film was amusingly cute and did reunite Reagan with Charles Coburn, one of his favorite actors from *Kings Row*, it did nothing to solve Reagan's career dilemma.

Reagan had initially been enthusiastic about the project because of the director Alexander Hall, who had led Robert Montgomery in one of the few genuinely funny and sophisticated "fantasy" movies that were so popular in the forties, 1941's *Here Comes Mr. Jordan*. In 1947, Hall would score another hit with a romantic fantasy that was a sequel of sorts to *Jordan* called *Down to Earth*, about Terpsichore (Rita Hayworth), who floats down to help a dancer (Larry Parks).[*] Unfortunately, none of Hall's talent transferred well to *Louisa*, whose characters were too down to earth, giving Reagan little opportunity to soar.

Reagan couldn't really complain, however, because Universal had intended to use him

---

[*] The characters of Mr. Jordan and Max are reprised from the hugely successful *Here Comes Mr. Jordan*, with Roland Culver replacing Claude Rains as Mr. Jordan, and James Gleason returning as Max.

in the superior *Woman in Hiding* until he'd taken himself out of it by breaking his leg. Nonetheless, *Louisa* represented nothing so much as a continuation of the slow slide of his postwar career, not quite steep enough to cause alarm, nor level enough to maintain the status quo of whatever remained of his stardom.

Nancy, meanwhile, kept up her pursuit, unaware that for all the women Reagan had been linked with, there was one who meant more to him than even the gossips ever knew about. He was crazy about gorgeous, leggy Christine Larson, different from all the others because he actually wanted to marry her.

On the night Reagan actually got down on one knee, his proposal to the twenty-six-year-old actress (she might have been as old as thirty-three; like many actresses, including Nancy, her true birth date is hard to verify) came with a ring and a diamond wristwatch as a deal sweetener. Larson turned down the proposal, returned the ring, but kept the watch.

She liked Reagan well enough, slept with him regularly, and was amused rather than annoyed by his political meanderings, but she just wasn't in love with him. Gary Cooper was the unrequited love of her life. Moreover, she was also a practicing Baha'i, something that would have been more of a problem for her than for Reagan, whose official religion was always more externally ritualistic than a reflection of any internal spirituality.[*]

Reagan may have been attracted to Larson but what he so desperately wanted, if not needed, was a luxe female to confirm his sex appeal to the world. His long list of paramours is a testament to that obsession, and his proposal to Larson the climax of it.

Nancy, who lived only a few blocks away from Larson, correctly suspected that on those nights when Reagan did not stay over with her, he was at Larson's, sometimes staying the entire night. She never dared to follow his car or drive past Larson's home to see if her suspicions were correct, but it wouldn't have mattered. She had a much better plan for her Ronald and it didn't include ensnaring him in a web of guilt.

In February 1950, Reagan decided he didn't want to celebrate his thirty-ninth birthday alone, especially since that year the Friars Club Los Angeles division's dinner to honor his service to the industry happened to fall on his birthday. To be his date, he invited Nancy, who saw it as a turning point, especially when, the next day, he told her he was going to nominate her to serve on the board

[*] The Baha'i believe that a new Messiah arrived after Moses, Jesus, and Muhammad and that his mission was to bring world peace through spiritual enlightenment.

of the Screen Actors Guild.

For Nancy, this was far better than any diamond watch. Still, Reagan was moving slowly and cautiously.

In the fall of 1950, Reagan reported for work at Universal to appear in the film that would forever expose him to ridicule and haunt him throughout his political career, particularly after he became president of the United States. *Bedtime for Bonzo* was directed by Frederick de Cordova, who would go on to produce *The Tonight Show Starring Johnny Carson* for more than two decades, a show where *Bedtime for Bonzo* became the subject of constant ridicule by Carson, most of it directed at Cordova, but it was difficult for Reagan to avoid the scattershot of Carson's sharp humor.

From the very beginning, however, the *Bonzo* humiliation factor for Reagan ran high. In a December 12, 1950, theatrical newsreel trailer narrated by "Preview Pete," the film was publicized by giving the chimpanzee all of the attention: "In the office of producer Mike Kraike, with Francis the mule and a strangely visible Harvey for witnesses, Bonzo signs the contract to appear in *Bedtime for Bonzo.* Terms of the contract? In return for a stipulated number of bananas, Bonzo agrees to do all his own stunts without benefit of a double . . . agrees to accept Ronald Reagan and Diana Lynn as his costars . . . and above all agrees to make monkies [*sic*] out of people . . . with which he is an expert!"

In truth, the film wasn't all that bad, or the pairing of animal with man that unusual for Hollywood. Actors had costarred alongside "monkeys" and "chimps" for as long as film existed, and few actors, no matter how big, managed to escape the so-called curse of working with scene-stealing animals and children at some point in their careers. From Charlie Chaplin to Cary Grant to Clint Eastwood, it has been tried with varying degrees of success. Chaplin most famously appeared opposite a child in his 1921 production of *The Kid* with Jackie Coogan, and in 1925 opposite a chicken and a bear in his 1925 film *Gold Rush.* Only his comic genius allowed him to get away with it. Fay Wray managed a career out of her heated relationship with King Kong in Merian C. Cooper's 1933 blockbuster, the only film of hers anybody really remembers. Jimmy Stewart successfully costarred with a giant rabbit in Henry Koster's 1950 *Harvey,* but at least it was invisible (Walter Slezak even makes reference to an invisible six-foot rabbit in *Bonzo*). Donald O'Connor practically made a career out of partnering up with a talking donkey named Francis, appearing with him in several movies, a forerunner to TV's *Mr. Ed.* A year after

Reagan made *Bonzo,* Grant appeared in Howard Hawks's *Monkey Business,* a very successful comedy costarring Ginger Rogers, a very young Marilyn Monroe, and Esther, the Chimp. Eastwood hit box-office paydirt in James Fargo's *Every Which Way but Loose* opposite Clyde the orangutan.

It wasn't just the fact that Reagan had to play opposite Bonzo that bothered him as much as it was being in another stale comedic role he felt he was completely miscast for but could not escape. Despite strong reviews when it opened (*The Hollywood Reporter* called it a "smash comedy," *Variety* called it "first-rate"), the film did nothing for Reagan's career goal to be accepted as a serious actor.

After *Bedtime for Bonzo,* Reagan, his tail hanging a bit longer between his legs, went back to Warners for the first film under his nonexclusive contract with them. It wasn't something he was particularly happy about but his only real option to keep himself working was to take whatever Warners offered, in this instance Stuart Heisler's *Storm Warning,* a film out of Jerry Wald's A unit.

Reagan was lucky to have any job these days, and he knew it. The lack of options wasn't just because he had done *Bonzo,* but was also due to the overall state of the film industry. By 1951, the year of *Bonzo*'s release, Warner's film production schedule was down to just twenty-eight films, from a prewar high of more than a hundred annually. Television, independent productions, and the ongoing public battles over communist infiltration that had fueled HUAC's latest round of investigations had taken much of the fun and nearly all of the fantasy out of the weekly American habit of going to the movies.

Stuart Heisler's best work would come in television episodics after an undistinguished career as the director of dozens of forgettable films, of which *Storm Warning* was one. It costarred Ginger Rogers, whose career was in decline following her smashing series of dance musicals with Fred Astaire; Doris Day (whom Reagan was reported in the gossips to have started dated again during the filming, which Day later denied); Steve Cochran, a holdover from the war years of interim leading men; and a host of faceless studio contract supporting players. And despite Jack Warner's public oath on the eve of the HUAC hearings to never again make socially relevant movies, that's exactly what *Storm Warning* was. Above all, Jack Warner, despite his pledge to HUAC, knew how to make pictures that sold, and politics and the stories dealing with the social order drew the biggest audiences, so he continued to make them. In a way, *Storm Warning* is a progressive film ahead of its time dealing with racist vigilantism in the South. In the film, crusading prosecutor Burt Rainey (Reagan) decides to take on and break up the Ku Klux Klan (the last time Warner had dealt with any degree of depth with this subject was Archie Mayo's 1938 *Black Legion,* starring Humphrey Bogart).

Although not a major box-office success, the film was one of Reagan's better efforts, well supported by an able cast and a good, realistic story. If it wasn't strictly an action picture, it was closer to the kind of film Reagan wanted to do. *Storm Warning* did well in theaters and Reagan agreed to go on a countrywide promotion tour to support it, one of the last the studio would underwrite before shifting much of its promotional budgets to television advertising.

Reagan hoped for some measure of career revitalization from this work, but unfortunately it wasn't to be. The box office for *Storm Warning* was lukewarm and became Wald's last production for Warner before he, too, like Wallis before him, left to form his own, independent filmmaking company.*

While Reagan was on location for *Storm*

---

* Despite Wald's long friendship with Reagan — they had met early in both their studio days, when Wald was still a contract screenwriter — he never hired Reagan for any of his independent productions.

Warning (in Corona, California, a town chosen by Warner for its ability to reasonably pass for the Deep South), Nancy bided her time, waiting patiently for Reagan to spend some of it with her. However, after completing *Storm Warning,* he flew directly to Arizona and into *The Last Outpost,* a film that Wasserman had arranged for him to make for Paramount. Reagan was paid only $45,000 to make the picture, and took it without complaint. He knew as well as anybody his recent film's track records had left him no bargaining power. And he was running short on cash.

Wasserman knew that Reagan wanted to make a *real* Western, something that — in his thirty-one feature films he made in the six years he spent in Hollywood prior to (and during) World War II, and the eleven in the four years since the war had ended — he had never had the chance to do. The genre had been the requisite stepping-stone to stardom in the early years of filmmaking. Now it was the last refuge for older Hollywood stars like John Wayne, Jimmy Stewart, Gary Cooper, and Spencer Tracy, all of whom had been aged out of their original youthful personae but eased into the leather saddles of the horse operas that would ultimately extend and in some cases come to define their careers — Wayne with John Ford in films like 1955's *The Searchers,* Jimmy Stewart in his fifties

Western cycle for Anthony Mann, Cooper in Fred Zinnemann's 1952 *High Noon,* Tracy in John Sturges's 1955 *Bad Day at Black Rock.* Reagan desperately wanted to become a member of that club.

Wasserman arranged for the veteran production team of William H. Pine and William C. Thomas, in place for a decade at Paramount where they made dozens of B movies, to use Reagan in the role of the cavalry officer in their Civil War Western, 1951's *The Last Outpost.** The film was directed by Lewis R. Foster, a veteran whose résumé stretched all the way back to silent film (and would move forward to TV episodics, mostly for Walt Disney's Daniel Boone and Andy Burnett miniseries). Foster had a good feel for Westerns, and with *The Last Outpost* delivered a solid B oater, no more, no less. As with previous efforts, it ultimately did nothing for the descending arc of Reagan's career.

As a single film, it remains in the margins of American cinema, but as an American historical landmark, it hit a home run. Here, for the first time, the American public saw Ronald Reagan sitting tall in the saddle, an image of what would one day become the one iconic vision of the future president of the United States, the rough and tumble leader of the free world. Up there on Tarbaby, his

* Aka *Cavalry Charge.*

own favorite horse that the studio agreed to ship from Reagan's L.A. ranch to Arizona, Reagan looked the part of a man marked for greatness. Unlike his role in *Santa Fe Trail,* which was really Flynn's picture and showed off the callow side of supporting-player Reagan, in this film he is fully formed, the man, the leader, the John Wayne–in-waiting inheritor of the mantle of the mythic all-American hero.

Finishing *The Last Outpost* capped a busy four-picture burst (*Louisa, Storm Warning, Bedtime for Bonzo,* and *The Last Outpost*) that, at the time, did nothing so much as replenish Reagan's dwindling bank account. With alimony, child support, taxes, and a lifestyle befitting a bigger movie star than he was, and having not worked for over four years during the war, Reagan had been nearly tapped out before Wasserman had come through with these four movies. And, as always, the soft-spoken, bespectacled, suit-and-tie agent kept a marker for his favors, ready to cash in when the time was right.

With Reagan, Wasserman knew, that time was rapidly approaching.

Back home, Reagan resumed his bachelor lifestyle. Davis quietly resumed her quest to put an end to it. To do so, she enlisted the help of every available gossip columnist, all of whom were only too eager to help. One of the lieutenants she enlisted in her campaign was the ever-reliable Louella Parsons, who was more than eager to see the two get together, especially if she could have the story as a scoop. In 1951, she wrote: "I sincerely believe there's not a chance in the world of Jane Wyman and Ronald Reagan being married lovers again . . . I introduced them. You might say I practically threw them together when I invited them to come out with me on my first personal appearance tour . . . and one of the lovely girls Ronnie seemed interested in for a while told me he recently said to her, 'Sure I like you, I like you fine. But I think I've forgotten how to fall in love.' "

Two months later, Parsons reported in her regular syndicated column that Reagan and Davis were seen dancing at Ciro's, and that their romance was a "very big thing" in Hollywood.

In May, Jim Burton wrote in *Modern Screen:* "No matter how you look at it, Ronald Reagan, the shy, quiet, executive-type actor, just *has* to be in love with Nancy Davis. Five will get you 10 anywhere in Hollywood that wedding bells will ring for them before many months have passed . . . it would be hard to find a girl more suited to Ronnie Reagan's somewhat split nature than Nancy Davis . . . In a wonderfully ordinary way, Nancy Davis has a great gift for homemaking, a real attribute as far as a man of

Reagan's tastes is concerned."

Nancy was especially pleased with the piece; Reagan was infuriated by it. He felt the magazines were prying into his private life, and profiting from his involuntary return to bachelorhood. If he thought Nancy was behind it, he never said anything to her or anyone else about it. If Reagan hoped his complaints would make the press go away, he seriously miscalculated the reaction of his complaints to the publishers, who were quick to point out that he had no problem posing for pictures when it benefited him and helped sell his movies. What had especially rankled the press were Reagan's continual self-important articles he wrote for various magazines during these blacklist years about the precious entity of "freedom."

The print news media was far less convinced of his nobility, and when he threatened to try to put the muzzle on one of them for making his private love life a little less so while he dated Nancy Davis, they returned fire with all cannons loaded. Here is the complete open letter from the editors of *Motion Picture* to Reagan that was published in the June 1951 issue of their magazine:

According to newspaper reports, the Screen Actors Guild, of which you are president, plans this summer to launch a campaign to prevent fan magazines from running any stories about the private lives of established film stars. You implied that such stories might be all right for young actors on their way up, but that, once a person becomes a star, the only news that should be published about him ought to be stories which the star himself considers acceptable.

We think you should know that, regardless of what rules your organization sets up concerning what is and what is not legitimate news for movie fans, every reporter and editor worth his salt is going to remember that his first responsibility is to his readers, and, in the good old American tradition, he is going to print the legitimate news he thinks those readers want him to print.

What's legitimate news about a movie star?

The answer is virtually everything a star does or says. You are paid a large salary because you are a public figure. If you were an unknown, you could be just as handsome as you are now, just as good a performer and just as hard a worker. But your salary probably would be no bigger than that of a competent engineer, taxicab driver, machinist or manicurist, all of whom are just as accomplished in their professions as you are in yours. But their jobs don't depend on the size of their public.

You made a personal appearance in Miami last winter to promote the box-office of your latest movie. During that visit to Miami, everything you did was news — or it is assumed you wanted it to be so. Whether you made a visit to a veterans' hospital, addressed a luncheon or — should it have happened — engaged in a brawl in a night club, you must have expected to find something about it in the papers next day, because that's why you were in Miami in the first place. But you should remember that you were news because publicity *made* you news.

You cited fan magazine stories about your divorce from Jane Wyman as "false and irresponsible invasions" of your privacy. We disagree. We disagree because you apparently didn't feel the marriage itself was a private affair (in 1943 our photographers were permitted to take all the pictures they wanted of your home, your wife and your family, and in 1941 you talked freely to our reporter concerning your expected baby, and posed buying toys, baby powder and bassinets). But, if the happy marriage was news, then it seems to follow that the *break-up* of that marriage also was news.

As for your reported feeling that publicity is all right for young actors, are we to assume you mean your fans are important to you only when you need them and that what you do once you gain stardom is none of their business?

Yours is a business, Mr. Reagan, which is built on publicity. In this sense, actors are like politicians; and, while Harry Truman could have written all the letters to music critics he wanted when he was a haberdasher in Missouri, once he became president such letters become news in every paper in the country. Although, since Mr. Truman's letter concerned his daughter, I imagine you felt his privacy had been invaded.

We suggest you take another look at your bank account, Mr. Reagan. And look around at your home, your present way of life, your success. If you decide they aren't worth the price you have to pay for them, then we think you've got a point. But, regardless of your conclusions, as long as our readers are interested in Ronald Reagan, or any other important movie star, we're going to give them stories that satisfy that interest.

The Editors, "Motion Picture"

On the surface, the piece was a direct rebuke to Reagan, but it also symbolized the general feeling that the print media had had enough of being told what they could and couldn't say. It was a direct outgrowth of the madness of what had been going on in Hollywood.

By now, the sick frenzy of the blacklist was in full fever and Reagan was one of its most intense supporters. Even as the studio system was collapsing into free fall, pictures that had once been seen as routinely patriotic, even if the hero was reluctant, as in *Casablanca* (Rick's loyalties were never in question), the notion of how to portray patriotism had became infinitely more difficult. Films like *High Noon* and, not long after, *On the Waterfront* were held up to the dark bright lights of freedom in search of hidden anti-Americanism (both films are replete with future blacklistees or capitulators, including *High Noon*'s producer/writer Carl Foreman and *On the Waterfront*'s director Elia Kazan, both of whose careers were wrecked as much by accusation and innuendo as fact, and in Kazan's case, secret testimony in which he "named names").

In truth, few who made or appeared in these movies were able to escape the collective taint.[*] Even those who were innocent found it difficult, as the nature of movies and

---

[*] For further information and background, the author recommends Larry Ceplair and Steven Englund's *The Inquisition in Hollywood*.

the whole point of the star system was to make the actors and actresses "become" the roles they played in the minds of audiences. Inside the industry, those who wrote and directed the movies were as vulnerable as stars to the public. Those who refused to testify at HUAC were blacklisted after the Waldorf Statement, and in some cases, such as the Hollywood Ten, went to prison on charges of contempt. Those who did testify were also blacklisted; besides Kazan, there was the unfortunate case of Larry Parks, the star of the dazzlingly successful *The Jolson Story,* who wound up publicly pleading for mercy (even though he had no idea what he had done wrong, if anything) and got none. In order to keep working, those on the fence, such as Humphrey Bogart, went through verbal contortions to explain what they really meant whenever they said what they said. John Garfield, arguably the hottest male star of the forties, was blacklisted and died at the age of thirty-nine of a heart attack. Some, such as actor Phillip Loeb and attorney Bartley Crum, committed suicide.** Some were

---

** Loeb died of an overdose in 1955 at the age of sixty-three. He had gained fame as the husband of Gertrude Berg on the popular radio and TV series *The Goldbergs,* but was forced off the show in 1950 after being listed in *Red Channels* and named by Elia Kazan and Lee J. Cobb during the HUAC hear

blacklisted simply because those in charge didn't like them (Disney's naming of Sorrell). Some, whose artistic friendships were long and deep, like Elia Kazan and Arthur Miller, saw them permanently ruptured. And some fled to foreign countries to avoid arrest and persecution and in many instances never returned to Hollywood, Carl Foreman and Robert Rossen among them. Others simply stopped working, sometimes for years, forced to sell everything they owned to feed their families as they suffered exile from their own industry. Superpatriots like John Wayne, whose real-life foundation for bravado was, to say the least, wobbly and weak, who nevertheless easily fit into the uniform of hero on the screen and stood in the posture of a patriot off it, cashed in on their oaths of loyalty and continued to earn their livings. Other "friendly witnesses" came through it all unscathed, as was the case with Gary Cooper, the Academy Award–winning star of *High Noon.* Hollywood in the fifties was in a fever of madness, paranoia, and confusion, built on chauvinism, profit, and vendetta.

And it was one of the reasons, overlooked among the usual histories of "what happened," that cite the rise of "free" television

---

ings as being a former communist. Loeb never worked as an actor again. Crum was an attorney who had defended several of the Hollywood Ten.

as the main culprit, Americans largely turned away from going to the movies. The messages coming off the screen were as twisted as the politics of those making the movies. A film such as Don Siegel's 1956 *Invasion of the Body Snatchers,* which carried subliminal anti-communist messages — our individualism is being snatched by people who look like our friends but aren't — did nothing to promote the notion of a family outing to the neighborhood theater. By the midfifties, the annual box-office take had been cut in half from a decade before. Suspension of disbelief was difficult with a box of popcorn in one hand and a "commie" scorecard in the other.

Even Reagan couldn't completely escape the pervasive hysteria. Although he had never liked either the communists he knew personally nor the policies they preached, his once Jeffersonian-based idealism — despite having taken a harder, more corrosive edge, unlike most who wanted to lynch anyone suspected of being a communist from the nearest cherry tree — still addressed the issue of whether a person's politics, no matter how unpopular, should automatically disqualify him from the opportunity to make a living in America, if that was really the American way. In "How Do You Fight Communism?," which appeared in *Fortnight* magazine in the January 22, 1951, issue, he addressed this dilemma and appeared to support the political minority but qualified that support with an indirect warning to anyone, meaning any communists, who would use freedom as a weapon against freedom. In that sense, he was actually one of the few voices of tolerance and moderation in an increasingly intolerant and immoderate time. He ended a long attack on those film-makers he saw as dangerously subversive with the following: "Democracy does guarantee the right of every man to think as he pleases, to speak freely and to advocate his beliefs. *Democracy also provides defense against those who would deliver our nation into the hands of a foreign despot.*" [Italics added].

During all of this, Reagan's attention to Nancy had necessarily fallen off. As a tap on the shoulder to remind him she was still around, she told him over dinner one night at Ciro's that since her last movie, William Wellman's highly touted 1950 production of *The Next Voice You Hear* (a bit of neo-Christian fluff about God deciding to go on the radio one Sunday night to have a fireside chat with the world), had bombed at the box office, she was thinking of accepting an offer to do a play in New York City. That meant she would have to move there, at least for the run of the production and probably a whole lot longer if she was going to make a living in the theater.

Reagan, unflappable as always, thought that

that might be a great move for her career.

That week she turned down the offer (if there ever actually was one).

She gradually began to hint she might start dating other men.

Okay by him, Reagan said.

Then one night, alone at his house, over drinks, she told him she was pregnant and that in another month she would start to show.

The next day he called her stepfather, Loyal Davis, and asked for his daughter's hand in marriage.

And the day after that, Nancy Davis voluntarily terminated her contract at MGM to devote herself full-time to making plans for the wedding.[*]

---

[*] Sources differ on whether Nancy Davis voluntarily ended her career at MGM or if the studio did it. Kelley claims in her biography of Davis that the studio canceled her contract after the failure of *The Next Voice You Hear;* Davis claims in her memoir that it was a voluntary decision on her part. Colacello suggests the studio allowed her to resign as a face-saving act.

■ ■ ■ ■

CHAPTER TEN:
FALLING UPWARD

■ ■ ■ ■

The Reagans were always the poorest
people in the richest crowd.

— CAROL TROY

Ronald Reagan and Nancy Davis in the 1957 production of Hellcats of the Navy, *the only feature film in which they appeared together.*

Nancy Davis was the perfect second wife for Ronald Reagan. He had made all his mistakes the first time around; he had chosen for sex and glamour, and had taken advantage of his position in the industry to get Wyman. Once they were married, when his career slipped as hers soared, he found himself locked in an emotional prison for which there was no other key to freedom, no matter how distasteful, than divorce. It wasn't until the arrival of Nancy Davis that Reagan would be able to even begin to break his lovelorn free fall. He was able to do it because she was utterly unlike any other woman he had ever been with, even Mugs, because she, Nancy, was totally willing to give up the watch and keep the man. Not that it was not going to be easy. For one thing, there were very real obstacles to be overcome. Reagan's career, already on the decline, was about to fall off a cliff, along with a lot of others as the studios downsized their contract talent to try to figure out how to stay in business. Not long before the wedding ceremony, Reagan realized that for the first time in a long time, he was, for all intents and purposes, flat broke.

MGM, Nancy's studio, made the announcement of the wedding date — March 4, 1952 — to the public almost as an afterthought to the news release that Nancy Davis had "asked out of her contract" (March 4 was a Tuesday, not the traditional Saturday wedding day). The publicity department, in a nod to Schary and company, had put her departure in the best possible light and, in keeping with the mores of the day, played down the fact that although it was her first marriage, it was Reagan's second. For a variety of reasons, Reagan, too, did not want a lot of attention focused on the wedding, not the least of which being that he absolutely did not want anyone to know that Nancy was already pregnant when they tied the knot.

Reagan's best man at the wedding was William Holden, his only invited friend. Reagan liked Holden, one of those he would always describe as a "man's man," a tall, dark, and handsome type who projected an on-screen combination of strength, heat, and vulnerability that was his bread and butter. Holden's wife, actress Brenda Marshall (Ardis was her real first name, the one her friends used), was also part of the wedding party, even though they'd had had too much to drink and had something of a brawl the night before and weren't speaking to each other at the wedding.

Left out of the ceremonies were Reagan's two other movie buddies, Glenn Ford and Jimmy Stewart. Ford was scratched because Reagan didn't want Eleanor Powell, Ford's wife, one of the biggest stars in Hollywood, to attract undue attention from the press; Stewart, then one of Hollywood's most eligible bachelors, because he would have to bring someone and Reagan didn't want to leave open the possibility she might be someone he wouldn't want to see. He and Stewart had dated many of the same women.

The ceremony took place at the Little Brown Disciples of Christ Church in the Valley, on the southern edge of the San Fernando Valley. No children, no stepchildren, no relatives, not even Reagan's mother was invited. No press was told where the wedding was going to take place. No gossip columnists covered the event. There was only a single set of photos, taken with the Holdens, at the Reagans' home prior to leaving for the church. After the simple exchange of vows, Mr. and Mrs. Reagan, he in a dark blue suit, she in a gray wool suit with a white collar and cuffs and a small hat, left to spend their wedding night at the Old Mission Inn in Riverside, a small, countrified upscale motel buried even deeper in the valley. There, a single bouquet of roses adorned the room, courtesy of the management. Having parked Reagan's children with his mother, the next morning they left for a two-week honeymoon in Phoenix, Arizona, where Edith and Loyal Davis flew out to share in the happy occasion. Ronald Reagan spent the first full day of his second marriage with his wife and her parents.

Nothing that day could have made him happier.

Back in Hollywood, Wasserman had bad news for his client. Universal wanted to part ways. The production unit led by Pine and Thomas could no longer financially justify putting Reagan into the final two movies of the four-movie nonexclusive deal he had been contracted to (at $75,000 per film); it exercised an escape clause based on the box-office returns and informed Wasserman his client was out. The timing of the cancellation couldn't have been worse. Reagan had just purchased a small but gorgeous piece of Malibu Canyon property on the corner of Mulholland Drive and Cornell Road in Agoura, California, undeveloped except for a small farmhouse and a caretaker's shack that had been built in 1918 and had seen better decades. The land itself was totally surrounded by 2,500 acres of Twentieth Century back lot, a purposely undeveloped stretch beyond the sightlines of billboards and other highway telltale identifications that served as the location backdrop for most of the studio's Westerns. Reagan's new house was located a half hour from Beverly Hills proper, far from the exclusive neighborhood of the film industry's biggest names. And that was just fine with him. As far as he was concerned, it was only "a hop, a skip and a Cadillac" away from Hollywood.

To finance the $85,000 purchase, Reagan had to sell the smaller ranch he had acquired while married to Wyman and managed to hold on to in their divorce agreement, using whatever he netted as the down payment. He also decided to keep the Londonderry apartment in Hollywood, for storage space. The purchase had taken all his available cash, but Reagan was unconcerned, believing his Universal deal was solid and that in a pinch there would always be a place for him at Warner.

When he returned to L.A. and got the bad news from Wasserman about Universal, he went directly to his office, sat down with his agent, and read him the riot act. He told Wasserman he needed something, and fast, to help pay the new mortgage and the stack of bills piling up behind them like waves on the Malibu surf. Well, there was something, Wasserman told him. Television. He could get him all the work he wanted in it and make them both (Wasserman and Reagan) a lot of money.

Reagan frowned, shook his head slowly, and said no. He didn't want to be in a medium dominated by clowns, comics, and game shows, he said. Nor did he want to be overexposed, giving away for free what audiences paid to see in theaters — not that anyone was lining up to pay to see him on the big screen these days, he joked. Reagan stood up, asked Wasserman to keep trying, and left.

When it came to television, Wasserman knew what he was talking about. As early as 1943, at the height of the war and with Jules Stein's enthusiastic approval, MCA had formed a subsidiary production company called Revue to capitalize on the big-band craze, to produce bigger and more sophisticated stage productions — "revues" — that would employ MCA clients. The idea was to package an entire evening's presentation rather than a single band and to charge appropriately for it.

Revue had proved incredibly lucrative to MCA until the war ended and the bottom fell out of the big-band craze, replaced by radio, records, and the hot new fad called rock and roll. By 1950, Revue's only remaining viable assets "were a corporate seal and reams of unused stationery," leaving Wasserman to figure out a way to resurrect it.

For a decade MCA had been packaging a radio show for NBC, *Stars Over Hollywood,* which had been one of the more successful ventures into the medium for both the network and the agency. The latter quietly stocked the program with its own clients, thereby earning both production and talent fees, technically a violation of the strict conflict-of-interest regulations that were set by the government to prevent actors' (and writers' and other talents') agents from also being their bosses. The problem was obvious; one side would be trying to get the most money it could get for its client, the other would be trying to pay the least possible. When both sides doing the negotiating were the same, there was a problem. A serious one.

Wasserman's particular brilliance in this venture shone early on, when he got the idea to turn the radio program into a television show. Whereas most early TV shows were live, the quality was usually poor compared to film, due to the technical limitations of the infant medium. Wasserman wanted the show, the name of which he changed to the *Armour Playhouse,* for its new canned-food sponsor, to be filmed at MCA's own in-house Revue studios, updated and modernized for TV.

To compensate for the cost of the renovations, Wasserman decided to pay talent the minimum allowable, or scale, $500 a show, via Revue, rather than the competitive rate they might have gotten if MCA were hiring them for an outside production. Name-brand stars such as Basil Rathbone, Phil Harris, Alan Ladd, and Merle Oberon were worth $5,000 a show. They were all MCA clients, they had all appeared on the radio show, and were all scheduled to appear for scale, on the TV version.

The brilliance of Wasserman's plan was not in the low-balling of his own clients, but the larger vision behind it. "Live" shows shot on film in the new studio could be played over and over again with no loss of quality, unlike what was already the TV norm, kinescopes — movies crudely made through the television lens during live productions that looked like they were shot through a magnifying glass (think of the filmed quality of *I Love Lucy* versus the kinescoped quality of the original thirty-nine episodes of *The Honeymooners*).

Although the *Armour Playhouse* lasted only a year on the NBC television network, MCA, under its Revue banner, in 1951 started selling its pristine filmed TV episodes on a syndicated basis to individual local stations across the country. The agency made huge profits while paying no residuals to either the show's performers or writers.

As the popularity of the new medium grew,

MCA expanded Revue's production schedule to include TV versions of the most popular radio shows of the forties, including *Truth or Consequences,* Groucho Marx's *You Bet Your Life, Kay Kaiser's Kollege of Musical Knowledge, The Red Skelton Show,* and *Abbott and Costello,* among dozens of others that were quickly and easily adapted to the new medium. Audiences were thrilled to see on their black-and-white screens what they could only "see" in their minds when listening to the radio.

Early on, Wasserman knew it was only a matter of time before the various talent unions, especially SAG, would realize what the game was and insist that MCA could not produce and represent talent at the same time. But he also knew that in postwar, post-monopolistic Hollywood, where as much, if not more, TV was being made as feature films, unreasonable union demands might not go over so well with a membership increasingly desperate for work. And he also believed he had an ace in the hole. The president of the Screen Actors Guild was not only a client but also a close and loyal friend. And one who needed work.

With a new wife, a mortgage, alimony, child support for two children, a third on the way, and no real work in sight, Reagan was hit with a back-tax assessment of $21,000 from the Internal Revenue Service that he knew he had to pay before he could appeal.*

That March, the cash-strapped Reagans agreed to attend the Academy Awards held at the RKO Pantages Theater in Hollywood. Hosted that year by Danny Kaye, they walked through the flashing bulbs to their seats, where they had a perfect view of Kaye and Jane Wyman performing what would be that year's Best Song winner, Hoagy Carmichael and Johnny Mercer's "In the Cool, Cool, Cool of the Evening" from Frank Capra's

* In his first memoir (*Where's the Rest of Me?*, page 247), Reagan claims the bill was the result of a miscalculation by the business department of Universal, which did not take into account the canceling of the last two of his contracted films when computing his annual salary. The story isn't completely accurate. The debt actually came from income Reagan had deferred prior to his entering the army, when he was still in the 95 percent tax bracket. It was Reagan's loss of anticipated income from breaking his contract at Universal that cost him anticipated revenues of $100,000, some of which he planned to use to pay off that tax bill. He managed to scrape together the $21,000, and a year later, Reagan won his appeal of the penalties (based on the fact that they had accrued while he was in the service) and the $21,000 was refunded to him — at a time when he was $18,000 in debt and sorely in need of cash.

Here Comes the Groom. Wyman, at the top of her game, had costarred in the film with Bing Crosby. Wyman was also once again nominated for Best Actress, this time for her performance in Curtis Bernhardt's *The Blue Veil* (she lost to Vivien Leigh in Kazan's *A Streetcar Named Desire*). When the duet ended, Reagan and Nancy politely applauded, their faces frozen in smiles.

Reagan finally got some film work early in the spring of 1952 at Paramount, where he made *Hong Kong* for the Pine/Thomas/Foster unit.[†] *Hong Kong* was directed by Lewis Foster and costarred Rhonda Fleming, although she was not Reagan's main interest in the film. This time he had to cope with a boy as one of his costars, once more breaking the cardinal rule of actors — to never appear opposite children or animals. *Hong Kong* turned out to be a mishmash of cracked romance, paranoid politics, the most unexotic exotic adventure tale imaginable. It is most notable not for anything inherently cinematic but for the interesting parallel between the life of the character Reagan played (Jeff Williams) and his own real life.

In the film, Williams is an ex-G.I. whose luck has gone sour after World War II. He

† Aka *Bombs Over China.*

seeks his fortune in Hong Kong and somehow gets caught up fighting communist insurgents (the film's time frame is pre-1949). Williams rescues a Chinese orphan boy, and takes him to a mission run by the most beautiful missionary in the history of organized religion (Rhonda Fleming). Eventually, after more plot than there are choices on a Chinese menu, Reagan decides to stay in Hong Kong and marry the missionary, conveniently depositing the boy in an orphanage and promising he will come back often to visit. The film disappeared from theaters faster than Chiang Kai-shek from the Chinese mainland.

Rhonda Fleming recalled how it was to work with Reagan on this film: "On the set, nobody else was talking; Ronnie was doing the talking and yarn-telling. We'd laugh, then we'd go into our scenes and, of course, they were not the greatest roles in the world, nor did we have the greatest director. Ronnie would talk about whatever was going on in the world at the time. That's when he seemed to be glowing. And he was funny, vibrant, open, outgoing. He was a totally different person off screen. He seemed to change when he performed — it was something that made me believe he was not comfortable. I don't think he was all that happy being an actor.

"In *Hong Kong* he was playing a bum, running away, trying to steal this little Oriental boy's valued possession. It was hard for Ronnie to be serious. For his scenes, he would have to make an effort to prepare his face to look very serious. In fact, he did it, but it was unlike his character. The minute they yelled 'cut' instead of rehearsing, he'd be into something else. Of the four movies I made with Ronnie, *Hong Kong* was the part he emerged the strongest in. The marriage to Nancy seemed to solidify him because she was very supportive of his career.

"Ronnie wasn't Errol Flynn — his sex appeal wasn't obvious. That electric something just didn't project. It was a very quiet type of sex appeal; understated. I was married and Ronnie was just married. His love scenes were very gentlemanly, sweet, and tender. He did not exude sex. We didn't kiss a lot on screen. We actually just had moments. Very tender, very gentle, not rough, not macho."

Reagan did two more films for Warner in quick succession, deals put together by Wasserman strictly for the money. The first, H. Bruce Humberstone's *She's Working Her Way Through College,* paired him once more with Virginia Mayo, whose legs walked off with the picture. It was a Warner Bros. recycle job, based on the old James Thurber and Elliott Nugent play that had been made by Warners in 1942 as *The Male Animal* (which was directed by Nugent and starred Henry Fonda and Olivia de Havilland in the parts now played by Reagan and Mayo). A couple of new songs by Sammy Cahn were thrown into the mix of the original Heinz Roehmheld score.

In it, Reagan plays a college professor who improbably gets entangled in the love life of one of his students, a burlesque queen who wants to be a writer. Reagan, of course, remains innocent and aloof of any sexual involvements, and the film, stripped of the more dramatic aspects of the original comedy, was primarily a showcase of skin for Mayo, in a part quite similar to the one she played in *The Girl from Jones Beach.* The film did well enough for her to be offered a sequel, *She's Back on Broadway,* which Reagan was not asked to be in.

Instead, he made what would be his fortieth and final film for Warner Bros., as Grover Cleveland Alexander in Lewis Seiler's biography of the great Philadelphia Phillies early-twentieth-century pitching sensation, *The Winning Team.* Warner initially had high hopes for this one. Jack L. Warner believed it might be as big a success as *Knute Rockne.* Both pictures were biographies of sports figures and were given a veneer of hallowed accuracy by the subjects' widows (in this case Alexander's widow, Aimee, played on-screen by Doris Day), who generously added a great deal of inside information but also insisted that the darker sides of their husbands' lives — where all the drama was usually rooted — be ignored. In Alexander's case, his alcoholism was glossed over and downplayed and his epilepsy eliminated altogether, leaving the story without much drama.

Warner assigned the film to its venerable Bryan Foy unit, which automatically made it less important (*Knute Rockne* had been a Hal Wallis production). Doris Day gave her portrayal a sexless purity that was both nonthreatening and not all that interesting. The film didn't do much at the box office, and with the kind of money he was making these days — about $75,000 a film — Reagan couldn't make ends meet; that July, after the film was dumped onto the bottom half of a double bill, Reagan had to go back to Wasserman once more to ask if there was anything else that could be done for him. Anything at all.

Wasserman came through for Reagan with the lead in a Paramount production, where Pine and Thomas agreed to use him again in something called *Tropic Zone,* directed by Lewis Foster, Pine and Thomas's favorite director for his speed, economical schedules, and general no-hassle delivery of quickly movable (and instantly disposable) product. While it was Wasserman who personally went to Pine and Thomas and pled for them to give Reagan another shot, in his first memoir,

Reagan remembers it differently, as Pine and Thomas coming to him: "The two Bills [Pine and Thomas] corralled me and talked me into doing one of those sand and banana epics. . . . I knew the script was hopeless, but there was a little matter of a debt of gratitude because they had given me *The Last Outpost.*"

In what was to be his final film of the year and the last he would appear in for fourteen months, Reagan accepted an offer from Universal to appear in a Western (the only reason he took the deal), *Law and Order,* directed by veteran art director Nathan Juran and costarring the sultry Dorothy Malone. In the film, Reagan plays a retired gun marshal who must rescue his town from an evil band of outlaws led by Preston Foster, who wants revenge and threatens to burn down the entire town to get it. Reluctantly, Frame Johnson (Reagan) must put the badge back on and defend the town to preserve its "law and order."

It was the kind of script Reagan loved and a role he wished he'd gotten more of, a tough but tender lawman who happily carries the burden of civilization on his broad shoulders, and settles all differences with a six-gun. Although the film had faint echoes (*very* faint) of Fred Zinnemann's *High Noon,* it was, in reality, a tired remake of a hundred similar Westerns from the thirties and forties. Unlike the distinguished and beautiful work of John

Ford, cinema's premier poet; and Howard Hawks, its best action and adventure man; and a bit later on, Anthony Mann, the king of nightmarish Westerns, *Law and Order* had nothing lyrical, transcendent, or redemptive about it. It was strictly shoot-em-up, with issues of right and wrong relegated to might-over-right. No one reloads his weapons, washes up before dinner, worries about the weather or where his next dollar is coming from. It was strictly old-hat, B movie-making already headed for cinema's Boot Hill with the coming of TV's deluge of one-hour Westerns able to cover this turf faster, cheaper, and better.

Reagan had made a cluster of films that had all but ensured he'd have no future in features, and he knew it. He had made them mostly for money, and less so with the dwindling hope that he might somehow strike lightning with one of them and find himself back on top. But in his heart he knew that wasn't going to happen. Reagan would, however, return to the top of the Hollywood heap, only not in films, but as a union leader, playing a key role in yet another crisis that was about to change the very definition and direction of fifties Hollywood.

It all began with a visit to Wasserman.

By 1952, it was clear that opposition by the studios to the new medium of television was fading. Those in charge who once saw TV as the great enemy of Hollywood had now banded together and formed the Alliance of Television Producers (ATP), a united front in what everyone knew was eventually going to come down to a battle over how to compensate talent for a medium that hadn't been invented when most actors, writers, and directors had first signed their film contracts. Even as talks had begun with SAG and the Writers Guild of America (WGA), Walt Disney struck a deal with the ABC network for the lease of his back library that paid him enough to build his Disneyland amusement park (with none of the money trickling down to his animators). And tightwad Harry Cohn, whose Columbia Studios were known throughout the industry as "Poverty Row" for his penny-pinching ways, vested his nephew $50,000 to start a TV subsidiary for Columbia called Screen Gems. Electronic entertainment had become the new frontier, and Wasserman (and Stein) wanted in. However, unlike Disney and Columbia, MCA was still a talent agency; both Wasserman and Stein knew if they were to remain players in television, they were going to have to overcome the additional obstacle of their inherent conflict of interest by serving also as producers.

Wasserman thought he had figured out a solution by the time Reagan came to see him after the disappointing returns of *Law and Order.* He knew that Reagan was having a tough time of it and that it might work to MCA's advantage. Wasserman greeted Reagan with open arms and took him for lunch with Taft Schreiber, Reagan's day-to-day agent who was also the head of Revue.

Later that afternoon, back at Wasserman's office, after Schreiber politely bowed out, the two got down to business. Wasserman told Reagan he wanted to discuss something with him, not in his capacity of actor, but as president of SAG: the discussions between the ATP and SAG over the issue of paying residuals to actors whenever the TV shows they appeared in were sold to new markets or repeated on the networks. Reagan knew what Wasserman was talking about. The talks had hit an impasse, with the producers angrily refusing to pay one cent more to what they considered hired help and SAG threatening to call a general strike that would shut down all production if their membership was not given a portion of the additional monies the studios made reselling the same product over and over again. The studios insisted that selling to new markets was no different from adding individual theaters to a feature's run. SAG said the influx of additional advertising revenue made TV a whole different ball game.

Reagan listened respectfully but with increasing unease. He already knew that the lawyer Revue Productions had hired to represent them in the talks — their man on the ATP side of the table — was Laurence Beilenson, the same lawyer who had represented Reagan during his divorce from Wyman. Moreover, Beilenson had represented the Guild for years, all throughout the turbulent forties, before resigning, lured away by Wasserman and MCA. On those grounds alone, Reagan should have immediately recused himself from any further discussions that afternoon and from any and all further negotiations, as had Beilenson, who had already agreed not to participate in any direct negotiations that involved the ATP and the Screen Actors Guild.

But Reagan wasn't able to do that; he couldn't walk out on Lew Wasserman without at least listening to what he had to say. He owed everything to Wasserman, and in Reagan's playbook of rules, loyalty was number one. Nor could he say no when Wasserman said he wanted Reagan's help in getting the Guild to agree to grant a blanket waiver to allow MCA to continue to represent talent while producing shows for television. Do that much, Wasserman suggested, and in return he would see to it that the ATP would agree to some form of residual payment for all actors. That was a deal that would work for everybody, Wasserman added. Reagan left Wasserman's office that afternoon worried and confused, aware that he was in the middle of a very sticky situation.

Beilenson, for his part, had seen the complexities of the conflict more clearly than Reagan. A strong, across-the-board move by the film industry into a medium that had gained enormous popularity in a very brief period of time — nothing like it had happened since movies had shifted from the nickelodeon to the big screen — was inevitable. And if SAG wasn't somehow mollified, that move could be physical as well as creative. The new capital for filmed entertainment would be New York City, where a ready pool of hungry stage actors, most of them non–SAG members, would get all the work. If the film industry proved unable to compete, it could spell the end of big-screen Hollywood, something no one wanted. The only solution, he knew, was a residual agreement that would keep filmed TV production in Hollywood. Beilenson also knew that because of the reach and power of Stein and Wasserman, the waiver issue for MCA and the matter of residuals were inevitably tied together.

Not surprisingly, it was Beilenson who first came up with what he believed was a workable formula. He informally suggested to SAG that they allow the initial rerun of a program to air without residuals, thereby giving producers a chance to recoup their investment and make some profit, and then a descending scale of royalties for talent, so they could get a piece as well. It wasn't a perfect plan — each side had to give up a little, but there was enough in it for everyone.

In response, and to show it meant business, SAG brought IATSE's national president, Richard Walsh, into the discussions, to keep on the table the threat of an industry-wide strike as their bargaining chip. SAG's position was further strengthened by the declaration of the American Federation of Musicians (AFM) that, hoping for an eventual piece of the pie, they, too, supported the idea of residuals for actors.

Things came to a head at a SAG meeting that took place on June 16, 1952, between Wasserman and SAG, Reagan presiding, over the issue of MCA's conflict of interest. Wasserman had decided to make his move and apply for that blanket waiver and promised, as he had Reagan, that in return for the waiver, he would get the ATP to accept the concept of graduated residuals.

Less than a month later, on July 14, 1952, SAG's board of directors approved MCA's written application for a blanket waiver for MCA.* It was one of the most sweeping

---

* Although Reagan voted in favor of the waiver, it was vice president Walter Pidgeon who put the motion before the board. Technically, it was Pidgeon's

agreements in the history of entertainment and would ultimately redefine the way business was done in Hollywood.

And it was almost totally ignored in the trade press, which buried the story on its inside pages. The national media ignored it completely, as did Reagan, then and for the rest of his life. There is no mention of it in his second memoir. Nor is Beilenson ever mentioned by name, either in his role as Reagan's divorce lawyer from Wyman or his indirect help in getting MCA its waiver. Nor, in his memoirs, does Reagan ever address the relationship between MCA's acquisition of that waiver and the turnaround in his own

---

motion, but Reagan had worked long and hard lobbying the board. The full board was made up of Walter Pidgeon, Ronald Reagan, Nancy Reagan, Leon Ames, Edward Arnold, Gertrude Astor, Richard Carlson, George Chandler, Rosemary de Camp, Frank Faylen, Wallace Ford, Paul Harvey, Robert Keith, Grafton Linn, Philo McCollough, George Sowards, Kent Taylor, Regis Toomey, Audrey Totter, and Rhys Williams. Because of the confidentiality of the minutes of these meetings and votes, it is unclear which of the six board members were present, but the vote was unanimous. Those members of the board who were represented by MCA included, besides the Reagans, Pidgeon, Ames, Arnold, Carlson, de Camp, Faylen, Toomey, and Williams. Everyone went on to successful careers in television.

career that would come about directly as a result of it, beginning with his unexpected resignation as the president of the Screen Actors Guild shortly after the granting of the waiver (although he remained on the board of directors). Many in Hollywood old enough to remember still believe that Reagan's actions were a clear conflict of interest. But there are many others who believe Reagan did what he had to do and that the waiver probably kept Hollywood as the capital of television production and saved numerous careers, if not the industry itself.

At the time of his June 1952 resignation from SAG's presidency, Reagan initially cited his wife's difficult pregnancy as the reason. With the baby not due until December, he said he needed to be able to spend more time with her, to make sure she was properly cared for. However, the real reason he resigned was far more complex. "They stop thinking of you as an actor," he later told reporters. "The image they have of you isn't associated with your last role, but with the guy who sat across the conference table beefing. And that's death." He appeared to be blaming his union activism for his inability to land the big picture and hoped stepping down might somehow help to resurrect his career. When the resignation became effective, on November 10, Reagan became the longest continuous president of the Screen Actors Guild. At the end of the last meeting he presided over, he was given a standing ovation.

On the afternoon of October 21, Nancy went into labor while she and Reagan were sitting in their box seats at the International Horse Show at the old Pan Pacific Auditorium. She was rushed to Cedars of Lebanon Hospital, where it was determined that for her own safety, and the baby's, the delivery would be by Cesarean section.

Everyone agreed that baby Patricia was beautiful, and Reagan, now forty-one years old, announced to the press that neither he nor Nancy would be making any more movies for a while so he could devote all of his time to care for his wife after the difficult delivery. Yet just five months later, Nancy took a role in a small science fiction film that had been offered to her, despite her still weak physical condition and her highly publicized proclamation immediately followed her wedding to Reagan that she was retiring from films because "I don't want to do anything else except be Mrs. Ronald Reagan."

The film was *Donovan's Brain,* directed by Felix Feist, a last-minute substitute for Curt Siodmak, the author of the cult novel who had wanted to direct the screen adaptation himself. When he finally gave up, MGM gave the film to Feist, a journeyman around from the silent days who would go on to work another decade in television. The only notable thing about this cheaply made and cheap-looking film is that Nancy Reagan's costar was Lew Ayres, Wyman's lover during the making of *Johnny Belinda.*[*] If it bothered Reagan, he didn't show it, and besides, they desperately needed the $18,000 the studio offered Nancy for the six-week shoot.

Reagan, meanwhile, kept returning to Lew Wasserman, who said he simply couldn't get him anything, but that he should be patient and something would turn up. In September 1953, just as Nancy was completing her gig in *Donovan's Brain,* something finally did: an offer from MGM to star in a film to be directed by Andrew Marton called *Prisoner of War.* The offer reached a grateful Reagan just in time: "I swear, it came down the chimney to the sound of sleigh bells and tiny hoofs on the roof."

The film deals with a group of GIs captured and brainwashed during the Korean War, a story and a role Reagan thought he could really sink his teeth into. He was cast as officer Web Sloane, who parachutes into enemy

* That same year, Wyman married Fred Karger, an actor/musician/conductor/arranger, thereby relieving Reagan of his alimony payments. Karger and Wyman divorced in 1955, remarried each other in 1961, and divorced again in 1965.

454

territory to discover the truth about the rumors of torture, allows himself to be captured, and undergoes all of it firsthand.

It was really nothing more than a B movie, no matter what Reagan believed, or wanted to believe, about its potential. The truth was, the Korean War was not World War II; it didn't produce clear-cut good guys and bad guys, there were no decisive victories that meant anything, and it didn't have an enemy leader like Hitler or Hirohito to galvanize the public. Besides, the public was getting all its information about the war from television, which covered it much better as an ongoing news story (the film itself was based on factual accounts that had originally appeared on TV, the film's producers hoping to cash in on the story's headline potential). Because of its so-called timeliness, the film was rushed to completion and released, where it laid a big fat bomb and disappeared from theaters and memories with all deliberate speed.

For his effort, Reagan was paid $30,000, less than half of the $75,000 he had received for *Law and Order.* Nonetheless, it was the first money he'd made in more than a year, and he took it because, with the combined salaries of his and Nancy's film work that year totaling all of $48,000, there was a real chance they might lose their home.

It was money that also forced him finally to give up his stand against appearing on television. Although he still maintained the new medium was not for him, the question of overexposure was no longer relevant. Any exposure at all was now the goal. While he refused to commit to any series (it's not clear whether he was offered one at this time), he quietly accepted a small role in an episode of *Medallion Theater,* an independently produced CBS live anthology program. Because of the high quality of its theatrical presentations, it was able to lure some of the biggest actors in the business, at least those who needed work, such as Henry Fonda, whose film career had fallen off the ledge following World War II and the persistent rumors of his too-leftist loyalties. Fonda appeared in the first episode of *Medallion Theater,* which aired on July 11, 1953. By the end of the year, Claude Rains, Janet Gaynor, Jack Lemmon, Robert Preston, and Charlton Heston, a good mix of the up-and-coming and seasoned screen veterans, were all lining up to be on the show.

Nevertheless, by 1953, as *Medallion*'s ratings began to fall against such regular television fare as game shows, live variety, and the early and hugely popular sitcoms, Wasserman managed to get Reagan an appearance in an episode called "A Job for Jimmy Valentine." It wasn't very good and was never broadcast again, but after the live performance, Wasserman pulled aside Reagan and asked him to audition to host a new Revue program to be sponsored by and called *General Electric Theater*. Reagan read for it and came off relaxed, clear voiced, authoritative, and amiable. When no decision was immediately forthcoming, Wasserman told Reagan to sit tight, that he was going to get the job.

In the meantime, Wasserman, increasingly taken up with MCA and Revue matters, assigned Arthur Park, a vice president whom Reagan knew but had never worked with before, to handle him. Park continued to get Reagan bookings on TV shows; the Christmas special "First Born," a half-hour drama for the Ford Television Theater in which he appeared with Nancy, who played his wife; and at least nine more episodes for him and two for her, which kept them afloat through 1954.[*] Although it sounds like a lot of work, in those days television paid relatively little and if the Reagans, combined, made as much as $15,000 a year from their TV work, it was a fortune compared with what other one-off actors were making (the average for a single guest appearance in those days was about $750, according to standard television contracts of the period).

And then, late in 1953, Wasserman approached Reagan with what he termed as a

[*] For more details and the complete compilation, see "Filmography and TV Appearances."

457

request but that was really an order. He wanted him to play Las Vegas.

In one of the most misunderstood (and incorrectly reported) incidents of his life, Reagan had became an involuntary player in yet another of Wasserman and Stein's expansion visions for "the octopus," as MCA was now being called because of the power and reach of its many tentacles. Wasserman and Stein had long wanted in on the action of the Vegas Strip and had earmarked the increasingly desperate Reagan as the entertainer they had who could bring respectability to the seedy gambling mecca just over the Nevada borderline, where there were no taxes and no unions but lots of money. It was a place where, it seemed, anything went. That's what made it popular with high rollers and also what attracted Wasserman and Stein.

Neither was bothered by the known mob influence in Vegas; far from it. Stein had begun to build his empire in Chicago, not just under the nose of Al Capone but with his blessing. And Stein had been a virtual one-man welcoming committee for Bioff and Browne when they first arrived in Hollywood as Capone and Frank Nitti's corrupt union emissaries (analyses of the degree of MCA's alleged involvement with organized crime are plentiful and don't always agree).[†]

Now, however, Reagan's financial situation was so desperate — the nonsmoking actor (he had given up the pipe after his divorce) had taken to doing magazine advertisements for Chesterfield cigarettes ("Not one proven case of throat irritation!"), which ran in all the national magazines — that when Wasserman said he could get him $30,000 for approximately eighteen hours of work (one ninety-minute show a night for six nights a week), Reagan, even aware of the type of activities and clientele the place attracted, did not say no. Instead, he talked it over with Nancy, and with her okay reluctantly agreed. Later that fall, Reagan signed a contract with Beldon Katleman, the owner of the El Rancho Vegas Hotel and casino, for a one-week stint to host the club room. Katleman was no stranger to Reagan, which made the whole thing a bit easier for the both of them. Katleman's father owned a string of parking lots in L.A. (and other cities), was a member of the Friars Club, and had been present that night in 1950 when the organization had honored Reagan. This was a deal among friends, Reagan wanted to believe, and that took some of

[†] The best and most detailed is Dan Moldea's *Dark Victory,* a book-length indictment of MCA's alleged mob entanglements. Also good on the subject is Lou Cannon's *Governor Reagan.*

the sting out of the humiliation.

Then the trouble set in. The engagement was for February but in early December, Reagan got a call from Park saying that Katleman wanted to move Reagan up to the end of that month, to play the Christmas holidays, when they expected their biggest crowds. Reagan said no because, as he told Katleman, he couldn't imagine hearing "Silent Night" over the sound of one-armed bandits jangling in the night and strippers giggling to the "12 Days of Christmas"; it was either February or nothing. When Katleman insisted, Reagan said he wanted out of the whole thing.

He thought that was the end of it until Wasserman stepped in and tried to convince him to do the show anyway, promising there would be no strippers in his act. He told Reagan he hoped that Reagan's presence in Vegas would give it a new respectability, so some of his show-business pals, like Frank Sinatra and Gene Kelly, might follow him to the Strip and play Vegas as well.

Wasserman was not at all happy when Reagan informed him that his decision not to play Katleman's place was final. Twenty minutes later, Wasserman booked Reagan into the Last Frontier for two weeks in February 1954.

If any of this has a familiar ring, it is because the story of Reagan's appearance is most likely the real basis for what became known as the Frank Sinatra saga from Mario Puzo's *The Godfather* novel and movies in which the character of Johnny Fontaine, a struggling singer, is sent to Vegas to make it a legitimate place for his more famous show-business friends to consider playing. Puzo was always evasive about whether or not his tale was based on certain events in Sinatra's life, and with good reason. The inevitable fury it enlisted in Sinatra from the book's first day of publication was double-edged; the famed crooner was furious because of what was true as much as what wasn't. What is unassailable is that Lew Wasserman, often referred to as the godfather of show business, asked Reagan to go to Las Vegas long before Sinatra ever brought his famed Rat Pack there and made the gambling mecca a "swinging" place.

Right down to the character's name — Johnny Fontaine — there was an undeniable association with Ronald Reagan (Johnny/Ronnie Fontaine/Reagan), as there was with Sinatra. It was true that Sinatra had gone to extraordinary lengths to get the part of Maggio in Fred Zinnemann's 1953 *From Here to Eternity.* Sinatra's career was at a low ebb, and that year he had little more to do than follow his then-wife Ava Gardner to Nairobi, where she was filming John Ford's *Mogambo* opposite the still-predatory Clark Gable, a notion that sent chills down Sinatra's skinny and insecure spine. To pass the time, he read the James Jones novel and determined to get himself the part of Maggio, the Italian soldier who eventually gets killed in the brig.

The only trouble was, Harry Cohn, the thuggish head of Columbia, like everybody else in Hollywood, wanted nothing to do with Sinatra. He had already cast Eli Wallach in the part. While stories abound about how Sinatra had his mob friends "lean" on Cohn, the truth is much less dramatic — no horses' heads or persuasive *consiglieres*. At the last minute, Wallach could not get out of a commitment he had made to Elia Kazan to appear in his Broadway production of Tennessee Williams's *Camino Real,* and had to turn down the film. Unwilling to hold up production, Cohn offered Sinatra a humiliating thousand dollars a week to play Maggio, which he accepted. A year later, he won a Best Supporting Oscar for his work in the film, which won seven in all, and Old Blue Eyes was back.

It was the other part of the story that *wasn't* true, and that's the part that always got Sinatra furious. Though Sinatra did appear in Las Vegas twice before Reagan, first at the Desert Inn on September 4, 1951, and again shortly thereafter, these shows happened at the lowest ebb of Sinatra's singing career, went largely unnoticed, and were quickly forgotten. It wasn't until the midfifties that Sinatra returned to Vegas at the behest of Jack Entratter, formerly general manager of New York's famed Copacabana and then general manager of the Sands. By then, Entratter boasted engagements at the Sands by some of the biggest names in show business, including former Copa headliners Lena Horne and Danny Thomas, and, true or not, Sinatra resented Puzo's suggestion that he was put there by the Mafia shill to attract other show business acts to the strip. It would, in fact, be years before Sinatra and his celebrated Rat Pack would make Vegas their legendary playground. It was Ronald Reagan who was first given that assignment by Lew Wasserman.* Sinatra never forgave Reagan for not coming out and saying the

* In 1962, according to FBI records, Chicago mobster Sam Giancana, outraged that Sinatra could not use his "influence" with the Kennedys to get Robert Kennedy to drop his investigation of MCA, considered killing Sinatra but instead ordered him and the rest of the Rat Pack to play the Villa Venice, in Chicago, as a way to give the club a bigger name. The first month the Rat Pack played the Villa Venice, it grossed more than $3 million. It is likely this is the real source of the Sinatra story that was then melded into the Reagan Vegas story by Puzo. (Additional information about the Villa Venice is from Dan Moldea's *Dark Victory: Ronald Reagan, MCA, and the Mob* [see "Sources"], page 154.)

463

character in *The Godfather* was based on him (or about the obvious and intended resemblance between the actor John Marley as studio head Jack Woltz and Lew Wasserman). The coolness between the two, despite some public displays of bonhomie, lasted the rest of Sinatra's life.[†]

That Christmas was a modest one at the Reagan home, cheered only by the news that he had been named the recipient of the second Annual Humanitarian Award for his work for the California Home for the Aged, in Reseda. It was much appreciated by Reagan, and well deserved, but it didn't put any food on his family's table.

As he had agreed, Reagan played the Last Frontier from February 24 through February 28, emceeing a show that featured the Continentals singing group, the Honey Brothers slapstick duo, the Blackburn Twins, and the

† It was Nancy Reagan who persuaded Sinatra to host the Reagan 1981 $10 million inaugural ball. Reports of her having had an affair with Sinatra remain unproved and unsavory. Much more likely, she chose Sinatra to host because the show was broadcast worldwide and Sinatra was at the peak of his current wave of popularity. He was not invited to the private party after but, in true Sinatra style, crashed it. None of the guards had the nerve to stop him from entering, despite the fact he did not have an official pass.

Adorabelles. Reagan once more insisted that none of the feather-headed, beaded and bodiced showgirls in his show appear topless, and none did, although a few well-placed pasties were all that kept that from happening. Even so, Reagan was somehow photographed one night visiting Katleman's casino sitting with famed stripper Lili St. Cyr, who was practically in flagrante, something he was not at all happy about. Many suspected (but could never prove) that Reagan had been set up for the photo by Katleman as payback for not playing the Christmas gig.

To prepare Reagan for his stint as a combination stand-up and sketch comic and master of ceremonies, Wasserman had hired comedy writer John Bradford to put together Reagan's patter for the ninety-minute show, of which a total of fifteen minutes involved Reagan. He worked closely with Bradford to learn his material, which was heavily weighed by tax jokes, to avoid any aha! headlines that might come about if some enterprising reporter discovered Reagan's debt to the IRS was approximately the same amount of money he was earning in Vegas.

The low point of the engagement, and Reagan's entire professional career for that matter, came when at one point in the show he had to wear an apron that carried an advertisement for Pabst Blue Ribbon beer, one of the sponsors of the engagement. In the sketch, he was forced to don a thick German accent and play straight man for a series of double entendres ("Vas you got under dere?" "Under where?" "Under dere!" "Underwear!") and was smacked on the head several times by the other performers on the show to accent the punch lines and cue the audience it was okay to laugh.

It was one small step above carrying a sandwich board and recalls nothing so much as the climactic scene in Josef von Sternberg's classic 1930 *The Blue Angel,* in which the once-proud and respected professor is reduced to playing a clown in a sleazy nightclub. To be sure, Reagan had not taken a sexual fall from grace as the professor had, and did not go crazy and die from his experience, but the idea that the former head of the Screen Actors Guild, the man who often took credit for having kept the doors open in Hollywood during the strikes, the man who decided who could get work and who couldn't, was reduced to playing the clown in a sleazy chorus-girl laden revue was, to say the least, not his finest hour.

When it was over, Reagan vowed never to do that to himself again, no matter how bad things got. He tried to put the best spin on it, that he and Nancy had had a wonderful time, that every seat had sold out for every show, that they did no gambling but stayed in their hotel suite together for most of the trip, except when he was required to be on stage. (The last part, like much of the rest of Reagan's reminiscences of the Vegas affair, simply was not true. Besides Reagan's visit to Katleman's casino, alone, both he and Nancy were seen gambling after his final show at the Last Frontier.)

Back in Los Angeles, the day-to-day drudgery of reality wasn't much better for the Reagans during this time. For one thing, Nancy had never been completely at ease playing the mother to Reagan's two children from his first marriage. She had always acted more as a friend of Maureen and Michael's father than their future stepmother and mother figure. And Patti had proved to be a difficult baby since her difficult birth. To make things worse, Maureen and Michael felt pushed aside by the arrival of their new stepsister, which Nancy did nothing to counter. Perhaps she adored her own baby and loved her more than she did the constant reminders that her husband had had a life and a family before her. She tried to be a good mother to all three, but she did not get close to her stepchildren in a motherly way, or give them the kind of reassurance that might have made them more secure in their childhoods and later on as adults.[*]

Reagan himself was never the attentive, hands-on kind of father his children might have wished, which might have offset their various insecurities and sibling rivalries. He chose to use his free time instead to concentrate on horse-breeding, in the hopes that somehow it might produce the additional stream of revenue he sorely needed.

It is fair to say that all families have some degree of trouble, that it is difficult to raise three children, perhaps even more so if one of the two from a previous marriage is adopted, but it is also fair to say that the personality attracted to the notion of mass, impersonal love from audiences who worship them as idealized figures, is often overly narcissistic. The need for mass devotion too often displaces the responsibility to give individual love to wives, husbands, siblings, parents, and children.

The Reagans' struggle in their individual lives for attention, for acceptance, ultimately for love from strangers — more from the public than from their families — may have produced in Nancy the desire for an externally perfect marriage. It's possible that to achieve this flawless image she assumed the

* All three have written extensively about their complicated childhoods, adolescences, and adulthoods.

leadership role as a mother to her husband, as well as his lover and companion, which left even less room for the children.

Reagan always wanted to play the role of leader, from the head of his union to the head of his household, as a way to gain respect and be adored. In a sense, he wanted to be what he wanted Jack to have been, and played numerous variations of him in movies: athletic Jack, amiable Jack, tipsy Jack, dark Jack, tough Jack, needy Jack (and in SAG, father-figure Jack to the extended family of union members). The gap between being able to rescue Jack and portraying him in idealized fashion on the screen translated in real life to a somewhat distant, aloof Ronald Reagan, reluctant, if not able, to meet the demands of real fatherhood. Reconciling his image with who he really was, for Reagan, was like trying to fit together two pieces of a puzzle that looked like they should but just didn't fit. In the end, it may have been easier to play the role, whatever that role might be, than to live it out in real life.

In the early spring of 1954, only weeks after Reagan completed his Las Vegas commitment, Lew Wasserman came through big-time. If he had wanted to pay back Reagan for helping to get the waiver and for trying to make some inroads in Las Vegas, he had found the perfect currency. Taft Schrieber,

Reagan's former day-to-day agent and a lifelong Wasserman loyalist, was by now in charge of Revue Productions, which had developed into a giant cash cow for MCA, and was pushing hard for Reagan to become the host and "pitchman" — the fellow who did the commercials — for the *General Electric Theater.* A new weekly half-hour anthology series to be shown every Sunday night on CBS at 9:00 p.m., it immediately followed one of the most popular television shows on the air, the *Ed Sullivan Show.*

Wasserman was careful not to tell Reagan about it until the deal was done, wanting his client and friend to believe that the giant corporate sponsor had wanted only him for the part, because the truth was, for the longest time they really didn't want him at all. He was, in fact, ninth on the list of nine possibilities MCA had submitted to G.E. as potential hosts. It was only when all the others — including Edward Arnold, Walter Pidgeon, and Kirk Douglas — turned down the job, that Reagan was officially offered it. This time he jumped into television. Although he had resisted the medium because of its early burlesque comedy image, things were beginning to change, largely because of the success of his predecessor at SAG. Robert Montgomery, after resigning from the presidency of the Screen Actors Guild, had produced his own television anthology, a show that had made him a bigger star than he had ever been in the movies. Following Montgomery's model, Adolphe Menjou, Gloria Swanson, Gene Raymond, and even Jane Wyman all became "hosts" of highly rated half-hour or one-hour dramas. "Uncle" Walt Disney had done the same, introducing his own backlog of cartoons and nature shows, and it had made him, relatively late in life and long after he had peaked as Hollywood's premier animator, one of the biggest names in television. Even directors wanted in, with Alfred Hitchcock agreeing to host a half-hour show for Revue that would turn him into a TV sensation above and beyond the stories his show offered; the success of *Alfred Hitchcock Presents* eventually helped spark a reevaluation of some of his greatest, if most overlooked, movies.

To become the face and voice of General Electric, Reagan was offered a starting annual salary of $125,000 (soon raised to $150,000), more than four times the amount of money he had made for his last feature. He happily jumped at the offer to remind people every week that, no matter what the theme or the moral was of the show's relentlessly uplifting mini-melodramas, "progress is our most important product." To Reagan, that slogan was a winner, one that contained in its six words a political direction, a reminder of the nonmaterial rewards of the

American way of life, and each time he delivered it he believed he forged an ever-deeper association between him and the viewing audience that inevitably merged the messenger with the message. The show debuted on September 26, 1954, and was an immediate hit in the ratings, coming in at number three that week, behind *I Love Lucy* (number 1) and the *Ed Sullivan Show.*

Over the next decade Ronald Reagan became more than the voice of General Electric; he became the physical embodiment of the credo of progressive corporate sponsorship, the notion that a better life was to be had living in America, because of the advantages to be gotten from the advantage of having cheap and abundant electricity.

Reagan's initial contract was for five years, unusually long for a television show but made possible by the combined power of Wasserman and Revue, who by contract controlled the Sunday-night half hour on CBS that it then leased to General Electric. Part of Reagan's deal called for him to spend sixteen weeks on the road, making speeches at G.E. plants to the employees, part of the company's "Community Relations" doctrine.

Reagan rubbed his hands at the thought of making speeches before live audiences. It was what he did best and a big part of what had appealed to him about hosting the show. Rather than having to play a character, he could be himself, or more accurately, play himself when he hosted.[*] He could talk directly to the American people and display his natural charm, wit, grace, and intelligence, all of which had eluded so much of his work on the big screen. On TV he came off as expansive, witty, and forthcoming, always dressed impeccably in western garb.

With the success of *General Electric Theater,* Reagan had risen from the ashes of his film career and the brink of financial ruin. The television resurrection of Ronald Reagan would take him on a journey that would change not only the parameters of his career, but the course and direction, and the definition of, his entire life.

And the world.

---

[*] Reagan occasionally did play characters on the show, for additional money, as did Nancy Reagan, who joined him on the third episode, "The Long Way 'Round," a bit of sanctimonious treacle about a loving and supporting wife who saves her husband from the brink of having a nervous breakdown, as all loving wives in America did for their overworked, underappreciated-at-work husbands. For a more complete listing of Reagan appearances on TV, see "Filmography and TV Appearances."

■ ■ ■ ■

CHAPTER ELEVEN:
THE FORGETTING OF
THINGS PAST

■ ■ ■ ■

I don't want to appear as though I am trying
deliberately to be vague. . . .

— RONALD REAGAN

Cover of an album Reagan recorded in 1960 to fight against what he believed was John F. Kennedy's platform for broadening medical coverage.

The success of the *General Electric Theater* television show made Ronald Reagan's face newly familiar to millions of family households, a friend who came into America's living room every Sunday evening with a filmed dose of the West Coast to offset the CBS network's weekly dose of live East Coast show business via Ed Sullivan direct from Broadway. Because of Reagan's renewed stardom, the show was able to attract top Hollywood talent, most of whom had long refused to do television — Jimmy Stewart, Joan Crawford, Fred Astaire, and Joan Fontaine among them.

The show's producer for the first six years was William Frye, a veteran of the glory days of dramatic radio plays and movie adaptations, and one of the pioneers of live film and kinescope television. "I had just finished producing a TV pilot for *The Halls of Ivy,* starring Ronald Colman, who had done the show for years on radio. When it looked like that wasn't going to go, I got a call from Lew Wasserman asking me if I'd be interested in this new show, *G.E. Theater,* hosted by Ronald Reagan. My first reaction was, well, here I'd just finished working with one of the most elegant and sophisticated stars, this male Garbo in his way, one of the so-called Brit Pack who only socialized with the other Hollywood Brits, Greer Garson, Basil Rathbone, and people like that, and now they wanted me to produce something that was the complete opposite of all that. I told Wasserman I wasn't sure I could do it and he said, 'Of course you can. You're just going from one Ronald to another!'

"At the time I was hired by Revue Productions, the company was so new, there were only about five producers, and I'm sure I was the only Gentile and the only Republican.

"It was a big change, for sure, going from an actor who was the most elegant man imaginable and an Academy Award winner, to one who was not really a big star. I feared I might be coming down a bit if I took it. But happily, I did."

To show Reagan his appreciation, a delighted Lew Wasserman promised him he would try to get him back into features. Reagan was grateful but insisted he would only do Westerns, and Wasserman readily agreed.

Meanwhile, Nancy Reagan focused on their home life, trying to do her best to balance the raising of the children (with the help of full-time nannies and a household staff) while she organized, refined, tightened, and elevated the Reagan social calendar. She carefully eliminated all functions that wanted Reagan to appear unless they were tied to a legitimate political cause she felt was in his best interests, such as a fund-raiser for the Actors Fund that took care of retired and often-destitute onetime film stars. She also eliminated all but six Hollywood couples from their social calendar, allowing dinner only with the Holdens, the Stewarts (Jimmy Stewart's recent, relatively late first marriage to a socially prominent nonactress saved him from joining the ranks of the outcasts), Robert and Ursula Taylor, who lived across the street, and of course, the Wassermans and the Steins. Other good friends such as the liberal Dick Powells, who had remained good friends with Wyman, were slowly phased out by Nancy. She didn't want Reagan to be reminded of his first wife in any way, and besides, the Powells were old hat.

It didn't help that Dick was also an actor. No matter how much money successful actors and actresses made, to L.A.'s elite, the whole business was considered crude and overwhelmingly left-leaning, and because of it, most performers remained at the bottom of Hollywood's real social register. That was driven by the publishing industry, headed by the Chandler dynasty, and real estate, led by the Dohenys and those who had relocated from the East Coast to supervise and direct the banking interests of the film industry.

By Nancy's decree, Ciro's and the Brown Derby were out, their obligatory front-bar cocktail scene too déclassé now for the Reagans. She preferred the private banquettes of Chasen's, where the older, more burnished Hollywood clique liked to socialize. They became regulars, often dining there with friends four or five times a week.

Reagan's first theatrical feature film after his success in television was Allan Dwan's *Cattle Queen of Montana,* in which he starred opposite Barbara Stanwyck. The film was shot in color and on location in Glacier National Park, Montana, a welcome change from the drab grays of the black-and-white back-lot features he had been pushed into in recent years. It was produced by Benedict Bogeaus, at RKO, a studio that had more or less gone into free fall, thanks to the not-so-funny eccentricities of Howard Hughes, whose manic Red-baiting and long string of overpriced moneymakers had managed to bring the studio to the brink of collapse. By the time *Cattle Queen of Montana* was made, the studio was nearly bankrupt, and it maintained distribution only because Hughes personally bankrolled it. He was willing to lay out enormous amounts of money to maintain the illusion that RKO was still a viable name-brand studio of some value on the open market.* It was for that reason that Hughes tried to hire big-name stars such as Stanwyck and the resurrected Reagan, to try to put some heft into the company's bottom line.

To direct, Hughes hired Dwan, a veteran who'd made nearly a thousand films by the time he made this one, including silents with Mary Pickford, talkies with Shirley Temple, and war pictures with John Wayne. He was reliable, he was good, and most important to Hughes, he came cheap. In the film, a rancher whose herd is stolen by the Indians (really by a rival rancher who hires the Indians to do his dirty work) hires Reagan as an underground operative (something Reagan knew a little about) who not only saves the herd but marries Stanwyck as well.

Although Reagan's heroics were as action oriented as ever, for the first time the facial etchings of middle age were impossible to hide from the magnifying glass of the big screen. Completely gone was the boyish look that Reagan had used to radiate the innocence that had gotten him so far. Now he

* Hughes sold RKO in 1957, to Desilu Productions, owned by TV stars Lucille Ball and Desi Arnaz, who used it primarily as a TV production studio.

481

looked beyond the far side of youth, on the borderline of grizzled, which actually made his performance look grittier than it really was. *Cattle Queen of Montana* once and for all proved that Reagan's days of playing the young leading man were over.

And it quickly joined the list of RKO box-office duds. The one lasting thing that came out of it was Stanwyck's TV series a few years later, *The Big Valley,* in which she virtually re-created her character from the film and found a whole new legion of followers.

Wasserman had gotten Reagan the film because he had promised to find him something, although he knew that nobody wanted Reagan for movies any more than they did Lucille Ball, Groucho Marx, or Red Skelton. He was TV now and he was going to remain TV. However, when the opportunity for the Hughes film came along, he positioned it to Reagan as evidence of how hot he still was.

Reagan shrugged off the film's flop and happily continued his duties at *General Electric,* emphasizing to one and all what a great idea it had been for him to go into the small-screen medium. In one interview he justified his relatively late but highly successful decision to move into television this way: "Television is now being produced in much the same manner that the film industry turns out their product. For a long time — too long, in fact — TV was handled by strictly radio people. In short, you were getting nothing but radio — with a picture. Actually, television is the same as the motion picture. Only the size is different. And it didn't take long for the big video network executives to realize that the best way to make a good picture was to film it — take out all the bugs before they cropped up."

Ann Sheridan found Reagan's enthusiasm for television a little hard to believe and a bit contradictory as well: "I remember Ronnie telling all of us not to join TV because it was the enemy of the movies. Next thing, he was on *G.E. Theater* with his contact lenses reading the commercials."

Reagan's response to Sheridan and to all the others who questioned his downsizing to the tube became a familiar mantra for Reagan, one that he would use again and again: He hadn't changed, television had. He had only come to it when it was worthy of his talents.

Despite the commercial failure of *Cattle Queen of Montana,* Hughes instructed the Dwan/Bogeaus unit to develop a follow-up and offered it to Reagan, who immediately said yes. This one was called *Tennessee's Partner,* and it was set in a California mining camp with a plot loosely based on a Bret Harte short story, one of several that he had written while traveling to California to experience firsthand the gold rush. It was a trip that provided fertile ground for his writing. As reformulated for the movie, the story concerns the fate of Tennessee, a cowboy gambler whose girlfriend, Elizabeth (Rhonda Fleming) runs a "saloon" (i.e., whorehouse) called, quite cleverly, "The Marriage Market." One night, Tennessee nearly gets killed over a misunderstanding in the saloon but is saved by another cowpoke passing through, played by Ronald Reagan. The two become pals, and it's Tennessee's turn to save Cowpoke (Reagan) when one of the rougher babes from the saloon tries to seduce him from a fleece job. Cowboy misunderstands, thinks his friend is trying to steal his girl, but comes to his aid anyway when Tennessee once again finds himself in a jam. This time his unselfish heroics cost Cowpoke his life. At his funeral, Tennessee decides to go straight and asks Elizabeth to marry him. Apparently the ghost of Cowpoke has infused Tennessee with a moral uplift, and in memory of his friend, to whom he owes his life, he decides to dedicate the rest of his to Cowpoke.

Despite having the better of the two roles — a character who dies a heroic death is a hard one to beat — Reagan's role came off as a supporting one rather than the lead, partly due to the poor script. The taller, younger, and ruggedly handsome John Payne happened to give what was perhaps the best performance of his career.* It didn't really matter in the end because the film did nothing and the moviegoing public ignored what would be Reagan's last big-screen Western. He would not get another feature for two more years, and when he finally did, it wasn't even a Western, but he didn't care. He was one of the biggest names in television, one of Revue's most important stars, and to him, that was, these days, where the real action was.

That same year, MCA, very quietly, asked SAG for and was granted a permanent extension on its waiver that was about to expire. Once again, the news was greeted with very little notice in the press, although later on it would become the linchpin for a federal investigation into the activities of MCA and everyone involved in the production and management end.

Including Ronald Reagan.

Besides his hosting duties, Reagan was slated

---

* Like so many other minor actors in Hollywood, Payne, whose most familiar role is Fred Gailey in George Seaton's 1947 *Miracle on 34th Street,* found his greatest success on TV, in the series *The Restless Gun* and as one of the later hosts of *Death Valley Days.*

to act in seven episodes of the *General Electric Theater,* and he served as the producer on all of them. Moreover, his first "tour" for General Electric (part of an overall multiyear campaign for him to visit every one of G.E.'s 135 operating plants nationwide) had been a resounding hit. It began in the East, in upstate New York, where G.E. had a gigantic thirty-one–acre plant in Schenectady, just outside of Albany, and traveled back across the country, making stops in Chicago and other major cities where G.E. had plants. Enormous crowds turned out everywhere for Reagan. To show its appreciation, in 1955, with as much fanfare as possible, General Electric built the Reagans their very own "House of the Future," an all-electric fully functioning home (actually a conversion of their Pacific Palisades residence). The deal was that G.E. would pay for all the upgrades and installments and improvements that would have normally cost hundreds of thousands of dollars, in return for the right to photograph it and use those pictures in its advertising. Everything was electric, from the dishwasher to the stove. "Everything except a chair," Reagan quipped to Louella Parsons.

While Mr. and Mrs. Reagan were seen smiling and luxuriating in their new house of the future, in private Nancy was less than thrilled with this arrangement. She was always on the lookout to make sure that her husband's image wasn't being exploited in any way. She was most concerned about maintaining his, meaning their, social dignity. "I wasn't wild about having my home turned into a corporate showcase," she said, but didn't complain for very practical purposes. "This was Ronnie's first steady job in years."

In the yards of both this house and their ranch, Reagan had drawn a heart in wet cement with an arrow through it as testament to his love and devotion to Nancy.

They continued their track on the upward mobility express by ensuring that the public's image of Ronald Reagan was not that of a bitter divorcé but of a happily married family man. To do so, Nancy enlisted the help of Reagan friend and always-ready-to-add-a-good-word-for-the-cause Louella Parsons. In a lengthy piece that ran in the *Los Angeles Examiner*'s weekend insert "Pictorial Living" in the spring of 1955, which was picked up in syndication all over the country, Parsons wrote:

"Today, Ronald Reagan is more fun and less serious about the world in general. I had dinner with Ronnie and his pretty wife, former actress Nancy Davis, and not once did he tell me anything that had to be done to reform conditions." When it came to baby Patti, Reagan beamed. "She's so bright!"

Quietly, a month later, Reagan, despite his producer's role with the series that was a clear violation of SAG rules and the reason that Montgomery and so many others had voluntarily resigned from the presidency of the Guild, was elected third vice president, replacing Howard Keel, after a spirited "Draft Reagan" campaign took hold, sparked by Jack Dales, SAG's executive director.[*] Reagan's election to office was a sharp indication that he would still have a hand calling the shots when it came to who could work in the industry and who couldn't. Reagan enjoyed that power and leapt at the chance to get some of it back, while Nancy continued to paint pretty pictures in the press of their perfect domestic life.

Every once in a while, little Patti, in one of her more upset moments of feeling neglected and confused, would run across the street to the Taylors', crawl up to their bedroom, and throw up all over it. Years later, Patti made this comment about her father that was a clue to her acting out: "I never knew who he was, I could never get through to him."

Gradually, Nancy eluded all but the most

[*] Before accepting the SAG presidency, according to Wasserman biographer Dennis McDougal, Reagan met with Wasserman to discuss whether or not he should. Wasserman encouraged him to do so.

carefully selected circle of friends, which grew to include the George Murphys, who'd gained admission due to his politics and his often-talked-of plan to run for governor or the Senate. Nancy liked that kind of ambition. For fashionable élan, Nancy kept Frances Bergen, former high-fashion model and wife of the onetime sensation Edgar Bergen, who had pulled off the interesting trick of making ventriloquism a hot item on the radio. Bergen's value was her social circle, which was a notable step up from the Reagans'. The Bergens threw regular dinner parties at their Bella Vista mansion on the right, or north, side of Beverly Hills, usually attended by the Steins, the Stewarts, and the Randolph Scotts. Scott was from southern aristocracy and acknowledged as one of the shrewdest businessmen in Hollywood, the only actor of his time to ever be given admittance into the Los Angeles Country Club, a highly restricted, upper-society, no-Jews-or-Catholics-allowed place.

The other thing about this social scene was that to a person, it was made up of Republicans. The Powells, the Murphys, the Steins, the Bergens, the Taylors, all were conservative-leaning Republicans; Reagan was the only die-hard registered Democrat among them. Nancy thought the exposure to their brand of politics was something of which her husband needed more. The higher up the social scale went, she carefully noted, the more conservative the politics became. Perhaps she believed that wasn't the worst thing in the world.

Deep into 1956, Reagan was still railing about communists, even though the public had finally begun to grow weary of the whole issue after the fall of Sen. Joseph McCarthy, who was given the world stage to prove his accusations of communist infiltration in government and could not do so. Even though at the time, there were many actors, writers, and directors who still could not work in Hollywood, the glass barricade was finally beginning to crack, due at least in part to the need for more talent to meet the growing demand for programming that television had produced.

Reagan, however, continued to take every opportunity he got to remind audiences about the dangers of communism in the entertainment industry. It had become his personal obsession, his platform of popularity. What he was especially incensed about was a plot that he concluded had been put into motion against the majors by a vengeful, too liberal government via the Supreme Court's upholding the 1948 U.S. [SIMPP] vs. Paramount lawsuit, which, he believed, hastened the end of the studio system.

On one of his many travels for G.E. to Youngstown, Ohio, he spoke before three hundred members of the Industrial Information Institute's ninth annual meeting, where he gave a highly revisionist history of Hollywood's battle with communists: "When we laid our findings before the House Un-American Activities Committee, not one word of it was published. Instead, the industry was castigated by government leaders 'for not doing anything about Communism' when at the time the film companies were facing $160,000,000 in suits filed against them for discharging Communists in their employ. The government reached a new height in its harassment of the industry when it told the movie industry to get rid of the Communists in its employ but also told the industry that if it got into any trouble doing so it couldn't get any help from the government."

Reagan was referring to SIMPP, believing that the government had simply chosen to attempt to destroy the entire industry as the best way of getting rid of its many communists, something akin to cutting out a whole body organ to get rid of a cancerous tumor. His reference to the information that wasn't published was something the thousands who suffered the blacklist dearly wanted brought out because they believed it might have saved their reputations and their jobs. In effect, Reagan was continuing McCarthyesque late-in-the-day Red-baiting, and it worked. Reagan's reputation as a fearless voice of freedom began to take on hallowed-halls echoes.

He usually ended this speech the same way, with a message that sounded for all the world like it was coming from a Republican, especially when he called for smaller, not bigger, government: "We in Hollywood have a suspicion that when you ask the government for help, you are likely to wind up with a partner . . . those taking away freedoms might be on your doorstep next and then it may be too late." It was all hell-and-brimstone: Big government helps you by helping itself to you; asking for government help of any kind means surrendering your individual freedom to the government.

It was evident that by 1956, there was very little liberal Democrat left in the political soul of Ronald Reagan.

Audiences, meanwhile, loved the speech, as did the corporate heads of General Electric, even if they worried that should the tide turn after the upcoming election that pitted Republican president Eisenhower against challenger Adlai Stevenson and somehow the liberal Democrat Stevenson won, it might indicate that the sentiment of the country as a whole was changing. It was always chancy to take sides, they knew, and they would have preferred it if Reagan was out there more heavily selling the virtues of refrigerators rather than Republicanism. To the corporations, those were two different and widely separate subjects. To Ronald Reagan, they were one and the same. People who used refrigerators also voted, he reminded G.E.'s corporate heads whenever they tried to rein him in. In the fall, Eisenhower won by a landslide, the blacklist, although diminished, continued, and Reagan's TV ratings on *General Electric Theater* hit an all-time high.

The following year Reagan signed on to do another feature, what would be technically his last, although he would make one more seven years later that was supposed to be made-for-TV but was briefly released in theaters. The 1957 film was Nathan Juran's *Hellcats of the Navy*. Juran had previously directed Reagan in *Law and Order. Hellcats* was produced by Charles A. Schneer at Columbia Pictures, a film Wasserman got the green light for because of his idea to have Nancy Reagan play opposite her husband. The film attracted Reagan because it was a World War II yarn, and Fleet Admiral Chester Nimitz had agreed to introduce it on-screen, the best kind of military movie gravitas one could hope for in Hollywood. Reagan loved the idea of playing opposite Nancy (also her next-to-last feature), the faint echoes of his pairings with Wyman cheering him on, helping him to level some playing fields only he could see. Nancy liked it for much the same reasons, if from the other side of the marital divide. She would have loved to have made more movies with her husband than Wyman had, but that was not likely to happen. So this one had to be great.

It wasn't.

Hellcats of the Navy was based on Charles A. Lockwood's and Hans Christian Adamson's book of the same name that chronicled the exploits of the Hellcats, a maverick group of submariners who took on the most difficult missions during the war. It was a strictly conventional job and might have made more sense had it been produced in 1947 rather than 1957, when words like "Japs" were no longer in vogue and the American enemy mind-set had shifted to the Russians.

The reviews it received were not very good, words like *mild* and *unconvincing* showing up in several of them, despite its generating more box office than any recent Reagan film, at a time when the studio itself was concentrating more and more on its Screen Gems TV subsidiary, the only branch of the operation that was making any real money.

After two miscarriages Nancy gave birth on May 20, 1958, to her second child, 8 1/2-pound Ronald Prescott Reagan, or "Skippy" as Reagan nicknamed him even before the baby was brought home from Cedars of Lebanon. Besides Reagan, Robert and Ursula

Taylor were there. Reagan beamed with pride at the first sight of his son, and even Patti seemed happy and excited about having a new baby brother. Using the techniques of the popular Dr. Spock, Nancy had taken special care in preparing her. With Patti's special personality problems, Nancy hoped that the Spock method would work and she would welcome her new brother with open arms.

Not surprisingly, Louella Parsons was the first reporter to get the story, which noted Reagan's insistence that the boy "was not going to be a junior. Because we've given him a middle name, but I am so excited and it's so early in the morning, I can't remember what it is."

If everything seemed for the moment idyllic in the Reagan household, all of that was about to undergo a profound change. It started innocently enough when William Holden resigned from the presidency of the Screen Actors Guild, for the same reason so many other board members and officers had over the years, because he wanted to start his own production company. It was no longer a novelty; anyone who still wanted to work in films as an actor either became a partner in the production or else had to be content with dreck like *Hellcats of the Navy*. Holden had acquired the rights to the steamy novel *The*

World of Suzie Wong, which he was interested in producing as a movie and starring in.

To replace him, the Guild overwhelmingly voted Reagan back into office, a post he graciously accepted, although the corporate heads of G.E. were less than thrilled. They were already concerned about Reagan's heavy emphasis on politics over products during his corporate appearances, and with national elections on the horizon, and Reagan once more the head of the always political SAG, their caution antennae were way up.

The first item up under Reagan's new administration sounded harmless enough — a proposal to create a welfare and pension plan for its members — but it nevertheless sparked a war that nearly shut down the industry for good. Although it didn't originate with him, before it was over, Ronald Reagan would once again play a key role defining in the way Hollywood did business.

As the fifties slipped away, the years of strikes, hearings, government antitrust actions, communist witch hunts, and the soaring popularity of television had left the industry of making motion pictures almost completely unrecognizable from the way it had functioned in its so-called golden era. At the height of its popularity, roughly from the midteens to the early 1950s, the studios operated on a tridivisional basis: production (making movies), distribution (selling and delivering movie prints to theaters), and exhibition (the ownership of the theaters where the movies were players). After the 1948 consent decree, the majors had to divest themselves of at least one of the branches of their three-part operation. Most chose to sell off the theaters, with the understanding that they could still take a huge percentage out of exhibition, the difference being they would now have to bid against independent productions for screens.

Universal-International, the oldest, and one of the largest and most venerated, of the majors, was also one of the hardest hit by the changing times. In 1957, it spent about $40 million on the production of only thirty-two films. Because of the new competition for the ever-decreasing number of venues, as people began staying home and watching the tube rather than going out for their evening's entertainment, Universal had to make the hard decision to either take on new partners, move into television, or go out of business.

Decca Records president Milton Rackmil was now calling the shots at Universal, the result of a hostile takeover in 1953 when the record company, flush with cash from the cresting popularity of .45 singles, bought the studio from its owner, British film magnate J. Arthur Rank. Rackmil then committed one of the most egregious miscalculations in

Hollywood's history. To raise much-needed cash, he sold off the studio's pre-1948 inventory of films (to Columbia's Screen Gems, which intended to lease them at a profit to television) and used the money to invest in a new in-house production company, United World Films. In other words, Rackmil put the money back into making movies for theaters, while Screen Gems made a fortune playing off its newly acquired inventory on every TV station in the country that needed to fill air time on weekends, after midnight, even in the early afternoons.

MCA, meanwhile, had done just the opposite of Universal. While making a fortune from its wholly owned TV subsidiary, Revue, it then acquired Paramount's pre-1948 film library. As TV became the new repository of Hollywood's golden age, those perceptive enough to see there was gold in those round cans of film collecting dust in the studio vaults managed not only to survive the shift in the direction of the industry, but made a fortune out of endlessly recycling them for no more than the cost of the occasional fresh print.

Key to the whole plan was the year 1948, the year that the original 1952 residual deal, the MCA-engineered give-back for its acquisition of the waiver, used as its point of demarcation. In return for the waiver that allowed it to go into television production,

MCA had successfully lobbied SAG to allow for residuals to be paid to actors for all movies they were in *after 1948.* It was a deal that MCA pushed through before anyone realized the value of old movies, the majority of which were made *before 1948.* On paper, it was a great deal. In reality, it was awful, and because of it, there were hard feelings, a growing sense among the actors who had appeared in them, that they had been taken. For most of the 1950s, they struggled to find a way to overturn the deal and get residuals for all the movies they were in.

MCA, meanwhile, was taking full advantage of the waiver and making so many TV shows that Revue desperately needed more physical space. Lew Wasserman set his sights on Universal's ample and mostly unused back lots along the Cahuenga Pass, which connected Hollywood to Burbank and north to the Valley. He knew that Rackmil needed cash. Wasserman soon came up with a complicated plan he knew would both appeal to and appease Rackmil, while getting MCA all the additional space it needed.

By December 1958, a deal was in place for MCA to merge with Universal for just under $12 million — that is, to buy everything but the studio itself, or what today would be called its brand, or brand name. That meant all of Universal's land, soundstages, warehouses, vaults, and office buildings went to

MCA, in return for which Universal would lease back all the production facilities for a flat fee of $1 million per year. That gave Revue unlimited access to Universal's back lots and whatever physical studio space remained.

As a result of the deal, MCA was able to increase Revue's production and in turn reap enormous additional profits from its television division. At the same time, Lew Wasserman, flush with Revue cash, cut a fancy new deal with Reagan, who was about to start his fifth season as host of the enormously popular *General Electric Theater.*

The show had made Reagan wealthy, but his money was nothing compared with the profits the show generated for both G.E. and Revue. To show his appreciation, Wasserman made Reagan a 25 percent owner of the show. This meant, among other things, that Reagan, the newly installed president of the Screen Actors Guild (with Wasserman's blessing), was not only a producer but a partner operating in direct conflict with the SAG bylaws, which explicitly prohibited board members and officers to serve in that or any management capacity. If he hadn't done so before, he now should have resigned as soon as the ink dried, as everyone else who held office had when they became producers. Reagan, who had been a line producer of the show almost from the start, was now an owner, and that eliminated any wiggle room that may still have existed.

And yet incredibly, nobody seemed to care — Wasserman didn't, CBS didn't, nor did the SAG membership who considered Reagan their hero, the man who'd kept them working in the 1940s and who they believed they *needed* now more than ever, as a confrontation over the residual factor loomed on everyone's horizon.

By the end of the fifties, all of the acquisition-merger actions between Universal and MCA finally caught the eye of the federal government. In 1960, the same year that Reagan was made part owner of the *General Electric Theater,* the buoyantly anti-Hollywood Justice Department began a major investigation into the practices of MCA, including possible mob connections reaching all the way back to the Bioff and Browne years. The investigation would prove time-consuming and costly for both Wasserman and Stein.

At the same time, something else was happening in Hollywood that was to have a far more profound effect on its future than yet another visitation by the FBI — the fading power of the decade-old blacklist. By 1959, Kirk Douglas had joined the brigade of actors who had begun their own production companies. Douglas's Bryna Productions had acquired the rights to Howard Fast's epic novel *Spartacus.* He hired Stanley Kubrick to direct and, in a bold move, also Dalton Trumbo, one of the so-called Hollywood Ten, to not only cowrite the screenplay with Fast but also to do so under his own name. The hypocrisy of the blacklist era had reached such nightmarish proportions that many of its talented but officially barred screenwriters were forced to write under assumed names, because they needed the money and, more important, because the studios that had refused to hire them still needed their talent. Douglas helped break that invisible wall of hypocrisy, and soon enough, the house of cards, which was what the blacklist had become, fell hard and fast.

As Douglas later recalled, "I personally broke the blacklist by using Dalton Trumbo's name as the writer of *Spartacus.* He started out the project as 'Sam Jackson.' So when we were debating what name we should use, I suddenly said, 'The hell with it. I'm gonna put his name on and see if the sky falls in.' It never did. Then Otto Preminger announced that he was going to use a blacklisted name and it all just sort of melted away."

One of the most immediate effects was the rehiring of those blacklisted actors, writers, and directors who had suffered through the years in creative oblivion. Another was a reduction in the power of intimidation-by-association. With the threat of being called a communist greatly reduced, if not eliminated altogether, the reinvigorated talent unions, led by SAG, now wanted their most long-standing unresolved issue to be readdressed — the question of residuals.

Unable to get the studios to budge, for the first time in its existence, the Screen Actors Guild called a strike against the majors, all except Universal. Universal was exempted, along with several larger independent production houses, because before the walkout, through Wasserman, it had negotiated a separate agreement with SAG promising that Universal would abide by the terms of any industry-wide settlement.

During the early stages of the strike, there was, as always, anything but unity among the ranks of labor. Richard Walsh, IATSE's strike leader, threatened to cross SAG's pickets, perhaps remembering how SAG had done the same thing to them during the '45 strike. Reagan was outraged at Walsh and went directly to the AFL-CIO's president, George Meany, to lodge a formal complaint. Duly noted, Meany told Reagan, then privately took him aside and urged him to settle his differences with his real adversary, the studios, and not to cause further problems between fellow union leaders.

The strike dragged on for six weeks until, on April 18, the union accepted a compromise:

a onetime payout of $2.65 million for all film residuals as seed money for SAG's pension and welfare fund, and 6 percent of the gross of films and television shows made after 1960 that were sold to TV (films for one-offs, shows for syndication), minus distribution costs that went directly to the Guild fund. There was no provision for pre-1948 films that were to be freely licensed to TV or for post-1960 films and TV shows, only the right to negotiate for residuals with no implicit guarantees. Reagan and Jack Dales, the executive director of the Screen Actors Guild, pushed hard for the membership to accept the deal, believing it was the best one they were going to get from a troubled industry.

The rank and file, desperate to go back to work (the majority were under the age of forty-five and believed the residual factor was not that important to them), approved it 6,399 votes to 259. After the vote was announced, Reagan received a ten-minute standing ovation.

As always, while Reagan loved to play the hero on screen and off, this time once again for his union, in truth the deal was all Wasserman's. At one point during the course of the negotiations, Wasserman had met secretly with Milton Rackmil at Universal, who then gave Reagan the terms both he and Wasserman wanted — payouts of up to 7 percent residuals for principal actors for all movies on a graduated scale related to when they were made and then rented to television (less royalties for older films, more for newer ones), with all the money not going directly to the actors but into SAG's pension and welfare fund. Not surprisingly, throughout the strike, Universal-International, owned by MCA, was the only studio not opposed to paying some royalties. The others — Allied Artists Productions Inc., Columbia Pictures Corp., Walt Disney Productions Inc., Metro-Goldwyn-Mayer Inc., Paramount Pictures Corporation, Twentieth Century Fox Film Corporation, and Warner Bros. Pictures Inc. — did not want to pay any royalties.

In truth, most of the minority, older actors and actresses with diminished earning abilities, whose film careers had peaked before 1960, were angered by the settlement; their early movies had by now become a staple of TV programming (and a huge source of fresh advertising revenue). In his 1991 memoir, Mickey Rooney says this about the deal: "The studios could sell the TV and videocassette rights to any pre-1960 movies without paying the actors and actresses a red cent. Why do you think Sony Corporation paid billions for Columbia Pictures? For its real estate? No, for what they call its software. Hey, to me it's not software. Those are my pictures, and Cary Grant's and Jimmy Cagney's and Jimmy Stewart's and Frank Capra's. And *that's* why

505

Sony coughed up millions for Columbia Pictures . . . Ronald Reagan was president of SAG in 1960 when the Guild sold us down the river." In another interview, Rooney added, "The Screen Actors Guild has never done anything for either the actors or actresses except to give them a home to die in."*

Even Bob Hope, one of Reagan's most fervent supporters, disliked the deal: "I made something like sixty pictures and my pictures are running on TV all over the world. Who's getting the money for that? The studios. Why aren't we getting some money? Mickey Rooney's started a whole campaign about this. I mean, when they got the money back that they paid for [those movies], why couldn't we start cutting in for a little chunk? . . . But you know, we're talking about thousands and thousands of pictures and Jules Stein walked in and paid [something like] $50 million for Paramount's pre-1948 library of films and

---

* Rooney may have had more reasons to complain about the deal than he let on, as his independent production company had settled with the Guild and agreed to pay residuals while the strike was going on. And he wasn't the only one. Larry Fine, of *Three Stooges* fame, and many others did as well, betting that their deals would become the standard. When it didn't, Rooney was particularly angry that he had given up more than he would have had he waited out the strike.

bought them for MCA. And if you get down and figure out the numbers, he got his money back in about two years and now they own all those pictures. They show them locally, regionally, nationally, and all over the world. And what does it mean? It would have been nice to get a little of that for the grand-children, wouldn't it?"

There was talk of a general boycott of all the studios and perhaps a class-action suit, all of it instigated by Rooney, but nothing came of it. Nevertheless, the prevailing feeling among the older membership was that the Guild, under Reagan's leadership, had sold them out, in what would come to be known in Hollywood as "the great giveaway."

Two months after he helped executive director Jack Dale work out the settlement to end the strike, Reagan, the man who had been returned to power to help get performers a fair share of the enormous profits being generated by their work, resigned his SAG presidency and gave up his seat on the board of directors. He may have left, but the anger and disappointment among all factions within the union remained as the younger members quickly came to feel that they, too, had been sold a suspect bill of goods. According to Reagan biographer Edmund Morris, "Wheelchair wisdom at the Motion Picture Country Home still has it that 'Reagan traded away our residuals.' Bitterness over the deal was at least a contributing factor in SAG's decision, twenty-one years later, to deny him its lifetime achievement award."

In his official letter of resignation, Reagan pointedly omitted any mention of his part-ownership of the *General Electric Theater,* or his eight years as one of the producers of the show. "Up to now I have been a salaried employee with no interest in profits. Now I intend to change that status by becoming a producer with an interest in profits. Therefore, with deep regret, I must tender my resignation."

Reagan spends exactly one paragraph on the SAG strike in his second memoir, and in it suggests that their performing services were sold, not rented, to studios by actors and that the notion of getting paid more than once, in different media, was something no one could have anticipated when the films in question were made.

Differences still linger in Hollywood as to whether the deal was a good one, and even if Reagan had all that much to do with it. According to Dave Robb, former labor reporter for both the *Daily Variety* and the *Hollywood Reporter,* who covered the unions in Hollywood for more than twenty years, a period of time that included the SAG settlement, "As far as deals go, I don't think that one was so bad because it set up the pension and health plan. Today that plan is huge, worth nearly two billion dollars in assets. True, it was set up in exchange for no pre-'48 residuals, but that was basically the principle of all the studios with every union at the time. They weren't about to pay for something that had not been covered in the original contracts and remained firm in their belief that it was unheard of to pay residuals on films that were made before the onset of television. It was, to them, like someone having to go to jail for committing a crime that wasn't a crime when they committed it.

"Either way, Reagan didn't have that much to do with it, even being SAG president at the time. It was Jack Dales, SAG's executive director, at the time called the executive secretary, who was the real big boss at the time. He was making hundreds of thousands a year at his post; Reagan was making nothing. The guy who's making the money runs the show. In recent years, the president has gotten more power, but it has been a struggle inside SAG."

Film documentarian William Gazecki said, "Some viewed Reagan as having sold out the union. Others insist the studios would never have shifted their position on the post-'48 pictures and that the engineering of a lump sum payment to start SAG's pension plan was indeed the best possible outcome. In general, the fallback position of SAG is that all final decisions were made by the Board of

Directors, and pinning the outcome of the strike on Reagan is inappropriate from that perspective. That being said, it is also true that Reagan was never a believer in the residual principle. Even in those early times, he ascribed to the same 'trickle down' theory that become popular when he was president of the United States. He felt that the producers should continue to own the products outright, in that their increased profits (sans residuals) would then create more jobs. It can likely be said that Reagan both supported the lump sum payment and did not support the demand for residuals on pre-sixties pictures, but it would be inaccurate to characterize him as the solo decision-maker. It was always the SAG Board of Directors that made the final decision. Did Reagan lobby the Board? Likely so. This was SAG's first real theatrical strike, and they did not have the solidarity then as was seen in later strikes. This was as big a factor in settling when they did on the pension deal. Also, the pressure to create a pension fund and health plan was significant — it was not an idle solution used only as leverage to make the deal and end the strike. The fact that they secured post-sixties residuals was a very significant gain, as it established the principle and first basic formula. This was not a minor achievement.

"It should be remembered that this was SAG's first real theatrical strike, and the pressure to make a deal grew, even though it didn't have the full support of the stars."

Earlier in 1960, while Reagan was busy trying to keep the peace at SAG, young Michael, who had been living with his mother and her next husband, Fred Karger, was ordered by the child psychiatrist he was seeing to start living with his father. Wyman's marriage was once more on the rocks, and because of her unstable domestic situation, she was no longer considered by the courts to be capable of providing a sound environment for the boy. Michael, fourteen, had been making regular weekend visits to the Reagans'. Now he was ordered to move in with them (Maureen would have had to as well, but she was attending Marymount College in Arlington, Virginia).

This didn't please Nancy at all, who reacted with a bizarre duality; she continued to want more than anything to be alone with "Ronnie," as she still called him, on what may best be described as her notion of an extended, never-ending honeymoon, while at the same time she railed against Wyman for being such a bad mother. When the courts shifted responsibility to the Reagans, Nancy insisted the only way they could take in the fourteen-year-old was if he was immediately enrolled at Loyola High School, a five-days-a-week live-in private school. Reagan agreed, as long as he could take the boy to the ranch on weekends. The net effect was that Michael was never actually in the Reagans' main home for any amount of time. When he was, his bedroom was the living-room couch.

Nancy just couldn't deal well with any of it. Between caring for her new infant and Patti's uncontrollable screaming, temper tantrums, and frequent vomiting during meals, it was too much for her. She wanted her warm nights by the fireplace with "Ronnie." A year passed before Nancy agreed, at Ronald's insistence, to add on a bedroom to their regular home for Michael and separate facilities for a full-time nurse to help care for Patti.

The situation was so unusual that Patti did not realize Michael was her stepbrother until the extra room was finished. As for the boy, quite understandably, he felt unwanted and went to his father to find out why Nancy, like Jane, didn't like him. Reagan reassured the boy, but perhaps in the worst possible way. She's busy with Patti and Ron, he said, which had the effect of making the adopted boy feel even further alienated.

Nancy much preferred to spend her time away from Reagan cultivating close friendships with Armand "Ardie" and Harriet Deutsch; Walter and Lee Annenberg; Earle and Marion Jorgensen; Bill and Betty Wilson; entertainment lawyer Charles Wick and his wife, who both owned a lucrative chain of nursing homes; former actress Bonita Granville and her husband, real estate baron Jack Wrather; Virginia and Holmes Tutte, who owned auto dealerships; Grace and Henry Salvatori, who had made their fortune in oil; and Alfred and Betsy Bloomingdale at the forefront. This wealthy Republican group of friends became known as The Group (and later on as the Kitchen Cabinet). It was this socially elite, moneyed advisory core that would provide the financing, the moral support, and finally the management for Reagan's transition out of movies and television and into full-time politics.[*]

Interestingly, with the exception of Bloomingdale, all the men were self-made and all

---

[*] Armand Deutsch, the only Democrat in the group besides Reagan, was a successful film producer and the grandson of one of the founders of Sears, Roebuck, and reportedly its largest single shareholder. Walter Annenberg was a publishing giant, whose *TV Guide* was at the height of its influence and popularity in the relatively new world of television viewing. His wife, Lee Annenberg, was the niece of Columbia Pictures founder and head of the studio Harry Cohn. Earle Jorgensen had made his millions in steel and aluminum and was one of Southern California's biggest single contributors to the state and national branches of the Republican Party. Alfred Bloomingdale was the heir to the Bloom-

their wives human dynamos. In the late fifties, "women of leisure," as those of a certain class were known, almost never worked, and if they once did, as with Granville and Nancy, they were quickly retired by their husbands. Their main focus became running their households and maintaining their social status. Many of them were the dominant personality between the two, and had, in midlife, adapted a more maternal regard for their husbands. Sex, if still a factor in their marriages at all, was something these women considered a bit too déclassé (which caused at least one husband, Alfred Bloomingdale, to enter into a series of sordid sex scandals that followed him to his grave). Nancy, whose quiet but highly effective nurturing of Reagan always had a mommyish tone, as if she were the proud mother of an older son, rather than his wife, fit quite neatly into the role of "the woman behind the man."

Arthur Park, who had taken over the day-to-day agenting of Reagan's acting career, recalled how well Nancy fit that role: "Nancy [was always] a very ambitious woman. Ambitious women do anything to meet their ends. She was very important in promoting Ronald

---

ingdale's department-store fortune, and his family was part of New York's German-Jewish elite that was known as and celebrated in literature as Our Crowd.

Reagan's activities politically from the time she married him. She wanted to be the First Lady. Definitely. Ronnie had a very strong marital relationship with Nancy Davis — very strong."

The couples shared dreams of a world whose sun rose and set by their schedules. They believed their future was limitless, and before they settled on Reagan, they had backed a number of politicians they believed had the potential to relocate the social and political nexus of the group from the West Coast to the White House. At the moment, their man of choice was Richard Nixon, whose 1960 campaign for the presidency had turned into a barn-burner.

Nixon was, indeed, the heir-apparent to the Eisenhower Republican administration that had controlled the White House for the past eight years. Despite a near career-wreck during Eisenhower's first run for president, when Nixon was accused of accepting illegal campaign funds, the dark and moody vice president had managed to survive the crisis and eventually curry the favor of the party for a run at another eight years of Republican power and leadership, until young John Kennedy made a horse race out of the campaign.

It was an odd group of bedfellows, to say the least. In 1946, Nixon, a lifelong Republican, had been elected to Congress as a representative of the 12th District of California, where he became part of HUAC's investigative team under the chairmanship of J. Parnell Thomas. While he took a background role during the hearings into the alleged subversive activities, he made his bones prosecuting Alger Hiss for being a spy. The success of that case led to his election in 1950 to the Senate. If there ever was an avowed anti-communist, it was Richard Nixon.

As for John Kennedy, he was Nixon's polar opposite. Handsome, charismatic, and youthful, Kennedy was born into great wealth, raised on the East Coast, was a legitimate war hero, an intellectual, and a rising star in the Senate; he seemed the natural choice to take over the leadership of the Democratic Party. After a failed attempt at upsetting Adlai Stevenson to win his party's nomination in 1956, he succeeded in 1960 and took on Richard Nixon, the Republican nominee in the presidential sweepstakes.

Bobby Kennedy, John's younger and far more intense brother, had gone into private practice as a lawyer until, at the request of his father, Joseph P. Kennedy, he joined the Senate committee staff of Senator Joe McCarthy as an assistant counsel on the Senate Permanent Committee Subcommittee on Investigations. Although Bobby resigned early in the McCarthy witch hunt for communists (many believe it was because his brother, one of the two senators from Massachusetts, was about to vote in favor of censuring McCarthy), he remained a personal friend of McCarthy's, who was the godfather to several of Robert Kennedy's children.

On paper, Reagan, who was still a registered Democrat, would have seemed a natural to back his party's youthful presidential candidate. Yet he had become a staunch supporter of Nixon, and publicly supported him after sending Nixon a letter that compared John Kennedy to Karl Marx. Reagan even volunteered to officially switch to the Republican Party, and likely would have if Nixon and his advisors hadn't advised him against doing so, believing it would be far more effective if a Southern Californian Democrat of such prominence was also a loud vocal supporter of Nixon's campaign for president.

There were many reasons Reagan was so supportive of Nixon. To begin with, he had an intense dislike and distrust of both Kennedy brothers. Like Nixon, he believed they were too rich, too young, and too opportunistic to properly serve the country at its highest level. And, most of all, he was certain that despite RFK's having briefly served as an assistant to Senator McCarthy, JFK was too soft on communism, at the very least not tough enough to take on the Soviet Union. On the other hand, no one was more anti-communist than Richard Nixon, and that credential was good enough for Reagan.

But there was another reason for Reagan to give his support to Nixon. Walter Annenberg was a huge Nixon man, and his influence on Reagan was enormous. Annenberg had already let it be known to Reagan that he, Annenberg, had told the corporate heads at G.E. what a great asset to the company Reagan was. He had also put Reagan's face on the cover of *TV Guide,* the single most coveted cover in the fifties. *TV Guide* was the general public's single indispensable publication, and to be on its cover was among the most prestigious "gets" of the times.* If The Group's unacknowledged leader was supporting Nixon, than Reagan, always eager to please strong, charismatic leaders, would as well.

Kennedy's slim victory over Nixon in the fall of 1960 cast a pall over The Group, including Reagan, but it was nothing compared to how he felt when Robert Kennedy, appointed attorney general by his big brother John, ordered the Department of Justice to open an extensive investigation into MCA. It was the culmination of nearly ten years of hard-edged research led by chief prosecutor Leonard Posner, originally set off by Lew Wasserman's involvement with Ronald Reagan and SAG's 1952 waiver deal, which Pos-

---

* Reagan was on the cover of *TV Guide* twice, once in 1958 and once in 1961.

ner believed had violated regulations governing the relationship between talent agencies and industry unions.

MCA's long association with established organized crime figures — names like Al Capone (reputed to once have been a silent partner of Jules Stein) and Sidney Korshak (otherwise known as "the enforcer" for his abilities to "get things done" while serving as one of MCA's top lawyers) — and the agency's long involvement with Bioff and Browne in the early corrupt days of the Hollywood division of IATSE, did not help. The Justice Department had never been satisfied with the terms and conditions that had made possible SAG's granting of the waiver, coming as relatively quickly after the 1948 Consent Decree that had been intended to curb what it considered the industry's unfair, antilabor business practices.

Robert Kennedy's reinvigorated investigation into MCA dragged on for months, with stars, executives, and department heads regularly subpoenaed to testify. Unlike the HUAC investigations of a decade earlier, the hearings into the illegal and possibly mob-infiltrated practices at MCA received almost no coverage in the general media. Only the local Hollywood trades seemed interested. And Ronald Reagan, who knew that it was only a matter of time before the Committee would get around to him.

At times Reagan thought that Robert Kennedy was setting him up to be the government's hoped-for ace in the hole, and that under oath he might reveal some fact or transaction that might bring down the entire house of cards he believed the government's investigation was built on. Other times he feared the investigation was really a retaliatory action on the part of the Kennedys against him personally, for his enthusiastic support of Nixon during the presidential campaign.

Reagan was also convinced that the big reach of the new Democratic administration, which believed in sticking its nose into the business of private enterprise, was an enormous financial burden to the rest of the country. Reagan saw all of that as part of a larger communist conspiracy to morally and financially corrupt the nation. He believed that the Communist Party had "renewed its infiltration of the movie and television industry" and that communists were crawling out of the rocks with plenty of misguided people willing to give them a hand. And who were they? The liberal left wing of the Democrat Party, whose belief in big government and high taxes were destroying the United States. According to Reagan, in May 1961, "The tax foundations offer the quickest means of Red victory. . . . No country that collects one-third of a man's income as taxes has ever been able to hold off a socialist or communist revolution." And he was outraged that the government was going after such all-American, upstanding entertainment giants as Jules Stein and Lew Wasserman while ignoring the real threats to the country.

Despite the warnings of everyone around him — including several corporate officers of G.E. who did not want to be associated adversely, through G.E.'s chief spokesperson and TV representative, with any government investigation — to tone it down, Reagan kept ramping it up. Wherever he appeared for his contractual speeches for General Electric, he talked to his audience more about elections than electricity. And he continued his thinly disguised attacks against the Kennedy administration, accusing the country of turning soft on communism and hard on the working man. He went so far as to suggest that inherited wealth kept those in power who had it out of touch with the needs of the everyday American.

On February 5, 1962, Ronald Reagan went directly from the Revue Studios, where he was completing the wraparounds for a new episode of *General Electric Theater,* to downtown Los Angeles, to testify under subpoena behind the closed doors of a federal grand jury. Reagan's testimony, kept sealed for years but eventually made public, is a remarkable document in evasiveness, charm, and self-justification cut with a fair measure of self-aggrandizement and loyalty to his friends and the company he worked for, MCA. Reading through it today, one cannot help but recall Reagan's testimony several years later, while president, during the so-called Iran-Contra hearings, where he experienced a curiously similar lack of memory.[*]

Reagan testimony was conducted by John Fricano of the Trial Section of the Federal Antitrust Division. After being sworn in, and his stature acknowledged by the court as a way of dispensing with certain formalities of identification, the questioning began. The first part of his testimony involved his early days in Hollywood, his representation by Bill Meiklejohn, and how that agent and his company were acquired by MCA, which then became his, Reagan's, agency.

FRICANO: "Do you recall when MCA acquired the William Meiklejohn Agency?"

---

[*] The complete testimony first appeared in Dan E. Moldea's *Dark Victory: Ronald Reagan, MCA and the Mob* (see "Sources"), an account of the history and dealings of the agency. Various excerpts of the entire investigation have appeared in various form in several other publications. The excerpts taken here are edited from the entire transcript, but the parts included are verbatim, except for purposes of clarification.

REAGAN: "I think around 1939 or '40 but my memory is a little hazy there . . . could I volunteer something here? I wouldn't want these ladies and gentlemen to think that I wouldn't wear a shirt and necktie to come down here. They caught me at the studio. I had no choice."

"Who was your personal agent at MCA when you first went to the organization?"

"Lew Wasserman."

"Have you ever had any other personal agent?"

"Yes, as Lew went more into the administrative end, becoming president of the company, Art [Park] has been my particular agent."

"What unions are you a member of, Mr. Reagan?"

"Screen Actors Guild and AFTRA. I have been a member, in addition, of the American Guild of Variety Artists for a brief time when I made personal appearances."

"Do you recall when you became a member of SAG?"

"Yes, when I came here and signed my contract with Warner Brothers."

"1937?"

"Yes."

"What positions have you held in SAG since you became a member in 1937?"

"Well, I have probably held twenty years of membership total as a board member. I briefly was a vice president and I had six and a half terms as president."

After some more questioning involving SAG dates and certain other negotiations, the questioning turned to the 1952 issuance of the blanket waiver for MCA, on Reagan's watch:

FRICANO: "What was the biggest point in the negotiations with TV film people of residual payments for actors in films once made, that they would be paid again when those films were run?"

REAGAN: "Well, that was to get — naturally the studios after fifty years of operating on a basis of once they had the film in the can it was theirs, they resisted at this idea of anyone having a lien against that film and they did not have complete ownership of it. One studio head said, 'It's mine to throw off the end of the dock if I want.' I made some that I wish I had."

"In point of fact, television was a dirty word in the motion picture industry in 1952?"

"That's right."

"It's also a fact, is it, Mr. Reagan, that the first company to capitulate with respect to repayment for reuse was a TV production company?"

"I am sure that would have been the Alliance [of Television Producers — ATP], yes."

"Which company, whether a member of the Alliance or not, was the first to capitulate with respect to repayment for reruns?"

"There you have me. I wouldn't know where we cracked that and if you tell me, I'll have to take your word for it."

"Well, you were president of the Screen Actors Guild in 1952, were you not?"

"Yes."

"That was a very important matter which Screen Actors Guild was taking up and it was the most important part of the Guild?"

"Yes, and I don't want to appear as though I am trying deliberately to be vague, but, as I say, I would like you to realize in my history of holding an office with the Guild, my memory is like a kaleidoscope of meetings, that I am sure if I sat down with someone and started in, I could then recall the details. But I met for seven months twice a day five days a week in an attempt to settle the big jurisdictional questions in 1946 and '47. I mean personally for more than eight or nine weeks almost every day in 19— Before 1947 as a member of negotiating committees. I mean, it's the length of negotiations that led to the stopgap that led to the release of feature motion pictures to television and I went to New York and I met out here for countless meetings with AFTRA when they were attempting to evade what was our right and jurisdiction."

"I think the grand jury understands, sir, at this time you were very busy and the memory of man is not the greatest faculty he possesses. I will attempt to refresh your recollection with respect to this time period. In the first place, does the fact that I state to you now that MCA was the first, MCA-Revue, that is, was the first to acquiesce to the residual payments help you out in your recollection? Can you substantiate that statement?"

"No, I can't. I honestly can't. I know that many times Jack Dales reported to me as president, he is the executive secretary of the Guild, that he had talked off the record to Lew Wasserman about this problem and about the recognizing of this principle and so forth. When did this occur, when did you say?"

"July 1952. July 23, 1952."

"Well, maybe the fact that I got married in March of 1952 and went on a honeymoon has something to do with my being a little bit hazy."

"I'm glad you raised that point. If we might digress, who is your wife?"

"Nancy Davis."

"Was she a member of the board of directors of SAG in 1952?"

"Yes."

"Do you recall any other unusual or momentous events in 1952 with respect to SAG's relations with one or more TV film production companies?"

526

"Well, now, what kind of events?"

"In 1952, when you were president of the Screen Actors Guild, did not the Screen Actors Guild grant to MCA what is known in the trade as a blanket or unlimited waiver to produce TV films?"

"Oh, we have granted — I don't know when it exactly started, we granted an extended waiver to MCA to be engaged in production as we had done with other people. Mr. Feldman, who was an agent and produced feature pictures, we gave him a waiver also."

"I think that was a limited waiver, limited specifically to two or possibly three productions a year. It was not a blanket or unlimited waiver."

"That's right."

"Was it SAG's history with respect to granting waivers in either media, motion pictures, or television prior to 1952?"

"Oh, well, I would have to say there must have been, I am sure, there must have been times when for some reason or another we refused but I am sure also — I can tell you what our general attitude was. Our attitude was where we could see no harm to one of our members, to our membership, that we should do everything we could to encourage production because the great problem we have had has always been unemployment. Even in times of prosperity actors are unemployed. They sit out and wait. If somebody comes to discuss and tell us they want to make pictures, we are inclined to go along with them."

A little while later, the questioning focused in still tighter on the granting of the waiver to MCA:

FRICANO: "You are familiar, are you not, with the waiver granted to MCA, in 1952 during your term as president?"

REAGAN: "Yes."

"Can you tell this grand jury why Screen Actors Guild gave to MCA a blanket or unlimited waiver?"

"Well, my own reasoning and one of the reasons perhaps why this doesn't loom so importantly to me is I personally never saw any particular harm in it. I was one who subscribed to the belief, and those were times of great distress in the picture business, I was all for anyone that could give employment. I saw no harm in this happening. Now, anything I would answer from there would be hearsay. I have been told that Revue grew out of MCA's efforts to enter the motion picture industry, in moving into the field of television, and they wouldn't touch it. And when Revue had in their hands the possibility of these packages and couldn't get anyone to produce them, that they set up shop to produce them themselves."

"Do you recall how early this was in point of time?"

"I don't know. I think it was prior to '52."

"It would have been either the latter '50s or 1950?"

"Yes."

"Because Revue had been in production since that time?"

"Yes."

"Do you recall the year Revue first went into production, Mr. Reagan?"

"No, I don't. Television at that time, you must recall, was mostly live and was mostly centered in New York and I knew there were shows called package shows, that you got a chance to do a guest shot. You went to do yours and it was a Revue package. I wasn't even familiar with the name too much. I just called it an MCA package but then that wasn't strange because we had the same thing in radio."

"You have given us your rationale behind your reasons for the blanket waiver to MCA in 1952. What was Screen Actors Guild's reason for granting the waiver?"

"Well, that is very easy to recall. Screen Actors Guild board and executives met in meetings and very carefully considered these things, weighed them at board meetings. I remember discussions taking place about it and usually the result of the discussion would be that we felt we were amply protected, that if any harm started from this, if anything happened to react against the actors' interests, we could always pull the rug out from under them. No great harm would be done before we could ride to the rescue, that our feeling was, here was someone that wanted to give actors jobs and that is the way it would usually wind up."

"How many more waivers did Screen Actors Guild grant to talent agents subsequent to the blanket waiver to MCA in order to give actors jobs?"

"I don't recall. I don't know if we did to William Morris or not.[*] When I say I don't know if we did, it was because I was more familiar with William Morris in the live field of packaging."

"Do you know whether any talent agents applied for blanket waivers subsequent to the time SAG granted one to MCA?"

"No, I don't."

"Did Screen Actors Guild attempt to induce agents to enter TV film production subsequent to the time it granted a blanket waiver to MCA?"

"No, I don't think we ever went out and asked anyone to do that."

"That would be consistent with the rationale behind the granting of a blanket waiver, would it not?"

"No, I don't think the Screen Actors Guild is an employment agency. I think we can well

[*] They did not.

recognize our not putting out blocks in the way of anyone who wanted to produce but I don't think ours was the point of trying to go out and get someone to produce."

"In other words, had the blanket waiver been asked by talent agents subsequent to 1952 in July when SAG granted the blanket waiver to MCA, such requests would have been considered by the Guild and granted, correct?"

"If all of the circumstances were the same as, they would be."

Fricano then went to the heart of the matter, the apparent, secret, and illegal quid pro quo between MCA and the Screen Actors Guild:

FRICANO: "Did you ever hear it said, Mr. Reagan, that Screen Actors Guild granted a blanket waiver to MCA due to the fact that MCA was willing at this time to grant repayment for reuse of TV films to actors?"

"No, sir."

"I will show you a document marked Grand Jury Exhibit Number 41 from Laurence W. Beilenson; do you know who Mr. Beilenson is?"

"Yes."

" 'To Mr. Lew Wasserman. MCA Artists Limited, re. amended Revue-MCA-SAG letter agreement of July 23, 1952.' This letter is dated June 7, 1954. I will ask you to read Paragraph 1 of this document and see if that doesn't refresh your recollection as to the reason why Screen Actors Guild granted a blanket waiver to MCA. May I read it for you, sir? 'Should the letter be a superseding letter or an amendment?' And I might add for your information that this dealt with the renewal of the blanket waiver which had been granted in 1952. The original agreement in 1952 extended to '59 but for some reason which we hope to elicit, in 1954 another year was tacked on to that waiver. Continuing, 'I prefer the latter because the letter of July 23, 1952, was executed under a specific set of circumstances where Revue was willing to sign a contract giving the Guild members reuse fees when no one else was willing to do so.' "

"Well, then I was wrong but, and I can understand that, but I certainly, I am afraid when I answered before that I was under the impression you were trying to make out that in negotiating a contract we saw this as a bargaining point of giving a waiver."

"Isn't it conceivable from this language?"

"Mr. Beilenson is a lawyer and in charge of negotiations. It's quite conceivable then if he says it in this letter."

"Does that refresh your recollection, sir?"

"I don't recall it, no."

"In your capacity of president of SAG it was your belief at this time that a waiver should be granted MCA because it would give actors work, is that right?"

"Well, this was always our thinking, yes."

After identifying the members of the board, and ascertaining how many of them were represented by MCA at the time of the granting of the waivers, a back-and-forth in which Reagan simply could not or would not give definitive answers to almost every single inquiry, Fricano returned once more to Reagan's alleged participation in the granting of the waiver.

FRICANO: "Did you participate in any negotiations in 1954 on SAG's behalf with respect to a waiver to MCA? I refer specifically to June 4 of 1954 when the Letter Agreement of July 23 was extended another year. Did you participate in any way in those negotiations?"

REAGAN: "I don't honestly recall. You know something? You keep saying 1954 in the summer. I think maybe one of the reasons I don't recall was because I feel that in the summer of 1954, I was up in Glacier National Park making a cowboy picture for RKO . . . so it's very possible there were some things going on that I would not participate in but I have no recollection of this particularly."

"I would like to know, sir, if you can tell the grand jury why in June of 1954 the blanket waiver to MCA was extended and the negotiations which SAG held with MCA was extended, whereas twenty-four days later, negotiations were held for other talent agencies, who had also requested waivers and the waivers which these agencies received were limited waivers?"

"I wouldn't be able to tell you."

"Were you aware of the fact?"

"I will say one thing. I don't know what you are getting at with the question and I am certainly in no position to infer that I want to tell you what to do or not. I can only say this. I have tried to make plain why my memory could be so hazy on a great many things whether it had to do with this or not because of the long years and participation in all of these in which days of meetings would be devoted to one particular point in a producer's contract or something. I can only say this, that in all my years with the Screen Actors Guild, I have never known of or participated in anything, nor has the Guild, that ever in any way was based on anything but what we honestly believed was for the best interests of the actor and, however it may look now as to the point of private negotiations or anything else, if there was —"

At this point the questioner cut off Reagan, agreed that he might have reasons not to remember details across a decade, and then once again returned to the issue at hand:

FRICANO: "I would just like to see if you can shed any light with hindsight on negotiations which took place at this time between

SAG and MCA."

REAGAN: "In view of what is shown in Mr. Beilenson's letter, it is very possible at that time, in spite of my not remembering, it is very possible that we saw an opportunity to break the solid back of the motion picture industry with regard to residuals and if we saw that kind of thing we moved in, as we did in the most recent strike when we found one studio, Universal, which would break the unit of the motion picture studios and we signed a separate contract with them. You can refer to those as secret negotiations. I met in an apartment in Beverly Hills —"

"I didn't use the word 'secret' in speaking of the negotiations that took place between SAG and MCA. That was your word."

"Well, I met privately with the president of Universal Studios and we walked out with the contract and were about to face the rest of the producers with one of their number who had broken this rank and willingly signed a contract to pay repayments. This could very well have taken place. I can see where MCA would be in an untenable position. They couldn't represent actors and deny actors the right to residual payments."

"But the fact remains that according to Mr. Beilenson's letter, he states that 'we gave you residuals when no one else in the industry would' and you have already stated, sir, that residuals at this time were a very important bargaining point between the Guild, not only the TV producers, but also the motion picture production companies, is that right?"

"Yes."

After several dozen more questions on this issue, Fricano now focused on one final subject; whether or not Ronald Reagan owned any part of the *General Electric Theater* prior to his resignation from the Screen Actors Guild in 1960:

FRICANO: "When did you first start with *G.E. Theater*?"

REAGAN: " '54."

"What were the terms under which you appeared in the *G.E. Theater*?"

"I was not to exceed six shows. That was my own contention because I didn't want to overexpose myself. I introduced all of the shows and closed them out. I specifically refused to do commercials and I don't think an actor should, and I did a number of weeks of touring for the company, visiting plants and employees, meeting the employees and appearing publicly, speaking and so forth, speaking speeches as a part of General Electric's employee and community relations program, because our show is under the institutional program."

"This was as early as 1954?"

"That's right."

"That was part of the contract?"

"That's right."

"Who negotiated your contract for *G.E. Theater?*"

"Well my first approach — do you mean with me?"

"No. Who represented you?"

"Art Park."

"With whom did he negotiate?"

"Art would have negotiated — well, first of all, it was Revue through Taft Schreiber who approached me. I turned down regular television shows a great deal. I did not feel — most actors were a little gun-shy of a series. . . . I kept holding out for motion pictures. . . . Anthologies had been singularly successful and they felt the reason was because there was no continuing personality on which to hang the production and advertising of the show. So, they were going to solve it by having a host, me, if I would do the job. . . . At this point now came the discussion about me and where I sit and then Art negotiated with Revue and I am sure with representation by BBD&O, because I ended up as an employee of the advertising agency."

"How did that happen?"

"Well, it happened because the agency did not want me to be an employee of Revue. They felt that this, as later I was told, they felt this would put Revue, if this thing clicked and if I were the principal character of the show, it would give Revue more bargaining power than they wanted them to have with regard to future productions. So they wanted control of me as an employee. Usually it's done that way. The sponsor won't have us as an employee. The sponsor doesn't want to have to justify an actor to the stockholders but he can justify so much for advertising and you are part of advertising. So I was employed by BBD&O."

"You were salaried?"

"I was salaried."

"Had Art Park attempted to obtain any ownership interest for you in the *G.E. Theater*?"

"No, when the show started the show was basically live so this was not an issue. We did a few pilots because we knew there were actors who still work on live television. The bulk of the show was made of live television shows."

"Is it unusual for an actor, a performer as yourself, to have an ownership in a live program?"

"This is very possible also but you must recall the only thing I would have been able to bargain for at this point was with the few shows I was in because my opening and closing did not go on beyond *General Electric*. There was no residual in my introduction of the show. No one else can ever use that."

"Did you discuss the possibility of an ownership interest in *G.E. Theater* in 1954 with anyone?"

"No."

"You did not discuss it with Art Park?"

"No, the main point of contention, and this became a great point of contention between Revue and MCA, was over a little idiosyncrasy of mine. In all the time I had ever done guest shows when I had done them on film, I had always refused to sell the foreign motion picture rights. Many actors who do film television, when it's on film, they give up their television fee for the right to show that picture in foreign theaters. As a practical point, I never wanted my pictures, which I know are made at a different budget for television, to ever have to compete on a motion picture screen with motion pictures made at a cost of millions of dollars. I didn't think it was fair for me as a performer. Revue wanted, if I wanted any of the show, they wanted the right to show them as they did other actors in the motion picture theater. It finally came to a point where Art, on my behalf, wouldn't give in. So Art, who is a vice president and Taft Schreiber who is a vice president in charge of Revue, went and took the problem to the head school teacher, Lew Wasserman, who is the president of the whole works, and Lew Wasserman asked Art what he thought in a decision of this kind was best for me as a performer, and both Taft and Art had to admit naturally it was best for me as a performer not to give up the motion picture rights and it was Wasserman who said then, there is no question he shouldn't give up his motion picture rights."

"So Mr. Wasserman arbitrated the dispute between Park and Schreiber?"

"And ruled in my favor."

"So then ownership never came into the picture in 1954?"

"No, television — it's hard to think those few years back — television was pretty new. I had been offered ownership in some series that had been offered to me in which I would play a continuing part but, you see, the main bargaining value that an actor has in getting that kind of ownership is in his service as an actor. We are talking about a thing in which at the moment I would only appear in three or four of these. . . . I didn't have much bargaining power and I practically sat for fourteen months without a day's work in the motion pictures. . . ."

"Yet, in 1954 when you signed the contract to perform in *G.E. Theater,* the ownership interest angle never occurred to you?"

"No, because that was not the kind of show supplemented [*sic*] to that. . . ."

"When did it first occur to you, sir, that you should have an ownership interest in *G.E. Theater*?"

"Along the end of the [initial] five years. We had been moving up the number of pictures [shows] we were making instead of live, and I was very instrumental, I never missed a chance to bedevil General Electric, that they would do better on screen than live. . . . At the end of the five-year contract I had had with MCA expiring with General Electric and BBD&O, [I wondered if] there wasn't some way I could cut down my senior partner, the Department of Internal Revenue, and start building something for the future, instead of taking everything in straight income . . . this was my own idea."

"Would you restate again because I lost the thread, directly what ownership interest did Wasserman say Revue would give you?"

"That it was comparable to the salary I was getting plus the fact that by becoming an employee of Revue, I no longer paid MCA commission. So that automatically gave me a ten-percent raise in salary and they gave me twenty-five percent ownership in all films made in the *G.E. Theater,* not just those I appeared in but all of them."

It had taken awhile, but under oath, Reagan finally admitted to his financial stake in the production of *General Electric Theater.* He also finally acknowledged that it was a conflict of interest because of his role as SAG president, even if he didn't seem to think it was that important.

One week after his testimony, his and Nancy's tax returns were subpoenaed by federal investigators for the years 1952 through 1955.

And barely a month after that, the government's chief prosecutor from the very beginning of the investigation, Leonard Posner, suddenly died of a heart attack. MCA then immediately began talks to settle the government's antitrust investigation by offering to dissolve its talent agency and wholly acquire Universal Studios (and Decca Records). With some modifications, the deal was pushed through; on September 18, Robert Kennedy announced that a proposed consent decree had been filed in the United States District Court in Los Angeles and that the settlement would become effective in thirty-five days. All criminal proceedings against MCA and its alleged coconspirators were dropped. Jules Stein, Lew Wasserman, Taft Schreiber, and Ronald Reagan were excused from all further testimony, including the much-anticipated public trial, which many in the Kennedy administration had wanted to be broadcast in the same uninterrupted manner as the *McCarthy vs. the United States Army* hearings a decade earlier.

No sooner had the investigation come to its abrupt end, than Reagan immediately resumed his vocal attacks on the Kennedy administration, accusing Robert Kennedy of having conducted a meat-ax operation against

MCA. He publicly bemoaned the fact that thanks to Robert Kennedy's insistence that MCA divest itself of its talent agency, hundreds of actors were now without adequate representation. These were strange and ironic sentiments from someone for whom a great many of those actors had little good to say about after the so-called Great Giveaway. Moreover, most of the agents who left MCA simply took their clients with them, either to the William Morris Agency or to the newly formed Ashley-Famous, which several former MCA agents had formed.

A month after the consent degree was signed by MCA that officially put an end to the federal government's investigation, Reagan was dropped as the host of *General Electric Theater.* He was angered by this decision and believed because he was so good and the show was so popular, it was a political rather than a business one, and that somehow, the Kennedys were behind it all.[*]

There may have been some truth to Rea-

---

[*] Despite his legendary status as a great communicator, G.E. executives were constantly sending corrective memos to Reagan, imploring him to be more careful in his use of words like "Frigidaire," a brand name for refrigerators, manufactured by one of G.E.'s competitors.

gan's suspicions. His promotional speeches on the stump for G.E. had continued to skew toward the political, even before his grand jury testimony. Earlier that same year, he had launched a vicious attack on the Tennessee Valley Authority, one of the hallowed pillars of Franklin Roosevelt's New Deal policies. During one particularly vitriolic speech, he told the crowd that the annual interest on the TVA deal was five times as great as the flood damage it prevented. The only problem was, G.E. held $50 million in contracts with the agency. When Reagan became aware of it, he personally telephoned Ralph J. Cordimer, the gracious but increasingly distant president of G.E., the guiding light of the corporation and the one who had originally come up with the idea of making Reagan the company's roving ambassador of goodwill. Reagan offered to drop the reference to the TVA, but after talking with Cordimer, he correctly sensed that some damage, probably irrevocable, had been done.

The last straw may have indeed been the convening of the grand jury, but in truth, even with the investigation, and with or without Reagan, *General Electric Theater*'s days were numbered. In 1962, Revue was at the top of its game, with hit shows that included *Wagon Train, Leave It to Beaver, McHale's Navy, Alcoa Theater, It's a Man's*

World, Laramie, Wide Country, The Jack Benny Show, and *The Alfred Hitchcock Hour,* a hit roster that cut across all three of the networks and dominated prime time. At the same time, *General Electric Theater* was about to start its eleventh season, shot in a format that was considered old hat and quickly disappearing from TV, the half-hour black-and-white, star-hosted, twenty-two-and-a-half-minute anthology melodrama. Even Hitchcock, who had dominated the 1950s with his show, had expanded to an hour to suit the viewers' changing habits. Moreover, NBC, sensing a weakness on CBS's part in the 9:00 prime-time hour following the untouchable *Ed Sullivan Show,* put in that slot the spectacularly popular *Bonanza,* a color extravaganza that made "the Ponderosa" a household expression.

Lew Wasserman, hoping to save the show (and Reagan's job), went to Jimmy Stewart, someone whose stalled postwar career Wasserman had helped revive in the early fifties by pairing him with director Anthony Mann in a percentage deal that had not only brought Stewart back into prominence but made him a millionaire. Now, when Wasserman needed a favor, Stewart could not refuse and despite having previously declined to appear in any television series, did a half-hour version of Dickens's *A Christmas Carol* for

G.E. Theater.[*]

While ratings temporarily rose because of all the star wattage, it was still too late to save the show. General Electric wanted to retain the time slot but wanted a new format. Reagan was then brought to New York City and offered the job of continuing as a field spokesperson, not as host or narrator, for *General Electric Theater.* Reagan declined, politely reminding G.E. that he was an actor, not a corporate speech maker. Seeing no other way out, G.E. fired him.

The show was canceled at the end of the 1962–63 season.

That fall, Ronald Reagan officially changed his party affiliation to Republican.

[*] In an interesting twist, Stewart had appeared in Frank Capra's 1946 *It's a Wonderful Life,* loosely based on *A Christmas Carol,* to help the director revive his flagging career.

■ ■ ■ ■

CHAPTER TWELVE:
RENDEZVOUS WITH
DESTINY

■ ■ ■ ■

You and I have a rendezvous with destiny. We can preserve for your children this, the last best hope of man on earth, or we can sentence them to take the first step into a thousand years of darkness. If we fail, at least let our children and our children's children, say of us we justified our brief moment here. We did all that could be done.
— RONALD REAGAN

In his final film, The Killers *(1964).*

In the summer of 1962, after eight years as the star of TV's *G.E. Theater,* the fifty-one-year-old Ronald Reagan once again found himself out of work, with no real acting prospects. And this time around, there was no powerful agency for him to fall back on. Lew Wasserman was no longer his agent because Lew Wasserman was no longer an agent. Having moved into a position of Guiding Light, for lack of a better or more precise term, of the new MCA–Universal Pictures, because of the recent settlement with the federal government, Wasserman was overseeing plans for the construction of the company's new corporate headquarters in "Universal City," what the trades had already dubbed The Black Rock. From there, Wasserman would rule over his ever-expanding entertainment dynasty of television, movies, music, and studio tours that under his supervision would grow into a billion-dollar empire.

It wasn't that he didn't feel an obligation to

Reagan. There just was nothing he could do for him at the moment, he told his former client. Be patient, Wasserman said, and something will happen.

Something did, only it wasn't anything that Reagan had been expecting. On July 25, his seventy-nine-year-old mother, Nelle Reagan, suffered a cerebral hemorrhage and died in her sleep. She had spent her last years in a nursing home in Santa Monica, paid for by Reagan after the house he'd bought for his parents had accidentally burned to the ground. Only her Bible had survived that, the same Bible she had next to her bed when she passed. If Reagan was shattered by the loss, he didn't show it. Instead, he sought comfort in the arms of his wife, and when he did comment publicly on it, in characteristic (for him) fashion, he reverted to the stoic and the philosophical. He was grateful, he said, that his mother had died peacefully.[*]

Two weeks after the funeral, held at the

* In light of Reagan's later health problems, it may be of some significance that, according to Reagan biographer Edmund Morris, Reagan believed his mother had "gone senile" the last years of her life, based on the fact that Nelle had noted to one of Reagan's fans that she was suffering from a hardening of the arteries in her head, which made it hard for her to think.

Hollywood Beverly Christian Church, attended by Reagan, his wife and children and his brother, Neil, now a vice president of the McCann-Erickson advertising agency, Reagan began making a series of paid speeches in and around Los Angeles he titled "The Price of Freedom." With nothing else really going on, Reagan had turned to speech making as a way to produce income. Also, for the first time since he had moved to California, after much thought, he decided he should back a specific candidate in the upcoming 1962 state elections.

Reagan's primary political focus that fall would be his support of Richard Nixon's run for the governorship of California. When questioned on the campaign trail about his recent switch to the Republican Party, Reagan trotted out his favorite response to all questions dealing with his political affiliations: "I didn't leave the Democrats, they left me." Nixon's eventual defeat that fall not only disappointed Reagan, it deeply angered him. He began looking toward the 1964 presidential campaign, determined to unseat the Kennedys and everything he believed they stood for. He would never forget or forgive Robert Kennedy for leading the charge against MCA that left him, Reagan, almost completely shut out of the entertainment mainstream after his disclosure that he had been a secret part-owner of his television show while representing his fellow SAG members. Ironically, he felt blacklisted as a result of his testimony. Whether he was or was not, the fact was there was nobody beating down his door to give him a job, and for that there was no one else to blame, he believed, than the Kennedy brothers.

It wasn't until almost a year later, in the fall of 1963, that Reagan was finally able to get a part in a new motion picture, his first feature-length film in seven years, although it wasn't exactly what he had hoped for. Lew Wasserman brokered the deal for a made-for-TV movie for Reagan, to be coproduced by Revue Productions and Universal Pictures. When Reagan read the script, he hated it because for the first time in his career he was going to have to play "the heavy." The character's name was Browning, the film a remake of Robert Siodmak's 1946 screen adaptation of Ernest Hemingway's short story "The Killers." It had been the vehicle Universal had used to launch Burt Lancaster's film career, and the rights to the original story still belonged to the studio.*

The new version was to be directed by Don Siegel, whose work Wasserman liked and

* As part of the 1961 consent decree, to avoid any possibility of reestablishing a monopoly by its merger with MCA, Universal agreed to divest itself

who, he believed, could bring the film in fast and cheap. The remake, originally titled *Johnny North,* was to be part of a Revue Productions TV series called *Project 120,* but it was rejected by NBC's censors and at that point Wasserman decided to retitle it *The Killers,* in an attempt to cash in on the revival of interest in the famed novelist following his July 1961 suicide. Any links to the original short story were hard to find, other than the plot line involving two contract killers who are part of a larger robbery scheme that has, predictably, gone wrong. In one scene, Reagan slaps Angie Dickinson (Sheila) across the face, and it was that very moment that caused the film to be pulled from the small screen.

Wasserman, looking to recoup his investment, released it in theaters, where it died as premature a death as most of the characters in the script.[†] It also marked the official end of Ronald Reagan's thirty-seven-year, fifty-four-feature-film career. For the rest of his days, Reagan regretted not only having made

---

of all but fourteen titles in its extensive film library it could retain for eventual remakes. *The Killers* was one of those titles.

† The film ran into problems with the outdated and now all but meaningless Production Code, which, among other objections, wanted to prohibit it from being shown in theaters on Sundays.

the film, but that his final appearance on the big screen was of a tough and violent psychotic who was abusive to women. That wasn't him up there, and that wasn't his idea of what film was supposed to be.

Or as he might have so aptly and succinctly put it, he hadn't changed, the movies had.[*]

Filming on *The Killers* had begun November 23, 1963, the day after John F. Kennedy was assassinated in Dallas, Texas. To Reagan, that was a much more significant event than the awful little film he had been talked into making by Wasserman. It was the murder that changed the world, changed America, and changed Ronald Reagan's life.

Now, with former vice president Lyndon Johnson suddenly in the White House, the dynamics of the 1964 presidential campaign had profoundly changed. Out of the deep national mourning of the days, weeks, and months that followed the tragedy in Dallas, a dark-horse Republican conservative by the name of Barry Goldwater gained a significant national following by offering a diametrically

---

[*] Per James C. Humes in his *The Wit and Wisdom of Ronald Reagan* (page 101), years later Reagan tried to make light of the film, insisting that he had been talked into making it and that it flopped because "I think the viewers kept waiting for me to repent and become a good guy in the end."

opposed alternative to LBJ's "Great Society" — something that Reagan considered to be too far over the line that divided liberalism and socialism. Goldwater offered a viable alternative to New York State's liberal Republican governor Nelson Rockefeller, at the time considered the favorite to win the Republican nomination. After careful consideration, Reagan volunteered his services in support of Barry Goldwater's campaign to become the Republican candidate in the upcoming presidential campaign. Kennedy was dead and Reagan wanted to make sure his legacy perished as well. As Hollywood movies always liked to remind audiences, vengeance dies hard.

The Republicans knew they had an uphill fight in 1964. In his fourteen years in the Senate, Johnson had always been a popular figure as a proud disciple of Roosevelt liberalism, and the death of JFK was a huge emotional wound to a country where the majority of its citizens felt a combination of individual grief and a collective loss over the assassination of the youthful, energetic, charismatic leader of the "New Frontier." "Camelot" had come and gone in a killer's blast, leaving the second-in-charge, Johnson, to carry on the unfinished doctrine of what people could do for their country.

The party of Dwight Eisenhower, the only Republican president in thirty-two years of otherwise Democrat domination of the White House, put all its electoral eggs into Barry Goldwater's basket. As the party leader, Goldwater surprised and disappointed a lot of Republicans, including former president Eisenhower, who found him too much of a right-wing extremist. The fact that Goldwater had summed up Eisenhower's eight years in office as nothing more than "dime-store New Deal politics" did nothing to help win over the former president's support.

Ronald and Nancy Reagan attended the convention held at the Cow Palace in San Francisco, where, as the premier celebrities in the house, they watched from a private box with pride and satisfaction as Goldwater took the nomination from not just Rockefeller but also long-shot challengers and comparative moderates Richard Nixon, Sen. Margaret Chase Smith, and former senator and UN ambassador (and Nixon's running mate in 1960) Henry Cabot Lodge.

Hosting the Reagans for the week they spent in the state capital were friends Holmes and Virginia Tuttle and Henry and Grace Salvatori, two of the wealthy, elitist, and socially upscale "Group" couples from Los Angeles. Holmes Tuttle had worked his way up through the world of banking until, in 1946, he was able to secure enough funding to open his own Ford and Lincoln-Mercury car dealerships in Beverly Hills. Through the years he used those franchises to build an empire of wealth and influence throughout Southern California. He had become a familiar face to Los Angelenos through television advertising and the ubiquitous Tuttle Ford dealerships that dotted the city's main thoroughfare. His dealerships were so well known that they became one of the unofficial signposts of L.A. In 1956, Holmes Tuttle became a California player in national politics when he supported Eisenhower's successful run for reelection to a second term. Tuttle, who prided himself on always being at the forefront of the fluid American political landscape, thought he knew something no one else did in 1964 when he looked for the future of the Republican Party and saw Barry Goldwater at the head of it.

Henry Salvatori, the head of the Western Geophysical oil company, volunteered to serve as Goldwater's finance chairman in California. When Tuttle asked Salvatori to help sponsor their friend Reagan's trip to the convention, he enthusiastically agreed. Reagan then got his brother, Neil, to help Goldwater put together his TV commercials for the upcoming fall campaign. Neil devoted the next two months to flying around the country constantly at Goldwater's side, supervising the filming of virtually every waking moment of the nominee, hoping it would yield something even remotely television friendly from Goldwater's decidedly nontelegenic white-haired, scowly visage adorned with thick, heavily framed eyeglasses and a face held in place by rough, reddish skin (some of which was reportedly attributable to Goldwater's nasty drinking habits — his campaign went to great lengths to keep them from the public; the night he had won the nomination, Goldwater had nearly passed out drunk and had to be loaded onto a private plane, by Holmes Tuttle, to get him back to Arizona). Goldwater was about as far away from Camelot as it was possible to get. In McLuhanesque terms, Lyndon Johnson seemed advantageously "cool" by comparison.

Goldwater had done himself no favors at the convention with his acceptance speech when he declared to his fellow conventioneers and the rest of America watching on television that "extremism in the defense of liberty is no vice! And let me remind you also that moderation in the pursuit of justice is no virtue!" It was that speech more than anything else that convinced most viewers that Goldwater was too hot wired with a dangerously short fuse, an impression reiterated by Johnson's classic one-minute commercial of a little girl picking petals off a daisy followed by a nuclear bomb going off, sixty seconds that were probably as responsible as anything else for Johnson's landslide election victory.

Reagan, however, liked and admired Goldwater's speech, hearing in it a much-needed resumption of a broadside against what he (and Goldwater) believed was the resurgence of a dangerous communist movement in the country and of its spoiled second cousin, liberalism. Reagan was convinced Goldwater was on the right track and was determined to help him get to the White House.

As Labor Day approached and Goldwater remained far behind Johnson in all the polls, Tuttle hit upon the idea of having Reagan, rather than Goldwater, be the principal speaker at a $1,000-a-plate fund-raiser to be held at the Ambassador's Cocoanut Grove nightclub in downtown Los Angeles. Reagan enthusiastically agreed, and the senator bowed out at the last minute due to, his representatives said, irreconcilable "scheduling conflicts." As soon as Reagan was named as the substitute speaker, the event quickly and completely sold out.

After his introduction, Reagan took to the podium and began what he called his "A Time for Choosing" speech; with slight variation, the same talk he had been giving for years. He knew it backward and forward, inside and out, and performed it as if it was his favorite dramatic monologue. He knew where all the strong points were, as well as every laugh. He knew just the right moments to pause. He knew when to shake his head and to slow down his words for emphasis. He knew how to look directly into the camera, into the eyes of everyone and no one at the same time and hold for the inevitable applause that dotted the high points, and he always knew at the end he would be given the inevitable standing ovation.

As the introductory applause subsided, he began as he did every speech he called "A Time for Choosing," partly as a way to convey his message about where he felt the increasing liberal/left direction of the country was headed and partly as an appeal for money. It had been written by Reagan himself in bits and pieces over the years, an amalgam, really, of the hundreds of speeches he had delivered on the corporate trail during his years with General Electric. Like any good script, it had been tried out numerous times before live audiences, with the best parts kept in and the ones that didn't work taken out. Despite Reagan's desire to appear progressive, in a conservative way (not difficult to do in contrast to Goldwater), his speech really recalled a different America, one that the movies had celebrated since the beginning of film itself as an uncomplicated paradise of freedom, individuality, equality, and democracy for all. Thus, it was peppered with many references and lines from other great speeches and speakers, including one that declared the

Republican Party, led by Barry Goldwater, offered not just America, but the world, its "last best hope for man on earth."

It was a punch line that never failed to make audiences sit up and take notice. It had all the eloquence and power of Kennedy's inaugural directive to his fellow Americans, to "ask not what your country can do for you — ask what you can do for your country." This is not surprising when the origins of "Reagan's" line are revealed (something Reagan never did in "A Time for Choosing"). Reagan's hero, FDR, had used it several times, although he, too, borrowed it without citing its original user (and author), Abraham Lincoln. It was altogether fitting and proper that Reagan's speech would echo both FDR, the savior of the twentieth century, and the savior of the nineteenth. However, because this was Reagan, who was neither a great intellectual nor a particularly insightful student of history, this was an echo of the *image* of both FDR and Lincoln. Reagan's face hardened into a granitelike visage that recalled Rushmore's Lincoln, rather than Hollywood's. It was as if FDR's aged wisdom had combined with Lincoln's youthful (forever) virtue in the guise of a modern-day American hero: Reagan as FDR, as Lincoln, all cut with a generous dose of everyone's favorite Hollywood patriot, John Wayne.

The speech was filled with a defense of

Republican policies and a denunciation of liberal/communist theories that, he reminded his audience, did not work, could not work, and because of it only brought misery in the past to any country that had tried it. He talked for about twenty minutes, stopping during the frequent breakouts of applause, and then, as he reached the end, paused, shook his head once, looked out into the audience, and declared, "You and I have a rendezvous with destiny. We will preserve for our children this, the last best hope of man on earth, or we will sentence them to take the last step into a thousand years of darkness!"

The room was frozen. No one moved, including Reagan. After what seemed like an eternity, the applause began and then rose to a crescendo and did not stop until everyone in the room had risen to their feet, cheering and stomping the floor in a thunderous ovation. Tuttle and Salvatori, who had been watching from the back of the room, looked at each other in amazement as Reagan smiled and waved while the audience continued its frenzied, passionate outburst.

After, while Reagan and Nancy greeted the attendees, Tuttle and Salvatori huddled, Tuttle scratching notes on the small spiral pad he always carried with him, looking at it as he wrote, while Salvatori dictated.

The next day Salvatori called Goldwater

and told him the plan: They were going to buy a half hour of national time for Reagan to give his speech, tweaked ever so slightly to make his support of Goldwater even more enthusiastic to the viewing audience.* The candidate, whose personal appearances more closely resembled a college poli-sci lecture, did not go for the idea at all. Besides, he was ideologically opposed to some ideas expressed in it, such as what he perceived to be Reagan's attack in it of Social Security. However, his real fear was the correct perception that the image of Ronald Reagan would not merely overshadow but dwarf his own.

Besides Goldwater's reluctance, which he would eventually be talked out of, there was another, very real problem the friends of Reagan faced. There simply wasn't enough money to buy a half hour of national network airtime. They were rescued by the unlikeliest of sources — another Hollywood movie star. John Wayne, the image of uberpatriotism, had long harbored desires of his own to one day run for office, but knew his age, health problems, and the lingering questions over his nonservice in the military during World War II made it impossible. Like so many others, he saw an idealized version of himself in

---

* Goldwater's name was added exactly one time to the generic core of the speech. In all previous versions of it Reagan had delivered, he had not mentioned him at all.

Ronald Reagan, a Central Casting version of what an American president should look like. And, crucially, Reagan was of the same political persuasion as Wayne, although Reagan had come to the right decades after Wayne had.

Just two weeks before the speech was scheduled to be telecast, it had not as yet been paid for and the network was threatening to cancel it. At the same time, during a rally held at Madison Square Garden, a group that called itself The Brothers for Goldwater, members of the Sigma Chi fraternity (Goldwater was a member), presented a check to Goldwater for $60,000, the same amount needed to pay for the Reagan telecast. The chairman of The Brothers for Goldwater was John Wayne. Another member was G.E. employee J. J. Wuerthner, the director and chief operating officer of the Garden event. When Wayne discovered there was no specific use designated for the money, he suggested it be used to buy the time for Reagan's speech.[*]

"A Time for Choosing" was broadcast nationwide on NBC on Tuesday night, Octo-

[*] For a fuller and more complete examination of events surrounding the speech and Reagan's subsequent rise to power, the author suggests Thomas W. Evans's book-length study, *The Education of Ronald Reagan* (see "Sources" for further details).

ber 27, 1964, one week before the election. Although it appeared to be live (coming in at a half hour, exactly the amount a typical episode with commercials ran), it was, in fact, a carefully edited videotape of the speech that had been delivered a week earlier in a Phoenix television studio. According to Patti Davis, in her 1992 memoir, the whole place was in tears by the time Reagan had delivered his declaration of a shared date with destiny.

Everyone in the audience at the Phoenix studio knew they had just seen and heard something special. By the time it was broadcast, there was an anticipatory buzz across the country. That night, the Reagans watched the speech together with the Salvatoris and the Tuttles, in the living room of another couple they were all friendly with, Bill and Betty Wilson. Tuttle beamed with pride as Reagan's image flickered its way to greatness.

And greatness it was. The impact was immediate, something that "live" television could do better than any other medium. This was not going to be just a water-cooler moment; it was the political equivalent of the night Elvis Presley burst on the scene on the *Ed Sullivan Show.* Everyone knew that night, as everyone knew this one, even before the applause had subsided, that a new political star had been born.

In Reagan's case, of course, it was nothing less than a moment of rebirth, into a new career, for a new audience, at a new time. He had finally found a way to marry the medium that loved him to the message he loved. As he had whenever he delivered the earlier versions of the speech, he delivered it (and himself) with all the confidence, charisma, charm, and magnitude that he had never been able to project playing characters on-screen.

The next day, the *Washington Post* was the first, but not the only, major publication to declare that, indeed, during the broadcast, "a new political Star was born." It was a multiple deliverance. That week a half-million dollars in fresh contributions from the public found their way into Goldwater's campaign coffers. No one had ever seen anything like it before. It was as if God had, indeed, appeared (as he hadn't in Nancy Reagan's *The Next Voice You Hear*), and delivered a special electronic Sermon on the Mount. Thanks to Ronald Reagan, Goldwater was going to be able to make a decent end run at what looked like an impossible goal: victory in November.

However, when the votes were counted, they added up to the end of Goldwater's presidential aspirations.

But for Reagan, it was the start of a new beginning.

That December, only a few weeks after the landslide loss, Reagan and Nancy invited the

Tuttles over to the house for a postmortem election dinner. It was an informal affair, although the topic at hand was an obvious one. How, Tuttle wondered, were they going to resurrect the Republican Party after the consecutive defeats of Nixon for governor and Goldwater for president? As the evening went on, the conversation turned to the next significant challenge for the party, the 1966 gubernatorial campaign against the Democratic incumbent, Edmund Brown. Brown was considered weak and beatable, and if the party could capture that one important seat, it could mean the springboard to a second national challenge to Johnson in '68. Everyone agreed that a lot could happen between the landslide LBJ of '64 and then. Four years was a long time to build a record.

Finally, over coffee, after going over dozens of names, Tuttle looked up with a slight smile as he brought his cup to his lips. "What about you, Ronnie?" he said softly.

Reagan smiled. He wasn't surprised. Talk of his running had begun immediately after "The Speech." He knew that Tuttle had already discussed the possibilities with Salvatori and other high-ranking California Republicans. Everyone wanted him because everyone had been turned on by "The Speech." Even Lew Wasserman, a die-hard Democrat, had suddenly gotten an offer for Reagan to return to prime-time TV to do another series, something called *Death Valley Days,* where he could essentially do the same thing he had done on *G.E. Theater,* that is, to serve as the host and occasionally appear in some episodes. Reagan liked the idea because the next gubernatorial election was still two years away. The show would not only bring in steady money but also keep his face on the air and in the consciousness of the American public until it was time to formally declare his candidacy. His weekly intros could be mini-variations of "The Speech" that would be seen in living rooms across the state (and country). No other candidate could buy that kind of exposure.

"What do you say, Ronnie," Tuttle asked. "Are you ready to dip your feet into a bigger pond?"

"Well," Reagan said, with a shake of his head, "I've always been a pretty good swimmer. I was a lifeguard, you know." Nancy got up from the table and came over to him, as he smiled and shook his head again. He felt Nancy's arm go around his shoulders. As it had his whole life, opportunity had come to him like a beautiful woman in some movie, her arms wide open, her beautiful face smiling, wanting to wrap herself around him and smother him with kisses.

No one spoke. No one had to. Everyone could sense the obvious. This time the possibilities were endless.

SOURCES

Several research facilities were used in the preparation of this book. They include:

The Margaret Herrick Library of the Academy of Motion Picture Arts and Sciences, Beverly Hills, California. Several private collections were examined, including extensive diaries of Louella Parsons, private interviews with Ronald Reagan, and the library's collections related to the Screen Actors Guild and HUAC.

The New York Public Library, main branch, New York City.

The New York Public Library for the Performing Arts, New York City.

The Ronald Reagan Presidential Library and Museum, Simi Valley, California.

Ronald Reagan's FBI file #100-382196, code name T-10.

Special research materials were made available by the Screen Actors Guild.

Miles Kreuger's Institute of the American

Musical, Inc., Los Angeles, California.

Special additional material, including never-before-published interviews conducted by Martin Kent, Ray Loynd, and David Robb, were generously supplied to the author by David Robb, former Labor reporter for *Variety* and the *Hollywood Reporter.*

BOOKS

Anger, Kenneth, *Hollywood Babylon II,* Dutton, New York, 1984.

Aylesworth, Thomas G., *The Best of Warner Bros.,* Gallery Books, New York, 1986.

Black, Shirley Temple, *Child Star: An Autobiography,* McGraw-Hill, New York, 1988.

Boller, Jr., Paul F., and Ronald L. Davis, *Hollywood Anecdotes,* Morrow, New York, 1987.

Bosch, Adriana, *Ronald Reagan: An American Story,* TV Books, New York, 2000 edition (based on the Public Broadcast Television [PBS] series *The American Experience*).

Brownstein, Ronald, *The Power and the Glitter: The Hollywood–Washington Connection,* Pantheon, New York, 1991.

Bruck, Connie, *When Hollywood Had a King,* Random House, New York, 2003.

Cagney, James, and Douglas Warren, *Cagney: The Authorized Biography,* St. Martin's Press, New York, 1983.

Cannon, Lou, *Governor Reagan,* Perseus

(Public Affairs), Cambridge, Mass., 2003.

Ceplair, Larry, and Englund, Steven, *The Inquisition in Hollywood,* University of California Press, Berkeley, Calif., 1979.

Colacello, Bob, *Ronnie and Nancy: Their Path to the White House — 1911 to 1980,* Warner Books, New York, 2004.

Davies, Marion, *The Times We Had,* Ballantine, New York, 1985.

Davis, Patti, *The Way I See It,* G. P. Putnam's, New York, 1992.

Day, Doris, and A. E. Hotchner, *Doris Day: Her Own Story,* William Morrow and Company, New York, 1975.

Edwards, Anne, *Early Reagan: The Rise to Power,* William Morrow and Company, New York, 1987.

Eliot, Marc, *Walt Disney: Hollywood's Dark Prince,* Birch Tree, New York, 1993.

Evans, Thomas W., *The Education of Ronald Reagan: The General Electric Years and the Untold Story of his Conversion to Conservatism,* Columbia University Press, New York, 2006.

Gabler, Neal, *An Empire of Their Own: How the Jews Invented Hollywood,* Anchor edition, New York, 1989.

Greenberg, Joel, and Charles Higham, *The Celluloid Muse,* Angus and Robertson, Sydney, Australia, 1969.

Harmetz, Aljean, *Round Up the Usual Sus-*

pects: *The Making of Casablanca,* Wiedenfeld and Nicolson, London, 1992.

Harris, Warren G., *Clark Gable: A Biography,* Random House, New York, 2002.

Hirschorn, Clive, *Warner Bros. Story,* Random House, New York, 1987.

Holden, Anthony, *Behind the Oscar: The Secret History of the Academy Awards,* Simon & Schuster, New York, 1993.

Humes, James C., *The Wit and Wisdom of Ronald Reagan,* Regnery Publishing, Washington, D.C., 2007.

Jackman, Ian, ed., CBS News, *Ronald Reagan Remembered,* Simon & Schuster, New York, 2004.

Kanfer, Stefan, *A Journal of the Plague Years,* Atheneum, New York, 1973.

Kelley, Kitty, *Nancy Reagan, The Unauthorized Biography,* Simon & Schuster, New York, 1991.

Kennedy, Mathew, *Edmund Goulding's Dark Victory,* University of Wisconsin Press, Madison, Wisc., 2004.

Kent, Martin, Ray Loynd, and David Robb, *Hollywood Remembers Ronald Reagan* (unpublished).

Kinn, Gail, and Jim Piazza, *The Academy Awards,* Black Dog and Leventhal, New York, 2002.

Leamer, Laurence, *Make-Believe: The Story of Nancy and Ronald Reagan,* Harper & Row,

New York, 1983.

McClelland, Doug, *Hollywood on Ronald Reagan,* Faber and Faber, Boston, Mass., 1983.

McDougal, Dennis, *The Last Mogul, Lew Wasserman, MCA and the Hidden History of Hollywood,* Crown Publishers, New York, 1998.

Meyers, Jeffrey, *Gary Cooper: American Hero,* Cooper Square Press, New York, 1991.

Moldea, Dan, *Dark Victory: Ronald Reagan, MCA, and the Mob,* Viking Penguin, New York, 1986.

Morris, Edmund, *Dutch: A Memoir of Ronald Reagan,* Random House, New York, 1999.

Neal, Patricia, *As I Am,* Simon & Schuster, New York, 1988.

Perrella, Robert, *They Call Me the Showbiz Priest,* Trident Press, New York, 1973.

Reagan, Maureen, *First Father, First Daughter,* Little, Brown, New York, 2001.

Reagan, Nancy, with William Novak, *My Turn,* Random House, New York, 1989.

Reagan, Ronald, *An American Life,* Simon & Schuster, New York, 1990.

Reagan, Ronald, and Richard Hubler, *Where's the Rest of Me?,* Kars Publishers, New York, 1981.

Rooney, Mickey, *Life Is Too Short,* Villard, New York, 1991.

Sarris, Andrew, *You Ain't Heard Nothin' Yet,* Oxford University Press, New York, 1998.

Sheed, Wilfrid, *The House That George Built,* Random House, New York, 2007.

Spada, James, *Ronald Reagan, His Life in Pictures,* St. Martin's Press, New York, 2000.

Summers, Anthony, *Official and Confidential,* G. P. Putnam's, New York, 1993.

Thomas, Bob, *King Cohn: The Life and Times of Harry Cohn,* G. P. Putnam's, New York, 1967.

Thomas, Tony, *The Films of Ronald Reagan,* Citadel Press, Secaucus, New Jersey, 1980.

Vaughn, Stephen, *Ronald Reagan in Hollywood,* Cambridge University Press, England, 1994.

Wallis, Hal, and Charles Higham, *Starmaker: The Autobiography of Hal Wallis,* Macmillan Publishers, New York, 1980.

Wiley, Mason, and Damien Bona, *Inside Oscar: The Unofficial History of the Academy Awards,* Ballantine Books, New York, 1986.

Wills, Garry, *Reagan's America: Innocents at Home,* Doubleday, New York, 1984.

Wilson, Earl, *Hot Times: True Tales of Hollywood and Broadway,* Contemporary Books, Chicago, 1984.

NOTES

INTRODUCTION

Reagan anecdote about Casablanca. The source is Rich Little, author interview (AI).

Reagan always called The source of this information is Nancy Reagan, who wrote in her memoir, *My Turn,* ghostwritten by William Novak, that Reagan called her Mommy. After the memoir was published, she had this to say about the revelation: "Yeah, well, that's us . . . that's the way it is . . . a lot of men like to be mothered." (The source for the postmemoir quote is Kelley, p. 502. Kelley also cites Reagan's pet name for Nancy as "Mommy.")

CHAPTER ONE: THE NEXT VOICE YOU HEAR

"At Eureka . . ." Reagan, *An American Life (AAL),* p. 60.

pronounced RAY-gun In his memoir *Where's the Rest of Me? (WTROM),* Reagan claims the name was always pronounced this way, although feeling the need to mention it recalls that for all of his movie and TV career he was referred to as Ronald "Ree-gun." He changed to "Ray-gun" only after formally entering politics, perhaps as a point of demarcation between his former and future careers. This memoir, cowritten with Richard G. Hubler, was originally published in 1965, the first year of Reagan's governorship of California, and updated in 1981, the first year of his presidency. Both editions are more fanciful than objective, and spend relatively little time on Reagan's acting career. The 316 pages are heavily weighted with information and anecdotes of a political rather than artistic nature, particularly in reference to Reagan's decision to switch political parties, from Democrat to Republican.

"For such a . . ." Numerous sources, including Spada, p. 2. Variations of the quote, all of which are surely apocryphal, include "So much noise for such a little bit of a fat Dutchman, but who knows, he might grow up to be president!"

analyzing the bones . . . Reagan, *WTROM.* Reagan does not elaborate how this might have been done, considering the family's dire financial straits.

"home to me . . ." Ibid., p. 17.

"[Reagan] was often . . ." Vaughn, p. 9. Helen

Cleaver was interviewed by Vaughn for her study of Reagan's early life.

"I would have been . . ." Reagan, *WTROM.*

"The fact was . . ." Spada, p. 10.

Dutch hit the campus Some of the information regarding Reagan's extracurricular activities at Eureka College are from Bosch (who references Cannon) and the *Peoria Star Journal,* October 17, 1980.

"any Oscar show . . ." The quote is from Reagan, *WTROM,* (p. 44), in which he claims the play "came in second." Other sources, including Spada, place it third.

"If I had told . . ." Reagan, *AAL,* p. 59.

"hold on . . ." Ibid., p. 64.

"make me see it," Reagan, *WTROM,* p. 49.

"Here we are . . ." Reagan, *AAL,* p. 65.

"Ya did . . ." Ibid.

"one of those . . ." Ibid., p. 70.

"shattered" Ibid., p. 76.

CHAPTER TWO: FROM MUGS TO THE MOVIES

"Although I've managed . . ." George Ward, October 2, 1981, quoted in McClelland, p. 180.

"The Cubs and . . ." Reagan, *AAL,* p. 73.

"I made only . . ." All Hodges quotes are from McClelland, p. 154.

"heartwarming role of himself" Wills, p. 179.

Nash convertible Details on the purchase of

Reagan's new car are from Myron S. Waldman, "Growing Up in the Midwest," *Newsday,* January 18, 1981.

"We became quite close . . ." George Ward, October 2, 1981, quoted in McClelland, p. 180.

CHAPTER THREE: THE IRISH MAFIA

"Pat O'Brien . . ." Reagan, *WTROM,* pp. 97–98.

"Leadingladyitis" Reagan, *WTROM,* p. 79.

Background on the Warner Bros. There are several sources for the background of the brothers and the origins of the studio. They include Gabler, Aylsworth, Ceplair and Englund, Hirschorn, Sarris, and others.

abortion clinics Many sources, including the author's biography of Jimmy Stewart (Random House, 2006), in which the notorious MGM brothels and the studio's participation in abortions is discussed in detail.

"When I first came . . ." Reagan, Hall, p. 7.

"Thanks to Pat O'Brien . . ." Ibid.

RONALD REAGAN SHOWS The Reagan/Hayward quote is from an illustrated article that appeared in "A Swimming Lesson from Hollywood," *Chicago Daily News,* July 23, 1938.

"I was twenty-one . . ." Rhodes, *New York Post,* December 18, 1980. Additional informa-

tion on Rhodes comes from diaries she kept
that the author has been given access to,
portions of which, including photos and
other materials that confirm their engagement, may be found on the Internet.

CHAPTER FOUR: DUTCH AND BUTTON-NOSE

"I hope my Ronald . . ." Nelle Reagan, quoted
in Morris, p. 165.

"Neither Ronnie or I . . ." Wyman, quoted in
"Making a Double Go of It!," Mary Jane
Manners, *Silver Screen,* August 1941.

"Small parts . . ." Leamer, p. 104. Leamer
forgets that Wyman had been married twice
before she met Reagan.

"My part . . ." Reagan, *WTROM,* p. 87. Neither
the film nor Eddie Albert receives even a
single mention in Reagan's second memoir,
AAL.

Reagan joined SAG in 1937 and became a
member of the board thanks to a recom-
mendation from his wife. The recommenda-
tion may be found in the minutes of SAG
meeting of July 14, 1941.

"When I arrived . . ." Reagan, *AAL,* p. 89.

"I was as brave . . ." Reagan, Tony Thomas, p.
69.

"I went around . . ." Wyman, Edwards, p. 201.

"my naked dress . . ." Davis quoted in the
film's production notes, on file at the Mo-

tion Picture Arts and Sciences Library.

"We came . . ." Reagan, Tony Thomas, p. 75.

"I was in London . . ." From a previously unpublished interview with Irving Rapper conducted by Kent, Loynd, and Robb, provided to the author for this biography. (Note: all interviews by Kent, Loynd, and Robb, unless otherwise noted, are previously unpublished and have been provided to the author by them.)

"We used to . . ." Huntz Hall, quoted from a guest appearance on *Late Night with David Letterman,* February 23, 1983.

"The next thing . . ." Ruth Waterbury, "Wanted — One Honeymoon," *Movie Mirror,* March 1940.

Reagan's pipe collection and Wyman's designation of a place in the den "to be occupied by each new pipe" is from Fredda Dudley, "Pipe Collector," *Hollywood,* 1942.

CHAPTER FIVE: THE GAMUT FROM A TO B

"Until I got . . ." Slight variations of this quote appear in both Reagan memoirs. It is quoted here in this version from Humes, p. 131.

"stretch a four-line" Warner, quoted in Vaughn, p. 68.

"I got in . . ." Reagan, *AAL,* p. 91.

Background on O'Brien's involvement in

Reagan's landing the role of George Gipp is from the following sources: Cannon, p. 55; the Warner Bros. Archive of Historical Papers housed at Princeton University, which includes the Wallis-Warner letters; and various newspaper and magazine clippings at the Margaret Herrick Academy library.

Reagan's and O'Brien's salaries for *Knute Rockne, All American* were reported in the *Los Angeles Herald-Examiner* on January 8, 1981.

"Win one for the Gipper!" In one of the more ironic twists of Reagan fate, in 1981, the first year of Ronald Reagan's presidency, there was a rush by every independent TV station (in the days before all-classic movie channels) to show as many Reagan films as they could get their hands on. The two most popular were *Bedtime for Bonzo* and *Knute Rockne All American.* Everyone wanted to see him as George Gipp tell Pat O'Brien as Rockne to "win one for the Gipper." However, whenever the film was aired, there was no trace of Gipp's character. As it happened, when Warner Bros. included the film in a package of pre-1948 films sold to Associated Artists Productions for television broadcast, all fourteen minutes of Ronald Reagan were cut out of the film. Over the years, many theories have been put forth to

explain what happened to the footage, including retribution by the Screen Actors Guild for Reagan's participation in a deal that effectively cut them out of all pre-1948 royalties; copyright problems stemming from the Gipp family's claims; and dozens of others. However, the real story was far more complex. The original screenplay was loosely based on a radio script by John H. Driscoll that was broadcast on December 5, 1939, on the DuPont-sponsored *Cavalcade of America* series. When Robert Buckner developed the film's screenplay, he "borrowed" a couple of scenes a little too closely, and the result was that Warner quickly bought the film rights to the radio broadcast for $300. However, the deal only covered the film's opening scenes. When the film opened, Driscoll sued for copyright infringement when he was able to identify seven additional scenes that too closely resembled his radio script, including the Gipper deathbed scene. The studio settled the case for an additional $5,000. The settlement did not include TV rights, and when the film was sold to TV, to avoid yet another lawsuit, Warner's legal department, rather than paying any more money to Driscoll, cut all the questionable scenes, including that one. The original director of the film, Bill Howard, may have been fired for his knowingly using several aspects of the Driscoll script without informing Warner. He was replaced by Lloyd Bacon, the only credited director of the film. The deleted scenes were eventually restored for the film's DVD and future cable releases. (Some of the information for this note is from an article by Tom Singer that appeared in the *Los Angeles Herald-Examiner.*)

Variety review of *Knute Rockne* appeared October 19, 1940; *Hollywood Reporter,* October 7, 1940; *New York Post,* October 19, 1940; *Saturday Evening Post,* December 15, 1945, re O'Brien and January 1, 1949, re Reagan.

"Vell, Jock . . ." Curtiz, quoted in Vaughn, and taken from the Warner Bros. studio archives at the University of Southern California.

Santa Fe Trail's film gross is from IMDB (Internet Movie Database).

In Reagan, *WTROM,* he writes that sometime in the late forties, Jimmy Roosevelt (FDR's son) had told him that some members of the Hollywood Independent Citizens Committee of Arts, Sciences, and Professions, or HICCASP, an organization that Reagan belonged to, might have been infiltrated by "communists." At a meeting, he saw Olivia de Havilland, whom he remembered less than fondly from the set of *Santa Fe Trail.* He began to suspect she, too, was a communist. After, when he discovers that de Havilland also suspects the organization has been infiltrated, she calls upon Reagan and Dore Schary, then the head of MGM, to find out what can be done. "I remember that I kept grinning at Olivia until she asked me what was so funny. 'Nothing,' I said, 'except that I thought *you* were one.' " Apparently, Reagan hadn't made much of an impression on de Havilland, because her reply was "I thought *you* were one, until now." Interestingly, what Reagan had seen as a moral issue during *Santa Fe Trail* had, in his way of seeing things, melded into, rather than progressed to, a political one. As will become clearer, he made most of his "choices" regarding who was a communist and who wasn't a communist, including his then–future wife, Nancy Davis, based on an emotional, morally founded value personal "system" rather than a politically, fact-based one.

Santa Fe Trail reviews: *Variety,* December 16, 1940, and *New York Times,* December 21, 1940. Additional information about the film's premiere is from the December 16, 1940, *New York Times* companion piece that ran alongside Bosley Crowther's review, and Warner Bros. publicity information housed at the Margaret Herrick Library.

CHAPTER SIX: KINGS ROW

"My soul . . ." Reagan, quoted in Maureen Reagan.

"You ask . . ." Wyman, quoted in Wilson, p. 219.

"We'll lead an ideal . . ." Leamer, p. 115.

Earning figures are compiled from Gallup reports and some additional reporting that appeared in Vaughn.

Some information on the Parsons/Reagan celebration in Dixon are from Parsons's scrapbook in private collection at the Margaret Herrick Library.

Some of the casting background information for *Kings Row* is from the original production notes that were quoted in the program notes of a retrospective of the film produced by Hal Wallis at the Los Angeles County Museum of Art that ran from July 4 through September 21, 1974.

In 1922, Postmaster General Will H. Hays retired from that position to become the first head of the MPPDA (The Motion Picture Producers and Distributors of America), which established the official guidelines for what could and could not be included in a film. These guidelines were also known as the Hays Code. No film could be distributed via the studio's various theatrical webs without a seal of approval from Hays. In 1934, Hays was replaced by

Joseph Breen, who was a far more rigid and powerful an enforcer of the production code. As to his fears that a filmed version of the book could not be made, Robinson was not wrong. In one of his early directives on the submitted script, Breen had this to say about it: "The specific unacceptability of this screen story is suggested by the illicit sexual relationships between Parris and Cassandra, and Drake and Randy, without sufficient compensating moral values: as well as the general suggestion of loose sex — the suggested relationship between Drake and the Ross girls — which carries through the entire script. In addition, the suggestion, in the characterization of Cassandra, of gross sexual abnormality; the mercy killing of the grandmother of Parris; and the sadistic characterization of Dr. Gordon; all add to the specific unacceptability of this particular story. Before this picture can be approved under the provisions of the Production Code, all the illicit sex will have to be entirely removed; the characterization of Cassandra will have to be definitely changed; the mercy killing will have to be deleted; and the several suggestions of loose sex, chiefly in the attitude of Drake, will have to be entirely eliminated. In addition, the suggestion that Dr. Gordon's nefarious practices are promoted by a kind of sadism will have to be completely removed from the story. You will have in mind, also, I am sure, that a picture of this kind could not be released in Britain, where *any* suggestions of insanity is always entirely eliminated from the films. Very truly yours, Joseph I. Breen — *Breen's comments from documents on file at the Herrick Academy Library.*

According to Hal Wallis in his *Starmaker: The Autobiography of Hal Wallis* (see "Sources"), "Censor Joe Breen raised endless petty objections to the script of *Kings Row*. He said we could not have a scene in which Drake McHugh said to his friend Parris, 'You have to bunk with me. I hope you don't mind the change.' We protested that these two men and the actors who played them, Ronnie Reagan and Robert Cummings, were entirely masculine and the line contained no suggestion of homosexuality, but Breen was adamant. We had to change the line to 'You have to bunk with me. I hope you won't mind, Mr. Mitchell'!"

"I rehearsed . . ." Reagan, *WTROM,* pp. 4–5.

"He was a hell . . ." Cummings, by Kent, Loynd, Robb.

"Ronnie did expound . . ." Robert Cummings, in an otherwise unidentified interview, possibly with Doug McClellan on July 2, 1982.

"All the cast . . ." Cummings, by Kent, Loynd, Robb.

"did not expect" Sheed, 24.

"I did another film . . ." Cummings, by Kent, Loynd, Robb.

"I'll never forget . . ." Cummings, by Kent, Loynd, Robb.

"Flynn and Ronnie . . ." Kennedy, by Kent, Loynd, Robb.

Some biographers and researchers have questioned whether or not Reagan was ever actually up for the role of Rick in Michael Curtiz's 1942 production of *Casablanca.* In her book-length study of the making of *Casablanca,* Aljean Harmetz states, "Several rumors and misconceptions have grown up around the film, one being that Ronald Reagan was originally chosen to play Rick. This originates in a press release issued by the studio early on in the film's development, but by that time the studio already knew that he was due to go work for the army, and he was never seriously considered." In fact, Jack Warner was hoping to get Reagan one more deferment and released the item to the press as a way of being able to claim later on that the film had already been in production and therefore Reagan should be allowed to make it. Warner's motives were clear: Reagan was one of his hottest actors and he wanted to put him in as many movies as possible. Finally, Gail Kinn and Jim Piazza in their unofficial history of the Academy Awards (see

"Sources") claim that Jack Warner really wanted Reagan to be paired with Hedy Lamarr rather than Ann Sheridan.

CHAPTER SEVEN: THIS IS THE ARMY

"Kings Row was . . ." Reagan, *AAL,* p. 96.

"You really should . . ." Berlin, quoted in Thomas, p. 143. Variations of the story are told in several Berlin biographies as well.

The statement announcing the MPA appeared as a full-page ad in the February 7, 1944, edition of *Daily Variety.*

Some of the background information on Reagan's involvement with wartime and postwar organizations is from Eliot *Disney,* Ceplair and Englund, Cannon, and Colacello. Other sources include several background files on HICCASP at the Margaret Herrick Library.

Details of the HDC preelection radio broadcast are from the *New York Times,* April 23, 1944. Additional information regarding Reagan's contributions and Wyman's participation in the show are from Vaughn and Brownstein.

"It's Ronnie who's Irish . . ." Zeitlin, *Modern Screen,* October 1944.

"When rumors started . . ." *Modern Screen,* January 1945.

"All I wanted to do . . ." Reagan, Morris, p. 221.

Brewer letter It was a three-page form letter written on IATSE stationery, signed by Roy Brewer, from the Hollywood Democratic Committee Collection, and quoted in Ceplair and Englund, p. 219.

Faulkner and Longstreet conversation Boller and Davis, p. 358.

"give its last groan . . ." Reagan, *WTROM,* p. 165.

anonymous midnight phone call Numerous versions of this story exist. Reagan retells it several times, with the details varying. In *AAL,* he claims he received the call while refueling his car at a gas station, from a public telephone. Other times he relates it as a midnight call. Every one of his biographers has some version. The Herrick Library has several articles that contain still other versions. The one used here is the most consistently told, and the most verifiable, although, as the narrative states, parts of it, such as the acquisition of the pistol, remain thus far unproven.

"I was the man . . ." Brewer, quoted in Bruck, p. 97.

"Thereafter, I mounted . . ." Reagan, *WTROM,* p. 179.

"I remember Ron . . ." Stewart, by Kent, Loynd, Robb.

Reagan's FBI file and his informing Reagan himself spoke and wrote several times about his informing activities, claiming they were acts of patriotism. Unlike Disney, once his participation was made public (it is not mentioned in either of his memoirs), he never tried to deny what he had done, although he never revealed what names he may have given or specific activities he reported on. Those names are redacted in Reagan's FBI file, which was first obtained by the *San Jose Mercury News* in 1985. It was only after the file was made public that Reagan acknowledged his secret activities. Among the many sources cited by Vaughn and Colacello, both of whom write extensively about this incident in their books, is the author's book on Walt Disney and the *New York Times* article published on May 5, 1993, that disclosed the author's having uncovered Disney's connection to the FBI, and others, via the Freedom of Information Act, while researching *Walt Disney: Hollywood's Dark Prince.* An important source for this chapter and others is Reagan's FBI file #100-382196, in which he is first described as "6.1: tall, weight 173 lbs., blue eyes and brown hair." Upon Hoover's death, in 1975, Reagan said of J. Edgar Hoover: "No twentieth-century man has meant more to this country than Hoover."

"Ronnie Reagan . . ." Jack L. Warner public statement, October 1946.

"His first significant . . ." William Gazecki, interview with author (via e-mail).

591

"I never had . . ." Dunne, quoted in Bruck, p. 107.

CHAPTER EIGHT: MR. REAGAN GOES TO WASHINGTON

"The night before . . ." Gladys Hall, "Those Fightin' Reagans," *Photoplay,* February 1948.

"If only . . ." Black, p. 406.

"long on quips . . ." Ibid.

"I'm especially proud . . ." Reagan, *AAL,* p. 116.

"My only beef . . ." From an unidentified interview with Reagan, most likely conducted by Hedda Hopper, found among the Ronald Reagan files at the Margaret Herrick Library.

"Right now . . ." Reagan, quoted by Hedda Hopper, "Guild Chief Views Told by Reagan," *Los Angeles Times,* May 18, 1947.

"You and I . . ." Wyman, *Movies,* August 1947.

Reagan and Montgomery testimony at HUAC Some background is from Kanfer, pp. 55–57, as well as Ceplair and Englund.

" 'I've got along . . .' " Wyman, quoted by Hopper, "A Good Man Is Hard to Find," *Modern Screen,* March 1948.

The details of the deterioration of the Reagan marriage are from many sources, including Reagan's first memoir, and several articles in the trades of the day, most by Hedda Hopper, who chronicled the dissolution of the Reagan marriage in her columns and articles in detail. It is unproved whether or not Hopper had been instructed by Warner, or Wasserman, to make Reagan look like a victim to Wyman's adulterous ways, but that is overwhelmingly the tone of Hopper's many, many pieces. It should be remembered that her magazine had an eight- to twelve-week lead time, which is why stories were usually published long after the events reported had taken place.

"The trouble started . . ." Louella Parsons, *Los Angeles Times,* February 9, 1948.

"They would not . . ." Dick Powell, quoted by June Allyson, in an article she wrote with Frances Spatz Leighton entitled "June Allyson: Shocking Truth Behind Tinsel of Hollywood Life," *Star,* July 6, 1982.

"wept and wept . . ." Neal, *People* Magazine, August 10, 1981.

"[Wyman] admits it was . . ." Perrella, pp. 130–31.

brand-new shoes Humes, p. 113.

The Waldorf Statement was a two-page press release issued on December 3, 1947, by Eric Johnston, president of the Motion Picture Association of America, following a closed-door meeting by forty-eight motion picture company executives at New York City's Waldorf-Astoria Hotel. The statement was a response to the contempt of Congress charges against the so-called Hollywood

Ten and marks the more than three hundred employees in the motion picture and related industries as communists or communist sympathizers (past or present). Besides its presumption of guilty until proven innocent, it did not allow for anyone accused to face his accuser in a court of law.

The Waldorf Statement: "Members of the Association of Motion Picture Producers deplore the action of the 10 Hollywood men who have been cited for contempt by the House of Representatives. We do not desire to prejudge their legal rights, but their actions have been a disservice to their employers and have impaired their usefulness to the industry. We will forthwith discharge or suspend without compensation those in our employ, and we will not re-employ any of the 10 until such time as he is acquitted or has purged himself of contempt and declares under oath that he is not a Communist. On the broader issue of alleged subversive and disloyal elements in Hollywood, our members are likewise prepared to take positive action. We will not knowingly employ a Communist or a member of any party or group which advocates the overthrow of the government of the United States by force or by any illegal or unconstitutional methods.

"In pursuing this policy, we are not going

to be swayed by hysteria or intimidation from any source. We are frank to recognize that such a policy involves danger and risks. There is the danger of hurting innocent people. There is the risk of creating an atmosphere of fear. Creative work at its best cannot be carried on in an atmosphere of fear. We will guard against this danger, this risk, this fear. To this end we will invite the Hollywood talent guilds to work with us to eliminate any subversives: to protect the innocent; and to safeguard free speech and a free screen wherever threatened. The absence of a national policy, established by Congress, with respect to the employment of Communists in private industry makes our task difficult. Ours is a nation of laws. We request Congress to enact legislation to assist American industry to rid itself of subversive, disloyal elements. Nothing subversive or un-American has appeared on the screen, nor can any number of Hollywood investigations obscure the patriotic services of the 30,000 loyal Americans employed in Hollywood who have given our government invaluable aid to war and peace."

"They agreed . . ." Reagan, *WTROM,* p. 226.

"His favorite food . . ." Skolsky, Sidney, February 26, 1948. Syndicated.

"After he and Jane . . ." Andrews, by Kent, Loynd, Robb.

"We were in . . ." Sherman, McClelland, p. 160. The quote is dated July 25, 1981.

Mervyn LeRoy phone call Several versions of this story appear, in both Reagan memoirs, in Cannon, Colacello, Kelley, and others.

CHAPTER NINE: LOVE IS LOVELIER

"When I opened . . ." Nancy Reagan, Humes, p. 83.

Nancy Davis early background Sources include Davis's autobiography; Kelley; Harris; Colacello; the unpublished and unsigned interview with Reagan in the Herrick private collections; the Herrick files on Reagan, Davis, and Parsons; and interviews with several primary sources, including a 2008 author interview with William Frye.

"With that kind of power . . ." Gottfried, quoted in Kelley, p. 58.

The dinner background and details are from Kelley, Reagan (both memoirs), Colacello, and several other sources, including the diaries of Louella Parsons archived at the Herrick.

"I had just arrived . . ." Underwood, by Kent, Loynd, Robb.

"I wish I could report . . ." Nancy Reagan, p. 97.

Background on Larson Kelley, p. 81.

"I sincerely believe . . ." Louella Parsons, *Modern Screen,* February 1951.

"The Reagans . . ." Carol Troy, "A Hollywood Producer," *The Village Voice,* March 16, 1982.

Details of the wedding Some information is from the *Citizen-News,* March 5, 1952. Additional information is from Colacello, Davis, Kelley, Cannon, and Reagan *(AAL).* Further research comes from the Reagan files at the Margaret Herrick Library.

"a hop, a skip . . ." Morris, p. 294.

". . . were a corporate seal . . ." McDougal, p. 158.

"On the set . . ." Fleming, by Kent, Loynd, Robb.

"The two Bills . . ." Reagan, *WTROM,* p. 241.

Wasserman and Reagan and the blanket waiver Some of the background for this is from Moldea, Bruck, and from McDougal, with additional source material from the files at the Herrick Library.

"They stop . . ." Reagan, quoted in "Reagan's Multiple Duties," by Richard Dyer Mac-Cann, *The Christian Science Monitor,* December 21, 1954. Similar views are expressed by Reagan in *AAL.*

"I don't want . . ." Kelley, p. 90.

"I swear, it came . . ." Reagan, *WTROM,* p. 248.

Reagan and Sinatra The problems between Reagan and Sinatra had begun long before the Vegas situation. Despite Sinatra's having been a board member of SAG in the midforties, he was in danger of being blacklisted for his performance of the then-controversial "The House I Live In" song from the 1945 eleven-minute short of the same name, written by Albert Maltz, who not long after became one of the Hollywood Ten. The film, which preached racial tolerance, was built around the song, written by Earl Robinson, who was also subsequently blacklisted. Sinatra was also a member of HICCASP and openly sympathetic to the communists, although never a party member, which was what saved him from being blacklisted. Reagan, however, did not approve of Sinatra's many associations with entertainers on the left, and when Sinatra expressed his strong support for Herb Sorrell during the 1945 strike, even after SAG did not back the CPU, it ended any chance of his ever being a friend of Ronald Reagan. In later years, Reagan tolerated Sinatra because of Nancy's fondness for him.

Reagan gambling on the last night of his gig in Vegas is from Colacello, p. 270.

CHAPTER ELEVEN: THE FORGETTING OF THINGS PAST

"I don't want to appear . . ." From Reagan's testimony before the grand jury investigating MCA, February 1962.

"I had just . . ." William Frye, interview with author.

"Television is now . . ." Reagan, quoted by Howard McClay in his column in the *Los Angeles Daily News* on November 24, 1954.

"I remember Ronnie . . ." Ann Sheridan, *Anger,* p. 314.

By his own admission, Reagan first officially violated the Guild tradition prohibiting officers and board members from producing when he produced the "Seeds of Hate" episode for MCA's *General Electric Theater* while a member of the SAG board. Reagan admitted as much in a letter to the *Hollywood Reporter* published November 14, 1955: "Now I am getting the biggest change of my entire career. My *General Electric Theater* bosses have permitted me to produce 'Seeds of Hate' for their series. It's an exciting challenge and I'll have a chance to blame only myself if it doesn't pan out. I started right out by signing a top star in this attraction." Less than a month later, on December 11, 1955, "Seeds of Hate" aired, starring Charlton Heston in the lead.

"Everything except . . ." Reagan, Louella Parsons, *Chicago Tribune Magazine,* February 26, 1956.

"I wasn't wild . . ." Nancy Reagan, p. 128.

"Today, Ronald Reagan . . ." Louella Parsons, *Los Angeles Examiner,* April 3, 1955.

Patti Reagan throwing up . . . Colacello, p. 277.
"I never knew . . ." Patti Reagan, quoted in Humes, p. 73.

The 1948 Supreme Court decision in *U.S. v. Paramount Pictures, et al.,* dealt a crushing blow to the Hollywood studios, and effectively brought an end to the studio system of classic cinema. This Great Hollywood Antitrust Case was actually two major suits (and numerous minor ones). In effect there were two "Paramount cases." The Hollywood studios' antitrust problems began with a Federal Trade Commission investigation in 1921. The FTC declared block booking anticompetitive, and brought into question other studio practices related to their theater monopolies. In 1928, the FTC took Famous Players–Lasky (the forerunner to Paramount Pictures) to court, along with nine other major Hollywood studios. In 1930, the major studios were declared guilty of monopolization. However, the effects of the decision were nullified by a controversial deal arranged with the Roosevelt administration during the depths of the Great Depression. After having weathered the worst of the Depression, the major studios emerged more powerful than ever. In 1938, the Roosevelt administration turned the tables on the studios, ordering the Department of Justice to file suit against Hollywood's Big Eight. The case *U.S. v. Paramount* was delayed several times by consent decrees and World War II. However, largely due to the influence of the independent producers and the rise of the SIMPP (Society of Independent Motion Picture Producers), the case made it to the Supreme Court, where the famous 1948 decision led to the abolishment of block booking, and the forced divestiture of the studios to sell off their theater chains. This case was an integral part of SIMPP's mission, and had a profound effect on Hollywood history. — *Wikipedia*

"When we . . ." Reagan, quoted in *Variety,* October 24, 1956.

"We in Hollywood . . ." From a speech that Reagan wrote and developed over a ten-year period. It is unclear when this particular phrasing was first used.

"was not going . . ." Reagan, quoted in Louella Parsons, various news services, May 21, 1958.

"I personally broke . . ." Douglas, by Kent, Loynd, Robb.

"The studios . . ." Rooney, p. 327.

"The Screen Actors Guild . . ." Rooney, by Kent, Loynd, Robb.

"I made something . . ." Bob Hope, quoted in McDougal, p. 264.

"Mickey Rooney's . . ." Hope, by Kent, Loynd, Robb.

"Wheelchair wisdom . . ." Morris, p. 514.

"As far as . . ." Robb, interview with the author.

"Some viewed Reagan . . ." Gazecki, interview with the author.

"Nancy [was always] . . ." Park, by Kent, Loynd, Robb.

compared John Kennedy to Karl Marx Spada, p. 77.

"The tax foundations" Reagan speaking before a supermarket institute meeting, quoted by the *Hollywood Citizen-News,* May 9, 1961.

CHAPTER TWELVE: RENDEZVOUS WITH DESTINY

"You and I . . ." The conclusion of the speech Reagan had given, in various forms, for ten years, and, without mentioning Barry Goldwater's name, the one he delivered in his national broadcast on October 27, 1964, on national TV. The following is how the speech began: "I am going to talk of controversial things. I make no apology for this. I have been talking on this subject for ten years, obviously under the administration of both parties. I mention this only because it seems impossible to legitimately debate the issues of the day without being subjected to name-calling and the application of labels. Those who deplore use of the terms 'pink' and 'leftist' are themselves guilty of branding all who oppose their

602

liberalism as right-wing extremists. How long can we afford the luxury of this family fight when we are at war with the most dangerous enemy ever known to man? . . ."

Goldwater's disagreement over Reagan's Social Security policy Evans, p. 168.

Goldwater's fear that Reagan would overshadow him Humes, p. 182.

Funding for "The Speech" Ibid.

Leon Ames, a well-known Hollywood actor probably best-known for his appearance with Judy Garland, playing her father, in Vincente Minnelli's *Meet Me in St. Louis,* was a friend of Ronald Reagan's for over forty years, having served on the Screen Actors Guild board of directors with Reagan for fifteen of them. Here, in an exclusive, never-before-published interview, originally conducted by Dave Robb, Ames tells a story about Holmes Tuttle: "When I was in the car business [after leaving film], I sold Reagan three or four cars, but he probably got the Lincoln he used as governor for free from Holmes Tuttle, a member of Governor Reagan's 'kitchen cabinet,' a campaign fund-raiser and key appointment and political advisor during Reagan's eight years as Governor of California. Tuttle was very close to Reagan. He was the guy who spark-plugged Ronnie's first running for governor. I remember at a party one night there was a great cinematographer from

Paramount saying, 'Of all the stupid things — Tuttle, for Chrissake, is sponsoring Reagan for governor. He's got about as much chance as a snowball in hell to get that.' He was a big cameraman, and he thought it was a stupid thing for anybody to sponsor this actor for the job."

"What do you say . . ." This scene has been re-created many times, although the location and the recalled dialogue differ. In Colacello, the scene takes place at the Reagans' house, after a meeting Tuttle has with other "friends" (i.e., influential fund-raisers who supported Reagan for governor in 1966 and included William Clark, Edwin Meese, and Michael Deaver), where they decided that the only candidate who could resurrect the shattered Republican Party was Ronald Reagan, and that the only obstacle standing in their way was how to convince him to run. Virtually every source has Nancy Reagan eagerly supporting the idea. According to Colacello, Reagan initially turned down the offer because of the financial sacrifice, which is when Wasserman came up with *Death Valley Days.* Reagan's skepticism was tempered by the fact that his onetime fellow board member at SAG and costar in *This Is the Army,* George Murphy, a conservative Republican, had been elected to the Senate in 1964.

FILMOGRAPHY AND TV
APPEARANCES

Dates indicate year of release, which, in some instances, may differ from the order in which these films were actually made. Reagan's military films have been omitted, as they have not been commercially released. They are referred to, where necessary, in the main body of the text.

FILM

Love Is on the Air — 1937. Warner Bros. Directed by Nick Grindé. Produced by Bryan Foy. Based on an original story, "Hi, Nellie," by Roy Chanslor. Screenplay by Morton Grant. With Ronald Reagan, Eddie Acuff, June Tarvis, Ben Welden, Robert Barrat, Addison Richards, Raymond Hatton, Tommy Bupp, Dickie Jones.

Hollywood Hotel — 1937. Warner Bros. Directed by Busby Berkeley. Produced by Hal B. Wallis. Screenplay by Maurice Leo, Jerry Wald, and Richard Macaulay, from a story by Leo and Wald. With Dick Powell,

Rosemary Lane, Lola Lane, Hugh Herbert, Ted Healy, Glenda Farrell, Johnnie Davis, Frances Langford, Alan Mowbray, Mabel Todd, Allyn Joslyn, Grant Mitchell, Edgar Kennedy, Fritz Feld, Curt Bois, Louella Parsons, Ronald Reagan, Benny Goodman and His Orchestra.

Swing Your Lady — 1938. Warner Bros. Directed by Ray Enright. Screenplay by Joseph Schrank, based on the story "Toehold on Artemus" by H. R. Marsh and the play adaptation by Kenyon Nicholson and Charles Robinson. With Humphrey Bogart, Penny Singleton, Frank McHugh, Louise Fazenda, Nat Pendleton, Allen Jenkins, Leon Weaver, Frank Weaver, Loretta "Elviry" Weaver, Ronald Reagan.

Sergeant Murphy — 1938. Warner Bros. Directed by B. Reeves Eason. Produced by Bryan Foy. Screenplay by William Jacobs, based on an original story by Sy Bartlett. With Ronald Reagan, Mary Maguire, Donald Crisp, Ben Hendricks, William Davidson, Max Hoffman, Jr., David Newell, Emmett Vogan.

Accidents Will Happen — 1938. Warner Bros. Directed by William Clemens. Produced by Bryan Foy. Screenplay by George Bricker and Anthony Coldeway from an original story by George Bricker. With Ronald Reagan, Gloria Blondell, Richard Purcell, Sheila Bromley, Addison Richards, Hugh

O'Connell, Janet Shaw, Elliott Sullivan, Anderson Lawlor, Spec O'Donnell, Don Barclay.

Cowboy from Brooklyn — 1938. Warner Bros. Directed by Lloyd Bacon. Produced by Hal B. Wallis. Screenplay by Earl Baldwin, based on the play *Howdy, Stranger* by Robert Sloane, Louis Peletier, Jr. With Dick Powell, Pat O'Brien, Priscilla Lane, Dick Foran, Ann Sheridan, Johnnie Davis, Ronald Reagan, Emma Dunn, Granville Bates, James Stephenson.

The Amazing Dr. Clitterhouse — 1938. Warner Bros. Directed by Anatole Litvak. Produced by Anatole Litvak (Hal Wallis and Jack Warner uncredited). Screenplay by John Wexley and John Huston, based on the play by Barré Lyndon. With Edward G. Robinson, Claire Trevor, Humphrey Bogart.

Boy Meets Girl — 1938. Warner Bros. Directed by Lloyd Bacon. Produced by George Abbott. Screenplay by Bella and Sam Spewack based on their original Broadway play. With James Cagney, Pat O'Brien, Marie Wilson, Ralph Bellamy, Dick Foran, Frank McCugh, Bruce Lester, Ronald Reagan, Penny Singleton, Dennie Moore, James Stephenson, Bert Hanlon, Harry Seymour, Peggy Moran.

Brother Rat — 1938. Warner Bros. Directed by William Keighley. Produced by Hal B. Wallis. Screenplay by Richard Macaulay and

Jerry Wald, based on the play by John Monks, Jr. and Fred Finklehoffe. With Wayne Morris, Priscilla Lane, Eddie Albert, Ronald Reagan, Jane Wyman, Jane Bryan, Johnnie Davis, Henry O'Neill, Larry Williams, William Tracy, Gordon Oliver, Jessie Busley, Olin Howland, Louise Beavers, Frank Coghlan, Don DeFore.

Girls on Probation — 1938. Warner Bros. Directed by William McGann. Produced by Bryan Foy. Screenplay by Crane Wilbur from his original story. With Jane Bryan, Ronald Reagan, Sheila Bromley, Anthony Averill, Henry O'Neill, Elizabeth Risdon, Sig Rumann, Dorothy Peterson, Susan Hayward, Larry Williams, Lenita Lane, Peggy Shannon, Janet Shaw.

Going Places — 1938. Warner Bros. Directed by Ray Enright. Produced by Hal B. Wallis. Screenplay by Sig Herzig, Jerry Wald, Maurice Leo, from the original play *The Hottentot* by Victor Mapes. With Dick Powell, Anita Louise, Ronald Reagan, Allen Jenkins, Walter Catlett, Harold Huber, Larry Williams, Thurston Hall, Minna Gombell, Louis Armstrong, Maxine Sullivan, Joyce Compton, Robert Warwick, John Ridgeley, Eddie Anderson, Rosella Towne.

Secret Service of the Air — 1939. Warner Bros. Directed by Noel Smith. Produced by Bryan Foy. Screenplay by Raymond Schrock, based on the files of ex-chief of Secret Service

William H. Moran. With Ronald Reagan, John Litel, Ila Rhodes, Rosella Towne, James Stephenson, Eddie Foy, Jr., Larry Williams, John Ridgely, Anthony Averill, Bernard Nedell, Frank M. Thomas, Joe Cunningham, Morgan Conway, Raymond Bailey.

Dark Victory — 1939. Warner Bros. Directed by Edmund Goulding. Produced by Hal B. Wallis. Screenplay by Casey Robinson, from an original play by George Emerson Brewer, Jr., and Bertram Bloch. With Bette Davis, George Brent, Humphrey Bogart, Ronald Reagan, Geraldine Fitzgerald, Henry Travers, Cora Witherspoon, Virginia Brissac, Dorothy Peterson, Charles Richman, Herbert Rawlinson, Leonard Mudie, Fay Helm, Lottie Williams, Ila Rhodes.

Code of the Secret Service — 1939. Warner Bros. Directed by Noel Smith. Produced by Bryan Foy. Screenplay by Lee Katz and Dean Franklin, based on the files of ex-chief of Secret Service H. William Moran. With Ronald Reagan, Rosella Towne, Eddie Foy, Jr., Moroni Olsen, Edgar Edwards, Jack Mower, John Gallaudet, Joe King, Steven Darrell, Frank Puglia, Maris Wrixon.

Naughty But Nice — 1939. Warner Bros. Directed by Ray Enright. Produced by Hal Wallis (executive) and Sam Bischoff (associate), both uncredited. Original screenplay by Jerry Wald and Richard Macaulay (original title: *The Professor Steps Out*). With

Dick Powell, Gale Page, Ann Sheridan, Helen Broderick, Allen Jenkins, Zasu Pitts, Ronald Reagan, Maxie Rosenbloom, Jerry Colonna, Vera Lewis, Peter Lind Hayes.

Hell's Kitchen — 1939. Warner Bros. Directed by Lewis Seiler, E. A. Dupont (Seiler found he could not "direct" the Dead End Kids; E. A. Dupont helmed most of their scenes). Produced by Bryan Foy and Mark Hellinger (both uncredited). Screenplay by Crane Wilbur, Fred Niblo, Jr., from a story by Crane Wilbur. With Billy Halop, Bobby Jordan, Leo Gorcey, Huntz Hall, Gabriel Dell, Bernard Punsley, Frankie Burke, Margaret Lindsay, Ronald Reagan, Stanley Fields, Grant Mitchell, Fred Tozere, Arthur Loft, Vera Lewis, Robert Homans.

The Angels Wash Their Faces — 1939. Warner Bros. Directed by Ray Enright. Produced by Robert Fellows. Screenplay by Michael Fessier, Niven Busch, Robert Buckner, from an idea by Jonathan Finn. With Ann Sheridan, Ronald Reagan, Billy Halop, Bonita Granville, Frankie Thomas, Bobby Jordan, Bernard Punsley, Leo Gorcey, Huntz Hall, Gabriel Dell, Henry O'Neill, Eduardo Ciannelli, Berton Churchill, Margaret Hamilton, Jackie Searle, Grady Sutton, Marjorie Main, Frank Coghlan.

Smashing the Money Ring — 1940. Warner Bros. Directed by Terry Morse. Produced by Bryan Foy. Screenplay by Anthony Coldeway and Raymond Schrock, from an idea by Jonathan Finn. Based on the files of ex-chief of Secret Service H. William Moran (although this was a completely original story). With Ronald Reagan, Margot Stevenson, Eddie Foy, Jr., Joe Downing, Charles D. Brown, Elliott Sullivan, Don Douglas, Charles Wilson, Joe King, William Davidson, Dick Rich, Max Hoffman, Jr.

Brother Rat and a Baby — 1940. Directed by Dan Enright. Produced by Robert Lord. Screenplay by Jerry Wald, Richard Macaulay, based on characters from the play *Brother Rat* by John Monks, Jr., and Fred F. Finklehoffe. With Priscilla Lane, Jane Bryan, Jane Wyman, Wayne Morris, Eddie Albert, Ronald Reagan, Peter B. Good, Larry Williams, Arthur Treacher, Moroni Olsen, Jessie Busley, Paul Harvey, Berton Churchill, Nana Bryant, Mayo Methot, Ed Gargan, Richard Clayton, Alan Ladd.

An Angel from Texas — 1940. Warner Bros. Directed by Ray Enright. Produced by Robert Fellows. Screenplay by Fred Niblo, Jr., Bertram Millhauser, based on the play *The Butter and Egg Man* by George S. Kaufman. With Eddie Albert, Wayne Morris, Rosemary Lane, Jane Wyman, Ronald Reagan, Ruth Terry, John Litel, Hobart Cavanaugh, Ann Shoemaker, Tom Kennedy, Milburn Stone, Elliott Sullivan.

Murder in the Air — 1940. Warner Bros.

Directed by Lewis Seiler. Produced by Bryan Foy. Screenplay by Raymond Schrock, based on his original story "Uncle Sam Awakens." With Ronald Reagan, John Litel, James Stephenson, Eddie Foy, Jr., Lya Lys, Robert Warwick, Victor Zimmermann, William Gould, Kenneth Harlan, Frank Wilcox.

Knute Rockne All American — 1940. Warner Bros. Directed by Lloyd Bacon. Produced by Hal B. Wallis. Screenplay by Robert Buckner, based on the story "Spirit of Knute Rockne" by Robert Buckner and material from Mrs. Rockne and Rockne's friends and associates. With Pat O'Brien, Gale Page, Ronald Reagan, Donald Crisp, Albert Basserman, John Litel, Henry O'Neill, Owen Davis, Jr., John Qualen, Dorothy Tree, John Sheffield, Kane Richmond, George Reeves, Richard Clayton.

Tugboat Annie Sails Again — 1940. Warner Bros. Directed by Lewis Seiler. Produced by Bryan Foy. Screenplay by Walter De Leon, based on characters created by Norman Reilly Raine. With Marjorie Rambeau, Jane Wyman, Ronald Reagan, Alan Hale, Charles Halton, Clarence Kolb, Paul Hurst, Victor Kilian, Chill Wills, Harry Shannon, John Hamilton, Sidney Bracy, Jack Mower, Margaret Hayes, Neil Reagan.

Alice in Movieland — 1940. Warner Bros. (short). Directed by Jean Negulesco. Produced by Gordon Hollingshead (uncredited). Written by Owen Crump and Cyrus Wood from a story by Ed Sullivan. With Joan Leslie, Nana Bryant, Clara Blandick, and Clarence Muse. Frank Faylen, Alan Hale, Alexis Smith, Jane Wyman, Ronald Reagan, and dozens of other Warner stars play themselves in cameos and are officially uncredited.

Santa Fe Trail — 1940. Warner Bros. Directed by Michael Curtiz. Produced by Hal B. Wallis. Screenplay by Robert Buckner. With Errol Flynn, Olivia de Havilland, Raymond Massey, Ronald Reagan, Alan Hale, Guinn Williams, Van Heflin, Henry O'Neill, William Lundigan, John Litel, Gene Reynolds, Alan Baxter, Moroni Olsen, Erville Anderson, Susan Peters, Charles D. Brown, David Bruce, William Marshall, Ward Bond, Joseph Sawyer.

The Bad Man — 1941. MGM. Directed by Richard Thorpe. Produced by J. Walter Ruben. Screenplay by Wells Root, based on an original play by Porter Emerson Browne. With Wallace Beery, Lionel Barrymore, Laraine Day, Ronald Reagan, Henry Travers, Tom Conway, Chill Wills, Nydia Westman, Chris-Pin Martin, Charles Stevens.

Million Dollar Baby — 1941. Warner Bros. Directed by Curtis Bernhardt. Produced by Jack L. Warner, Hal B. Wallis. Screenplay by Casey Robinson, Richard Macaulay, Jerry Wald, based on a story by Leonard Spigelgass. With Priscilla Lane, Jeffrey Lynn, Ronald Reagan, May Robson, Lee Patrick,

Helen Westley, Walter Catlett, Richard Carle, George Barbier, John Qualen, John Ridgely, Fay Helm, Nan Wynn, John Sheffield.

International Squadron — 1941. Warner Bros. Directed by Lothar Mendes. Produced by Edmund Grainger. Screenplay by Barry Trivers and Kenneth Gamet, based on the original play by Frank "Spig" Wead. With Ronald Reagan, James Stephenson, Olympe Bradna, William Lundigan, Joan Perry, Julie Bishop, Tod Andrews, Cliff Edwards, John Ridgely, Selmer Jackson, Addison Richards, Holmes Herbert, Eddie Conrad, Reginald Denny, Richard Travis, William Hopper, Frank Faylen, Helmut Dantine.

Nine Lives Are Not Enough — 1941. Warner Bros. Directed by A. Edward Sutherland. Produced by William Jacobs, Bryan Foy, and Hal B. Wallis. Screenplay by Fred Niblo, Jr., from the novel by Jerome Odlum. With Ronald Reagan, Joan Perry, James Gleason, Peter Whitney, Faye Emerson, Howard da Silva, Edward Brophy, Charles Drake, Vera Lewis, Ben Welden, John Ridgely.

Kings Row — 1942. Warner Bros. Directed by Sam Wood. Produced by Hal B. Wallis. Screenplay by Casey Robinson, from the novel by Henry Bellamann. With Ann Sheridan, Robert Cummings, Ronald Reagan, Betty Field, Charles Coburn, Claude Rains, Judith Anderson, Nancy Coleman, Kaaren Verne, Maria Ouspenskaya, Harry Davenport, Ernest Cossart, Ann Todd, Scott Beckett, Douglas Croft, Mary Thomas, Joan Du Valle, Ludwig Stossel.

Juke Girl — 1942. Warner Bros. Directed by Curtis Bernhardt. Produced by Hal B. Wallis. Screenplay by A. I. Bezzerides, adapted by Kenneth Gamet from a story by Theodore Pratt. With Ann Sheridan, Ronald Reagan, Richard Whorf, George Tobias, Gene Lockhart, Alan Hale, Betty Brewer, Howard da Silva, Willard Robertson, Faye Emerson, Willie Best, Fuzzy Knight, Spencer Charters.

Desperate Journey — 1942. Warner Bros. Directed by Raoul Walsh. Produced by Hal B. Wallis. Screenplay by Arthur Horman, based on the original story "Forced Landing" by Arthur Horman. With Errol Flynn, Ronald Reagan, Nancy Coleman, Raymond Massey, Alan Hale, Arthur Kennedy, Ronald Sinclair, Albert Basserman, Sig Rumann, Patrick O'Moore, Felix Basch, Ilka Gruning, Elsa Basserman.

This Is the Army — 1943. Warner Bros. Directed by Michael Curtiz. Produced by Jack L. Warner and Hal B. Wallis. Screenplay by Casey Robinson, Claude Binyon, based on the original stage productions *Yip, Yip, Yaphank* and *This Is the Army* by Irving Berlin. With George Murphy, Joan Leslie, Ronald Reagan, George Tobias, Alan Hale, Charles Butterworth, Rosemary DeCamp, Dolores Costello, Una Merkel, Stanley Ridges, Ruth

Donnelly, Dorothy Peterson, Kate Smith, Frances Langford, Gertrude Niesen, Joe Louis, Victor Moore, Irving Berlin.

Stallion Road — 1947. Warner Bros. Directed by James V. Kern. Produced by Alex Gottlieb. Screenplay by Stephen Longstreet, from his original novel. With Ronald Reagan, Alexis Smith, Zachary Scott, Peggy Knudsen, Patti Brady, Harry Davenport, Angela Greene, Frank Puglia, Ralph Byrd, Lloyd Corrigan, Mary Gordon.

That Hagen Girl — 1947. Warner Bros. Directed by Peter Godfrey. Produced by Alex Gottlieb. Screenplay by Charles Hoffman, based on the novel by Edith Roberts. With Ronald Reagan, Shirley Temple, Rory Calhoun, Lois Maxwell, Dorothy Peterson, Charles Kemper, Conrad Janis, Penny Edwards, Jean Porter, Nella Walker, Harry Davenport, Winifred Harris, Moroni Olsen, Frank Conroy, Kathryn Card, Douglas Kennedy, Barbara Brown, Milton Parsons.

The Voice of the Turtle — 1947. Warner Bros. (aka *One for the Book* in its TV release). Directed by Irving Rapper. Produced by Charles Hoffman. Screenplay by John van Druten, based on his original play. With Ronald Reagan, Eleanor Parker, Eve Arden, Wayne Morris, Kent Smith, John Emery, Erskine Sanford, John Holland, Nino Pepitone, Helen Wallace, Sarah Edwards, William Gould, Frank Wilcox, Ross Ford.

John Loves Mary — 1949. Warner Bros. Directed by David Butler. Produced by Jerry Wald. Screenplay by Phoebe and Henry Ephron from the original play by Norman Krasna. With Ronald Reagan, Jack Carson, Patricia Neal, Wayne Morris, Edward Arnold, Virginia Field, Katherine Alexander, Paul Harvey, Ernest Cossart, Irving Bacon, George B. Hickman, Larry Rio, Nino Pepitone.

Night Unto Night — 1949. Warner Bros. Directed by Don Siegel. Produced by Owen Crump. Screenplay by Kathryn Scola, based on the novel by Philip Wylie. With Ronald Reagan, Viveca Lindfors, Broderick Crawford, Rosemary DeCamp, Osa Massen, Art Baker, Craig Stevens, Erskine Sanford, Johnny McGovern, Ann Burr, Lillian Yarbo, Ross Ford, Irving Bacon, Almira Sessions.

The Girl from Jones Beach — 1949. Warner Bros. Directed by Peter Godfrey. Produced by Alex Gottlieb. Screenplay by I.A.L. Diamond, from an original story by Allen Boretz. With Virginia Mayo, Ronald Reagan, Eddie Bracken, Dona Drake, Henry Travers, Lois Wilson, Florence Bates, Jerome Cowan, Helen Westcott, Paul Harvey, Lloyd Corrigan, Myrna Dell, William Forrest, Gary Gray, Mary Stuart, Jeff Richards, Dale Robertson, Lola Albright, Betty Underwood, Joi Lansing.

It's a Great Feeling — 1949. Warner Bros. Directed by David Butler. Produced by Alex Gottlieb. Screenplay by Jack Rose and Melville Shavelson from an original story by I.A.L. Diamond. With Dennis Morgan, Doris Day, Jack Carson, Bill Goodwin, Irving Bacon. Cameos by David Butler, Gary Cooper, Joan Crawford, Michael Curtiz, Errol Flynn, Sydney Greenstreet, Danny Kaye, Patricia Neal, Eleanor Parker, Maureen Reagan, Ronald Reagan, Edward G. Robinson, King Vidor, Raoul Walsh, Jane Wyman.

The Hasty Heart — 1949. Warner Bros. Directed by Vincent Sherman. Produced by Howard Lindsay and Russel Crouse. Screenplay by Ranald MacDougall, from the play by John Patrick. With Ronald Reagan, Patricia Neal, Richard Todd, Anthony Nicholls, Howard Crawford, John Sherman, Ralph Michael, Alfred Bass, Orlando Martins.

Louisa — 1950. Universal. Directed by Alexander Hall. Produced by Robert Arthur. Screenplay by Stanley Roberts from his own original story. With Ronald Reagan, Charles Coburn, Ruth Hussey, Edmund Gwenn, Spring Byington, Piper Laurie, Scotty Beckett, Connie Gilchrist, Willard Waterman, Jimmy Hunt, Marjorie Crosland, Terry Frost, Martin Milner.

Storm Warning — 1951. Warner Bros. Directed by Stuart Heisler. Produced by Jerry Wald. Screenplay by Daniel Fuchs, based on the original story "Storm Center" by Daniel Fuchs and Richard Brooks. With Ginger Rogers, Ronald Reagan, Doris Day, Steve Cochran, Hugh Sanders, Lloyd Gough, Raymond Greenleaf, Ned Glass, Walter Baldwin, Lynne Whitney, Stuart Randall, Sean McClory.

The Last Outpost — 1951. Paramount. Directed by Lewis R. Foster. Produced by William H. Pine and William C. Thomas. Screenplay by Geoffrey Homes, George Worthington Yates, Winston Miller. With Ronald Reagan, Rhonda Fleming, Bruce Bennett, Bill Williams, Peter Hanson, Noah Beery, Jr. (aka Noah Berry), Hugh Beaumont, John Ridgely, Lloyd Corrigan, Charles Evans, Richard Crane.

Bedtime for Bonzo — 1951. Universal. Directed by Frederick de Cordova. Produced by Michel Kraike. Screenplay by Val Burton and Lou Breslow from an original story by Raphael David Blau and Ted Berkman. With Ronald Reagan, Diana Lynn, Walter Slezak, Jesse White, Lucille Barkley, Herbert Heyes, Leslye Banning, Midge Ware, Ginger Anderson, Bridget Carr, Harry Tyler, Ed Gargan, Billy Mauch.

Hong Kong — 1952. Paramount. Directed by Lewis R. Foster. Produced by William H. Pine and William C. Thomas. Screenplay by Winston Miller from a story by Lewis B. Foster. With Ronald Reagan, Rhonda Fleming, Nigel Bruce, Lady May Lawton, Marvin Miller, Claude Allister, Danny Chang, Mary Sommerville, Lowell Gilmore.

The Winning Team — 1952. Warner Bros. Directed by Lewis Seiler. Produced by Bryan Foy. Screenplay by Ted Sherdeman, Seeleg Lester, and Merwin Gerard, from the story "Alex the Great" by Seeleg Lester and Merwin Gerard. With Doris Day, Ronald Reagan, Frank Lovejoy, Eve Miller, James Millican, Rusty Tamblyn, Gordon Jones, Hugh Sanders, Frank Ferguson, Walter Baldwin, Dorothy Adams, Bonnie Kay Eddy, James Dodd.

She's Working Her Way Through College — 1952. Warner Bros. Directed by H. Bruce Humberstone. Produced by William Jacobs. Screenplay by Peter Milne, based on the play *The Male Animal* by James Thurber and Elliott Nugent. With Virginia Mayo, Ronald Reagan, Gene Nelson, Don DeFore, Phyllis Thaxter, Patrice Wymore, Roland Winters, Raymond Greenleaf, Norman Bartold, Amanda Randolph, Henrietta Taylor, Eve Miller, The Blackburn Twins.

Tropic Zone — 1953. Paramount. Directed by Lewis R. Foster. Produced by William H. Pine and William C. Thomas. Screenplay by Lewis R. Foster, from an original story by Tom Gill. With Ronald Reagan, Rhonda Fleming, Estelita, Noah Beery, Jr., Grant Withers, John Wengraf, Argentina Brunetti, Rico Alanez, Maurice Jara, Pilar Del Rey.

Law and Order — 1953. Universal. Directed by Nathan Juran. Produced by John W. Rogers. Screenplay by John and Gwen Bagni, from the story "Saint Johnson" by W. R. Burnett. With Ronald Reagan, Dorothy Malone, Alex Nicol, Preston Foster, Ruth Hampton, Russell Johnson, Barry Kelley, Chubby Johnson, Dennis Weaver, Jack Kelly, Valerie Jackson.

Prisoner of War — 1954. MGM. Directed by Andrew Marton. Produced by Henry Berman. Screenplay by Allen Rivkin. With Ronald Reagan, Steve Forrest, Dewey Martin, Oscar Homolka, Robert Horton, Paul Stewart, Henry (Harry) Morgan, Stephen Bekassy, Leonard Strong, Darryl Hickman, Jerry Paris, Stuart Whitman, John Lupton.

Cattle Queen of Montana — 1954. RKO. Directed by Allan Dwan. Produced by Benedict Bogeaus. Screenplay by Howard Estabrook and Robert Blees, from a story by Thomas Blackburn. With Barbara Stanwyck, Ronald Reagan, Gene Evas, Lance Fuller, Anthony Caruso, Jack Elam, Yvette Dugay, Morris Ankrum, Chubby Johnson, Myron Healey, Rodd Redwing, Paul Birch, Byron Foulger, Burt Mustin.

Tennessee's Partner — 1955. RKO. Directed by Allan Dwan. Produced by Benedict Bogeaus. Screenplay by Allan Dwan, Milton Krims, D. D. Beauchamp, Graham Baker, and Teddi Sherman, based on a story by Bret Harte. With John Payne, Rhonda Fleming, Ronald Reagan, Coleen Gray, Anthony Caruso, Leo Gordon, Myron Healey, Morris

Ankrum, Chubby Johnson, Joe Devlin, John Mansfield, Angie Dickinson.

Hellcats of the Navy — 1957. Columbia. Directed by Nathan Juran. Produced by Charles H. Schneer. Screenplay by David Lang and Raymond Marcus, from a story by David Lang, based on a book by Charles A. Lockwood and Hans Christian Adamson. With Ronald Reagan, Nancy Davis, Arthur Franz, Robert Arthur, William Leslie, William Phillips, Harry Lauter, Michael Garth, Joseph Turkel, Don Keefer, Selmer Jackson, Maurice Manson.

The Young Doctors — 1961. United Artists. Directed by Phil Karlson. Produced by Stuart Millar and Lawrence Turman. Screenplay by Joseph Hayes, based on the novel *The Final Diagnosis* by Arthur Hailey. With Fredric March, Ben Gazzara, Dick Clark, Ina Balin, Eddie Albert, Phyllis Love, Edward Andrews, Aline MacMahon, Arthur Hill, Rosemary Murphy, Barnard Hughes, Gloria Vanderbilt, James Broderick, Joseph Bova, George Segal, Matt Crowley, Dick Button, Addison Powell, Dolph Sweet, Ella Smith, Nora Helen Spens, Bob Dahdah.

The Killers — 1964. Universal. Directed and produced by Don Siegel. Screenplay by Gene L. Coon, based on the short story by Ernest Hemingway. With Lee Marvin, John Cassavetes, Angie Dickinson, Ronald Reagan, Clu Gulager, Claude Akins, Norman Fell,

Virginia Christine, Don Haggerty, Robert Phillips, Kathleen O'Malley, Ted Jacques, Irvin Mosley, Jimmy Joyce, Scott Hale, Seymour Cassel.

TELEVISION

Hollywood Opening Night "The Priceless Gift" (1952)

Law and Order "Frame Johnson" (May 1953)

Medallion Theater "A Job for Jimmy Valentine" (1953)

The George Burns and Gracie Allen Show (aka *The Burns and Allen Show*) episode 3.38 (August 3, 1953), himself

The Milton Berle Show (aka *Texaco Star Theater* [USA] and *The Buick-Berle Show* [USA: new title]) episode dated November 13, 1953, himself

Revlon Mirror Theatre "Next Stop Bethelehem" (December 5, 1953), actor

Lux Video Theatre (aka *Summer Video Theatre* [USA: Summer title]) "A Place in the Sun" (January 28, 1954), actor, and "Message in a Bottle" (September 3, 1953), Merle Fisher

Schlitz Playhouse of Stars (aka *Herald Playhouse, Schlitz Playhouse, The Playhouse* [syndication]) "The Doctor Comes Home" (July 31, 1953), actor, "The Jungle Trap" (February 19, 1954), actor, and "The Edge of Battle" (March 26, 1954), actor

Prisoner of War (1954), Webb Sloane *The Ford Television Theatre* "The First Born" (1953), "And Suddenly, You Knew" (1953), Steve Wentworth, and "Beneath These Waters" (1954), Lt. Commander Masterson

General Electric Theater (aka *G.E. Theater* [USA: informal short title] and *G.E. True Theater* [USA: new title]). Reagan hosted all 11 seasons and appeared in these 41 episodes as an actor:

"Nora #1" (September 26, 1954)
"The High Green Wall" (October 3, 1954)
"The Long Way 'Round" (October 10, 1954)
"The Face Is Familiar" (November 21, 1954)
"The Dark, Dark Hours" (December 12, 1954)
"The Martyr" (January 23, 1955)
"The Return of Gentleman Jim" (February 6, 1955)
"War and Peace on the Range" (March 13, 1955)
"The Bounty Court Martial" (October 9, 1955)
"Prosper's Old Mother" (November 20, 1955)
"Feathertop" (December 4, 1955)
"Let It Rain" (December 18, 1955)
"Try to Remember" (February 26, 1956)

"The Lord's Dollar" (April 22, 1956)
"The Professor's Punch" (September 30, 1956)
"Orphans" (December 2, 1956)
"No Skin Off Me" (February 3, 1957)
"Bargain Bride" (April 7, 1957)
"A Question of Survival" (May 12, 1957)
"Father and Son Night" (October 13, 1957)
"Cornada" (November 10, 1957)
"The Coward of Fort Bennett" (March 16, 1958)
"No Hiding Place" (April 6, 1958)
"The Castaway" (October 12, 1958)
"A Turkey for the President" (November 23, 1958)
"Deed of Mercy" (March 1, 1959)
"Nobody's Child" (May 10, 1959)
"Signs of Love" (November 8, 1959)
"The House of Truth" (December 13, 1959)
"The Book of Silence" (March 6, 1960)
"So Deadly, So Evil" (March 13, 1960)
"Mystery at Malibu" (April 10, 1960)
"Goodbye, My Love" (October 16, 1960)
"Learn to Say Goodbye" (December 4, 1960)
"The Devil You Say" (January 22, 1961)
"The Iron Silence" (September 24, 1961)
"Money and the Minister" (November 26, 1961)
"The Wall Between" (January 7, 1962)

"Shadow of a Hero" (February 4, 1962)
"My Dark Days: Part 1" (March 18, 1962)
"My Dark Days: Part 2" (March 25, 1962)

What's My Line? episode dated July 19, 1953, himself (mystery guest), and episode dated May 20, 1956, himself (guest panelist)

Disneyland (aka *Disney's Wonderful World* and aka *The Wonderful World of Disney* [USA: new titles]: "The Pre-Opening Report from Disneyland/A Tribute to Mickey Mouse" (July 13, 1955), himself; "Walt Disney World's 15th Anniversary Celebration" (November 9, 1986), himself; "Disneyland's 35th Anniversary Celebration (February 4, 1990), himself (also archive footage)

The Name's the Same (1 episode), himself as a contestant (date unknown)

I've Got a Secret episode dated October 5, 1955, himself; episode dated February 8, 1961, himself

General Electric Summer Originals "Jungle Trap" (September 18, 1956), actor

To Tell the Truth episode dated September 23, 1958, guest panelist

Toast of the Town (1955–58), himself

Tennessee Ernie Ford Show episode dated November 7, 1957, himself

The DuPont Show with June Allyson (aka *The June Allyson Show*) "The Way Home" (January 18, 1960), Alan Royce

Startime (aka *Ford Startime* and *Lincoln-*

Mercury Startime) "The Swingin' Singin' Years" (March 8, 1960), host

This Is Your Life "Charles Coburn" (June 29, 1960), himself

The Young Doctors (1961), voice-over narration

Zane Grey Theater (aka *Dick Powell's Zane Grey Theater* and *The Westerners*) "The Long Shadow" (January 19, 1961), Major Will Sinclair

Heritage of Splendor, 1963, narrator

The Dick Powell Show (aka *The Dick Powell Theater* [USA: new title]) "Who Killed Julie Greer?" (September 26, 1961), Rex Kent; "The Last of the Private Eyes" (April 30, 1963), guest host

Wagon Train "The Fort Pierce Story" (September 23, 1963), Capt. Paul Winters

Kraft Suspense Theater "A Cruel and Unusual Night" (June 4, 1964), Judge Howard R. Stimming

The Celebrity Game episode dated August 23, 1964, himself

Death Valley Days (aka *Call of the West* aka *The Pioneers* aka *Trails West* aka *Western Star Theater*). Reagan hosted all episodes and appeared in eight:

"Tribute to the Dog" (December 24, 1964), George Vest

"Raid on the San Francisco Mint" (March

10, 1965), William Chapman Ralston

"The Battle of San Francisco Bay" (March 18, 1965), David Farragut

"No Gun Behind His Badge" (March 25, 1965), Bear River Smith

"Temporary Warden" (September 30, 1965), Warden Hume

"The Lawless Have Laws" (October 1, 1965), Lt. Col. Martin Burke

"No Place for a Lady" (October 21, 1965), William Burt

"A City Is Born" (October 22, 1965), Charles Poston

The Carol Burnett Show (aka *Carol Burnett and Friends* [USA: repeat compilations title]) Episode 3.16 (January 26, 1970), himself

The Tonight Show Starring Johnny Carson (aka *The Best of Carson* [USA: rerun title]) episode dated November 26, 1970, himself; episode dated October 2, 1972, himself (as Governor Reagan)

The Sonny and Cher Comedy Hour episode #3.1 (September 15, 1972), himself

This Is Your Life "Joel McCrea" (December 3, 1972), himself

The Dean Martin Show (aka *The Dean Martin Comedy Hour* [USA: new title]) "Celebrity Roast: Ronald Reagan (September 13, 1973), himself

V.I.P.-Schaukel episode #5.4 (November

21, 1975), himself

Today (aka *NBC News Today* [USA: promotional title] and *The Today Show* [USA]) episode dated November 13, 1979, himself

NBC White Paper "Reagan: The First 100 Days" (April 23, 1981), himself

ESPN SportsCentury "Pete Rose" (December 22, 2000), himself (voice-over)

AUTHOR'S NOTE AND ACKNOWLEDGMENTS

During the years I spent at Columbia University's School of the Arts, where I earned an MFA and then pursued my PhD in film history, and where dozens of films were screened every day in various classes, I don't remember a single film with Ronald Reagan in it ever being shown. Looking back, it surprises me how many movie stars of the forties had developed cult followings among my college generation of the 1970s — the Marx Brothers (holdovers, who peaked in the thirties, but still making movies in the next decade), Humphrey Bogart, of course, Bette Davis, John Garfield, Jimmy Cagney, even Fred Astaire, but not Ronald Reagan. Although he would outlive all the others and go on to become the president of the United States, his film career, except for *Bedtime for Bonzo,* was, then and today, largely forgotten.

The reason we didn't focus on Reagan at Columbia (and I suspect other film schools didn't as well) was because his film career suffered from a fatal lack of opportunity; with one or two exceptions, he never worked as the lead for a great director (or, as we at Columbia's film school called them, auteurists). The closest he ever came was probably Raoul Walsh, but *Desperate Journey* belonged to Errol Flynn. Reagan also worked two times for Don Siegel, but neither film, *Night Unto Night* or *The Killers,* was typically "Reagan" or, arguably, typically Siegel (who today is still not fully recognized as the major director he was). I had never even heard of *Night Unto Night* until I started writing this book, and then had to track down a VHS copy of it in Los Angeles (it was not then and I don't believe is available today on DVD), only to realize it was much more Broderick Crawford's movie than Reagan's, even though Reagan was the ostensible male lead. *The Killers* is on DVD, but its principal appeal is how it foreshadows Siegel's far superior work a decade or so later when he learned how to pinpoint violence in the persona of Dirty Harry. Of course, having Clint Eastwood as his leading man, who in many ways became the actor (but not the politician) that Reagan wasn't (and was), didn't hurt.

For me, the best director Reagan ever worked with was, without question, Michael Curtiz. But we didn't see much of Curtiz either at Columbia — he was generally shunned by the so-called Sarissites, of which I surely was (and still am), because of the sheer number of assigned films Curtiz had turned out in his career at Warner Bros., and the lack in his enormous body of work of a unifying, singular, identifiable personal style, or "vision," amid the many genres he seemed to so easily cross. The one film of Curtiz's that stands out above all the others is the one Andrew Sarris used to refer to as the "exception" to the Auteur Theory (which, to him, proved it at the same time). That, of course, was *Casablanca,* in which, as noted earlier, Reagan had hoped to star. *The Santa Fe Trail* was the best of the films Curtiz directed Reagan in, but, alas, that one, too, belonged to Errol Flynn, in whose shadow Reagan's leading-man career unhappily (to Reagan) forever remained.

The other director of note who has been seriously overlooked in both Reagan's career and by the auteurists is Sam Wood (he gets the barest of mentions and no critical overview in Sarris's landmark *The American Cinema*). Wood directed Reagan in what was arguably the best picture of both their careers, *Kings Row.* But that film, too, was in a sense lost to auteurists, because it was overwhelmed the year it was released by Orson Welles's far superior *The Magnificent Ambersons.* Let me add before I suffer the fury of armchair film historians everywhere that I am well aware that *Kings Row* was a commercial and critical success when it was released, and *The Magnificent Ambersons* a commercial and critical disaster. However, thirty years later, it was *The Magnificent Ambersons* that was rightly hailed by my fellow film students and our mentor/scholars alike as the classic, while *Kings Row* was not even granted a thought, let alone a look. I would hate to think that Sam Wood's far-right politics had anything to do with this omission, but I do believe his career did suffer in his lifetime for his ultra-right extremism. The obituaries that followed his death in 1949 of a heart attack put his film career far behind his political one, where it has remained forevermore. There is no doubt that a serious reexamination of his body of work is overdue.

One lesson I learned at Columbia was that often, in film, the action lies in the margins of what is considered the mainstream. Time and time again, I have found that to be true in my biographical work, and with Ronald Reagan, it is an excellent way of beginning to understand what it was about the career of this relatively minor actor who played such a strong part in the off-screen actions that engulfed Hollywood in the forties and all that followed. To me, his presidency was underscored by a powerful unifying presence nurtured and developed during that time.

His formative years in Hollywood have been

looked at before, but only in the most perfunctory of ways, beginning with his own memoirs, where his movie career serves as a fast setup to get to the "real action" of his second, more successful political life. His glossing over of this period was a mystery to me until I began to dig deeper into that period of his life (and the period itself), both in terms of his politics as well as his films.

Generally speaking, a creative person's best work comes when he or she is young, and often it is the key that unlocks the secrets of their artistic souls. How does one do a biography of, say, Vincent van Gogh without delving into his paintings as the pathway to understanding who he was? How does one begin to understand Charlie Chaplin's greatness by looking only at his politics or tragic childhood and not at his films? To study van Gogh or Chaplin without studying their art (or in today's jargon, their "product," which probably makes it easier to include Reagan in the mix) is to not study them at all.

As I read the related works of others, which proved quite useful to me — especially Lou Cannon's massive two-volume biography of Reagan, Bob Colacello's dual bio of Reagan and Nancy, Dennis McDougal's solid biography of Lew Wasserman, Stephen Vaughn's strong sociopolitical study of Reagan's Hollywood years, and Dan Moldea's crackling exposé of Reagan's relationship to MCA and what Moldea perceived as their connection to organized crime — it occurred to me that as good as they all were, they shared a similar problem, either a lack of interest in and/or an inability to look at Reagan's movies from a creative rather than a sociological point of view. None of these books, or any others I have found thus far, looked at Reagan's films as works of cinematic art, failed or otherwise. Rather, they all put them into a social, chronological, and/or political context, what Andrew Sarris once defined as missing the forest for the trees.

To be able to fully comprehend Reagan the man, then, one must also understand Reagan the actor. How else to truly comprehend how "Win just one for the Gipper" and "Where's the rest of me?" became not only political slogans for him but life-defining ones as well, and how the characters he played during his film career led directly to the persona he inhabited that eventually served as the God-like narrator of *General Electric Theater*, the forerunner to his greatest role of all, the president of the United States. Was Ronald Reagan a great actor? Probably not, if one bases that judgment only on his film career, but certainly yes if one considers his Hollywood years as the foundation that allowed Reagan, as he himself suggests in the beginning of this book, to successfully play the greatest role of his career, the "president of the United States."

Finally, I should say that I have seen every one of Reagan's movies and most of his TV work, thanks to DVDs, videos, Turner Classic Movies, my own extensive film collection, and the kindness of various higher institutions, museums, private collections of friends, and even a benevolent stranger or two. In sum, as the Eagles rock band once sang, "This could be heaven or this could be hell." Because of the span of time this book covers, from the early twentieth century to the first years of the sixties, it is, by necessity, a historical, rather than a journalistic, enterprise. Most of those involved in the story have passed on. To those few who survive and consented to interviews, I am deeply grateful. While I have discussed, debated, argued, and agreed with many of my contemporary film critics, scholars, and political experts, much of what has been written here has come from my own academic and professional background, journalistic investigations and interviews, an immersion into the ample available historical data, the films, and many original never-before-published materials and interviews generously supplied by veteran Hollywood reporter Dave Robb.

Having already expressed my debt to Andrew Sarris, among the many participants in the research for this book I also emphasize the special contributions of Mary Steifvater;

David Herwitz; Miles Kreuger; Rich Little; Robert Wagner; William Frye; Barbara Hall in Special Collections and the rest of the extraordinarily well-informed and endlessly helpful staff of the Herrick Library; filmmaker and historian Stephen Litwinczuk; William Gazecki, director and producer of *Behind the Masks: The Story of the Screen Actors Guild;* and the many, many others along the way who helped, either with valued opinions, the unmistakably authentic detail of memory, or a shove in the right direction to documents, films, and other people, places, and things.

I also wish to thank my agent, Alan Nevins, of The Firm.

At Harmony Books, I also wish to thank my terrific editor, Julia Pastore, my great publisher and dear friend, Shaye Areheart; and the entire Random House family, of which I am extremely proud to be a member. They include Mark McCauslin, Lauren Dong, and Norman Watkins.

And so I leave you now but will see you again a little further on up the road.

ABOUT THE AUTHOR

Marc Eliot is the *New York Times* bestselling author of more than a dozen books on popular culture, among them the highly acclaimed biographies *Cary Grant* and *Jimmy Stewart;* the award-winning *Walt Disney: Hollywood's Dark Prince; Down 42nd Street; Take It from Me* (with Erin Brockovich); *Down Thunder Road: The Making of Bruce Springsteen; To the Limit: The Untold Story of the Eagles;* and *Death of a Rebel.* He has written on the media and popular culture for numerous publications, including *Penthouse, L.A. Weekly,* and *California Magazine.* He divides his time among New York City; Woodstock, New York; and Los Angeles, California.

Visit the author at www.MarcEliot.net.